ISA

Timba:
The Sound of the Cuban Crisis

In memory of my father Francesco

Ry Cooder, talking about old Cuban musicians who have died, indicates Ibrahim Ferrer:
So we have Ibrahim in 1998, we are very lucky.
Off-camera translator to Ferrer:
Year '98 will be very lucky for Ibrahim!
Conversation from the movie *Buena Vista Social Club*

I have music for those who know about music
for those who like music
for those who like dancing
and for those who like criticizing.
José Luís Cortés

The drum knows the mistery of pain,
of life and death,
because it has been extracted from the forest with the axe.
Yoruba proverb

Timba:
The Sound of the Cuban Crisis

VINCENZO PERNA

ASHGATE

Published by
Ashgate Publishing Limited   Ashgate Publishing Company
Gower House   Suite 420
Croft Road   101 Cherry Street
Aldershot   Burlington, VT 05401-4405
Hants GU11 3HR   USA
England

Ashgate website: http://www.ashgate.com

British Library Cataloguing in Publication Data
Perna, Vincenzo
    Timba: the sound of the Cuban crisis – (SOAS musicology series)
    1. Dance music – Cuba 2. Popular music – Cuba 3. Music –
    Social aspects – Cuba
    I. Title II. Series
    781.5'54'097291

Library of Congress Cataloging-in-Publication Data
Perna, Vincenzo, 1957–
    Timba : the sound of the Cuban crisis / Vincenzo Perna.
        p. cm. – (SOAS musicology series)
    Includes bibliographical references and index.
    Discography: p.
    Filmography: p
    ISBN 0-7546-3941-X (alk. paper)
    1. Dance music – Cuba – History and criticism. 2. Popular music – Cuba –
Social aspects. I. Title. II. Series.

ML3486.C8P48 2005
781.64'097291'09049–dc22
                                                            2004004246

ISBN 0 7546 3941 X

Typeset in Times by Laserscript, Mitcham, Surrey, Great Britain
Printed and bound in Great Britain by MPG Books Ltd, Bodmin

Contents

Plates

Unless otherwise specified, all the photos were taken by the author.

(between pages 158 and 159)

1   José Luis Cortés, aka El Tosco
2   El Tosco with NG La Banda during a concert in Havana
3   CD artwork for *La bruja* ('The Witch') by NG La Banda
4   Notice-board for activities at the Hotel Capri, announcing 'NG La Banda and guests'
5   NG La Banda doing their 'waist-shaking contest'
6   Los Van Van's singer Pedrito Calvo checking the dance style of a member of the audience
7 and 8   The provocative artwork for La Charanga's mid-1990s albums: *Pa' que se entere La Habana*; *Tremendo delirio* (Magic Music 1996 and 1997)
9   A hand-written poster at a crossroads announcing a concert by Paulíto FG
10   Cover picture from the CD *Una aventura loca* (Caribe, 1994), the first album of Manolin
11   Singer Paulíto FG at La Tropical
12   The latest 'boy band' version of La Charanga Habanera
13   A picture from Bamboleo's third album (*Ya no hace falta*, Ahí Namá, 1999)
14   Pianist and composer Lazaríto Valdés, leader of Bamboleo
15   Pianist and composer Manolíto Simonet, leader of El Trabuco
16   Giraldo Piloto, drummer, composer and leader of Klimax
17   An ecstatic audience during a timba concert in Havana
18   Female dancers dancing during a concert in Havana
19   Street classes: girls in a square of the largely Afro-Cuban suburb of Guanabacoa
20   'Socially contaminated area': *jineteras* in a discotheque in Havana
21   Street rumba (photo © Frédéric Vigneau 1997. Reproduced courtesy of F. Vigneau)
22   Players of *batá* sacred drums during a santería ceremony (photo © Frédéric Vigneau 1997. Reproduced courtesy of F. Vigneau)
23   Two protagonists of the Afro-Cuban cultural renaissance: Amado Dedeu and the visual artist Salvador González

Music Examples

Acknowledgements

In the course of my exploration of Cuban music, many people have helped me in many different ways, with commentaries, suggestions and even by simply telling me their personal stories. Among those people and the musicians I have met in all these years, and who keep on *luchando*, I wish to thank Lily and Marino, Maria Aurora and Monica in Havana, Rey and Ian (he knows why) in London, and Raúl in Torino.

I wish to acknowledge here the assistance of the Central Research Fund of the University of London, which has enabled me to undertake part of my research in Cuba. I also wish to thank Dr Olavo Alén Rodríguez, director of the Centro de Investigación y Desarrollo de la Música Cubana (CIDMUC) in Havana, for granting me access to the Centre, and Prof. Philip Baker of the School of Oriental and African Studies (SOAS) for putting me in contact with Armin Schwegler of the University of California at Irvine, who has helped me to trace the African roots of the word 'timba'. I am also grateful to Leonardo Acosta, Radamés Giro and Helio Orovio for sharing with me their encyclopaedic knowledge of Cuban music. A special thanks must go to Lucy Duran of SOAS for her help and encouragement throughout the research. All the opinions expressed in this book, of course, are exclusively my responsibility.

Finally, I should like to thank Irene and Francesca for their support (and endurance) of my wanderings between Britain, Cuba and Italy – especially since the final writing of this book has coincided with the arrival of baby Lorenzo.

Introduction

Timba lives on the streets, in the queues, in the way people talk
and dance. It's like an attitude to life here and now in Cuba, that
we as musicians reflect in our lyrics.

José Luís Cortés (quoted in Henry 1998)

In the 1990s, popular music from Latin America and the Caribbean has
received increasing scholarly attention. A number of books have
presented detailed ethnographic studies focusing on single Caribbean
styles (Guilbault 1993, Pacini-Hernández 1995, Austerlitz 1997, Averill
1997), while others have offered comprehensive surveys of the musics of
the area (Manuel et al. 1995). Some excellent non-specialist texts,
moreover, have made readers aware of the influence of Latin American
music on jazz and popular music produced in North America, Europe
and Africa (Roberts 1985 and 1999).

Together with Brazil, Cuba is probably the Latin American country
that during the 20th century has made the strongest impact on
international music. The acknowledgement of such importance in the
West has not as yet been matched by a comparable expansion in the
literature about Cuban music, and especially in the music made after
the revolution. While attention has been paid to pan-Latin styles of
Cuban descent such as *Latin jazz* and *salsa* (Gerard and Sheller 1989,
Glasser 1995, Aparicio 1998, Waxer 2002), Cuban music of the past
(Carpentier 1946, Moore 1997), Afro-Cuban religious music (Cornelius
and Amira 1992, Vélez 2000, Hagedorn 2001), the discussion on post-
1959 popular music in Cuba has mainly remained confined to
journalistic books written for a general readership (Steward 1999,
Sweeney 2001, Leymarie 2002, Roy 2002). With few exceptions (e.g.
Díaz Ayala 1981, Acosta 1983 and 2002, Manuel 1990, Padura Fuentes
1997), even the substantial body of literature produced by contemporary Cuban writers has tended to concentrate on panoramic surveys of
Cuban music (Linares 1974, León 1974, Alén Rodríguez 1994), popular
music of the past (Valdés Cantero 1988, Giro 1995), Afro-Cuban
folklore (Alén Rodríguez 1986, Vinueza 1986, Pérez Fernández 1987)
and organology (Elí Rodríguez, Casanova Oliva, et al. 1997), showing a
marked propensity of Cuban musicologists for 'collection, technical
analysis, documentation of neo-Africanisms and the like' (Manuel 1990,
xi).

For a series of reasons, the profound changes which occurred in Cuban music in the last forty years seem to have been difficult to perceive abroad, to the point of leading an expert such as Peter Manuel to claim, in the late 1980s, that 'since 1959 there have been no dramatic revolutions in the field of Cuban dance music' (Manuel 1987, 166), and to reiterate his view in the mid-1990s (1995). By that year, indeed, the fall of the Soviet Union had unleashed in Cuba changes that have created a totally new social and musical environment. The boom of tourism, in particular, has proved extremely beneficial to Cuban dance music, nurturing the success of a distinctive new style.

This book deals with timba, a type of contemporary Afro-Cuban dance music that has become the dominant popular style in Cuba during the *período especial*, the name given by Fidel Castro to the dramatic economic crisis that followed the demise of the Soviet Union. An eclectic fusion mixing *son* with Afro-Cuban rumba, timba incorporates influences ranging from US black music to Afro-Latin popular styles. An urban style mainly developed in Havana, timba in fact shows remarkable parallels with African-American hip-hop. It is symbolically and economically related to street-life; it comments in slang on sex, money and life in the *barrio* (neighbourhood); it is frequently controversial. Visually, it has developed a sexually provocative, individual dance style far removed from previous Cuban and Latin American codes of couple dancing, and related to lower-class Afro-Cuban dance genres such as rumba and conga.

With its nervous sound and its here-and-now attitude, timba appears diametrically opposed to nostalgic, revivalist products such as *Buena Vista Social Club*, which in the late 1990s paved the way to a global rediscovery of 'traditional' Cuban music. Far from indulging the exotic expectations of the foreign market, timba is a style of music that is listened and danced to by Cubans who do not live in the comfortable residential areas of Havana, but in the dark, destitute rooms of the inner city, in the worn-out concrete apartment blocks of Alamar, in the shacks behind Marianao, where one sees no palms or beaches, the heat is suffocating and the air stinks with sewage.

The cracking sound of the *período especial*

Musically, timba is the result of an innovative fusion of elements drawn from multiple directions. From one point of view, it can be seen as a development of a line of dance music (*música bailable*, here shortened to MB) that emerged during the 1970s with bands such as Los Van Van and Irakere, and which has since gradually 'blackened', incorporating multiple Afro-Cuban musical and cultural references. Yet from another point of view, timba has proved extremely porous, both musically and culturally. Eclectic and open to disparate and even contrasting musical influences, this style cannot be reduced to a model of national musical development, if that is ever possible in popular culture. Timba is as close to Afro-Cuban street culture as it appears receptive to African-American styles such as jazz (an element already strongly present in pre-1959 Cuban popular music), funk and rap, and to the influence of Caribbean and Latin American black popular styles such as salsa, dancehall and cumbia.

As a music style, timba crystallized in the late 1980s largely thanks to the experimentations of NG La Banda, a band led by black flute player and composer José Luís Cortés, who made his music into the voice of the marginal black barrios of the capital city. With the re-conversion of the Cuban economy caused by the *período especial*, in the early 1990s the novel style moved to the centre of the popular musical scene of Havana. Thanks to the fertile ground provided by the boom of international tourism, timba became the mainstay of night entertainment and the soundtrack of the new tourist *dolce vita*. In the context of the crisis and of the rapid changes occurring in Cuban society, its musicians acquired a position of exceptional popularity and economic power.

On the island, the success of timba has been of enormous symbolic relevance. By relating to the world of working-class Blacks through music, lyrical content and dance style, timba songs have brought to the fore previously marginalized aspects of Afro-Cuban culture, articulating issues of race, class and gender that rarely surface in official discourses, and reaffirming black identity in opposition to a generic notion of *cubanía* (Cubanness).

Ethnomusicologist Bruno Nettl once described popular music as a music 'performed by professional but not very highly trained musicians' (1972: 218). A particular feature of timba – indeed, something that sets it aside from most other popular styles – is the fact that its fusion has been brought about by musicians with a first-class conservatoire training, educated by the system set up by the Cuban revolution. This progression from classical music to the dance floor gives an idea of the complex nature of timba, of its ability to convey almost opposite cultural references and aesthetic aspirations.

Functional and commercial, timba is a sort of avant-garde dance music that combines the spirit of the popular barrio with sophisticated arrangements and lives in a duality between smoothness and street culture, dance and art music, which has led Puerto Rican jazzman David Sanchez to call it 'the smartest pop music I've ever heard' (Watrous 1997). For this reason, timba is a music style that poses serious challenges to distinctions between highbrow and lowbrow culture, and popular, folkloric and cultivated music, occupying perhaps a unique position in the international popular music scene.

While immensely successful with young Afro-Cubans, timba has developed an uneasy relationship with the Cuban political establishment. As a type of black dance music it resists cultural elitism, empowering Afro-Cuban culture and contesting visions of ethnic pacification and social harmony. Through its appropriation of foreign styles, timba challenges discourses that seek to construct a demonized image of capitalism, and evades notions of narrowly-defined cultural nationalism. Popular support and economic relevance, therefore, have not saved timba from a head-to-head collision with the Cuban authorities, who, in the late 1990s, attacked its perceived excesses and banned the activity of the most popular timba band.

In this book, I examine the emergence, the success and the downfall of timba, showing how in Cuba this music has come to represent the sound of a crisis not only economic, but also social and political. Through its lyrics, musical style, models of behaviour and closeness to street culture, timba articulates the values of a largely black youth subculture that has grown up in the shadow of the crisis, revealing the disorientation of Cuban society at the beginning of the new millennium, and ultimately symbolizing the difficult, contradictory opening of Cuba to the outside world. In the early 1990s, commenting on the consequences of the impact of tourism on Cuban society, Fidel Castro declared: 'We will be all the more pure if we are able to preserve our virtues amid the contamination certain things might bring with them' (Castro 1994). As both the result of and a challenge to the irruption of tourism in Cuba, in a sense timba represents Cuban society's bad conscience, embodying many of the things that its cultural and political establishment would not like to see, and to be seen.

Facing Cuban and Latin music: the role of timba

Cuban music is today unanimously recognized as a major historical force behind Latin American music, and as an important player in the development of US popular music and jazz. By investigating popular music made in Cuba after 1959, I believe, this work contributes to fill a gap in the study of modern Cuban music, showing how the revolution has created the conditions for profound (and generally little-known) musical changes, and for the birth of a type of sophisticated popular music that has developed relatively free from market pressures. These conditions have been the premises for the role attained by timba in the last decade.

The study of timba is, I think, important for a series of reasons. Musically, this style represents a unique combination of influences, artistic attitudes and technical abilities that has probably no match in other third world cultures. In Cuba, timba has been enormously successful, during the 1990s becoming the main recreational music of the black masses and a vehicle for the vindication of Afro-Cuban popular culture and music.

The meaning here of 'popular' is both crucial and controversial. On the island, certainly, people practise and listen to many different popular music genres. But only one enjoys the favour of the local masses, and that is without any doubt *música bailable*, a type of music that can draw together audiences in the order of tens of thousands. Not unlike popular music in the West, this music in Cuba has often been treated with cultural conceit. Why do we need to talk seriously about it? I think we need to do it for several musical, cultural, social and political reasons: its sheer popularity in Cuba; its novelty and originality as a music style; the skill of its practitioners; its relationship with both local traditions and the culture of the black diaspora; its meanings and the way its style brings to light the tension points within Cuban society. And last but not least, the fact that timba provides us with a brilliant example of a music that can be carnivalesque, complex *and* meaningful.

Dance music is crucial to both Cubans' self-representation and outsiders' perception of them. Even if frequently perceived to be associated with clichés of sand, sun and sex, in Cuba this music does not have a purely escapist role. In its musical structure, textual content and choreographic form, timba is often in contrast with dominant social and cultural canons. The study of timba, thus, offers an opportunity to explore how music can be significant and political in a society where information is almost entirely controlled by the state. Gage Averill once observed how the 'powerful appeal of music – its engagement with human emotions – is the reason it serves effectively as an instrument of politics and a medium of power' (1997: 19). As a style of dance music, timba owes its significant political power not so much to the content of its messages, but to the multiplicity and ambiguity of the meanings it generates. Contrary to conventional forms of political music – engaged, articulated, univocal, sexually restrained – timba is anthemic, streetwise, ambiguous and hedonistic. It is topical, culturally spurious and economically rewarding.

A style like timba, in fact, shows how the politics of popular culture is more about contesting cultural hegemony than trying to convey explicitly political content. Rather than politics *in* popular music, one might say, it is politics *through* popular music: as veteran jazzman Max Roach once put it to a US militant rapper, lyrics were not everything and 'the politics was in the drums' (quoted in Lipsitz 1994: 38). With its popular slang, its following among working-class Blacks, its celebration of individualism, lust and consumer values, timba represents a challenge to the power of the official word. Thanks to its own opacity, its resistance to being reduced to definite, closed meanings, timba has been central to the construction of a defiant youth subculture. Like so many popular music styles, timba is associated with licence and pleasure, two notions that – as Michel Foucault has pointed out – represent both a site of political control and a site of resistance to it.

The need for an examination of popular music in post-revolutionary Cuba, also, is made all the more urgent by the growing international popularity of Latin music, a conceptually untenable notion that nevertheless continues to be used as a discursive operator among musicians, listeners and the music industry. Certainly, not all Latin American popular music is related to Cuban music, but a considerable part of what circulates in the West under the nebulous label of Latin music is – be that Latin jazz, salsa, Santana's 'Corazón espinado' or the latest summer hit.

In the growth of popularity of the various styles of 'Latin' music and artists since the late 1990s – indeed, a real boom – a special role has been played by *Buena Vista Social Club*, a phenomenon that has totally redefined the international image of Cuban music and has constructed a romanticized representation of a society that is crossed by dramatic tensions. By confronting the definitions of Latin and Cuban music circulating in the global arena, the investigation of timba, I believe, tells us something important about the dialectics of tradition and modernity and local and global that generates and makes third world cultures so vital, and about the fantasies of isolation and cultural purity that inform so much of the Western perception of world music.

Timba in the black diaspora

Timba is not only a musical style, but also a subculture and a cultural movement of sorts. I say 'movement' not because the music has an explicit formulation or a manifesto, but because it closely parallels and complements similar trends in other artistic fields. In its commitment to Afro-Cuban culture, for example, timba relates to an interest in black arts and religion that is presently booming, both in Cuba and abroad. As a music with strong ties to the life of young urban Blacks, at the same time the new style is the focus for a subculture manifesting behaviours and values that appear in striking contrast to revolutionary ideals. Timba emerges therefore as a crucial, if ambivalent, point of articulation of the

Cuban black youth's symbolic resistance to social norms, both through its role as a voice of the pride of people of African descent and in its celebration of low life and materialism.

The loyalty of timba to Afro-Cuban life and values, in particular, calls strongly into question the position of Blacks in contemporary Cuban society, an issue that in the last few years has solicited a growing debate (De la Fuente 2001). Up to this day, on the island, race remains an extremely controversial and politically sensitive issue that is rarely mentioned in public discourse. For that reason, the tremendous strength of Afro-Cuban culture in contemporary Cuba – of which popular music and dance represent such a visible and primary element – may be paradoxically interpreted as an outcome both of the cultural policies of the revolution, and of their failure to understand the specificity of Afro-Cuban culture and make it accepted to the wider Cuban society. As a type of black dance music, timba in fact appears to have inherited biases and prejudices that have accompanied previous expressions of Afro-Cuban popular culture.

Another complex, related issue regards the meaning of terms such as 'Afro-Cuban' and 'Black', which in this book I have employed interchangeably to refer to people of African descent who in Cuba would generally be described as *negro/a* or *mulato/a*.[1] My usage of the word 'Afro-Cuban' has been consistent with that of various Anglophone scholars (for example Moore 1997, Hagedorn 2001), but not with the common Cuban usage of the adjective *afrocubano*. Cuban scholars, in fact, generally restrict the use of such a term to forms presenting evident African retentions. In the case of music, musicologists tend to define as *música afrocubana* folkloric forms of African derivation such as the music of santería, *palo monte* and *abakuá*, but not styles with a clear black cultural matrix and audience such as rumba and popular dance music (see, for example, León 1974 and Alén Rodríguez 1994). Such a conceptual distinction tends to hide the fact that the great majority of dance music made in Cuba after the revolution (as much of that made before) incorporates influences from Afro-Cuban folklore, has been mainly produced by Afro-Cuban musicians, and has a largely Afro-Cuban following. While popular dance music in Cuba enjoys a wide, inter-racial mass appeal, and no statistical data are available on the correlation of music consumption and race, both common opinion and empirical evidence suggest that the most devoted practitioners and followers of *música bailable* are Blacks.

---

[1] I am aware of the extremely intricate, mobile and contradictory nature of racial labels, a fact that is particularly visible in post-colonial societies such as Cuba, where popular language expresses an incredible range of racial distinctions (see Chapter 6).

By adopting the concept of subculture, I have not implied the existence of any unmediated relation between musical style and social class. Likewise, by talking of Afro-Cuban music and culture, I do not imply any essential relation between timba and black ethnicity. I make this clarification because timba and salsa, as Afro-Caribbean styles, are frequently perceived by outsiders as inherently primitive, 'tropical' forms, which share with the unclear category of 'black music' characteristics such as emotional immediacy, spontaneity, sensuality and physicality (Tagg 1989; Gilroy 1993).

As Negus (1996) has noticed, such a picture of black music tends to combine two related essentialisms: the view that black people are more natural, and the idea of a superior naturality of their music. While timba superficially conforms to these clichés, it actually challenges them in many important ways. Contrary to stereotypes of black music as direct, unmediated, joyous, bodily and rhythmic (and therefore not, or less, intellectual), timba is difficult to play, requires a remarkable technical mastery and entails a great deal of organization. In fact, it is not any more spontaneous than jazz, where improvisation is the result of technical dexterity and instant compositional skills developed by musicians over a long period of practice. Its references to past Afro-Cuban music are not 'natural': as one important black musician once put it, it was only thanks to his professional apprenticeship that he 'learned how to dominate the syncopation of Cuban music' (D. Calzado, in Goizueta 1996). Its festive character hides references to important social issues, and its celebration of sensuality, far from expressing a natural quality of Afro-Cubans, helps to articulate black and Latin male sexual myths and shifts in gender roles in Cuba.

The notion of the *black Atlantic*, elaborated by Paul Gilroy (1993), challenges views that imply a necessary, essential link between music and black ethnicity, and provides a flexible framework to look at black American identities and cultural forms not as fixed, but as continuously recreated throughout the African diaspora. In drawing on the previously marginalized world of Afro-Cuban language, religion, visual imagery, music and dance, timba shows parallels with analogous movements visible in places as different as Haiti, Colombia and Brazil, where these trends appear at the same time rooted in local African-derived traditions and informed by international black popular culture (Averill 1997; Wade 2000; Sansone 2003). The fusion of local and foreign elements made by *timberos*, and their transnational cultural ties with the black diaspora, represent in fact a serious challenge to Cuban dominant political ideology. This, I argue, not so much because timba represents the emergence of a form of black nationalism or separatism, but because it resists being framed in nationalistic terms, and totally bypasses the attempts to promote political cohesion with the old-fashioned tools of nationalism. As Lipsitz has suggested,

> Post-colonial cultural expressions are based on experiences of people and communities, rather than on the master narratives of the nation state.... The populations best prepared for cultural conflict and political contestation in a globalized world economy may well be the diasporic communities of displaced Africans, Asians and Latin Americans created by the machinations of world capitalism over the centuries. These populations, long accustomed to code switching, syncretism, and hybridity may prove far more important for what they *possess* in cultural terms than for what they appear to *lack* in the political lexicon of the nation state.
>
> (1994: 31)

Lipsitz' reference to syncretism leads me to a further point, related to the frequent use of this notion in discussions on Caribbean culture. Syncretism, I believe, may not be the best way to conceptualize this type of cultural process. In Herskovits' influential formulation, syncretism was based on a passive notion of cultural resistance, a somewhat mechanic blending of elements of two cultures into a third hybrid form, through which elements of African culture were retained in the Americas (Perna 2000b). What we actually have in a music like timba is an eclectic cultural mix, a stylistic and ideological bricolage including modernized dance music, elements of Afro-Cuban folkloric music, jazz harmony and instrumentation, rap-inflected vocals and pan-Caribbean influences. Timba juxtaposes elements taken from different and contrasting domains – secular/religious, folkloric/popular, artistic/commercial, national/foreign – and reconciles consumer culture with African deities in a process that is very reminiscent of contemporary African popular cultures (Barber 1997).

In its incessant movement between different spaces, times and ideologies, timba also cast doubts on the clear-cut distinctions between African and European music that are deeply embedded in the way Cuban authors discuss music, and that have been often taken for granted by Western scholars.[2] Rather than one of retention of African elements, the logic at work in timba seems to be that of a *practice*, a process of permanent re-appropriation and re-articulation. In the words of Cuban art critic Gerardo Mosquera,

> More than survival, the real feat of the culture of Africa on the other side of the Atlantic is its story of flexibility, appropriation, and transformation from its own essential character as dynamic function, achieved under conditions of extreme dominance – an anti-fundamentalist strategy of taking advantage of the opponent's strength.... On this last point [i.e.

---

[2] See, for example, León 1974, and Alén Rodríguez 1994. Manuel 1995 categorizes Cuban music under African-derived and European-derived styles.

religion] another word has been abused – 'syncretism' – to designate
something that corresponds more to the concept of 'appropriation', in the
sense of taking over for one's own use and on one's own initiative the
diverse and even hegemonic or imposed elements, in contrast to assuming
an attitude of passive eclecticism or synthesis.

(1996: 227)

Since the end of the 1980s, the interest of ethnomusicology in new forms
of urban, eclectic popular musical styles has greatly expanded around the
much-debated category of world music.[3] In this respect, my analysis of
the relationship between timba and the recent boom of Cuban
'traditional' music as embodied by *Buena Vista Social Club* raises once
more the thorny issue of the culturally and politically ambiguous role of
this musical label. Reflecting on the phenomenon, it seems to me that
timba has paid in terms of international marginalization for its resistance
both to stereotypes of tropicalism and to idealized notions of tradition
and cultural authenticity. On a more positive note, timba has provided a
perfect example of how it has become impossible to define 'local' styles
in reference to a purely national, culturally and geographically enclosed
context. Jocelyne Guilbault has suggested that the study of local popular
styles may be 'integral to an understanding of the emerging phenomenon
of world music' (1993: xv). In the case of timba, I would add, such a
study strongly needs to be focused on the 'struggle and competition
between different producers, tastes and money-makers' (Frith 1989: 3)
across both the local and the global scene, in order to dispel the
accumulation of stereotypes that afflict the Western perception of 'other'
musics and to shed light on the complex network of reciprocal influences
that connect localized styles with the symbols and meanings that
circulate around the globe.

About this book

In the past decade, non-Western popular music has been investigated by
ethnomusicology and popular music studies, two disciplinary areas that
both offer valuable methodological tools. The use of ethnographic and
musicological instruments, in particular, can help to overcome the lack
of empirical data and the risk of over-theorization often found in popular
music studies (Cohen 1993), and to integrate the cultural analysis of
popular styles with specific musicological investigation (as advocated,
for example, by Tagg 1982, Frith and Goodwin 1990 and McClary and
Walser 1990).

---

[3] On the debate on world music, see Frith 1989, Garofalo 1993, Mitchell 1993, Pacini
Hernández 1993, Goodwin and Gore 1995, Guilbault 1997 and Hesmondhalgh 1998.

In my research, I have deployed some classic ethnographic tools in order to give a voice to musicians and audiences and offer a view of timba from below, looking at how those who make and use timba explain and conceptualize it. I have conducted fieldwork on the island, attending bands' rehearsals and shows, and carrying out lengthy conversations and interviews with musicians, scholars and members of the audience. In order to describe timba's own 'musical logic', and to explore some possible relations between sound and social structure, furthermore, I have recorded my own material, and transcribed and analysed excerpts from timba songs (although for that last purpose I have used commercial rather than field recordings).

Music's own 'internal' logic, however, is affected, limited and directed by a variety of social forces, and perhaps more visibly so in socialist Cuba, where the state has a pervasive role and power. Ethnomusicology's general synchronic approach and emphasis on culturally integrated societies, therefore, appears less helpful when dealing with the complexities of modern popular culture and issues such as politics, class and gender.[4] It is clear that timba, while retaining strong ties with Afro-Cuban expressive traditions, is not a type of folk music, but an expression of contemporary urban black popular culture, a commodi-fied style circulated through media and records. In that respect, cultural studies have appeared to offer more sophisticated conceptual reference points that could help to make sense of timba as a subculture, and of its positioning within the global market and the black diaspora. This part of the investigation, therefore, has required looking at the economic, social and political framework that has made timba possible and successful, making use of a variety of cultural and historical material. Insiders' discourses from below, thus, have been put into context and related to the readings of timba circulated by the media and the music industry through records and articles in the Cuban and international press.

A final aspect of the work behind this book that I wish to mention here is the fact that my research in Cuba has been complemented by fieldwork in Europe, during which I have met a considerable number of Cuban musicians resident in Europe and have come into contact with a series of Cuban and European promoters, dance teachers, dancers and music fans. While initially motivated by practical reasons, this approach has eventually led to a conceptual re-focusing. The view of

---

[4] For a critique of ethnomusicology from the 'popular' side, see Middleton 1990 and Moore 1997. In my view, however, ethnomusicology's limitations are not conceptual but eminently operational, and do not avoid remarkable undertakings in the analysis of popular music (for example Manuel 1988).

Cuban music from afar has proved particularly important to appreciate timba's transnational nature and ability to shift its meanings across different places and contexts, and to understand the conflicting representations of Cuban music circulating in the West. By looking at timba not only from a local perspective but also through its 'global' dimension, I have been made aware not only of the way dance music is central to Cuban diasporic communities and the piecing together of their fragmented identities, but also of the necessity of reading popular music and culture considering circuits, not single places (Clifford 1992).

Overview of chapters

Part I sets the scene of *música bailable* in Cuba. In Chapter 1, I analyse the situation of dance music on the island prior to the 1990s, examining, in particular, the long stage of 'crisis' between the late 1960s and the mid-1980s, when the Cuban government shut down most dance clubs and the attention of the youth was mainly captured by foreign music. Due to a combination of musical and political factors, this period saw a decline in the popularity of local dance music, which was perceived as unfashionable by the media and associated by the authorities with marginal lifestyles – in an argument reminiscent of the polemics on early *son* which would later re-emerge in the criticisms against timba. Paradoxically, the revitalization of Cuban dance music was largely the result of the impact of US-born salsa in the mid-1980s, which revived an interest in Cuban *música bailable*, and constructed a popular audience that would become the platform for timba.

Chapter 2 describes the emergence of timba during the *período especial*, emphasizing the innovative role of the eclectic fusion of dance music, jazz and rumba produced by NG La Banda in the late 1980s. This chapter shows how the band exploited the fissures created by the crisis and the economic reforms of the early 1990s, and tied their experimental dance music to the expansion of the tourist industry. By the mid-1990s, timba had placed itself at the centre of the Cuban entertainment industry, enjoying a veritable boom, and leading to the emergence of new bands and solo singers who rose to the status of international artists and local superstars.

Chapter 3 examines the structural changes that occurred in professional music-making in Cuba during the 1990s. By producing a drastic downsizing of the welfare state, the economic crisis transformed Cuban musicians from state employees into small entrepreneurs, enabling them to negotiate contracts with foreign promoters and record companies, and retain most of their earnings. Foreign tours, the opening of new dollar-only clubs and the arrival of international record companies on the island, in particular, granted MB musicians a position of unprecedented wealth, and created the conditions for the export of timba. While providing quick cash to some artists and to the Cuban music industry, however, market oriented music reforms also remarkably marginalized local audiences and other musicians, and have not eliminated forms of institutional control on popular music.[5]

Part II looks at the origins of the term 'timba' and analyses timba as a musical style and a subculture. Chapter 4 traces the term back to its possible origins and examines its adoption as a label for contemporary dance music as an alternative to terms such as son and salsa. It then provides a description of timba as a musical style, looking at issues of sound, instrumentation, structure, rhythmic organization and improvisation. Using transcribed musical excerpts, the chapter discusses the relationship of timba to previous Cuban styles and its incorporation of foreign elements drawn from jazz, funk, salsa and rap. Chapter 5 examines timba's vocal style, language and lyrical content, looking at the complex and ambiguous way in which timba songs construct their meanings. Finally, the chapter investigates timba subculture, analysing aspects such as visual style and dance, and discussing their relationship with symbols of consumer culture and 'deviant' lifestyles associated with the emergence of new social actors such as *jineteras* (young women usually described as prostitutes).

Part III examines a series of issues raised by well-known timba songs, showing how these have often challenged official discourses on race, religion, gender and political ideology. Chapter 6 focuses on the relationship between timba and Afro-Cuban culture and religion, and correlates it to the position of Blacks under the revolution. As a music largely made by black musicians for black audiences, timba appears to incorporate references to their expressive culture in the form of both language and lyrical content, and music and dance forms. In the work of NG La Banda, these references have been used to articulate a poetics of marginality aimed at challenging racial prejudice by fusing street rumba

---

[5] As this book went to press, the Cuban government announced the end of the circulation of the US dollar in Cuba, which has been legal tender since 1993 (see Chapter 2). From November 2004 on, Cubans will not be able to use dollars for commercial transactions but will have to exchange them for a special currency called 'convertible peso', paying a commission of 10 per cent. The move has been announced by President Castro as the result of the aggressive policies of the Bush administration, who in 2004 imposed further limitations on travel to Cuba and on Cuban exiles' remittances. The measure will allow the Cuban government to withstand the increasingly difficult economic situation and tighten its control on the monetary mass, but it will also affect the living conditions of people depending on remittances from the US, and has created fears about the possibility of the emergence of a black market in currency trading.

with African-American popular music. The chapter then focuses on santería, a previously marginalized form of Afro-Cuban religion that has boomed during the *período especial*, and has found great resonance in timba songs. The last part of the chapter discusses issues of cultural authenticity, looking at how timba and Afro-Cuban popular culture have constructed a dialogic relationship that has resisted attempts of folklorization and control.

While the proficiency of dance musicians has made it extremely difficult to criticize timba on the grounds of its musical quality, the studied ambiguity of timba songs has made them impervious to attacks on its content. Not surprisingly, then, criticisms of timba in Cuba have mainly focused on the alleged vulgarity of its lyrics. In examining those criticisms, Chapter 7 reveals how they stem not only from timba's sexist depiction of women – which is indeed common to much Latin American and Cuban popular culture – but also from its references to sex tourism, a fact that has indirectly questioned the role of the state-controlled tourist industry. Analysing the phenomenon of prostitution in Cuba in the mid-1990s, Chapter 7 discusses how timba has been seen as a platform for *jineterismo*, producing songs that stage an ambivalent representation of the sensuality of the *mulata*.

Chapter 8 looks at how, in the second part of the 1990s, the crisis and the 'dollarization' (dual economy) divided Cuban society, fostering a generation of black youth disaffected with revolutionary ideals and increasingly looking to tourists as role models and economic resources. In the field of popular music, the new spaces for artistic expression and private entrepreneurship produced by the crisis resulted in the increasingly defiant attitude of timba musicians. The challenge was best personified by La Charanga Habanera, who articulated the new individualistic culture of Afro-Cuban youth and were seen to embody the role of popular musicians as proto-capitalists. By singing songs and exhibiting behaviours deemed offensive to revolutionary values, in 1997 the band eventually caused a violent, unprecedented institutional reaction that sent an ominous warning to all *timberos*.

That year represented a turning point for both Cuban music and Cuban society, with the end of a period of relative tolerance, a retreat from the economic liberalization of the early 1990s and increasing repression against crime, vice and dissidence. It saw, also, the beginning of the meteoric rise of *Buena Vista Social Club* in the Western market, where their record achieved a level of success greater than any other album of Cuban music. Chapter 9 examines the *Buena Vista* phenomenon, looking at how the album has embodied, in the person of its producer Ry Cooder, an equivocal notion of musical authenticity that relates to the ideology of folk revivalism. Its success has created a worldwide nostalgic representation of Cuban music (and, by extension, of Cuban society) and has produced endless controversies among Cuban musicians of opposite parties. These contentions have been appropriated by Cuban official discourses and employed to celebrate the truly national character of 'traditional' music as represented by *Buena Vista*, as opposed to the 'excesses' of commercial timba. The final part of the chapter brings in a critique of the ambiguous notion of world music, revealing how, in the Cuban case, the international success of a brand of 'traditional music' largely ignored by local audiences but appealing to the foreign market has resulted in the silencing of contemporary popular music.

Timba may have now lost some of the novelty value it had during the 1990s, but it is far from dead, and continues to enjoy in the new millennium an enormous popularity in Cuba. Before coming to the conclusions, Chapter 10 provides a short panoramic view of the current trends in Cuban black popular music. In doing this, it attempts to read timba as part of a wider musical and cultural flourishing of black arts in Cuba. This grass-roots movement, which I have provocatively dubbed the 'Havana Renaissance', has proved crucial both to the reaffirmation of Afro-Cuban identity on the island and to the re-entry of Cuba into world culture.

A final word

At the beginning of this research I knew that, like any topic that has to do with contemporary Cuba, my work would have to deal with the bipolar logic that informs all discussions of the 'Cuban question'. In a way, rather than deterring me, the task has made the subject more challenging. I love Cuba, its music and its people, and I find US policies towards the island both cruel and ineffective. During my visits to the island, I have witnessed how the Cubans of the *período especial* deal with unimaginable difficulties. As a European, at the same time, I could not avoid asking difficult questions about the present and the future of Cuba. In my work on Cuban music I have therefore tried to avoid oppositional logics and pre-fabricated political clichés, not least because I have therefore found it difficult to share the feelings of two categories of foreigners I have frequently met in Cuba: romantics uncritically supportive of the revolution and cynical tourists who have found there the ultimate sex paradise. Was it possible, I asked myself, to look at the music and culture of Cuba whilst avoiding the bottlenecks of ideology and cynicism, of political rhetoric and tropicalism? This book is an attempt to answer such a question.

Part I

Setting the Scene

Part I

Setting the Scene

Chapter 1

Música bailable under the Revolution, 1959–1989

[interviewer]: *Do you ever sing, Fidel?*
[Castro]: I have a terrible ear for music. I do like music, but I have
no musical talent.
Not even while taking a shower?
No, Tomás. Often the water is too cold, and it makes me quiver.
I do not have that habit. Unfortunately, I have a terrible ear for
music. I like music very much, especially the revolutionary songs,
the music of Silvio, of Pablito, of Sara....
I like classical music, and I have a special preference for marches.[1]

I'm gonna tell you something a bit daring. *Música popular* is
possibly more popular than our national anthem. Maybe some
people think that 'Guantanamera' is our national anthem.
                                   J. Betancourt (interview with the author, 1999)

At the opening of the new millennium, the extraordinary international
success of the album *Buena Vista Social Club* seemed to suggest the
existence of a continuity between the present-day accomplishments of
Cuban popular music and its 'golden era' in pre-revolutionary Cuba.
Such an idea has been reinforced by the emphasis placed by the Cuban
authorities on national cultural identity, which has given the impression
of steady, vigorous state support of local popular music. In the words of
Peter Manuel, '[t]he revolutionary government has regarded the
promotion of popular culture as a high priority; moreover, it has
enthusiastically promoted Cuban popular music as a vital part of
national heritage' (1988: 37).

Similar statements need to be qualified, because, since 1959, popular
music in Cuba has undergone alternating fortunes and a rather
complicated history. After the revolution, the Cuban state extended its
control over practically every area of music production, distribution and
consumption, also playing a central role in artistic education. At certain
stages, the Cuban authorities have supported and promoted selected
popular music styles and artists. For a complex series of reasons,
however, the most popular type of Cuban recreational music, *música*

---

[1] T. Borge, interview with Fidel Castro, *El Nuevo Diario* (Managua), 7 June 1992.
Unless otherwise specified, all the translations of songs, interviews and written sources
from Spanish are mine.

bailable, has often met with considerable institutional distrust. In fact, between the late 1960s and the early 1980s, local dance music underwent a period of deep crisis, reaching a stage that one Cuban author has defined as 'unprecedented paralysis' (Acosta 1999: 179).[2]

This chapter examines the situation of *música bailable* (MB) from the advent of the revolution to the end of the 1980s, that is just before the emergence of timba and the beginning of the *período especial*. Aspects of this period have been covered by authors such as Linares (1974), Manuel (1986, 1987, 1990b), Elí Rodríguez (1989) and Acosta (1990a, 1999). Here I intend to adopt a different, more critical perspective, looking at the correlation between changes in music and in cultural policies, and underlining how, during the period, Afro-Cuban popular music was often marginalized in favour of other musical styles. The identification of this process, occasionally hinted at but never openly addressed by scholars and writers, is, I believe, crucial to the understanding of the meaning, the popularity and the problems of contemporary timba.

In the first part of the chapter, I look at the changes of music under the impact of the reforms and the new policies adopted by the revolution. In particular, I discuss the way in which, after a period of great expansion during the 1950s, Cuban MB was affected by factors such as the decline of the tourist industry, the emigration of major popular musicians and the nationalization of the media and of music contracting.

I then examine the state of MB between the late 1960s and the 1970s, the stage of its most acute crisis, when the majority of music venues were shut down by the authorities, and Cuban youth turned their attention to international pop and rock. In the early 1970s, foreign popular music was denounced by the government as a manifestation of cultural imperialism and banned from the airwaves. Caught between political pressures and a need to please their audiences, the Cuban media found themselves in a difficult situation and responded by broadcasting a mix of sentimental *canción*, political songs and, once the ban was lifted, Anglo-American pop. At the end of the decade, to many observers, the decline of Cuban dance music appeared irreversible.

Paradoxically, the rescue of national dance music eventually came via salsa, a type of Latin music born in the USA and initially scorned by the Cuban cultural establishment as a capitalist appropriation of Cuban son. Here I look at the impact of salsa in the mid-1980s, underlining

---

[2] In dealing with post-revolutionary Cuba, I have loosely followed the periodization adopted by historians, who generally identify five stages of the revolution: the early years, 1959 to 1967; the period of the 'revolutionary offensive' and of the rapprochement with the Soviet Union, 1968 to 1975; the institutionalization and consolidation of the revolution, 1976 to 1985; the process of 'rectification of errors', 1986 to 1989; and the *período especial*, 1990 to the present day (Domínguez 1993; De la Fuente 2001).

how its influence, thanks to a generation of innovative popular bands that had emerged during the previous decade, eventually led to the resurgence of MB, preparing the ground for the subsequent boom of timba. Ironically, many of the new talents of Cuban *música bailable* came from the state music schools where popular music and jazz were proscribed.

This chapter reveals how, in its initial stage, the Cuban revolution indeed produced a 'remarkable improvement of material facilities for cultural expansion' (Mesa-Lago 1974: 97), particularly in music, but also created conditions that have had a deeply negative impact on dance music. Rather than to a creative crisis, then, the decline of the popularity of local dance music during the first two decades of the revolution can be traced to a combination of factors such as changes in music policies and in the organization of the music profession, and to social and cultural prejudice by the media and institutional bodies. This attitude, I argue, stems from both the persistence of pre-revolutionary cultural and social biases against black popular culture, and fears of a connection between that culture and 'marginal' behaviours that might nourish a distinct black identity and challenge the construction of a racially and culturally unified nation.

Popular music in Havana at the advent of the revolution

> Never mind political propaganda. . . . help your friends to the
> happiness which travel to Cuba can give them.
> > Fidel Castro, speaking to ASTA delegates in Havana in
> > October 1959 (Schwartz 1997: 201)

In the years immediately before the revolution, Cuba was a major musical scene in the Americas, boasting several radio and TV stations and a thriving music industry, with both subsidiaries of US record companies and music publishers, and a strong national entertainment industry. The main local record company, Panart, produced half a million records in 1954, and by the end of the decade sold half of its production abroad (Díaz Ayala 1981).

The island's capital was a place of intense musical interchange, with clubs and theatres playing host to international artists such as Edith Piaf, Sarah Vaughan and Nat 'King' Cole, and Cuban musicians enjoying popularity on the international market with styles such as mambo and cha-cha-cha (Roberts 1985).[3] Besides six major cabarets, Havana nightlife

---

[3] In fact, in Cuba Nat 'King' Cole recorded various albums, such as *Rumba a la King*, *Papa Loves Mambo* and *Cole Espagnole*.

offered at least a dozen second-line cabarets where patrons could see local stars of the calibre of Benny Moré or listen to jazz combos and jam sessions. Dozens of other little nightclubs and bars, mostly concentrated in the new Vedado area, offered regular live music (Acosta 2002).

The expansion of music during the 1950s, and especially of popular music for night entertainment, was closely related to the booming tourist economy. Under dictator Fulgencio Batista, Havana had become an important destination for US travel, famous for its nightlife, gambling halls, cabarets and prostitution industry. With a neo-colonial mix of economic underdevelopment, elite tourism, financial *laissez-faire* and political repression, Batista had created a favourable environment for the development of night entertainment and dance music and the exploitation of musicians, reminiscent of the position of jazz in the USA during the previous decades. Gambling, in particular, had become a key national economic factor, paying for the entertainment in hotels and cabarets such as the Tropicana. A world-renowned venue celebrated for its excellent orchestras and lavish shows, Tropicana had on its payroll 40 musicians and 70 dancers and singers (Schwartz 1997).

Dance music played a vital role not only in tourist nightclubs and hotels, but in the musical life of the whole city. With more than forty dance events per night, pre-1959 Havana provided different audiences with an ample range of music, catered by a variety of institutions such as bourgeois and aristocratic clubs, associations and dance academies, immigrant societies, 'coloured societies' (that is, associations of Afro-Cubans), professional guilds and beer gardens (Carrobello et al. 1991).

The triumphant arrival in Havana of the *guerrilleros* headed by Fidel Castro in January 1959 did not change the situation overnight. Despite a certain degree of social turbulence and administrative chaos, the early months of the revolution saw an effort to return to normality. Clubs and cinemas remained open, artists and bands kept playing and touring abroad, radio stations went on broadcasting a mix of local and foreign music (Díaz Ayala 1981). In the face of the rebels' publicized intent to eradicate the vice industry, in the first year of the revolution international tourism and gambling continued to represent the main financial source of the national economy.[4]

The uncertainty created by the new political situation, however, led to a rapid decline in the number of foreign visitors. In autumn 1959, the

---

[4] During its first months in power the revolutionary government indeed made an attempt at shutting down casinos in Havana. But realizing the disastrous impact of the measure on the national finances, and facing angry reactions by the workers of the tourist industry, it hastily reopened the gambling halls under its own supervision (Schwartz 1997).

Instituto Nacional de la industria turística (INIT) made a desperate attempt to rescue the local tourist industry. It issued a promotional booklet entitled *Cuba, 1959: Land of Opportunity, Playland of the Americas*, and hosted a convention of the (US) American Society of Travel Agents, where Castro 'unapologetically acclaimed tourism as Cuba's salvation' (Schwartz 1997: 201). Despite such efforts, international travel to Cuba did not return to pre-1959 levels and in the following years virtually disappeared from the island.[5] With tourism vanished a fundamental financial resource, gambling, wiped out not so much by the new government's moral crusade but by the decline of foreign travel to Cuba (ibid.).

At the opening of the new decade, the somewhat fluid political situation changed, and the international tensions between Cuba and the USA rapidly escalated. In 1960, the Cuban government expropriated all US companies, and the US government reacted by prohibiting exports to Cuba. In January 1961, Cuba–US diplomatic relations broke off. The US-sponsored, failed invasion of the Bay of Pigs in the same year, and the missile crisis in 1962, finally precipitated the international isolation and economic decline of the island, pushing it closer to the Soviet Union.[6]

Socialism without *pachanga*: the forging of a new identity

The young revolution met with ample support among popular musicians, whose working conditions during the 1950s had been far from easy (Díaz Ayala 1981). In the entertainment industry, cases of exploitation had been common, with artists having to play extremely long sets, receiving flat fees for their recordings and not being paid for the copyright of their compositions. Conditions had proved particularly bad for black artists, discriminated from their white colleagues both socially and financially.[7]

The decline of tourism, however, produced a sharp contraction in the number of jobs in the entertainment industry, affecting particularly

---

[5] Between 1960 and 1973, Cuba received an average of 3000 tourists per year (Hatchwell and Calder 1995).

[6] During the 1960s, however, the relationship between Cuba and the Soviet Union went through several ups and downs, and was fully normalized only after 1968. It is worth noting that, in that year, there was a covert conflict between the Cuban leadership and the USSR, with the latter supporting an anti-Castro faction. Only after the Soviet Union had slowed down its oil supply did Castro move closer to the East European bloc, announcing his support for the invasion of Czechoslovakia (Domínguez 1993).

[7] Racial discrimination, obviously, affected black audiences as well. In 1951, the famous US jazz drummer Max Roach visited Havana, but being black was refused entrance to Tropicana as a customer (Acosta 2002). On the conditions of black musicians in pre-1959 Cuba, see Valdés Cantero 1988 and Torres 1995.

musicians active in the lucrative hotel circuit. Hit by the fall in employment and by restrictions imposed on salaries and foreign travel, several important musicians decided to emigrate. The process intensified during 1961, when other popular musicians chose to settle either in Latin America or in the USA.[8] For Cuban music, the eventual break of the relationship between Cuba and the USA marked a turning point. From that moment on, virtually two different Cuban musics existed: one for the international circuit fed by Cuban expatriated and other Latin American musicians, and one made in Cuba by local artists for the local population, virtually cut off from the international scene and the foreign market.

In the field of popular music produced on the island, the years immediately following the revolution did not see dramatic stylistic changes, but witnessed a boom of songs, marches and hymns with a patriotic content, and the zenith of *filin* (or feeling) (Elí Rodríguez 1989). A jazz-inflected, refined vocal style emerged in the 1940s with composers such as José Antonio Méndez and César Portillo de la Luz and singers such as Elena Burke and Omara Portuondo, *filin* had developed a strong relationship with Cuban jazz, which had itself reached a remarkable level of sophistication and internationalization (Acosta 2002).

In a famous statement of the period, referring to the enthusiasm and the sense of joyful participation experienced by Cubans in the early 1960s, 'Che' Guevara described the Cuban revolution as 'socialism with *pachanga*' (a dance music style that surfaced in 1958 and was played by *charanga* bands).[9] While the government implemented nationalizations widening its control on the press, the broadcast media and the music industry, nightlife in the capital city continued to flourish. Without the racial and social barriers separating Cubans under Batista, and with clubs' prices subsidized by the state, Havana was full of cabarets and clubs, open-air balls and festivals patronized by racially-mixed audiences. Now supported by INIT, some of the big pre-1959 cabarets continued to function, including Tropicana, Capri, the Copa Room of the Hotel Riviera, the Salon Caribe of the Havana Hilton (now Habana Libre) and the Club Parisien of the Hotel Nacional (Díaz Ayala 1981).

'Che' Guevara's reference, however, proved ill-fated. In 1961, the creator of *pachanga* Eduardo Davidson defected to the USA, and entered the ranks of musicians eliminated from the Cuban airwaves. The last music fad to be exported from the island, pachanga symbolized the paradoxical position of much popular music and the dilemmas of the Cuban media and music industry during the 1960s. Because a great part

---

[8] For a list, see Díaz Ayala 1981. Between 1960 and 1962, as many as 200 000 people, mostly white and from the social and economic elite, left Cuba (Domínguez 1993).

[9] On *charangas*, see note 33 below.

of the catalogue of Cuban recorded music was represented by popular music made by émigré musicians, it was simply not usable. After their defection, the *charanga* band Fajardo y sus Estrellas were renamed on the records of the nationalized Panart label as 'Orquesta Típica Panart' (Díaz Ayala 1981).

The shift in the Cuban cultural climate was also signalled by episodes such as the censorship of *P.M.*, a documentary made by S. Cabrera Infante and O. Jiménez. To the accompaniment of Afro-Cuban music, the film showed working-class *habaneros* during their leisure time, dancing, drinking and relaxing. Initially praised by local artists and intellectuals, in 1961 the documentary was suddenly confiscated by the Institute of Cuban Film (ICAIC), which claimed that the work failed to reflect the new political realities and projected an image of Cubans as mainly devoted to dancing and drinking (Matas 1971). The incident represented an ominous sign of the change in the moral attitude of the political leadership towards popular culture, and of the uneasy situation in which music connected with public entertainment would find itself operating in the following years.[10]

The first significant changes in the type of popular music performed and broadcast in Cuba manifested around the mid-1960s with the appearance of *nuevos ritmos* such as *pa'cá*, *pilón* and especially *mozambique*. This last 'new rhythm', created by Pello 'El Afrokán' (Pedro Izquierdo, 1933–2000), employed a large percussion section playing a cyclical structure based on a combination of Afro-Cuban rhythms. To the mix of rumba, conga and *abakuá* percussive patterns, mozambique added a melody played by voices and trombones.[11]

The advent of mozambique 'made it possible to set free into the dance hall a musical and choreographic complex discriminated by the former social regime' (Elí Rodriguez 1989: 292–3). Based on group choreo-graphy and Afro-Cuban urban folklore, this 'new rhythm' articulated,

---

[10] On the discussion following the incident, Fidel Castro delivered his famous *Address to the Intellectuals* (Castro 1961). A few months after his speech, the declaration of the principles of the newly-founded Uneac (Union of Writers and Artists) stated that the organization 'regard[s] it as absolutely essential that all writers and artists ... should take part in the great work of defending and consolidating the Revolution. By using severe self-criticism we shall purge our means of expression to become better adapted to the needs of the struggle' (quoted in Thomas 1998: 1465). A similar line on culture and art was restated in the Havana Cultural Congress in 1968, and then in the Congress on Education and Culture in 1971 and in the First Congress of the PCC in 1975 (Otero and Martínez Hinojosa 1972; Madan 1982). Article 38 of the new Cuban constitution (1976) stipulated that 'artistic creativity is free as long as its content is not contrary to the Revolution'.

[11] So-called *nuevos ritmos* were a common feature in the history of Cuban popular music, and resulted from a process of 'restructuring' of sections of previous compositions (León 1974). On the *abakuá* cult, see Chapter 6.

even through its own name, an important opposition between collective black national forms and music and previous dance styles, and was enthusiastically supported by the Cuban media. Mozambique symbolized the new emphasis placed by the revolution on the black component of its population, and contrasted with that part of pre-1959 Cuban music seen as derivative of US music and economically and ideologically associated with the Batista regime. In the words of a Cuban author, 'in a period of intense class struggle, clubs, cabarets and other night centres ... [were] perceived by wide sectors of the population as symbols of opulence and corruption of the rich classes or as dens of vice of some marginal strata' (Torres 1995: 343). Jazz big bands, for example, formerly employed by hotels and cabarets and largely made up of white and mulatto musicians, declined as dance bands and were incorporated into music and dance shows.[12] Meanwhile, the honour of traditional Cuban dance music was defended by flute-and-violins *charangas* such as that of Enrique Jorrín, Neno González and the Orquesta Aragón, by trumpet-led *conjuntos* such as that of Roberto Faz and Chapottín, the revived Septeto Nacional, and by the band of singer Benny Moré, who died in 1963 (Díaz Ayala 1981; Acosta 2002). As their leader Rafael Lay later claimed, the Orquesta Aragón 'stood virtually alone defending Cuban popular music .... The mozambique arrived, and we did the mozanchá .... Forty-one years without interruptions, including thirty-three years of cha-cha-cha, always defending it' (Hernández 1986: 128–9).

Structural changes in music-making and education

During the 1960s, the policies of the Cuban government moved towards increasing nationalization and centralization, and introduced a series of structural reforms in the organization of culture and education, the media and the music industry that had far-reaching effects on the study, production and consumption of music.[13]

In the early 1960s, the government nationalized the broadcast media, merged record companies and music publishers into the state-owned EGREM (Empresa de Grabaciones y Ediciones Musicales, created in

---

[12] The big formats with many musicians only remained in fixed places such as Havana cabarets, all of which maintained a jazz band until the 1970s or the 1980s. These bands, apparently, accompanied the show but did not play *música bailable* (Crespo, interview with the author, 1998).

[13] Cuba had no Ministry of Culture until 1976, when the new socialist constitution was inaugurated. Before this time, cultural policies had been the responsibility of the National Council for Culture, an organization under the Ministry of Education.

1962) and put music clubs, venues and theatres under the management of a variety of state entities and cultural and political organizations. In 1968, completing a plan already in operation with classical music performers, it made all professional musicians into employees of state-controlled agencies (*empresas de espectáculos*). Under the new regulation, musicians were given a regular salary, paid rehearsal time and a retirement pension in exchange for a certain number of monthly performances (Robbins 1990b). The reform freed musicians from the uncertainties and economic constraints of the profession, but also inevitably increased their dependence on the state.

During the same period, the Cuban government also made extraordinary efforts to provide education for all its citizens. Mass literacy campaigns gave many Cubans access to education for the first time and, in the space of a few years, virtually eradicated illiteracy, eventually achieving the highest level of literacy in Latin America.[14] Such fervour also affected music education. In the capital city, the government nationalized a number of private self-styled conservatoires of uneven educational quality and created two new state conservatoires on the outskirts of the city (Ardévol 1969). It also designed a system of high-quality free music schools, modelled on the Soviet system of music education and initially staffed by East European teachers. The first and best known of them was the music school part of the Escuela Nacional de Artes (ENA), a National School of Arts established in 1962 in Havana in the formerly exclusive residential area of Cubanacán.

The establishment of these schools gave many underprivileged Cuban students – and among them, many Blacks – access to quality music education, and greatly improved the general technical level of Cuban musicians. The music education reforms appeared mainly set up to train classical performers who would bring culture to the masses, but also had some unpredictable effects in the field of popular music. The expansion of music education, in fact, led to the virtual disappearance of the musically illiterate or semi-literate popular musician, and produced generations of musicians who subsequently entered the professional circuit and became the backbone of Cuban popular music.

Prior to 1959, Afro-Cubans represented the majority of the Cuban population, but were socially and politically marginalized. Proclaiming its commitment to racial equality, the revolutionary government set out to give them a more prominent political role, dismantled institutional discrimination and introduced a series of economic and social reforms that benefited Blacks as the lower-income sector of the population.

---

[14] The illiteracy rate in Cuba dropped from 23.6 per cent in the early 1960s to 5.6 per cent in 1979 (Domínguez 1993).

Thanks to a demographic boom and the emigration of large sectors of the white bourgeoisie in the early 1960s, the Afro-Cuban population grew further and increased its social mobility (Domínguez 1993). For both political and demographic reasons, therefore, the presence of the black component became an important factor in the new national identity promoted by the revolution, in opposition to the *criollo*-Spanish identity of the white elite associated with the Batista regime.

At a cultural level, such emphasis on the black sector of the population was reflected in the support given by the state to research into black folklore, the creation of national performance ensembles such as the Conjunto Folclórico Nacional (1962) and the sponsorship of amateur music-making and dance.[15] This was consistent with the general acknowledgement of the Cuban revolution for the importance of art and culture, and its remarkable support of the promotion and diffusion of art and for the expansion of cultural consumption, testified by both official documents and the creation of several new cultural organizations (Otero and Martínez Hinojosa 1972; *La Cultura* 1982).

Many documents on the cultural policies of the 1960s and 1970s, however, also contained recurring warnings of the dangers of artistic practices that deviated from official ideological lines.[16] State sponsorship of music and other arts, therefore, remained firmly subordinated to projects and activities that appeared consistent with the revolutionary aim of promoting a unified national identity, and that avoided connections with aspects of popular culture that were deemed contrary to the ideals of the revolution and to Marxist materialist principles.[17]

The years of the 'self-blockade', 1968–1973

In the second half of the 1960s, Cuban youth turned their attention en masse to Anglo-American pop and rock. Trying to counterbalance the influence of international music, the media further championed mozambique and other types of national music. The attempt proved unsuccessful, and resulted in a further decline of the popularity of local dance music. As the leader of Los Van Van Juan Formell later recalled in an interview,

---

[15] According to Cuban statistics, amateur groups (music, dance and theatre) went from 1300 in 1965 to 22 600 in 1975, and 33 000 in 1980. In 1985, *aficionados* amounted to 900 000 (Otero and Martínez Hinojosa 1972; Madan 1982; Robbins 1990b)

[16] For example *Resolución 'Sobre la cultura artística y literaria'*, 1st Congress of the Partido Comunista de Cuba, 1975, in Madan 1982.

[17] For a detailed discussion of the issue, see Chapter 6.

[i]n Havana there was something called the Mozambique rhythm ... something that was not a ballroom dance but a street mass dance, which was such a hit that people got caught by it. And what happened? The government made a big mistake: as the music that was popular was coming from abroad – music such as The Beatles and rock from that period – they banned it from the radio, and by decree broadcast that guy Pedro Arrogan [sic] every half an hour. ... people eventually hated Gueiro [Izquierdo] so much that they never wanted to dance again. Van Van were born at a stage where people did not want to dance to Cuban music.

(Castellanos 1998)[18]

Although initially not forbidden, in Cuba listening to foreign music was actively discouraged by the authorities (Loyola Fernández 1997). In spite (or because) of that, the appeal of international music spread among the youth, and styles such as '*bossa nova, twist, self, yenka, gogó* and other played by Beatles ... [and] Beach Boys' became extremely popular (Linares 1974: 172).[19] The impact of these styles became palpable in the emergence of a variety of local 'new rhythms' which tried to accommodate foreign influences and bore names such as *bossa nova-son, chachacha-shake, afro-shake, bolero-blue* and *guajira-rock* (León 1974).

Towards the end of the decade, the increasing popularity of international popular music among the youth became a matter of concern for the Cuban leadership. The boom of Anglo-American rock was then associated with the emergence of anti-establishment youth subcultures across the USA and Europe, and had become a symbol of freedom in Eastern Europe as well, where the 'Prague Spring' signalled the existence of a rebel culture close to the heart of the Soviet Union (Ryback 1990).

The late 1960s, nonetheless, brought about a dramatic rapprochement of Cuba with the Soviet Union, caused by the failure of Cuban efforts at industrialization and of attempts to export the revolution. In 1968, the Cuban government announced a 'revolutionary offensive' which was intended to re-direct economic efforts from industrialization to agriculture. The offensive brought austerity into the life of *habaneros* and started a process of de-urbanization that moved many of them to the countryside.

Between 1969 and 1970, the government organized a colossal mobilization of the population, in an attempt to reach a record sugar harvest (*zafra*) that would appear to solve the problem of the economic underdevelopment of Cuba. The goal eventually proved unreachable and the effort left the whole economy shattered (Domínguez 1993). The

---

18 Los Van Van were founded in 1969.

19 The Beatles, in particular, were very popular in Cuba, making a strong, if belated, impact on local music. On rock in Cuba, see 'El rock por dentro', *Revolución y Cultura* 3/1986, De La Hoz 1987 and Mir 1997. On the Beatles' influence, see Castellanos 1997 and Villar 1997.

failure of the *zafra* signalled a 'sovietization' of Cuba, with a final process of nationalization that led to the abolition of all remaining private businesses and the creation of a totally state-controlled, centralized economy.[20]

This process included the nationalization of professional music-making and music contracting, and of the music cabarets and venues not yet under state control, in an apparent process of rationalization which eventually led to 'a far more irrational management of artists' (Acosta 1999: 54). In their effort to decentralize music activities, gain more popular participation and dismember the pre-existing star system, the authorities increased their support of amateur music-making and festivals (Linares 1974). In the late 1960s, rumours circulating in Havana talked of the government's intentions to eliminate professional music-making, on the model of sport (D'Rivera 1999).

The 'revolutionary offensive' had another unfortunate long-term effect, the shutting down of all Havana music clubs and dance venues, a closure that in many cases became permanent. During what Acosta has dubbed 'the most disastrous year for Cuban popular music' (2002: 137), the government imposed a dry-law and shut down all the cabarets, producing an almost complete paralysis of popular music performances and night entertainment (the only cabaret exempted was that of the Hotel Deauville, reserved for foreign delegations). As Acosta recalls,

> Havana has always been famous for her nightlife, her cabarets, her dance marathons in arenas and beer-halls, her carnival parties and *toques de santo* with Afrocuban dance and music. During the 1970s and 1980s, such Havana virtually disappeared, with the closure of many nightclubs, big and small, with the exception of the well-known Tropicana and of the cabarets in the most important tourist hotels. Restaurants, coffee-shops, bars and diners, as well, were closed down little by little, until the capital city... became a real ghost city, a fact twice as sad for those who knew her before 1968, the year when that inexplicable trend was started.
>
> (1999: 176)

The trend was perhaps less inexplicable if one considers the worldwide institutional fears that associate popular music and dance with deviant and anti-social behaviour. Initially motivated by the economic mobilization, with its moral crusade, the wave of closures revealed, if not an explicit attack, a deep distrust of popular entertainment on the part of the political authorities of the time. Not only would the closures help to

---

[20] The 'revolutionary offensive', part of a stage of the revolution dubbed by some scholars as 'Sino-Guevarist' (Mesa-Lago 1971), owed much to China's 'cultural revolution', and led to the closure without compensation of 50 000 small businesses, including bars and nightclubs. Private entrepreneurs were then portrayed by official propaganda as members of a persisting petit bourgeoisie hostile to the revolution (Thomas 1998).

avoid mass meetings that, in the face of the rebellious spirit of the youth of the late 1960s, must have looked particularly threatening,[21] they also conveniently helped to solve old problems of law and order related to music and dance, alcohol consumption and the meeting of 'marginal' people, many of whom were in fact Blacks. In subsequent years, the trend was partially reversed and some venues eventually reopened (albeit some for only a few days a week and others with live bands replaced by recorded music). As Acosta points out, however, the damage was irreversible: Havana never returned to what it had been, and 'popular balls disappeared from Cuban social and musical life, for the first time in history, for almost twenty years, until the end of the 1980s' (2002, 138).

The opening of the 1970s, therefore, saw a wave of austerity and moralization sweeping all aspects of Cuban public life, and hitting particularly hard the non-conformist behaviour of the youth. As in Eastern Europe, young Cubans leaning towards hippie culture, sporting blue jeans and long hair, listening to foreign music or manifesting 'deviant' sexuality were perceived by the political establishment as followers of bourgeois decadent values, and met with solemn condemnations and police repression.[22] In one of his speeches, Fidel Castro denounced people living in an 'extravagant manner': 'long hair and fancy clothes, he said, spelled moral degeneracy and would ultimately lead to political and economic sabotage' (Thomas 1998: 1435). Following his cue, other political leaders stigmatized people who played guitar and 'danced to epileptic music' (ibid.). In 1971, the First Congress on Education and Culture declared the necessity 'to contain any form of deviance among the youth', fight the infiltration of imperialist cinema, television and art, and revive the authentic roots of national culture (Lumsden 1996: 72).[23] In a move appropriately

---

[21] The signs of a rebel youth subculture were visible in Cuba as well. In his autobiography, dissident writer R. Arenas, for example, reports that in 1968 '[i]n spite of our government's official backing of the Soviet invasion, we did not remain indifferent. We organized a protest march in front of the Czechoslovakian embassy; it was a march joined by a great number of Havana's youth' (Arenas 1993: 126). Domínguez (1993) relates a massive (albeit unofficial) general strike of Cuban workers that took place during the summer and autumn of 1970. According to Pérez-Stable, 'many young Cubans were seduced by counterculture' (1983: 199).

[22] These years represented the zenith of the infamous UMAP camps (Military Units to Aid Production), agricultural forced labour camps employed to rehabilitate 'deviant' youths, among whom were many intellectuals and homosexuals (Lumsden 1996).

[23] The Congress provided a platform for Fidel Castro to criticize the 'neocolonial elements in the [Cuban] cultural movement' and attack foreign intellectuals such as J.P. Sartre, O. Paz, C. Fuentes, M. Vargas Llosa and G. García Márquez, who had criticized the arrest of poet Heberto Padilla. Shortly before the end of the Congress, Padilla was forced to read a letter of self-criticism and sign a confession (Mesa-Lago 1971).

described by Acosta as a 'cultural self-blockade', in 1973 the government banned the broadcasting of Anglo-American pop and folk music (Acosta 1990a; Mesa-Lago 1971).

The 1970s crisis of dance music: cultural nationalism, music and the media

According to Acosta, however, the Congress's declarations in favour of national culture remained essentially wishful thinking and 'were never put into practice by radio, television or other cultural organizations, with the exception of the Casa de Las Américas and, partially, ICAIC' (1999: 172).[24] The attitude of the Cuban media and cultural establishment towards local popular music styles, in particular, remained ambivalent. Throughout the 1970s, these styles received little attention from the broadcast media and remained excluded from the syllabuses of music studies.[25] The state subsidized Afro-Cuban music in the form of professionalized folklore, but discouraged aspects of black popular culture that did not conform to Marxist notions of progress. This included the practice of Afro-Cuban religious cults and the study of Afro-Cuban subjects in universities.[26]

The great popularity of foreign music and of its local imitations among the youth, on the other hand, revealed the failure of institutional attempts to regulate popular tastes. In the years between the end of the 1960s and the early 1970s, a host of local outfits inspired by foreign bands emerged, including groups such as Los Zafiros and Los Bucaneros, both modelled on US black vocal groups, and rock and jazz fusion bands such as 5U4, Los Dadas and Los Magnéticos. Trapped between cultural

---

[24] The Casa de Las Américas is a cultural institution promoting the research and diffusion of Cuban and Latin American culture. ICAIC is the Cuban Film Institute. Both institutions were set up in the early years of the revolution, were headed by prestigious figures like Haydée Santamaria and Alfredo Guevara, and enjoyed a remarkable degree of artistic autonomy.

[25] Popular music was taught in professional music schools such as the Escuela de Superación Profesional, but remained absent from the curriculum of ENA until the early 1990s (Ardévol 1969; Robbins 1989). When, in 1993, Irakere member Carlos Averhoff was eventually nominated teacher of popular music at the Instituto Superior de Arte (ISA) in Havana, he lamented the time-old institutional hostility towards popular music: 'I often ask myself why in my country they have blockaded the possibility to have a good school for popular musicians, because almost all academic profiles of our school were aimed at the formation of classical musicians' (Tesoro 1993).

[26] According to Moore (1997), during the 1960s and 1970s the authorities harassed university students and teachers interested in Afro-Cuban studies. On religion, see Chapter 6.

maximalism and the need to retain their audiences, radio stations found themselves forced to make concessions to popular taste and circumvented the broadcasting ban on foreign music by playing Spanish and Mexican versions of Anglo-American tunes. International music, also, kept entering the island through records brought in by diplomats and sailors, and through radio broadcastings from Mexico, the USA and Britain. In fact, several musicians I have interviewed, and who are now in their late forties, have stressed how, in the 1970s, Cuban youth showed little interest in local music:

> Many people started to listen to US radio stations, all those who travelled abroad came back with a lot of music, and Cuban radio stations started to broadcast that type of music. Even if we did not export any music, a lot of music entered the island, from Europe as well. Cuban music went through a deep crisis, where during the 1960s and the 1970s bands of Cuban dance music found it very difficult to find work. People did not like it, they preferred music from abroad.
>
> (Crespo, interview by the author, 1998)

Yielding to a situation they could not control, the authorities lifted the broadcasting ban on Anglo-American music after about a year. As a result, towards the end of the 1970s, Cuban radio stations began programming Abba, Boney M, Barry White, the Bee Gees and Miami Sound Machine around the clock. Cultural publications such as *El Caimán Barbudo* started to publish articles on rock, and a substantial 'alternative rock market' and a new generation of intellectual *roqueros* emerged in Havana (Villar 1997). Among them was amateur guitarist Juan de Marcos González, who would later play a central role in the revival of Cuban traditional music and in the making of *Buena Vista Social Club*.[27]

During the 1970s, the diffusion of foreign music was often blamed by the musicians of the older generation for the decline of Cuban dance music. Enrique Jorrín, the creator of cha-cha-cha, declared: 'Our youth dances to 30 per cent Cuban music, the rest is "international" music, mostly with the influence of The Beatles.' The leader of the Orquesta Aragón Rafael Lay added, 'today there are no dance-halls ... thus the youth's acceptance of North American rhythms, which they can see danced in the movies shown on TV'.[28] As a Cuban writer later commented, '[o]ur youth ... categorized as "old" the traditional Cuban rhythms, nearly all of which continued to be played, as in previous

---

[27] As a young guitarist, González recalls, he played music by 'Kinks, Rolling Stones, Jethro Tull, King Crimson, Procol Harum, Creedence Clearwater Revival, Grand Funk' (J. de Marcos González, interview with the author, 1999).

[28] Interviews in *Bohemia*, October 1976 (Jorrín) and *El Caimán Barbudo* 1977 (Lay), quoted in Díaz Ayala 1981: 315–16.

decades, by musicians older than the great mass of people who demanded new forms of musical expression'.[29]

At the end of the decade, the crisis of Cuban popular music became the subject of a long series of articles written by music reporter Mayra Martínez. The Cuban journalist eventually came to the conclusion that much of the blame was to be put on the broadcast media. She quoted one musician saying that radio stations 'have become, in practice, the musical policy-makers', and reported as a general opinion the view that the broadcast media 'do not respond ... to the people's needs' (Martínez, 1980c). In another of her interviews, she quoted music critic Helio Orovio lamenting the lack of interest by broadcasting and recording media in 'quality music', and their promotion of 'pseudo-Cuban' music consisting of Spanish pop and local covers of foreign songs (Martínez, 1980b).

The problems signalled by Martínez were also the object of a detailed analysis by distinguished jazz musician and music writer Leonardo Acosta. According to him, after the abolition of commercial music polls in the early 1960s, the absence of charts and any other type of survey on popularity had made the media prone to paternalism and manipulation, and generated a 'star system' not dissimilar to that of capitalist countries, where the same artists seen on TV were heard on the radio, performed at the most prestigious concerts and went on tour abroad (Acosta 1990a).[30] In the field of music, following foreign trends and going after 'catchy' songs, television promoted a series of (largely white) local imitators of Latin balladeers such as Roberto Carlos and Julio Iglesias. The music of these imitators consisted of a brand of *canción* which, as Manuel observed as late as 1987, 'identical in form and content to the international style of sentimental slow song, appears to be the single most predominant musical genre on the Cuban media' (1987: 172).

Damaged by the shutting down of clubs and largely ignored by the broadcasting media, Cuban dance bands also faced problems with the music industry. On the one hand, the Cuban record industry was technically obsolete and affected by problems of nepotism and public unaccountability similar to those of the broadcast media, and turned out a few, poor-quality records in a subjective, erratic fashion, releasing them with great delay (Acosta 1990a). On the other hand, the system created by the 1968 reform of the music profession generated a cumbersome

---

[29] A. Costales in *Universidad de La Habana*, no. 209, 1978 (quoted in Medin 1990: 125).

[30] Acosta's essay was written in 1983, and put in a systematic form observations he first expressed in 1978.

bureaucratic apparatus where, in order to receive their professional cards (*plantillas*) and be assigned to their own *empresas*, professional musicians had to be evaluated and pigeonholed into a system of classifications according to genre (Robbins 1989). During the 1970s, the rigid nature of that system (which was later modified) forced musicians to conform to a given style and repertoire, and made it extremely difficult to change band.[31]

Because of the byzantine nature of music regulations, for example, musicians without formal studies could not belong to an *empresa* and embark on professional work. '[B]ureaucratic mechanisms ... hindered attempts to form new bands, and made the professionalisation of artists of proved quality impossible only because they lacked academic titles. Silvio Rodríguez himself tried for years to form a band without success' (Acosta 1999: 97).[32] Under such a system, music employers could not contract musicians directly, but had to go through tortuous negotiations with their *empresas*, often to discover that it was impossible to hire the artist they wanted. Acosta quotes the cases of

> many professional musicians who managed to remain inactive, while still collecting their salaries .... Further, in the absence of indices of popularity ... and the impossibility of direct hiring by the tourist *empresas*, the mass media, or other organizations, sometimes one used to encounter the worst groups or soloists working, while others much superior (including high-level graduates of conservatoires) remained inactive.
>
> (1990a: 199)

As both Martínez and Acosta suggest, the crisis of Cuban popular music, and in particular that of MB in the 1970s, was essentially a crisis of visibility due to the marginalization of Cuban music by the broadcasting media and the cultural establishment. Despite the authorities' nominal commitment to cultural nationalism, a combination of obsolescence of old styles and bands, popularity of foreign music, law-and-order concerns and inefficiency and bureaucratization of the music industry pushed Cuban dance music to its lowermost.

---

[31] In a 1980 interview, jazzman Paquito D'Rivera complained about the scarcity of live shows and criticized the rigidity of the *empresas* system. 'We need an accurate study of this problem, so that every artist should be able to decide which band he belongs to or about his own working style. This will avoid the bureaucratic machinery becoming a restraining wall (*muro de contención*) where the aspirations and the chances of many artists, and mainly the youngest ones, would crash' (Martínez 1980a). On another occasion, trumpet player Arturo Sandoval declared that, in order to play concert jazz, he eventually had to set up his own band (Steward 1985). Both musicians later defected to the USA.

[32] Twenty years later, singer Manolín Hernández (aka 'El médico de la salsa') would face similar problems. Being self-taught, he could not find an *empresa* to represent him, and became possibly the first and most successful self-employed musician (Chapter 2).

**Precursors to timba: Cuban jazz, *songo* and the modernization
of Cuban dance music**

The 1970s represented the years of maximum isolation of revolutionary
Cuba and the zenith of institutional attempts at cultural control. But the
period was also a moment of generational change which led Cuban
popular music out of its impasse, and showed that the much-discussed
crisis of the period was all but a matter of creativity. The early 1970s, in
fact, marked the appearance of Los Van Van and Irakere, two bands that
gave a decisive impulse to the evolution of Cuban popular music.

Los Van Van (whose name came from a slogan for the giant *zafra*,
which assured them free publicity and an immaculate political
credibility) were founded in 1969 by bass player and composer Juan
Formell (b. 1942) and are still active today. A modified *charanga*, they
adopted electrified violins, electric bass and guitar, keyboard and drum
kit, and owed much of their initial success to their role as modernizers,
bringing into local dance music the influence of Western rock and pop,
and producing songs with vocal harmonizations reminiscent of US soul
and the Beatles.[33] As Formell later commented about his early years,
'before becoming a member of Revé [his first engagement with a dance
band, before founding Van Van] my plans were not about entering the
world of *música bailable*, because, to be frank, in my twenties I was
much more interested in jazz and rock than in Cuban popular music'
(Padura Fuentes 1997b).[34]

After their initial impact, Van Van increasingly Cubanized their sound
and developed a brand of modernized son dubbed *songo*, which can be
considered as one of the forerunners of timba. One of the most
important features of songo is the adoption of the drum kit, an
instrument notably absent both from Cuban *conjuntos* and *charangas*
and international salsa. The instrument represented not only a timbric
novelty, but coincided with the adaptation of rumba patterns to the
instrument, then played by renowned Afro-Cuban drummer José Luís
Quintana (aka Changuito).

---

[33] The *charanga* format emerged in the early twentieth century, playing mainly
danzones and featuring flute, clarinets, violins, piano, bass, timbales and guiro. Clarinets
were later abandoned, and the 'classic' 1950s *charanga* sound of flute and violins
became the hallmark of cha-cha-cha. For a taste of Van Van's early work, see their 1969
album reissued by Egrem on CD as *Colección Juan Formell y Los Van Van, Volumen I*
(1995).

[34] Formell's statement explains why the music of Van Van, now seen as the archetypal
Cuban dance music, in the past has sometimes been criticized by music writers as alien to
the true national style. Commenting in 1981 on their music, for example, Díaz Ayala
conservatively asked, 'Is that really Cuban music?'

In early songo, the drummer made sparse use of cymbals except for the hi-hat, and had its sound supplemented by two or three conga drums played by another percussionist, who stressed mainly the open tones. In Example 1.1, we can observe how the syncopated pulsation of the bass drum on the fourth eighth of the first bar, sometimes called *bombo*, coincides with the second stroke of the 3 + 2 rumba *clave* (here notated for reference in the lower staff). The rhythmic interplay between snare, tom and cowbell is reminiscent of the patterns played by *palítos* in rumba, and of the *cáscara* pattern derived from rumba and often played by the timbales in Cuban dance music.[35]

During their long musical career, Van Van have adapted to changes in popular taste, shifting their personnel and incorporating new stylistic features. In this respect, one of their most important moves was the adoption of trombones in the early 1980s. Under the pressure of the growing popularity of salsa, Formell modified his band's format with the introduction of a section of three trombones, instruments that had a marginal role in previous Cuban music but were central to salsa's sound. Musical aspects aside, Van Van have owed their enduring popularity in Cuba to the ability of Formell to produce topical songs with incisive lyrics, which have occasionally caused him trouble with the authorities (Acosta 1998).

Example 1.1   Songo drum kit pattern (adapted from Gerard and Sheller 1989)

[35] For a discussion of *clave* and other technical aspects of Cuban popular music, see Chapter 4.

Jazz is another musical style that has played a crucial role in twentieth-century Cuba, where the presence of jazz bands has been documented since the 1920s (Acosta 2000). From then on, Cuban musicians have had an intense interchange with this African-American style, making important contributions to its evolution (Roberts 1999). Although in Cuba jazz has had a relatively minor role as a genre of music for listening to, during the 1940s and 1950s it represented essential knowledge for musicians active in dance big bands. These drew abundantly on US commercial and danceable jazz, and were often staffed by excellent jazz soloists.[36] In the 1950s, while in Havana US jazz impresario Norman Granz produced *Cubano* (the first LP of Cuban jazz), a Club Cubano de Jazz organized performances inviting US jazzmen like Zoots Sims, Kenny Drew and Philly Joe Jones to play with local musicians. The club operated between 1958 and 1960, and was only dissolved after the break in diplomatic relationships between Cuba and the USA in 1961 (Acosta 2002).[37]

The fate of the Cuban Jazz Club highlights the uneasy position of the African-American style in Cuba during the 1960s, when the authorities alternatively tolerated and rejected it as a style associated with US imperialism.[38] Havana was full of excellent jazz musicians, but the word 'jazz' was not popular with the cultural establishment. In 1967, in a somehow contradictory move, the National Council for Culture (the predecessor of the Cuban Ministry of Culture, created in 1976) set up the Orquesta Cubana de Música Moderna (OCMM). This was essentially a big band staffed with young jazz musicians and created 'with the intention of somehow checking the wind of rock and fashionable music from abroad or, at least, to resist it with a product that was similar, but Cuban' (Orejuela 1999).[39] The OCMM was the only jazz band active on

---

[36] Without the influence of jazz, even the music of the most popular Cuban singer of all times, Benny Moré, and his *banda gigante* ('giant band', that is, big band) would have been inconceivable.

[37] Between 1957 and 1959, Cuban jazz musicians recorded in Havana the famous *Descargas* or *Cuban Jam Sessions*, which made a shocking impact on Latin musicians in New York.

[38] In the early and mid-1960s, for instance, many Cuban jazz musicians continued to work in the nightclubs of Havana, often backing the singers of *filin*, a style that had a strong jazz component. At the end of the decade, however, jazz life was greatly affected by the dismembering of the music industry and the closure of music venues (Acosta 2002). On the position of jazz in Cuba, see also Manuel 1987.

[39] The OCMM was directed by Armando Romeu, member of a family of distinguished musicians and formerly director of a leading jazz band. Saxophonist P. D'Rivera registers the surprise of young musicians at the news of the creation of the Orchestra, devoted to 'playing all sorts of music, mainly *jazz* and *rock* ... after so much repression precisely against all that' (D'Rivera 1999: 125).

the island after 1968 and played a varied repertoire consisting of standard and third stream jazz, jazz-rock, popular music and film soundtracks (Acosta 2002). Before eventually becoming a studio band and ending up backing mediocre commercial singers, the OCMM played a crucial role in the history of modern Cuban music as an incubator of talents who were to become part of the most important Cuban jazz group. In 1973, the Orquesta's pianist Jesús 'Chucho' Valdés (b. 1941), together with some of the youngest members of the band, formed a new group called Irakere (its name, meaning 'forest', originated from a Yoruba tale).

Today Irakere are the most respected Cuban jazz band and something of an international institution. Having made their debut in the year of the ban on foreign music, however, they initially found it difficult to be accepted by cultural institutions as a proper 'concert' band, and survived by playing during weekends for the perplexed and bellicose dancers of the Salón Mambí (D'Rivera 1999). That duality between jazz and popular music has characterized their repertoire over the years: while performing their Afro-Cuban jazz on the international circuit, in Cuba Irakere have very often continued to play popular music for dancing audiences (Martínez 1986).

Their brand of danceable (when not dance) music, in fact – with its fusion of jazz, rock and Afro-Cuban popular and folkloric influences – represents the most direct antecedent of timba. The same is true for their instrumental format (essentially that of the Cuban jazz band), which was the blueprint for the timba sound of the 1990s. Irakere's horn section, initially consisting of two trumpets and two saxes, was largely responsible for the introduction of the jazz-influenced phrasing now typical of timba bands such as NG La Banda.

One of the most innovative moves by Irakere is visible in the way they have revitalized Cuban music by conjugating a virtuoso, modern sound with rhythms extracted from the Afro-Cuban tradition. Strictly speaking, the integration of black rhythms into jazz and popular music had already a long history in Cuba. Apart from the symphonic compositions of *afrocubanistas* composers García Caturla and Roldán, musical attempts at drawing on Afro-Cuban folklore dated back to the experiments of Gilberto Valdés in the 1930s, dubbed by Alejo Carpentier as a 'tropical Gershwin'. In the field of popular music, similar attempts were visible in the piano production of Ernesto Lecuona as well as, obviously, in early son. As for jazz, one important antecedent was represented by the *ritmo batanga*, created in the early 1950s by pianist Bebo Valdés (the father of 'Chucho'). This short-lived fusion integrated the rhythm of the *batá* sacred drums of santería into a jazz big band that included two conga players and one *batá* drummer, in the person of the distinguished *batalero* Trinidad Torregrosa (Acosta 2002).

Outside Cuba, important contributions to the integration of Afro-Cuban music with jazz have been made by various generations of Cuban musicians resident in the USA, mostly percussionists. Besides the wave of mambo and the success of Machito's appropriately named Afro-Cubans, Cuban *rumbero* Chano Pozo was responsible with Dizzy Gillespie for the birth of Cubop, often considered the first Latin–Jazz fusion. After Pozo's death, between the 1950s and the 1960s in the USA several Cuban percussionists worked in the broad area between popular music (including Latin dance music, rhythm and blues, funk and salsa) and jazz, and particularly in the sub-genre often condescendingly called Latin jazz, where names such as Patato Valdéz, Mongo Santamaria and Armando Peraza greatly contributed to the evolution of the style (Roberts 1999).

Having said that, there are still good reasons for considering Irakere as the most important forerunners of timba. One is their extremely eclectic musical approach, which draws together styles with markedly different aesthetics and audiences such as jazz, rock, Cuban dance music, rumba, and Yoruba and *abakuá* cult music. In their popular production, such a fusion has been achieved particularly through the incorporation of elements taken from the black tradition of rumba and santería – and the adoption of Afro-Cuban instruments such as *batá* drums, *chekeré* rattlers and the *agógo* bell – into a modern language based on a fusion of jazz and Cuban popular music with influences from US funk and rock. Essentially a combination of Cuban and US black styles, the music of early Irakere clearly heralds the black aesthetics of timba.

In their own place and time – that is, in the Cuba of the 1970s – Irakere were the first modern Cuban band to give prominence and bring systematically Afro-Cuban sounds and themes into popular music.[40] In their work, these sounds did not simply represent a touch of colour, but constituted the very nerve of the composition. One of Irakere's early innovations was a fusion named *son-batá*, exemplified by tunes such as 'Bacalao con pan' (1973). The label referred to the fusion of son with *batá* drumming, there extracted from santería ritual context (see Plate 22)

---

[40] Irakere were later followed by bands like Afrocuba (1976) and Sintesis (1978), which both worked on fusions of, respectively, jazz and rock with Afro-Cuban folklore. Irakere's successful integration owes much to the contribution of individual musicians such as Oscar Valdés Jr., the first singer and percussionist of the band. Valdés (no relation to 'Chucho') was born in Havana in the predominantly black neighbourhood of Pogolotti and boasted an impressive musical pedigree (he was the son of percussionist Oscar Valdés I, and nephew of singers Alfredito and Vicentico Valdés). It is largely thanks to the influence of Valdés – who, inside the band, represented the 'popular' soul – that Irakere experimented with songs including rumba and other Afro-Cuban folkloric rhythms (D'Rivera 1999).

and placed into a steaming popular song amid electric guitar and brass riffs.[41]

Careful listening to a song such as 'Bacalao con pan', however, reveals that son and batá are not the only, and perhaps not even the main, reference points. The song opens with a rock guitar with wah-wah and bass à la early Santana, and progresses with a layer of melodic batá percussion supplemented by congas and drum kit which underlie all the first section. Although the piece may be called 'son' because of its bipartite structure made of a narrative part followed by an antiphonal section, its most obvious reference here appears to be rumba.[42] Such reference is apparent not only in the markedly *rumbero* singing of Oscar Valdés Jr. in the first section – which features minimal, improvised-like verses such as 'La rumba es lo más sublime para el alma divertir' ('rumba is the most sublime enjoyment for the soul', a variation of an oft-quoted verse of son composer Ignacio Piñeiro) – but also in the use of the rumba *guaguancó clave* and in the structure of the second part. This second section opens with a piano and organ *tumbao* to which are added the drum set and the *chekeré*. Then the *coro* 'Bacalao con pan' emerges, and the tumbao disappears under a seething accompaniment provided by Hammond organ, electric guitar, trumpet, bass, drum kit and percussions. With the exception of few instrumental breaks, this section is entirely constructed on call-and-responses between coro and solo singer, and then between coro and short phrases played by the trumpet. In short, the song, while labelled as son-batá, would be probably best described as a rumba with an insertion of batá drumming.

As in the case of Van Van's songo (initially sometimes spelt as *son-go*), the adoption of the label 'son' was probably due more to tactical reasons than to strictly musical ones: since son was (and is) considered to be the quintessential national popular style, nobody would dare to argue with the use of such term. Even though the subsequent work of Irakere has made extensive use of 'deep' Afro-Cuban folkloric rhythms taken from batá, *arará* and *ñáñigo* (*abakuá*) music, the most important Afro-Cuban musical influence on the popular side of their repertoire (and on the subsequent timba movement) seems to come from rumba, in terms of

---

[41] Now in the collection *Taka Taka-Ta*, Exotica, 1998. The fusion paralleled similar elaborations in the field of folkloric music and dance such as the *batá-rumba* of the ensemble Afro-Cuba of Matanzas, who aimed to create 'a new kind of rhythmic complexity by "crossing" rumba and batá drums, and by combining Kongo-based and Lucumí approaches to percussion and pulsation patterns' (from the liner notes of the CD *Afro-Cuba, A Musical Anthology*, Rounder Records, 1994). On *batá-rumba*, see also Daniel 1995.

[42] For a discussion of the musical terms employed here, see Chapter 4.

stylistic references, content and ambience. Consider, for example, another famous Irakere tune 'Ese Atrevimiento' ('Such an insolence').[43] Recorded in 1981, the song is essentially a rumba that starts with a straightforward voice-and-percussion *guaguancó*, and then proceeds to comment on the inappropriate behaviour of a black woman. Because of its direct language and macho attitude, the piece was criticized by the authorities and banned from public performances, representing an early hint to the underworld of the black *marginales* on which rumba feeds, and which would powerfully re-emerge in 1990s timba.

In a nutshell, one could say that, setting off from the two distinct directions of MB and jazz, both Van Van and Irakere engaged in a simultaneous process of modernization and re-Africanization of Cuban popular music. In such work, however, they have not been alone but have been by joined by other popular bands of the period such as the Orquesta Ritmo Oriental, an all-black, modernized *charanga* featuring a traditional flute-and-violins section alongside electric bass, keyboard and an innovative percussion section made by *pailas* (timbales), guiro, congas and drum set.[44] The mid-1970s recordings of the band present a dense sound where stylemes of US r&b, funk and soul interlock with rumba *clave* and swinging violin riffs. In the 1970s, the band was known in Cuba as the charanga with the best percussion, and had a powerful spectacular presence, featuring two musicians who would become key figures of timba, David Calzado (the future leader of La Charanga Habanera) and Tony Calà (the singer of NG La Banda).

When discussing musical innovators of the period, one must also mention GES, or Grupo de Experimentación Sonora del ICAIC (Group for Sonic Experimentation of ICAIC). Founded in 1969 and directed by young guitarist and composer Leo Brouwer, GES was a loose formation with a marked experimental character, a sort of workshop for artists with widely different backgrounds who met to study, compose and play a music that fused jazz, rock, classical and electro-acoustic music, and *nueva trova*.[45] Although GES had a minor presence in live performances, and did not make any dance music, they produced a quantity of recordings and incidental music for films of the era. The group's impact on contemporary music was to be felt mainly through its eclectic approach and the influence of artists who later became famous, such as composer and director Leo Brouwer, jazz pianist Emiliano Salvador, *trovadores* Pablo Milanés and Pedro Luís Ferrer, rock guitarist Pablo

---

[43] Now on the CD *Colección Irakere, Vol. V*, Egrem, 1995.

[44] The band was originally founded in 1958.

[45] Before *nueva trova* became officially established, in the early stage of their careers *trovadores* such as Pablo Milanés, Silvio Rodríguez and Sara González all worked with GES.

Menéndez, plus a number of young jazz musicians who would later join Irakere, such as Jorge Varona and José Luís Cortés (Acosta 2002).

Many of these young musicians came from ENA, whose music school, in the late 1960s and early 1970s, had expelled students caught playing jazz and popular music on the grounds (Acosta 1999). The ENA school had a crucial formative role in the new Cuban popular music, providing musicians for popular bands of the 1970s and 1980s such as Irakere, Afrocuba and Opus 13, and training future MB bandleaders like Adalberto Alvarez and José Luís Cortés, who all boasted a far higher level of technical expertise than previous MB musicians. Despite the categorical exclusion of non-classical music from their school's curriculum, ENA students avidly listened to foreign music. Composer and producer Joaquím Betancourt (b. 1952), a former student at ENA, was the founder of Opus 13, an experimental band that in the 1980s made successful incursions into MB. According to him,

> during the 1960s in a sense there was more US music than today.... I would say that, in the 1960s, the music less heard was Cuban music. In spite of good bands and composers, during the 1960s and 1970s Cuban music was never as strong as it is now, nor had today's importance, for different reasons .... Yes, really jazz was a little clandestine, we listened to it covertly, not officially. Because at the ENA the repertoire with the great names of classical music ... was [like] a cult. We did that secretly, we went on discovering that [jazz], and Cuban MB as well, and did that underground.
> (interview with the author, 1999)

The paradoxical role of Cuban music schools in training classical performers then led astray by popular music was tangible in the frustrated words of a classical musician in the late 1970s, who registered how 'the results of art teaching, while producing fruits in other directions, have not been able ... to give the country enough qualified personnel to fill the gaps of the Orquesta Sinfónica Nacional, which, even with the technical foreign assistance, today is still incomplete' (Fernández Barroso 1979: 121).

A further, apparent paradox is represented by the fact that many of the musicians who spearheaded the innovations at the roots of contemporary MB had entered the arena of Cuban music as modernizers. Contrary to the nominal nationalistic orientations of the government, the conservative academic practice of the schools and the cultural 'self-blockade' during their formative years, future leading figures of MB had fairly cosmopolitan tastes: Valdés played jazz, Formell was interested in rock and Cortés was mainly into classical and Brazilian music (Cortés, interview with the author, 2000). In a situation of isolation, experimentation and musical practice and consumption strongly based on live performance, their adventurous spirit prepared the ground for the rise of timba.

The impact of salsa and the resurgence of *música bailable*

Towards the end of the 1970s, the popularity of Van Van was in decline and Irakere steered towards Latin jazz, building an international arty profile that in 1979 won them a Grammy. In 1980, a Cuban survey revealed that about 80 per cent of 15 to 17-year-old students preferred 'contemporary international music', while only 13 per cent of them favoured 'contemporary national music' (Alén Perez 1988). At the time, the popularity and consumption of dance music, which offered black *conjuntos* such as Rumbavana and *charangas* such as Orquesta Revé, Original de Manzanillo, Aliamén and Ritmo Oriental, appeared essentially confined to sectors of the black population. White MB bandleader Juan Kemell recalled how, as a teenager, he used to listen mainly to US music, and at the time it was mainly Blacks who danced *casino* (the salsa-like Cuban couple dance style). Only after the phenomenal success of the TV programme *Para bailar*, he said, 'white people started learning how to dance' to Cuban music (interview with the author, 1998).[46] A further, if indirect, sign of the decline of local MB was represented by the emergence of revivalist band Sierra Maestra, which launched a traditionalist fad interpreting old *sones* and *guarachas*.

The preference for foreign music on the part of the youth contrasted with a new style that was then winning the support of political organizations. Towards the end of the 1970s *nueva trova* ('new song'), a singer-songwriter movement that had surfaced in the late 1960s, moved towards the centre of the official music scene. Described by some authors as the only new style of music to emerge from the revolution, the movement became for some years the international ambassador of Cuban music, and met with considerable success in the Spanish-speaking world (Manuel 1987).[47]

The *new trovadores* claimed they were inspired by old Cuban *trovadores*, a movement of nationalistic singer-songwriters that emerged in the last decades of the nineteenth century, but in fact appeared strongly influenced by international music, and particularly US protest song. With intellectual, self-conscious lyrics on social themes and anti-imperialism, nueva trova resonated of the international folk music of the time, showing influences ranging from Chilean 'new song' to US soft-rock, and

---

[46] *Para bailar* was a popular programme of the 1980s focused on dancing.

[47] Initially called *canción protesta* (protest song), in 1972 *nueva trova* became an officially-sanctioned movement under the sponsorship of the Communist Youth's Union (UJC). The Movement produced every year a Festival of Nueva Trova, and organized, in conjunction with the state, the Jornadas de la Canción Política (Days of Political Song). Its existence as an organization lasted until the mid-1980s (Benmayor 1981; Robbins 1990b; Nicola 1997; Villaça 2000).

instrumental formats featuring guitars and synthesizers (Manuel 1987).[48] Nueva trova may not have had that much in common with previous Cuban popular music, but it invented a new tradition of concert music that was eventually able to solicit official support (something never achieved by other styles of Cuban music) and gain regular space on Cuban TV.[49] In the opinion of one contemporary Cuban commentator, during the 1980s *nueva trova* enjoyed 'a tremendous official backing and support, ... [while] popular culture got marginalized' (R. Zurbano, quoted in Hernández et al. 2002: 70).

At the same time as *trovadores* were being hailed as the essence of revolutionary music, Cuban dance music started coming home from abroad. In the year of the survey quoted above, 1980, jazz singer and trumpeter Bobby Carcassés went on tour to Colombia with a group of musicians attached to the Cabaret Tropicana. On his return home, he declared, 'they play more Cuban music in Colombia than in Cuba' (Díaz Ayala 1981: 309). He was referring to salsa, a style that during the 1970s had peaked in New York City and then spread across the Hispanic Caribbean. As a then young popular musician recalls,

> In 1978 or 1979 I went to Panama, where I first listened to salsa. I've always been very fond of traditional music, it's our roots, our life. I brought back a lot of salsa to Cuba.... [some musicians friends of mine] travelled frequently outside Cuba and brought back a lot of salsa, music from Peru, Venezuela, and I used to listen to a lot of that.
>
> (Crespo, interview with the author, 1998)

Salsa made an official entry into Cuba during a phase of political rapprochement with the USA under the presidency of Jimmy Carter. In 1979, CBS organized a concert at the Karl Marx Theatre in Havana with a representation of US artists which included, among others, *salseros*

---

[48] Especially in its most politicized form, in the 1970s *nueva trova* was strongly influenced by the *nueva canción chilena* developed under the socialist government of Allende. The influence of *nueva canción* and Andean music in Cuba became stronger after the military coup in Chile in 1973 and the consequent Chilean political and cultural diaspora.

[49] That is not to say that *nueva trova* was simply the mouthpiece of the Cuban government. In fact, especially in its early stage, the movement faced strong official hostility. Moreover, authors such as Pablo Milanés, Silvio Rodríguez, Noel Nicola and Sara González have had quite a varied production, and taken rather different musical directions. Milanés, for example, had his background in *filin* and went on to explore Cuban traditional music. *Trovadores* of the younger generations such as Carlos Varela, at the same time, have moved close to rock and become strongly controversial. But it remains a fact that in post-revolutionary Cuba *trovadores* made the only type of explicitly political music, and came eventually to be seen, both at home and abroad, as the purveyors of revolutionary music. The supposedly stronger cultural and moral weight of their music was reflected in classification for purposes of work, which assigned *trovadores* to state-subsidized *empresas*. MB musicians, instead, were part of self-financed *empresas* (Robbins 1989).

Rubén Blades, Hector Lavoe and Roberto Roena, the Fania All Stars, and jazz-fusion band Weather Report. Due to poor publicity, the event faced a tepid reaction from the audience, and found little resonance in the media (Acosta 2002). Here is how a then young Cuban musician who was there remembers the event:

> In 1978 [actually 1979] a meeting Cuba–US took place, and Fania All Stars played at the Carlo Marx theatre. Many people in the audience ... were not very impressed by Fania.... Johnny Pacheco said: 'We came to Cuba to play for you for free, and you don't want to listen to us!' ... For the generation born in the 1950s and in the 1960s – to whom radio and TV had not given access to traditional music – that was obsolete music.
> (Crespo, interview with the author, 1998)

The same event was recorded from the US perspective by music critic John Rockwell:

> When I accompanied a group of American rock, jazz and Latin musicians to a Cuban music festival in 1979, the Cuban audiences gave the Puerto Rican, Panamanians and Dominicans a decidedly cool welcome .... To be fair, the Cubans hear Latin music all the time, and at this festival, the first of its kind under Fidel Castro's regime, they wanted more rock and jazz, which for them were the novelties.
> (Rockwell 1984: 200)

In 1983, the picture was completely reversed, and young Cubans gave an enthusiastic reception to the performance of Venezuelan *salsero* Oscar de León. His success in Cuba represented a turning point, igniting a boom of salsa that marked the beginning of a rethinking of the roots of Cuban music. As Juan Formell has acknowledged, 'with Oscar de León and Rubén Blades, our young people started to enjoy traditional Cuban music' (Rivero and Pola 1983). This is how another musician recalls the story:

> in the early 1980s, Oscar de León came to Cuba, and that gave the final push, so that people would look at what our music really was. [It was] [a]ll sold out, TV and radio producers started to realize. I think all Cuban musicians must be grateful to Oscar de León, because he turned Cuban music on its head.
> (Crespo, interview with the author, 1998)

Salsa offered to local audiences a music that sounded at the same time familiar and new. It was sung in Spanish, had a structure based on Cuban son and could be danced in the *casino* style. At the same time, through its representation of Latino life in the US city and its incorporation of elements of soul, jazz and various Latin American styles, it projected a decidedly cosmopolitan, modern feeling. The popularity of salsa fuelled in Cuba a veritable explosion of dance music, generating local imitations and adaptations. As Betancourt said, 'De León turned everything upside down. All Cubans started imitating salseros' (interview with the author, 1999).

Regardless of its popular success, however, salsa was initially rejected by the media and the cultural establishment on nationalist grounds, and accused of being a capitalistic appropriation of Cuban music (Rivero García 1979; Martínez 1981).[50] Considering the cosmopolitan character of much Cuban popular music, the argument appears rather chauvinistic and represents a strange contortion by cultural institutions that had ignored local dance music for years.

The boom of salsa produced a fracture between the new and the old guard of MB. Feeling threatened by salsa and unable to adapt to it, the latter launched an anti-salsa offensive, 'immediately supported by journalists, musicologists and all the apparatus of music diffusion, which decided to ban salsa (although this was never explicitly formulated)' (Acosta 1999: 177).[51] Younger musicians adopted a more flexible approach. Los Van Van, for example, revived their popularity by adopting the salsa sound, celebrating the move in their song 'Somos Los Van Van' (We are Los Van Van).[52] The tune narrates the history of the band, recalling the times when 'young people danced to rock and roll', and tells how the group had 'evolved' by adding 'more flavour' to son by adopting trombones (that is, the instruments characteristic of the salsa sound). The salsa frenzy also affected old institutions of Cuban MB such as the Orquesta Revé, who adapted their sound to the audiences' changing tastes, and became manifest in the work of musicians who acted as a transitional generation between previous dance music and timba. Composer and bandleader Adalberto Alvarez, for example, emerged during this period as the creator of a brand of modernized son strongly influenced by salsa, and had several of his compositions covered by international *salseros*.

In the second half of the 1980s, popular demand eventually forced the intellectual establishment to accept salsa, producing 'a U-turn in the policy of the music diffusion apparatus' (Acosta 1997). The move represented a crucial moment for Cuban dance music, which, from that moment on, earned more and more institutional acceptance, gaining a space and a visibility never enjoyed in the previous two decades. The

---

[50] In 1978, a cover of the magazine *El Caimán Barbudo*, for example, showed a picture reading 'La "salsa" es nuestra' ('Salsa belongs to us') (issue no. 131). In the early 1980s, British film-maker Jeremy Marre, who was then preparing a documentary on salsa, abandoned his project of filming in Cuba because, he said, the authorities insisted on dictating to him which music was 'politically acceptable' and did not want him to edit takes of Cuban musicians alongside those of New York *salseros* (Marre and Charlton 1985).

[51] The old guard of Cuban MB has never accepted the label salsa. In the 1980s, the Orquesta Aragón allegedly refused a recording deal with a Japanese company because they did not want to have their music branded as 'salsa'.

[52] From the album *Los Van Van*, Egrem, 1982, now on the CD *Colección Juan Formell y Los Van Van, Vol. VII*, 1995.

dance music boom also helped to revive some of the ancient dancing spaces of Havana. In 1985, after a long period of closure, the Salón Rosado de La Tropical reopened, quickly becoming the capital city's main popular music and dance venue. This open-air concrete arena in suburban Havana, formerly attached to a brewery, was, and still is, one of the few places where Cubans can dance and pay in national currency (most dance clubs now charge entrance fees in US$).

For all its popularity, however, La Tropical retained the social stigmas traditionally attached to black MB. Interviewed in 1991 by a Cuban journalist, one of its MCs assured the reporter that a selective door policy did not give 'any chances to the *lumpen*' (Carrobello et al. 1991).[53] The journalist reported that many Cubans considered the arena to be a place 'for bullies', and that neighbours complained about rows and fights taking place in the streets nearby (ibid.). Another article lamented 'the idea that dance, together with consumption of alcoholic drinks, inevitably causes problems' (Martínez 1988b). Even today, La Tropical is seen by many white Cubans as a dangerous and unpleasant place, and is heavily patrolled by armed policemen. In 1996, people trying to attend a timba concert there protested against the expensive entrance fees and ended up rioting with the police (De Motas 1996).

At the end of the 1980s, the official U-turn on dance music had extended to political organizations, state-controlled booking agencies and the media. Discovering the mass potential of MB, the UJC, the youth organization of the Cuban Communist Party, started to give people attending political meetings free tickets to dance clubs, and in 1991 organized the first Festival of Dance Music in Havana (*Granma* 155, 24 July 1991). In 1992, they took control of a popular Havana tourist disco formerly under Cuban–Spanish management, with the intention of 'making the place healthy' by eliminating the social ills generated by contacts between locals and foreigners (Elizalde 1992). As the then leader of UJC Roberto Robaina[54] told a foreign researcher,

> We've done away with the old ways of pressurizing people to come out to rallies .... Instead of hours of speeches, most of our rallies have none – just good music, dancing, singing, and maybe a short video clip commemorating a historic event.
>
> (Benjamin 1990a: 29–30)

---

[53] This policy was mainly enacted by restricting access to people holding a special card. 'To get the card', the MC explained, 'they need to be workers, students, or housewives'. Cards and tickets to music shows and clubs are often given out by mass organizations such as CTC, UJC or FMC, and, while nominally helping to give equal opportunities of entertainment to all the population, also represent an obvious form of political control.

[54] In subsequent years, Robaina's breath-taking political career culminated in his position as minister of foreign affairs. He was eventually disgraced in 1999.

The official acceptance of MB was finally sanctioned by the emergence of the once-despised term of 'salsa' in the public arena. At the opening of the 1990s, even ultra-conservative Cuban TV surrendered to popular demand and launched salsa music programmes. As the island entered the *período especial* and turned to tourism for economic salvation, booking agencies pushed the cause of *música bailable* with international promoters and the management of newly-opened tourist cabarets. Enjoying a level of popularity and institutional support unprecedented in revolutionary Cuba, MB musicians tried to exploit the popularity of salsa to re-enter the international circuit, dubbing their own music *salsa cubana*.

Conclusions

Undeniably, the revolution gave remarkable support to culture and art, establishing educational facilities such as art schools, subsidizing professional musicians and performing ensembles, and funding amateur productions and festivals. This support, in general, went to cultural and artistic activities that were seen as consistent with the interests of the revolution, or that could be mobilized in favour of its agenda.

In the early decades of the revolution, when compared to that of arts such as literature, theatre and cinema, the role of music was probably perceived as less ideologically strategic (and, after all, this was not very different to the position of music in the West). Musical cultural policies, therefore, seemed mostly concentrated on the creation of material facilities and on education, with a particular stress on cultivated music and 'high' art. Speaking at the First Congress of the Cuban Communist Party in 1975, Fidel Castro lamented that, in the musical field, before 1959 Cuba had 'suffered from a constant penetration of foreign forms, and mainly from North America' (1976: 125). He then mentioned achievements of the revolution such as the establishment of the Sinfónica Nacional and other orchestras, and praised the 'traditional line of political and social song carried on by *Nueva Trova*' (ibid.). In other words, the Cuban leadership of the time tended to perceive music either as high art or as art with a straightforward propagandistic value.

What then was the position of popular music and MB in Cuba in the early decades of the revolution? With the exception of *nueva trova*, popular music appeared to be mainly seen by the authorities as entertainment for the masses with no ideological content and use (Marshall 1988). Since popular culture rarely follows cultural policies, however, Cuban society of the 1960s and 1970s did not appear to adapt easily to the pervasive ideologization brought about by the revolution.

Despite official condemnations, previous cultural tastes persisted, foreign music maintained a strong presence, and Afro-Cuban cultural and religious practices survived. In fact, both statistics (Otero and Martínez Hinojosa 1972) and empirical observation confirm that after the revolution popular music remained the most popular cultural form. As Marshall suggested in the late 1980s, 'Cuban culture is still overwhelmingly oral. Music is the opium and the ecstasy of the people. Wherever you go in Havana you hear music' (1988:214).

Our long overview of *música bailable* prior to the 1990s, therefore, indicates that the support given by the revolutionary leadership to Cuban popular music has not always been as enthusiastic as suggested by Manuel at the beginning of this chapter. In fact, a combination of changing tastes, misguided policies, bureaucratization, law-and-order concerns, and cultural and social bias seems to have frequently marginalized MB in favour of other types of music. As in other parts of the world, the partially real, partially imagined association of dance music with deviant behaviour has brought about a discrimination of MB as the recreational music of the lower classes, mostly identified with Afro-Cubans.

In the early 1960s, the revolutionary government declared its political commitment to Afro-Cubans and their culture. The rise of ephemeral black *nuevos ritmos* such as mozambique seemed to provide the model for a new type of national popular music, and a response to the musical void created by the emigration of major Cuban artists and by the stylistic obsolescence of pre-1959 styles. When young Cubans proved more interested in pop and rock than local music, the authorities blamed cultural imperialism and declared the necessity of promoting an authentic Cuban culture. In practice, official statements did not translate into any significant support for local black popular music, and the attitudes towards Cuban black popular culture continued to waver between marginalization and control.

During the late 1970s, *nueva trova* seemed to offer a new solution to the old problem of identifying a brand of national popular music befitting revolutionary values. This new style, however, was itself strongly influenced by international music, and presented contents, attitudes and audiences that made it into a rather unique and intellectual type of popular music. Despite the emergence of new highly innovative popular dance bands, meanwhile, Cuban MB continued to be seen as unfashionable and socially problematic.

The criticisms of the media expressed at the time by MB musicians and progressive Cuban music writers – who accused them of cultural conservatism, elitism and social prejudices towards dance music – suggest that many of the problems that affected the relationship between popular music and the media in Cuba did not substantially differ from those of music in capitalist countries. The support given by the Cuban media to different, seemingly antithetical genres such as Spanish-inflected romantic song and *nueva trova*, for example, revealed a preference for certain common traits. Both styles were derivative of international music, focused on individual performers, were meant for listening to and not for dancing, and had a predominantly white audience. Both, also, took themselves extremely seriously and lacked the carnivalesque spirit of dance music, the expression of a black street culture that resisted both folklorization and neo-positivist notions of social progress.

The explosion of the salsa boom during the 1980s showed a rapid swing of the musical interests of Cuban youth towards dance music, but met with initial resistance from the cultural apparatus. By branding salsa as a commercial and exploitative product of US capitalism, the Cuban authorities seemed to miss, as they had often done with jazz during the 1960s, salsa's counter-hegemonic role in both the USA and the Caribbean as an expression of Afro-Latin identity.

Música bailable, therefore, appears to have been the site of convergence of different cultural, racial and political prejudices. Writing about son and dance music in Cuba in the late 1980s, Robbins reported that 'for many, mainly *mulato* and white Cubans, to be a *sonero* – a player of *son* – or to dance to *son* ... is to be *chéo* [vulgar], low, uncultured and unambitious' (1990a: 203). According to those people, Robbins continued, '"[m]*úsica bailable*" is "simple, crude, under-developed; it has no message". Its audience – as opposed to that of "concert music" – is represented by "the lowest of the low"' (ibid.: 204). Such representation of black music did not permeate only the everyday dominant discourse, but largely extended to the media and the entertainment industry, which perceived MB as a superficial and uncultured form of mass entertainment. In 1992, an officer of state agency Artex, then trying to sell a show by La Charanga Habanera to a journalist, told him with a broad smile on her face, 'they are some ugly little Blacks (*unos negritos feítos*), but they do some interesting things on stage' (Godfried 2000).

Because of its relationship with lower-class people, MB seems to have inherited the troublesome and licentious image attached to Blacks in pre-revolutionary Cuba, and retained old-time social stigmas and associations with marginality and crime. In some cases, as an occasion for mass drunkenness and disorderly behaviour, it has been seen as a source of nuisance and a matter for the police.[55] In other cases, as an activity

---

[55] In a recent interview with guitarist Pablo Menéndez, leader of rock band Mezcla, Foehr relates that *nueva trova* musicians 'insisted on a clause in their contracts that banned

associated with individuals with riotous and immoral conduct, MB could be considered as a potential focus for anti-revolutionary sentiment. In any case, as a celebration of sensuality and pleasure, MB conflicted with Marxist puritanical principles and seemed to bring a symbolic challenge to established social values.

The uneasy relationship of the Cuban authorities with MB may also have had its origins in the relative impermeability of dance music to instances of political control. As a foreign scholar noted in 1990, 'much of the music that Cubans listen and dance to today has no connection at all with the revolutionary message' (Medin 1990: 129). He continued,

> it is evident that the revolutionary leaders are very far from turning popular music to maximum advantage as a medium for transmitting the revolutionary message. Consequently, this highly important realm of Cuban popular culture still remains, for most part, immune to the monolithic politicisation process.

While underlining the extraordinary strength of popular music in Cuba, such a remark posits one important question. Why has the revolution failed to exploit the propaganda value of MB? One of the reasons, probably, lies in the very nature of popular music, and particularly of dance music. Consciously or not, as a form of entertainment that avoids 'serious' issues, MB has eschewed the responsibilities of politicized music, justifying itself simply on the grounds of its own popularity. In contrast to officially-sanctioned *trovadores*, thus, MB musicians have been able to avoid, generally, any direct association with political content. In this way, they have retained an ample margin of mass appeal and artistic independence, and kept open the option of making incursions into social commentary by hiding behind a screen of jocular comments.[56]

The position of music in Cuba between the 1970s and the 1980s shows some parallels with that in other socialist countries such as the Soviet Union, where the biggest selling artists were sentimental pop singers, and the early 1970s amateur rebel rockers were neutralized through a mixture of repression, professionalization and state sponsorship (Ryback 1990).[57] As John Street has observed, commenting on music in communist Eastern Europe,

---

the sale of alcohol and prohibited dancing during the performance.... "We were out to change the whole structure of music experience in Cuba," Pablo explained. "Here people had the knee-jerk reaction, 'Oh, music. Let's get drunk, dance, vomit, drink more beer and rum until we forget our bleak misery'. We wanted people to come listen to the lyrics of our songs.'" (Foehr 2001: 49).

[56] For a discussion on the content of MB, see Chapter 5.

[57] One big difference, of course, being that the Soviet Union had never had a popular music tradition in the least comparable with that of Cuba.

Popular music has been applauded and banned, it has been censored and sponsored; but whatever its treatment, it has always been mistrusted. There is a natural tendency for any institution that takes full responsibility for life in a community to be unnerved by change. What is new is never fully understood; what is not fully understood cannot be controlled. In the case of pop, this combination of ignorance and impotence can have two, quite opposite effects. For the fans, pop can come to represent an aspect of life that is beyond state control.... In the same way, pop can appear as a threat to the state's authority. 'If music fills a football stadium with raving youngsters', Josef Skvorecky wrote, 'it signals danger'.

(1986: 30)

Chapter 2

Music in Havana at the Dawn of the *período especial*: the Emergence of Timba

'A big hand for the black man struggling for his bread and butter!'
José Luís Cortés[1]

At the beginning of the 1990s, the disintegration of the Soviet Union precipitated Cuba into an abysmal economic and social crisis. Within the space of a few months, the island lost most of her foreign trade partners and saw the living conditions of her citizens reach fourth world levels. The beginning of the *período especial*, as it was euphemistically called, brought to Cubans material problems and spiritual suffering in every possible aspect of their lives, and marked dramatic social changes. To try to revive the country's waning finances, the government turned to tourism and introduced a series of previously inconceivable economic reforms, softening its position on ideological matters.

In this chapter, I look at the emergence of timba in Havana at the turn of the decade, revealing how the beginning of the *período especial* has coincided with the appearance of new actors in the field of *música bailable*. Propelled by the crisis, the expansion of tourism revived nightlife in the capital city, benefiting particularly the activity of MB musicians, and putting their music at the centre of the Havana tourist stage, as had happened in the Cuba of the 1930s and the 1950s. As the providers of entertainment for the tourism-driven renaissance of Havana, MB musicians rose to an unprecedented level of mass popularity and economic power.

At the centre of all the changes in the arena of dance music of the period was a new outfit called NG La Banda. The founder of the band was José Luís Cortés, a black musician with experience in the fields of both jazz and popular music, and who, at the end of the 1980s, had been able to tailor a type of dance music that had become extremely successful among young Blacks. As the blueprint for timba, in the early years of the 1990s that music moved from Afro-Cuban barrios into tourist clubs, where it offered its audiences – a mix of young attractive Afro-Cuban

---

[1] 'Aplauso pa'l negro que está luchando por los frijoles!', quoted in Galilea 1998.

women and middle-aged Western males – a platform for their encounters on the dance floor.

The years between 1993 and 1997 represented a period of boom for *salsa cubana*, as timba was then publicly called. Thanks to their work in tourist venues and to lucrative deals abroad, dance bands flourished, and new individual artists and bands appeared in the arena of MB. All these groups were modelled on the format of NG and adopted the structure of Cortés's popular compositions, with songs featuring nervous horns breaks and extremely long second sections filled with rap-inflected choruses. Amidst scarcity and the virtual collapse of the welfare state, the leaders of bands such as NG La Banda and La Charanga Habanera, and singers such as Issac Delgado, Paulíto FG and Manolín became the models of the successful entrepreneur in the new, market-driven Cuba.

In this chapter, I underline how the emergence and success of timba in the early and mid-1990s was due to its ability to negotiate between a series of opposite tensions. Musically, timba represented a convergence of the artistic aspirations of the 1980s with the economic opportunities of the 1990s, when musical innovators like Cortés were able to exploit the fissures opened by the crisis, navigating between art music and barrio culture, the legal and the submerged economy. With timba, formerly taboo topics such as Afro-Cuban religion and sex tourism filtered into popular music and made their irruption into the public arena, becoming the subject of a string of successful songs and countless polemics. The new style acquired an outstanding symbolic importance because it celebrated, connecting them, the culture and pride of the black barrio and the hedonistic mood of the youth of the *período especial*, unimpressed by political rhetoric and desperate to escape scarcity. For many young *habaneros*, thus, timba became both a subcultural manifesto and a practical means to gain access, via tourist dance clubs, to a world of sophistication and plenty.

Cuba into the 1990s: the advent of the *período especial*

The music and the cultural production of contemporary Cuba cannot be understood without looking at how the *período especial* has changed life on this Caribbean island almost beyond recognition. In negative terms, the crisis has brought a rapid and dramatic decline in the living standards of Cubans, which, in the previous decades, had reached levels far superior to those of most third world and Latin American countries.[2] Yet

---

[2] According to the 2003 UN *Human Development Report*, Cuba ranked 52nd in the global HDI (Human Development Index), and 6th among Latin American countries (<http://hdr.undp.org/reports/global/2003/>).

from another point of view the crisis has led Cuba to open itself to the world in an unprecedented way, making the island more dependent on global economy, exposing Cubans to Western models and ideas, and, also, spreading Cuban music and culture across the globe.

Until the end of the 1980s, Cuba was a rather isolated country. Frozen in the geography of the Cold War, it had a centralized, planned socialist economy based on trade with the East European bloc. Its citizens were seldom allowed to travel abroad, and had minimal contacts with foreigners. Foreign tourism was scarce, and represented mainly by East Europeans and a few Westerners. In comparison to the rest of Latin America, Cuban society was remarkably egalitarian, with work, housing, education and health care provided for free by the state to all its citizens. The economic and social situation of pre-1990s Cuba, however, was not idyllic. On the foreign front, the island had to contend with long-standing US hostility and the US trade embargo, and a high foreign debt. Internally, Cuba experienced difficulties similar to other socialist countries, such as economic inefficiency, corruption and chronic shortage of housing and consumer goods, coupled with political repression and social problems such as racial discrimination, youth disaffection and an increasing crime rate.[3]

The extreme dependence of Cuba on trade with the Socialist bloc made the fall of the East European regimes and the final collapse of the Soviet Union in 1991 an almost fatal blow. On losing its traditional trade partners (which accounted for about 80 per cent of foreign trade), the island plunged into its deepest economic crisis since the beginning of the revolution. This fact led many foreign observers to regard the fall of Fidel Castro as imminent and inevitable. Such a perception was particularly strong in the USA, where the Cuban–American lobby in Miami pushed for the stiffening of the US trade blockade against Cuba with the intention of speeding up the demise of Castro (the Torricelli Bill, 1992; the Helms–Burton Law, 1996).[4]

The depth of the economic and political crisis in Cuba became fully tangible between 1992 and 1993. Food and fuel became scarce, public transportation virtually disappeared and long power blackouts left Havana and the rest of the island in the dark. In 1994, in Central Havana a series of street riots took place, the first of this type since the advent of the revolution, with the destruction of state-owned stores and demands for social change and political freedom. The riots eventually led

---

[3] On the social and economic situation in pre-1990s Cuba, see Salas 1979b, Habel 1991, Domínguez 1993 and Eckstein 1997. On human rights and political repression, see the annual reports by Amnesty International and Human Rights Watch.

[4] Between 1989 and 1993, a vast US literature forecasted the imminent fall of Castro (for example Oppenheimer 1992).

to the *balseros* crisis, during which 35 000 Cubans fled the island on makeshift rafts (see Chapter 6).

The government reacted to the crisis by announcing wartime-like measures. In December 1990, Fidel Castro proclaimed the *período especial en tiempo de paz*, the 'special period in time of peace', still in place more than a decade later. This saw the introduction of strict rationing measures and the launch of economic reforms that tried to accommodate opening up to a market economy within a socialist framework.[5] The most striking effect produced by these reforms was the shift of the focus of the Cuban economy from sugar cane to tourism, seen as the quickest way of providing hard currency to the state. Castro declared, 'I envision an entire highway system north of Villa Clara, Ciego de Ávila, and Camagüey lined with hundreds of hotels' (quoted in Baloyra and Morris 1993). In 1991, the government inaugurated hotels built with Spanish capital in Havana and Varadero, and, in 1992, issued new laws devised to attract fresh foreign investments. Other reforms had a more immediately visible and direct impact on the life of ordinary Cubans. Between 1993 and 1994, to harness a flourishing black market and a booming inflation, the government de-penalized the possession of foreign currency, authorized self-employment and introduced private agricultural markets.[6]

Such measures provided a life-jacket for the sinking state's finances and, from the mid-1990s on, produced a slow recovery of the economy. At the same time, they induced changes that have had a deeply negative impact on Cuban society, generating an increase in inequality, race discrimination, sex tourism, AIDS and crime.[7] A particularly divisive effect has been that produced by tourism and 'dollarization', a form of dual economy that has created two parallel markets, one in local pesos, one in dollars. Most goods and services previously acquired by ordinary citizens in national currency have now become available only in exchange for dollars, through either the black market or state-owned shops called

---

[5] Rationing has been part of Cuban life since the 1960s. But in the early 1990s, the problem was not simply the scarcity of certain types of food or consumer goods, but the shortage of basic food stuffs such as milk, vegetables, eggs and meat. Many Cubans survived the years between 1992 and 1993 by eating just rice and beans, and sometimes drinking water with sugar.

[6] In 1993, the exchange rate between the US dollar and the Cuban peso fell from 1 : 1 to 1 : 120.

[7] For a description of the reforms, see Zimbalist 1992 and *NACLA Report to the Americas* 32: 5 (March/April 1999). For an assessment of the impact of the *período especial* on everyday life, see Azicri 2000. On the economic debate in Cuba about the role and effects of the reforms, see Carranza Valdés et al. 1996, Monreal 1997 and Dilla Alfonso 2000. For a discussion of the social impact of the reforms, see Molyneux 1996, Centeno and Font 1997, Elizalde and Perera 1997 and the *NACLA Report* above.

chopin. Goods sold there include many essentials such as clothing, vegetable oil, milk and soap, and carry a 240 per cent government tax (Holgado Fernández 2000).

As salaries continue to be paid by the state in devaluated pesos, however, Cubans have been forced to find other ways to obtain dollars, legal or illegal. Some of them have gained access to foreign currency through family remittances, which mostly come from the USA. These remittances are today one of the most important sources of hard currency in Cuba (if not the main one), but are not distributed equally. Black Cubans, for example, are far less likely to receive money from abroad, because most Cuban-Americans are white. The appearance of Westerners roaming the streets of the capital city, loaded with dollars, has thus made tourists into the most obvious providers of hard currency for the majority of the population. Numerous Cubans – including many professionals – have moved into the tourist sector, where wages are higher and tips are in dollars. It is a well-known fact that, in contemporary Cuba, hotel liftboys and parking-watchmen earn more than surgeons and university teachers.

Another way to earn dollars is by self-employed work. In the early 1990s, the inability of the state to provide basic services such as plumbing, building, transportation and car repairs, boosted the sector of the *trabajadores por cuenta propia*. In this sector, activities tied to tourism that provide foreigners with private transportation, accommodation and catering have become particularly profitable. Here, the line between legal and illegal activities is often very thin. The provision of services from the informal sector, legal and regulated since 1993, has thrived alongside less honourable activities such as black marketeering, prostitution, drug smuggling and the trafficking of goods counterfeited or stolen from state factories, such as rum, cigars and CDs. In Havana, the sight of middle-aged foreign men shopping with their teenage local fiancés has become part of everyday life.

In general, the impact of the crisis on Cuban society has been devastating. According to a Cuban sociological study produced in the mid-1990s, among the most significant effects of the *período especial* have been unemployment and sub-employment, school truancy, inversion of earnings (less qualified workers earning more than qualified ones), a growth in social inequality, an increase in administrative and police corruption, the decline of the living standards of families, a de-stabilization of couple relationships, the growth of individualism and violence, increased transgression of moral and juridical norms, and the growth of crime and prostitution (Díaz Canals and González Olmedo 1997).

The emergence of timba and the role of NG La Banda

The economic crisis, the ideological softening and the reforms of the early 1990s provided the background for radical changes in the field of music as well. On the one hand, the decline in the paternal role of the state during the *período especial* made it unable to subsidize culture and provide musicians with a meaningful salary. On the other hand, the arrival of masses of tourists and the free circulation of the dollar revitalized the lethargic nightlife of the capital city and opened up a whole new market for popular musicians. In an extremely fluid situation of economic shortages, ideological relaxation, tourism boom and semi-legal entrepreneurship, MB moved to the centre of the Havana music scene.

The musician behind the renaissance of the capital city's night scene was an experienced flute player, arranger and composer called José Luís Cortés, universally known in Cuba as 'El Tosco' (that is, 'the coarse one') (see Plate 1). Shortly before the beginning of the *período especial*, he had put together, under the name of NG La Banda, a pool of virtuosi who played an odd mixture of MB, funk and jazz and had quickly entered the elite of Cuban popular music.

Born in 1951 in a poor neighbourhood of Santa Clara, in central Cuba, Cortés was part of the first generation of those Afro-Cubans to whom the revolution had given access to a top-quality music education. Young Cortés studied at the famous school of music at ENA during the 1960s, but was expelled for his turbulent and rebellious behaviour. Instead of entering the field of classical music, he joined first Los Van Van (1970 to 1980), and then Irakere (1980 to 1988), the two single most important Cuban bands. The influence of these groups was crucial in determining the direction of Cortés's subsequent work, and the character of 1990s timba.

The popular side of Irakere's repertoire, that which insists on Afro-Cuban styles, themes and dance, had a particular influence on Cortés. With their powerful rhythm section, slapped bass lines and jazz-inflected phrasing of the horn section, the band represented for the young flutist a model for transferring the stylemes of jazz into popular music. In fact, it was during his stint with Irakere that El Tosco emerged as a popular arranger and composer, writing hits such as 'Rucu rucu a Santa Clara' (1984), which can be considered a forerunner of timba.[8] Starting out as a salsa ballad, the song progresses through a syncopated tumbao for piano solo into a lengthy montuno containing several coros (choruses) and mambos (instrumental interludes), and ending on a

---

[8] Now on the CD *Colección Irakere, Vol. IX*, Egrem, 1995. For a discussion of the musical terms contained here, see Chapter 4.

conga rhythm. NG's later production essentially differs from such early examples in its emphasis. By further expanding the space of montuno and vocal coros and focusing on dancing audiences, NG have played down the role of improvisations and instrumental solos, making room for dance and interaction with the audience.

Stylistically, Irakere appears as the single most evident musical influence on NG La Banda. In contrast to Irakere's artistic ambitions, the music of Los Van Van has provided Cortés with an insuperable model for capturing the mood of Cuban dancing audiences. With their ability to produce well-crafted tunes with topical lyrics, Van Van showed how popular songs could be used to comment on issues that were too trivial or too sensitive to find their way into the state-controlled media.[9] This view of the popular musician as a social chronicler, common to other Afro-Caribbean styles, re-emerged powerfully in Cortés's early work with NG, eventually becoming a central aspect of the poetics of timba. In the comparison with Van Van, however, profound differences in audiences and musical affiliations also emerge, which signal the originality of the project of NG. While Van Van's polished sound and humorous but always polite texts, for example, may be regarded as a successful attempt to reconcile the black and white elements of Cuban music, the music of NG appears instead to take resolutely the road to the barrio, emphasizing Cortes's idiosyncratic approach to Afro-Cuban popular culture.

In Cortés's music, this commitment to the urban barrio was not immediately apparent. In their first incarnation, in 1988, the band appeared under the name Nueva Generación (New Generation), a sort of supergroup formed by Cortés with other former members of Irakere (G. Velazco, C. Averhoff and J. Mungía). Adopting a similar instrumental format, the new band aimed, in the grandiose words of its founder, at 'looking for Cuban music of the future' (Lam 1997). The music of the band, documented by a few albums, was strongly marked by Irakere's dualism between jazz and popular music, with instrumental tunes that combined rock sounds, jazz improvisation and Afro-Cuban percussion, in what might be basically described as a brand of refined popular music for the listening crowd.[10] According to Cortés,

> at first we experimented with very well-crafted dance music in order to please musicians, critics and intellectuals, and it was a real flop; what we did was neither meat nor fish; and we did not manage to be successful in any way.... therefore we decided to make the music we felt and started to

---

[9] See, for example, Van Van's tunes such as 'La Habana no aguanta más', on the capital's housing crisis, or 'La Titimanía', on sugar daddies.

[10] *Siglo I* and *Siglo II (a.n.e.)*, *Abriendo el ciclo* and *A Través del ciclo* (Estrellas de la Salsa Cubana, Egrem, 1986–7).

enjoy it, the Cuban timba, where the real mark of our identity lies. Thus we reached the heart of the dancers.

(ibid.)

The legend has it that El Tosco, after his false start, during a tour in Colombia took the decision to narrow down the scope of his ambition and focus on popular music, and in particular on a type of music explicitly targeted at the dance floor. In doing so, he chose for his group the new name of NG La Banda – where 'NG' did not only refer to the previous name of the band, but could also mean 'no good', in a sarcastic reference to his detractors (Durán 1993). During the period 1988–9, Cortés put much of his effort into contesting criticisms, capturing the attention of the media and attracting the support of the music bureaucracy (Sarusky 1999). His breakthrough came in 1989. Under the slogan 'La banda que manda' (the band who rules), NG undertook a tour of the black barrios of Havana, something never previously seen in Cuban music. During that tour, the band played songs such as 'Los Sitios entero' and 'La Expresiva', which extolled the virtues of the black neighbourhoods of the capital city. There Cortés realized his barrio constituency, building a loyal following among young Blacks and establishing his street-credibility. His idea was perhaps simple, but extremely daring: to make a type of dance music rooted in barrio life, mixing jazz, salsa, rumba and rap, and employing elaborated arrangements played by virtuoso musicians that would combine artistic aspirations and popularity.

NG's first album was aptly titled *En la calle* ('On the street') and contained seminal timba titles such as 'La Expresiva' and 'La protesta de los chivos', a cover of 'Que viva Changó' by Celina González (dedicated to santería), and some tunes closer to the canons of then popular *salsa romántica*.[11] Their second LP, *No se puede tapar el sol*, also released in 1990, offered again a mix of timba and salsa ballads, with numbers such as 'Los Sitios entero' celebrating one of the *rumbero* areas of Havana (see Chapter 6).

Loved by many, feared by some and respected by everybody, in Cuba El Tosco is today widely credited as the inventor of timba. In fact, his music has made an original, clever montage of elements that were already floating in the space of Cuban popular music. Some were strictly stylistic features, others were textual aspects and others still – and these perhaps represented the most decisive factor – were modes of relating to its listeners. With these elements, Cortés was able to construct an audience for his cultural bricolage, and become the hero and musical

---

11 *En la calle*, LP, Egrem, 1990. That is not the CD with the same title published by Qbadisc.

vindicator of the black masses. As he would later explain, 'I am a barrio Black (*un negro de barrio*).... Everybody knows that marginal barrios are those which endure more sufferings, those that people label as bad, as bad as could possibly be' (Sarusky 1999).

With an initial audience mainly represented by low-class, Afro-Cuban youth, Cortés's innovations would have probably remained part of a long string of short-lived fads in the history of Cuban popular music. But the leader of NG was not only an experienced and charismatic musician, he was also a clever businessman. With the advent of the *período especial*, he spotted the new opportunities created by the expansion of tourism, and ferried his band to dollar-only clubs, taking with him part of his barrio audience. The convergence of Cortés's innovative musical conceptions, his poetics of marginality and the new, high profitability of MB prepared the way for the explosion of timba.

In that sense, Cortés became a leading figure of the Havana music and entertainment scene of the early 1990s. He supported local radio stations, set up the Casa de la Música in Miramar (since, NG's personal stronghold), inaugurated the Palacio de la Salsa and scouted for new talent. This role granted him unprecedented power, and gave his music a much wider resonance in terms of content and audiences. During the heated nights at the Palacio, among the local and foreign crowds cheering NG were US, Japanese and European promoters and executives of record companies.

The output of NG on record at the beginning of the decade shows an extremely eclectic repertoire of songs, with influences ranging from rock to Latin jazz, from mambo to rap. This wide-ranging approach differentiated NG from most other Cuban dance bands, and found its justification not only in the dual market of Cuban music (local and foreign), but also in the necessity to play down the aggressive reputation of the performances of NG in tough barrios, where fist-fights and stabbings were not rare. The repertoire of early NG contained, in a nutshell, all the trends developed by subsequent timba bands, such as the sophisticated approach of singers Issac Delgado and Paulito FG, the rhythmically and harmonically elaborated language of jazz-leaning Klimax and the commercial, provocative stance of La Charanga Habanera. The most original contribution by NG, however, is probably found in songs such as 'Los Sitios entero', where they were able to mix the rebellious spirit of rumba with the drive of US black popular music, producing an angular sound that resonated more of soul and funk than of polished salsa. This particular aspect of NG's work – which was clearly perceivable in their live performances in Cuba, but difficult (and politically risky) to translate onto record – set a standard for the sound and attitudes of the timba music movement.

The case of NG exemplifies a unique convergence, inside Cuban MB, of Afro-Cuban street culture and avant-garde artistic aspirations, brought about by a generation of artists who had been trained as classical musicians, had grown up dreaming of becoming jazzmen, and have found success and money as dance musicians. The artistic maturity of this generation coincided with a phase where the chances of making a living with *música de concierto* (that is, music for a listening audience) were quickly disappearing, and new free-market opportunities were materializing in the field of dance music. This dualism between artistic expression and commercialism is crucial to the understanding of timba, and translates into a constant oscillation between roughness and slickness, escapism and social commentary, creative ambitions and marketability.

The adventurous novel style championed by NG represented both a metaphor and an actor for the new, market-oriented Cuba. Acting as a focal point for night entertainment in the capital city, this music played a pivotal role in the informal economy revolving around tourism, bringing to the fore the culture of young urban Afro-Cubans and creating a symbolic and social space for their contacts with foreigners. These contacts developed in salsa clubs and, predictably, were centred on the display on the dance floor of young black bodies to the gaze of Western tourists. With an open form made of sequences of coros and improvised comments, the songs of NG created and, in a sense, institutionalized a new musical and narrative space, offering through their lyrics a bittersweet commentary on life in Cuba in times of crisis.

The mark of timba

In the following chapters I shall give a detailed account of timba, examining it analytically as a musical style and a subculture. Here, I think it useful to give a short description of the style, in order to show how NG have provided a blueprint, defining a musical model and a relationship with urban black popular culture that has been imitated by all Cuban dance bands of the decade.

In general, NG can be included in the trend of simultaneous modernization and re-Africanization of Cuban MB described in the previous chapter. Such tendency has shown itself in a propensity, on one side, to draw on Cuban black popular culture both in terms of musical references and content, and, on the other side, to show a marked eclecticism which has become one of the hallmarks of timba. While there can be no doubts on the 'Cubanness' of the music of NG, the movement of Cortés's production across different Cuban musical genres and domains (dance music present and past, jazz, folklore, bolero, song, etc.) and the range of their international stylistic references (which has shown their music open to influences as diverse as US jazz fusion, rap and funk, or Jamaican and Colombian popular styles), has made timba into a style where – much to the irritation of cultural nationalists – distinctions between what is local and what is foreign do not make much sense.

With their early music, for example, NG provided a model of song organization. Among their many experiments, the band have popularized a form of song consisting of a bipartite structure made of a first, quieter narrative part, followed by a second, more energetic section based on the alternation of call-and-response between chorus and solo singer. Superficially, the form is similar to son and salsa (hence the name *salsa cubana*). By giving far greater space and weight to the second part, however, Cortés has, as it were, stripped the narration to its bones and expanded the participatory and emotive part of the song. This innovation relates to aesthetic strategies, and also to the new social function of MB. The second section, where Cortés placed a quantity of choral refrains (coros), has become the most popular part of the song, and the one that can be stretched *ad libitum*.

The marked virtuosity of timba is another of NG's contributions to Cuban MB, and an aspect that differentiates modern Cuban music from most previous Cuban and Latin dance music. Compared to much dance music around the world, timba is a style with arrangements and instrumental parts that require careful rehearsing and a significant technical ability. In the panorama of Cuban MB, NG have put particular emphasis on the skill of individual artists, earning fame as the band with the best musicians, and making this into one of their trademarks (with a mixture of awe and respect, NG's horn section has earned the nickname of *los metales del terror* i.e, the frightening horns). This orientation certainly has to do with Cortés's musical tastes and the influence of Irakere, but is also related to factors peculiar to music-making in Cuba. The availability of highly-trained professionals willing to sell their work at a low cost has brought into timba creative aspirations and an aggressive edge, injecting into new Cuban music something of the competitive spirit at the core of jazz and other styles of African-American music.

Finally, NG's songs have supplied contemporary MB with a model through their language and content, which is frequently challenging and polemic. NG's pieces are often fragments of social chronicle depicting stories and characters familiar to dark-skinned Cubans. Some of them provide critical comments on issues such as prostitution, others contain references to racism, money, santería and everyday life in the barrio. In conformity with such aesthetics, their songs show none of the poetic, intellectual language of *trova*, and employ street slang and criminal jargon (one of these songs, indeed, is actually called 'El preso', that is, 'the prisoner'). As I will underline in the following chapters, this symbolic association with the street constitutes perhaps the most crucial aspect of the poetics of timba, the motivation for its mass popularity in Cuba and one of its most criticized facets.

The decline of the collective and the rise of dance popstars

The new musical style enjoyed its period of maximum expansion between 1993 and 1997. During that phase, it generally held in the music industry that MB was the only type of Cuban music that could be successfully exported. In 1991, Cuban television launched the enormously popular weekly programme *Mi Salsa* ('My salsa'). *Salsa cubana*, as timba was then often called, earned the support of state agencies and gained more and more space in the national printed and broadcasting media. In order to exploit the economic potential of popular music, the government authorized musicians to negotiate their own tours abroad and encouraged foreign record companies to set up offices in Cuba (see Chapter 3).

With the re-conversion of the national economy to tourism, MB developed strong ties with the new dollar-only clubs and venues that were springing up in the tourist areas of the country. The boom of tourism revived the capital city's dance circuit and had direct repercussions on the activity of popular musicians. After the lean times of the 1980s, where many of the surviving cabarets had been transformed into discos, Cuban night spots returned to featuring live music. Hotels reopened their faded cabarets and dancehalls, such as the Salon Rojo in the Capri, the re-named Palacio de la Salsa in the Riviera and the Turquino in the Habana Libre (see Plate 4). New sanctuaries of dance music appeared in the western, most exclusive part of the city, with names such as El Papa, La Mesón, La Cecilia, the Havana Club and La Casa de la Música.

The opportunities created by the new music market and the legalization of the dollar (1993) led to the emergence, between 1992 and 1995, of new bands and singers who came to dominate the arena of Cuban music during the decade. They all adopted as their main reference point the marks traced by Cortés's style: minimal narrative sections, extremely long montunos filled with coros and vortical horn riffs, street slang and topical content. For many of these new artists, NG represented not only a blueprint, but also a springboard. In 1992, NG's lead singer Issac Delgado went solo, and took with him as musical director drummer and composer Giraldo Piloto (later the founder of Klimax). In the same year, the singer of Opus 13, Paulo Fernández Gallo, organized a new band under the name of Paulíto FG y La Élite (see Plate 11). Between 1992 and 1993, also making their first public appearances were Manolín and La Charanga Habanera, who would later lead the phenomenal boom of dance music in Havana and challenge the leadership of NG.

The emergence of solo singers represented a relative novelty for Cuban MB, which before the *período especial* had mainly identified with bands. Outfits such as Los Van Van or Adalberto Alvarez y su Son, for example, avoided the focalization on singers by using more than one vocalist, and were not fundamentally influenced by changes of personnel. The focusing of popular music on individual artists and the rise of the new popstars of MB also affected the identity of established bands. From then on, the names of outfits such as Van Van, Irakere and NG appeared steadily associated with those of their leaders, who thus proclaimed their rights to the artistic paternity and the economic ownership of the band. On records, the names became 'Juan Formell y Los Van Van', 'José Luís Cortés y NG La Banda', 'David Calzado y La Charanga Habanera'. The sole presence of the picture of their leader on record sleeves signalled that the band's components had become interchangeable.[12]

In establishing the unprecedented figure of the musical popstar, the appearance of singers such as Delgado, Paulíto and Manolín not only reflected the repositioning of Cuba in the globalized economy, but also responded to functions specific to local society. The new stars of Cuban music signed five figure contracts with foreign record executives, but frequently continued to reside in the run-down barrios and tenement houses of the black areas of Havana, adopting flashy lifestyles and living in flats stuffed with all sorts of consumer goods. As the life of ordinary Cubans receded to fourth world levels, the stars of salsa projected a representation of success and sophistication, an image of escapism and self-empowerment which, in the context of the decline of the economic role of the state, acquired obvious political meanings.

The role of the popstar as the heart-throb was well interpreted by mulatto singer Issac Delgado (1963). Delgado, whose soft voice and style are close to the canons of salsa, in 1995 signed an exclusive recording

---

[12] That process would become clearly visible with La Charanga Habanera, which, between 1998 and 1999, replaced virtually all their musicians while keeping their name under David Calzado's leadership. Significantly, such a process of individualization and inter-changeability of personnel affected not only timba bands, but also revivalist groups. Since their respective leaders took part in *Buena Vista Social Club*, thus, the Afro-Cuban All Stars have become 'Juan de Marcos's Afro-Cuban All Stars' and Cuarteto Patria have been renamed 'Eliades Ochoa's Cuarteto Patria'.

deal with US top Latin label RMM (he was the only Cuban resident artist on the label's roster, and the first one to play in Miami, in May 1998). His *timbero*-crooner duality and his cultivation of a 'smooth' repertoire were the result of a decision motivated by his desire for a career as an international singer.

> I have been one of those making some musical concessions in order to integrate myself into what's going on in the world. At the same time, I have another repertoire for Cuba only. I have two repertoires, one international repertoire, and one for Cuba, so that I mix it with the international one because in Cuba, in order to dance, people need a very energetic, aggressive music.... Therefore, now, I don't make music only for Cuba, but for Cuba and the entire world.
>
> (interview with the author, 1998)[13]

While Delgado was trying to build an international career, in Cuba his popularity was overshadowed by that of Manolín González Hernández. Also known as 'El Médico de la salsa' ('the doctor of salsa'), Manolín rocketed to fame between 1994 and 1995. The comparison between Delgado and El Médico is particularly interesting, because these two singers, together with Paulíto FG, represent a generation of stars who worked an area halfway between salsa and timba.[14] With an emphasis on romantic and sometimes erotic lyrics, quiet *temas* and a sophisticated image and sound, they embodied the other side of the aggressive projection of NG and La Charanga Habanera, articulating relevant differences among the audiences of MB. According to Cuban research published in 1997, Delgado's music, with its pleasant sound, polite lyrics and romantic dance style, was particularly favoured by students and intellectuals. By contrast, manual workers and housewives with a lower educational level stated their preferences for 'more contrasting and aggressive rhythms' such as those of La Charanga and NG (Cruz Jorge 1997: 12).

Manolín (b. 1965) was a medical doctor-turned-crooner and a character perfectly tuned to the new social reality of the *período especial*. His career paralleled the changes in the economy of music and the rise of MB musicians as part of a quickly upwardly mobile class that could be seen around Havana driving Japanese cars and sporting designer clothes, golden chains and mobile phones. A protégé of Cortés, El Médico was a pioneer in self-promotion, who, at the start of his career, managed to produce a 'buzz' in Havana by staging a verbal war with Paulíto (a technique commonly employed by US rappers). He then assured the loyalty of local music journalists by taking them on tour abroad (a fact

---

[13] Delgado has since been dropped by RMM.
[14] After defecting to the USA in 2001, El Médico has considerably altered his style.

that, by his own admission, cost him between $2000 and $3000, an astronomical sum by local standards) ('Una aventura loca', 1997). Without any support from television and radio, by the end of 1994 he had been able to place songs such as 'La Bola' ('The ball') at the height of popularity in Cuba, starting a meteoric rise that would end with institutional ostracization and his defection to the USA.

The career of Manolín paradigmatically represented the rise of the new, proto-capitalist self-made man. At a press conference in 1997, the singer lamented how, at the start of his career, he had been boycotted by cultural institutions and Cuban *empresas* (the only organizations that can legally represent Cuban musicians). For that reason, he said, he 'had no other chance than to become a self-employed worker' (ibid.). With the uninhibited attitude to money manifested by young Cubans in the 1990s, he told a US journalist,

> It happens that developments in my career have coincided with certain changes in Cuba.... There was the legalization of the dollar, and to my surprise, people began associating the dollar with me.... People in Cuba have a prejudice against the dollar.... But everything costs money. I don't have anything against money at all. Money is a mediator.
>
> (Cantor 1998b)

His association with money, in fact, was not that illogical. According to the Cuban research quoted above, in 1996, by singing at one Havana tourist club, El Médico was making $9200 a month. In the same period, Delgado earned $1800, and a Cuban doctor around 15 dollars (Cruz Jorge 1997). One of Manolín's hits, 'Somos lo que hay' ('We are what there is'), probably provided the best manifesto for the new market-driven Cuba and the urban subculture that identified with timba. The song opened with a grandiloquent synthesizer quotation of the theme of *Star Wars* and then, in its enormously popular rapped coro, went,

> We are what there is
> What they sell like hot bread
> What people prefer and ask for
> What goes out of stock on the market
> What people hear everywhere
> We are the top.[15]

For the cultural and political establishment, the success of Manolín represented the very symbol of the triumph of materialism and individualism over revolutionary moral values. Much to their distaste, even his personal story – that of an individual without a proper artistic

---

[15] 'Somos lo que hay / Lo que se vende como el pan caliente / lo que prefiere y pide la gente / Lo que se agota en el mercado / lo que se escucha en todos lados / Somos lo maximo.' From the CD *De buena fé*, 1997.

pedigree who had been trained for a medical career – paralleled the widespread phenomenon of doctors and teachers abandoning their professions to become caterers and taxi drivers in the tourist industry. Not surprisingly, then, in the second half of the 1990s El Médico became the main target for the attacks on MB by the Cuban press, which criticized him for his allegedly extravagant, ostentatious lifestyle and his musical inadequacies. At a round table on culture, one panellist referred to Manolín, Cortés and Calzado as 'little entrepreneurs, successful artists, nouveaux riches'. Another panellist declared: 'Today the successful man wears a [golden] chain and has a Jetta parked in front of his house. The Médico de la Salsa is the model of the successful man: a chain, a car, and a lot of money' ('El rojo y el verde', 1997).

With Manolín, the structure of timba songs became fixed, almost formulaic, with extremely short, romantic temas on the model of salsa, and long montunos filled with coros and instrumental mambos. Manolín's half-spoken, half-voiced singing style has frequently been criticized by his Cuban detractors, who have cited his untrained voice and limited extension as an extreme example of the commercialization of contemporary MB. But perhaps the reason for the incredible popularity of El Médico in Cuba in the mid-1990s was to be found precisely there, in the commercial character of his music and stage persona. With his smart designer clothes, his optimistic message, his songs celebrating hedonism and flamboyant life, Manolín expressed the dreams of young Cubans who lived in scarcity and did not believe in the promises of the revolution. With catchphrases such as 'estar arriba de la bola' ('to be on the top of the ball', to be fashionable) and 'soy el rey' ('I am the king'), the coros of his songs coined expressions that have become part of the everyday language of the *período especial*.

Narrated through his intimate crooning, the stories of romance and casual love affairs of Manolín did not resonate of rumba and poor barrios, and made almost a counterpoint to NG's aggressive sound and topics. *Una aventura loca* (1994), El Médico's first album, contained songs about bohemian lifestyle ('Dicen que soy un farandulero', 'They say I'm a bohemian') and consumer culture ('La chica que busco lleva un jean Dakota Blue', 'The girl I look for wears Dakota Blue jeans'). With erotic ballads such as 'Una aventura loca' ('A mad adventure'), the album provided a sophisticated soundtrack to Havana nights, a soft sonic bed for young Cubans' love fantasies and sexual affairs with foreigners (see Plate 10).

For these Cubans, escapist dreams could sometimes materialize in the form of a passport and an exit visa to leave the island. 'A pagar allá' ('Reversed charge') was a tale of distant love where the narrator lamented, 'I gave you my soul, my deepest love, but your interest for all that money was more important.' As often happens with timba, it was the second part that contained the contextual crucial information: the woman had married a foreigner and now lived abroad. The song, therefore, did not simply tell a story of unfaithful love, but referred obliquely to sex tourism. Without making any explicit statement, the song indirectly questioned the nature of the relationships between locals and foreigners and, perhaps, of the whole boom of Cuban tourism.

La Charanga Habanera and the spectacularization of timba

> We aren't mad, we know what we want.
> Live your life, as if it were a dream
> La Charanga Habanera, 'No estamos locos'[16]

Another important name that emerged in the first half of the 1990s from the ebullient Havana musical scene was that of La Charanga Habanera, the band who best embodied the materialistic spirit of the decade and the acceleration of Cuban MB into postmodernity. At a time when popular musicians struggled to emerge and secure a contract with an international record label, La Charanga succeeded in building the image of a most spectacular and controversial band.

The group was originally founded in 1988 as a real *charanga*, working seasonally as house band at the Sporting Club in Monte Carlo. There, they played modernized versions of Cuban classics, sharing the stage with international stars such as Stevie Wonder, Whitney Houston and Tina Turner. Until 1991, La Charanga remained essentially an export band, virtually unknown to Cuban audiences. In that year, violinist and composer David Calzado (b. 1957) became their leader: sensing the impending changes in the economy of Cuban music, he decided to launch the group on the home market.

He kept the old name of the band, but radically altered their sound, choosing a format similar to NG, but with some important differences. Compared to Cortés's outfit, the new band cultivated an openly commercial and outrageous image, less focused on virtuosity and more on spectacularity. They paid great attention to visual details, giving much care to dress, stage presentation and choreography. Dropping traditional *guayaberas* and uniforms, La Charanga brought on stage the dress codes of hip black Cubans, with sneakers, baggy trousers, designer T-shirts and baseball caps. All this transformed the concerts of the band into theatrical shows where all the members of the group performed

---

16 'No estamos locos / sabemos lo que queremos / Vive la vida / como si fuera un sueño.' From the CD *Tremendo delirio*, 1997.

complex, sexually provocative routines that mixed rumba, break-dance and *despelote*, the new dance style of timba.

The appearance of La Charanga highlighted the transitional role of NG La Banda, their function in bridging the pre- and post-*período especial* musical and cultural spirit. Despite its compromise with the mercantile values of the 1990s, NG's work appeared centred more on artistic skill than on visual entertainment, more on social chronicle than on escapism. El Tosco wrote songs that seemed genuinely committed to Afro-Cuban culture, and presented himself as a devout follower of santería. With La Charanga Habanera and the new stars of *salsa cubana*, on the other hand, the references to the black barrio receded into the background. Rather than appealing to collective Afro-Cuban identity, the energetic shows of La Charanga and the performances of individual stars such as Delgado, El Médico and Paulíto FG projected an image based on individual charisma and sex appeal. The great popularity acquired by La Charanga in the late 1990s can be precisely explained by their incarnation of the dreams of success and money of the urban youth, who wanted to forget, rather than be reminded of, their social origins.

The novelty of La Charanga became apparent as well in their music. Without abandoning the basic model sketched by NG, they adopted references that appeared closer to disco, funk and rap than to jazz. Their tunes exhibited an electronic, emphatically artificial quality, reducing to a minimum the instrumental sections and shifting their emphasis to rapped *coros* and a very tight rhythmic fabric. On the whole, the new band's performances appeared focused less on the virtuosity of singers and more on their physical attraction and dancing skill.

In the context of the underdeveloped Cuban scene and music industry of the early 1990s, the extreme visual self-consciousness of La Charanga, acquired during their experience in Europe, represented an element of great novelty and impact, and contributed to securing them a contract with one of the first foreign record companies operating in Cuba, Spanish label Magic Music. As Calzado explained,

> We have caused a break in the canons of salsa, in its dress codes. We have started to dress in a very informal, modern way, performing uncommon scenic movements. In salsa bands only singers dance, while in La Charanga all the orchestra moves, with players leaving their instrument and coming front-stage. I saw people doing that in Monte Carlo and I got thrilled, so I transferred it into our music. It has produced good results, and many people imitated that. It's very difficult, and requires many hours of rehearsals.
> Q: Who creates the dance routines?
> I do, using musicians' ideas as well and developing them.
> (interview with the author, 1999)

Behind their image as a slick showband, however, La Charanga dealt also aggressively, if ambiguously, with social issues. One of their early hits, 'Quítate el disfraz' ('Take your disguise off'), for example, had young women taking off their shirts during the concerts and carried political references to the double standard that some consider typical of today's life in Cuba. The two albums published with Magic Music in 1996 and 1997, in particular, contained several controversial songs. Under the disguise of love stories, songs such as 'Superturistica', 'El temba', 'Lola, Lola' and 'Hagámos un chen' employed popular slang to touch on issues such as drugs, tourism and prostitution. The graphic artwork for the albums was no less contentious. The front sleeve of *Pa'que se entere La Habana* featured a $100 bill with the face of the US President disguised as a pirate. The sleeve of the following album showed a smiling black man wearing a condom over his head, and holding a flower made of coloured condoms (see Plates 7 and 8).

Conclusions

The emergence of timba in the early 1990s was the result of a very particular set of artistic factors and historical circumstances. The main musical factor was provided by the appearance of NG La Banda in the late 1980s, who originally set out as an experimental supergroup on the model of jazz-pop outfit Irakere. After their flop as a concert band, NG constructed a street-wise image and refocused their activity on dance music, establishing a large following among the Havana barrio youth.

The tourism-driven resurgence of nightlife in the capital city led to the appearance of new venues and the reviving of the old hotel cabarets, providing highly-paid work for MB musicians. In that context, NG established themselves as the most successful Cuban popular music group, the main catalysts for tourist night entertainment and the model for new bands and artists. From NG's ranks emerged various of the new names that, from 1993 onwards, fuelled the boom of *salsa cubana* (at that stage, the term 'timba' had not yet emerged in Cuban public use).

The popularity of the new Cuban MB with tourists, and the appearance of foreign promoters and music companies in Cuba, gave Cuban dance musicians a chance to reach an international audience through foreign tours and records. Some of those musicians, such as El Médico, Paulíto FG and Issac Delgado, were solo singers who worked a romantic, confidential side of MB closer to the canons of international salsa, and rose to an unprecedented level of popularity and status as local popstars. Others bands such as La Charanga Habanera, instead, promoted an openly commercial and controversial image that privileged choreography and spectacularity over purely musical values.

Stylistically, the model of song adopted by the new Cuban *salseros* appeared largely inspired by NG's blueprint, and showed a tendency to a progressive simplification and crystallization in the song's form, with a short, unimportant tema, followed by a coros-filled montuno, which became the focal point of the piece. Rather than being related to purely musical factors, such formalization of dance songs appeared strongly related to the new social context and economic function of dance music.

Thanks to their work in dollar-only clubs and abroad, around the mid-1990s the stars of Cuban salsa reached a position of outstanding popularity and economic power in Cuba. With songs and stage personas celebrating materialism and individualism, singers like El Médico and bands such as La Charanga Habanera became the symbols of the new, market-adjusted popular artist, articulating into a modern, cosmopolitan image the desires and aspirations of their young, black barrio audiences.

Chapter 3

Facing the Market: Cuban Musicians and Audiences into the 1990s

Until the end of the 1980s, the generous subsidies of the state had made the life of thousands of professional Cuban musicians markedly different from that of many of their Western colleagues. As in any other field of Cuban society, the *período especial* had a shocking impact on the music profession, producing changes that affected virtually all aspects of musical activity and consumption. Previously regarded as culture, music now became a commercial good and acquired a new economic role.

In this chapter, after looking at the particular situation of music production and consumption in Cuba before the 1990s, I analyse some of the most important changes in the organization and legal framework of the music profession introduced during the *período especial*. The economic reforms brought about the end of the state monopoly on music recording and contracting, with the aim of improving efficiency, bringing hard currency to the state and relieving it of the burden of subsidizing culture. New legislative measures attracted to Cuba foreign record companies, which financed new productions by local artists and gave them unprecedented international exposure.

The irruption of the market has had dynamic effects in some areas of musical life, but has not benefited equally all professional musicians. While initially favouring MB musicians, it has largely excluded artists of other musical genres and marginalized local audiences. The dollarization of the economy, in particular, has excluded Cubans from most music clubs and tied dance music to sex tourism and prostitution. The relative economic liberalization, moreover, has not been matched by a parallel widening of freedom of expression, and has not eliminated problems of political control on popular music through media manipulation, economic pressures and censorship.

In the final part of the chapter, I examine the contradictory impact of the US economic embargo on Cuban music. On the one hand, the international success of Cuban music in recent years indicates that the US restrictive policies have not prevented Cuban musicians from signing with foreign record companies and touring abroad (including in the USA). On the other hand, the confused legal situation and the potential economic risks created by the US embargo laws on Cuba appear to have largely discouraged record transnationals from investing in Cuban music.

Professional musicians before the 1990s

Before the *período especial*, professional musicians in Cuba led a rather comfortable life. According to their technical level, the genre and the function of their music, they were assigned to an *empresa de espectáculos*, a contracting agency which was under the authority of the Ministry of Culture and paid them a monthly salary. On the basis of the type of music and performance, professionals were required to fulfil a certain work quota, or *norma*.[1] Such a system granted professional musicians a prestigious job, earnings in the higher region of Cuban salaries and 'leisurely work schedules' (Manuel 1995: 46; 1990b).

At that stage, the activity of most musicians was focused on performances for local audiences. As international tourism in Cuba was scarce, only a few selected musicians – people thought to be close to the Communist Party and not likely to defect – were authorized to tour outside the island.[2] This emphasis on live performance marked one big difference with popular music in industrialized countries, where music consumption since the 1950s had increasingly revolved around recorded music. The only record company, state-controlled Egrem, paid flat fees to musicians and sold records at a low, subsidized price without collecting the performing rights (Robbins 1990b). As in other developing countries, records did not play an economically significant role in musicians' lives. Popular musicians made them to get exposure and fame, but earned their bread and butter mainly by playing live gigs. The centrality of live performance and the marginal role of the record industry, however, did not make the role of the broadcast media less important. As in pre-1959 Cuba, radio continued to be crucial in orienting musical tastes and determining the popularity and prestige of popular musicians (Acosta 1990a).

---

[1] The *norma*, for example, required recitalists to play six gigs per month, and MB musicians 19 gigs per month. Robbins describes *empresas* as 'a cross between a musician's union and a talent agency ... responsible for correlating musical services, pay scales, work quotas, and musicians' ratings' (1989: 381). An important distinction among these agencies is that between state-subsidized *empresas* (representing symphonic musicians, brass bands and *nueva trova*) and self-financing ones (dealing, among others, with *música bailable*). For a detailed description of the organization of musicians before the *período especial*, see Robbins 1989 and 1990b.

[2] When travelling to the West, these musicians were allowed to keep a percentage of their earnings in hard currency (most went to their *empresa*) and could thus obtain access to foreign goods difficult to find in Cuba.

Until the end of the 1980s, therefore, all sectors of music production and consumption were controlled by the state. Musicians worked for *empresas* supported by the Ministry of Culture, the media and the only record company were state-owned, venues and theatres were managed by a variety of institutional entities, and artists who travelled out of Cuba had most of their earnings skimmed off by their own agency.

Changes in music regulation during the *período especial*

The economic crisis of the 1990s hit Cuban musicians hard. While inflation eroded their salaries and made consumer goods disappear from stores, the lack of transportation and the daily power blackouts posed enormous problems for professional musicians. The crisis hit selectively, and had a different impact on musicians of different musical genres. The arrival of masses of tourists and the free circulation of the dollar, in particular, revived the Havana nightlife and offered new, attractive financial rewards to MB musicians. Pre-1990s cultural and financial hierarchies were turned upside down: whereas before 'concert music' had stood at the top and 'dance music' at the bottom (Robbins 1989), cultivated and non-commercial music was now largely marginalized in favour of music for entertainment.

The crisis and reforms of the *período especial* produced radical changes in economic legislation and in the organization of music. The economic restructuring process, in particular, pressed the state to make its companies financially self-supporting. This led to an attempt to diversify and improve the efficiency of the music industry, and to devise investment laws seeking to attract foreign record companies to Cuba. The new interest of the authorities in the export potential of music was related to recent changes in the US embargo law, which, after introduction of the Berman Amendment (1988), made it possible to export to the US 'informational material' such as films and sound recordings.[3] As a consequence, Egrem, owner of a substantial catalogue of pre- and post-1959 tapes, was encouraged to license archive recordings to Western record labels. In 1989, Cubartista – a highly bureaucratic booking agency managing the foreign engagements of Cuban musicians – was dissolved and supplanted by Artex, another state-owned but more independent agency.

The greatest changes in the life and activity of Cuban professional musicians, however, were produced by the legalization of the possession

---

[3] The Amendment, or 'informational materials exemption', is contained in the Omnibus Trade and Competitiveness Act of 1988 and in the Foreign Relations Authorization Act 1994.

of foreign currency in 1993 (formerly a serious crime). Along with the free circulation of the dollar, came the authorization for musicians to negotiate directly their foreign tours and recording deals.[4] Touring abroad, which for most Cuban musicians had previously been extremely difficult and cumbersome, became relatively easy and actually encouraged by the state. The reforms put an end to the egalitarianism of the old quota system, which limited the number of gigs and the earnings of musicians, and allowed them to charge fees according to demand (Vázquez, interview with the author, 1999). Musicians could now choose which *empresa* would best represent them, arrange their work contacts personally and, most importantly, retain between 70 and 80 per cent of their foreign earnings, provided they paid a percentage to their *empresa* and income taxes to the state.

Although not as crucial as tourism, the economic role of music in Cuba during the 1990s was remarkable, to the point of being acknowledged by Fidel Castro. At a meeting of the Communist Party in 1993, he declared:

> We all liked that argument very much about the recordings producing more than a five-star hotel, or five times as much as a five-star hotel. That is an argument to consider. Those are figures to consider.... They are statistical figures of what music could represent, which is barely considered today. Therefore, among the measures that we need to apply there are some that could have an influence among artists and intellectuals in an economic sense.
>
> (Castro 1993)

Accordingly, music has been catalogued by CEPEC (the Centre for Export Promotion of Cuba) as one 'item for exportation' and placed under the rubric 'Art and collection articles' together with films, works of visual art and handicrafts.[5] Music – and particularly popular music – can bring hard currency into the coffers of the Cuban state in a variety of ways, not only through the sale of records abroad. To give some examples: performances in tourist clubs in Cuba;[6] licences on archive material by local record companies; money brought in by foreign record companies operating in Cuba; revenues from performing rights collected abroad; percentages on the money earned by musicians from foreign tours paid to their *empresas*; income taxes paid by musicians at home; taxes paid by Cuban workers resident abroad, including musicians ($100–130 per capita/per month); all-inclusive courses and seminars on popular and folkloric music and dance organized in Cuba by cultural institutions; and

---

[4] Decree-Law no. 140, 13 August 1993 and Resolution of the Ministry of Culture no. 61, 4 November 1993.

[5] Website <http://www.infocex.cu/cepec/>.

[6] According to David Calzado, when La Charanga Habanera played there for four days at Christmas 1995 the Palacio de la Salsa made $29 000 from entrance fees (Delgado 1996).

money from voluntary contributions solicited to successful artists by political mass organizations. Among the cash that music brings into Cuba, one can also count the money spent in Cuba and earned by musicians during their foreign tours, and the remittances of those who live and work abroad. To all this, in a country also known as *la isla de la música*, that is, 'the island of music', one must add the paramount importance played by music in the promotion of foreign travel to Cuba (*Buena Vista docet*).

The economic reforms thus encouraged musicians to import foreign currency by playing in tourist venues and touring abroad, and transformed them into seasonal workers and economic migrants. With easier access to foreign travel and greater economic incentives, MB musicians started touring extensively, accumulating considerable wealth. In the mid-1990s, bands such as Van Van were spending months on international tours. In 1998, more than 3000, mostly popular musicians travelled abroad. In 1999, their number doubled (Váquez, interview with the author, 1999; Vicent 2000).

Under the new circumstances, musicians continued to receive a minimal level of subsidy from the state. But, with more freedom from the bureaucratic limitations of the *empresa* system of the past, more mobility and (when successful) much higher earnings, they have essentially become managers of themselves. Today, successful bandleaders handle substantial amounts of foreign currency and have on their payroll a string of people working for them, from musicians to PR assistants, from sound engineers to stage technicians and tailors. In some cases, they lend money and equipment to other musicians (it is rumoured, for example, that at the beginning of his career Manolín was generously helped by El Tosco, and had later to honour a substantial debt). According to one Cuban agent, in 1999 top bandleaders and singers (but not their musicians) could make as much as $10–12 000 a year (Vázquez, interview with the author, 1999). According to other sources, at the end of the 1990s the annual earnings of people like Calzado, Paulíto and Manolín were in the region of US$40 000 (Paternostro 1999). Modest by international standards, these figures represent an extraordinary amount of money when compared to the salary of ordinary Cubans, who today can earn around $150–200 a year, and even less. This has not eliminated problems of exploitation of musicians by band directors. Very often, against earnings that are sometimes substantial, during tours they pay their musicians very little ($50–70 per day). I have been repeatedly told of bandleaders who do not acknowledge the creators of arrangements or of compositions, and register these under their own names.

During the economic crisis, however, popular musicians have proved one of the most adaptable categories. Through their acquaintance with influential people and foreigners, travels abroad and some black marketing and smuggling, they have enjoyed in general a far better living than the average Cuban. For most of the 1990s, musicians working in Cuba could be paid only in local pesos, and had to resort to alternative means in order to get dollars. Top artists imposed under-the-counter payments in hard currency, while other bands had to find less elegant systems. One of these was to sell bottles of rum or resell free tickets before their show (a fact suggesting that such a practice was tolerated and even encouraged by club managers, who used free tickets as a form of payment) (Kernell, interview with the author, 1998).[7] In the late 1990s, the government eventually authorized the payment in dollars of musicians playing in tourist facilities and working for local record companies (Cantor 1999a).

The role of foreign record companies

Until the end of the 1980s, the performance of the Cuban recording industry had been 'particularly undistinguished' (Manuel et al. 1995). As a state-owned monopolistic company, Egrem was affected by a combination of negative factors such as lack of capital, low efficiency, technological obsolescence and international isolation (Acosta 1990a; Robbins 1990b). The limited number of vinyl records and cassettes produced by Egrem were sold exclusively on the national market at subsidized, non-remunerative prices.

In the 1990s, the process of diversification of the music industry led to the creation of new national record companies, still state-owned, but financially self-supporting and with a higher degree of independence. Among the new labels that appeared during the decade were Bis Music (subsidiary of Artex), RTV Comercial, Artcolor and Unicornio (set up by *trovador* Silvio Rodríguez). Egrem mainly concentrated its activity on reissuing and licensing archive material at a bargain price, a process that peaked after the success of the *Buena Vista Social Club* album. As the founder of a New York-based Cuban specialist label has observed, 'There is a deluge of product.... You're competing now against hundreds of compilations made all over the world' (Ned Sublette, quoted in Martin and Morales 1999). In effect, the catalogues of some Western 'Latin' labels, such as English Tumi and US Qbadisc, appear today almost entirely made of cheaply licensed, attractively repackaged Cuban archive material.

---

[7] In Europe, I have seen members of a top dance band selling Cuban cigars after their gig at a Latin club.

In the first half of the 1990s, Cuban record companies tried to make new products and launch new artists, but found it extremely difficult to compete with foreign companies when it came to paying advances on royalties to established artists, and to promoting and distributing their records (Benemelis, interview with the author, 1999).[8] The most dynamic role in the field of MB, therefore, passed on to a handful of European independent record labels, attracted to the island by economic incentives and low production costs. This unprecedented move in post-revolutionary Cuba brought into the capital city private enterprises such as Spanish-owned Caribe Productions, Magic Music and Eurotropical, who signed up local artists and produced a substantial amount of original material mainly in the field of MB. Caribe, the first foreign label to establish itself in Cuba (1992), boasted a roster including top MB names such as Los Van Van, NG and El Médico. Magic Music signed Paulíto FG and La Charanga Habanera, and Eurotropical put under contract Manolíto y su Trabuco and Klimax. Through their subsidiaries, even US-based labels landed on the island. RMM signed Issac Delgado, and Nueva Fania Paulíto FG. At the end of the 1990s, in Cuba there were four national and six foreign record labels in operation, with seven other companies in the process of being represented (ibid.).[9]

The international opening of the Cuban music industry led to investments in infrastructure, with the construction of new recording studios. In 1998, the government, in a joint-venture with Silvio Rodríguez, invested $6m in the building of digital Studio Abdala, defined by *Billboard* as 'world class'. Other studios were built by Egrem, Artex and ICRT (Institute of Radio and Television), with the intention of not only recording local music, but also attracting foreign productions with their low costs and the high quality of Cuban session musicians. Meanwhile, artists like *trovadores* Rodríguez and Milanés, as well as bandleader José Luís Cortés, set up their own personal recording studios (Vicent 2000).

Since in Cuba a CD costs $15, the equivalent of a month's average wage, Cubans cannot afford to buy records, and the Cuban home record market is non-existent. The earnings of record companies that operate in Cuba, therefore, are essentially based on sales on the international market, which include those to foreigners visiting the island. After radio, cassettes sold at $1 each represent the most popular local medium for music. In the last few years, illegally-duplicated CDs have made their appearance on the island, sold on the black market and sometimes even under-the-counter in state-owned stores.

---

[8] Arguably, such a situation was also due to the prohibition, in force until 1998, on local companies paying musicians in dollars.

[9] Since then, the situation has radically changed (see Chapter 10).

Despite the world popularity of Cuban music and the promotional work done by foreign labels, in real terms the international sales of Cuban recorded music have been quite modest. It is perhaps ironic that the only significant global hits of Cuban music – those of *Buena Vista Social Club* and rap outfit Orishas – have not been achieved by labels based on the island, nor made in the field of dance music. Many Cuban music executives, indeed, agree that MB has yet to produce a global success. In the USA alone, where a Latin gold record sells 50 000 units, the sales of Cuban MB in the late 1990s were estimated in the region of 10 000 copies (Cantor 1997).[10] In 1999, Alberto Segura, the manager of Eurotropical, reported world sales for his best-selling act Manolíto y su Trabuco in the region of 25 000 copies (Martin and Morales 1999). Asked about the chances of Cuban MB making a crossover into the global record market, Segura said,

> At the level of live shows, the market is good, it is growing in England, obviously in Spain, in Italy, and also in countries like Germany .... From the point of view of records, it is a bit more complicated, and maybe in Europe, [where] people do not understand the lyrics, it is more difficult to reach the audience, no matter how rhythmic the music is. I don't think that it will be very easy to make such a crossover, but anyhow [Cuban MB] will occupy an important market niche like blues or jazz.
> (interview with the author, 1999)[11]

What appears small by international standards, however, might look big from the point of view of local musicians. Little more than a decade ago, musicians recording in Cuba were paid with flat fees and their recordings had no foreign market. Today, foreign record deals generate international exposure and demand for international tours, granting sums that in Cuba seem enormous. The presence of the new record companies also indicates a shift in the economy of Cuban popular music, which has been partially reorienting from live performance to recording. Today, for top popular musicians, advances from recording deals and copyright payments from abroad may represent a significant part of their earnings.

The international opening up of the local music industry has also pressed the Cuban authorities to tackle the issue of copyright – one of the historical problems of music on the island after the breakdown of relations between Cuba and the USA. This has led to the signing of international agreements on authors' rights, and to the creation of a new society for the management of musical copyright (Caraballo Sánchez 1996).[12] The presence of foreign record companies, in particular, has

---

[10] In that article, Cortés stated that NG, with something like forty albums, have probably sold around 200 000 records worldwide.

[11] Since my interview the company has ceased to operate in Cuba.

[12] In 1967, copyright was dismissed as a bourgeois notion by Castro (Marshall 1988).

persuaded many Cuban musicians to sign agreements with European songwriters' societies. The Spanish SGAE (Sociedad General de Autores y Editores) manages the rights of about 700 Cuban musicians and in 1998 alone invested $871 000 in the promotion of Cuban culture. In 1999, 21 Cuban members of SGAE (among them Rodríguez, Milanés, Compay Segundo and the heirs of Lecuona and Matamoros) received payments of rights totalling around $850 000 (Vicent 2000).

A complex issue regarding international copyright is the payment of rights on Cuban music performed in the USA to songwriters who live in Cuba. According to current US law, it is illegal to transfer such money to the island. Recently, the Cuban music industry challenged in a British court the US company Peer Music over the case of 'Guantanamera'. Through Pete Seeger's and other versions, the song is said to have generated 16 million dollars of copyright money in the USA, none of which has ever reached its legitimate Cuban songwriter Joseíto Fernández (now deceased). If successful, the judgement of the British court is expected to constitute an important legal precedent against the stipulations of US embargo laws (E. Vila, communication at Cubadisco 2003, Havana).

Facing the market: musicians

The reforms have produced beneficial effects for the Cuban music industry, but not for all musicians or ordinary Cubans. The end of the generous state subsidies, the dollarization of society and the irruption of the market economy, in practice, have brought success and wealth to a handful of artists, but have not solved the problems of unemployment and underemployment of most of the island's 12 000 professional musicians. As in any other aspect of society, the dual economy has created a watershed between what is marketable in dollars (popular music, jazz, sometimes folkloric music) and what is not. The most obvious casualties of such a process have been classical musicians, in the past one of the prides of revolutionary Cuba.

In the field of popular music, the re-conversion to a market economy has marginalized bands lacking capital to buy musical instruments, technical equipment and recording time. Many groups have disbanded or have been 'broken down into small formats in order to work as trios or quartets in hotels or tourist places' (Crespo, interview with the author, 1998), recycling themselves as *músicos de sopa* ('soup musicians', that is restaurant musicians). In the field of MB, many musicians have lamented the existence of an artistic oligarchy represented by a small number of bands who hold a virtual monopoly on work in the tourist circuit.

The economic difficulties, the weakness of the local music industry and the desire to break into the international market have also exposed Cuban musicians to exploitative practices, in the fields of both recorded and live music. Since the early 1990s, foreign executives of dubious morality have raided the island in search of cheap music, commissioning recordings and reselling them without paying musicians, buying recordings from artists for flat fees or imposing exploitative contracts. In 2000, the Cuban music industry eventually announced the creation of a national organization seeking to 'avoid pirating and abuses from producers of no scruples' (Vicent 2000).

Local musicians are fully conscious of their weakness in the face of Western record companies. As the leader of Klimax, Giraldo Piloto, explained,

> For many years, we did not know what was going on in the world in terms of records, of the rights we had as artists.... we didn't know anything about royalties, contracts, how many years, exclusive, percentages ... nothing of this. That was totally new for us. I know what I'm talking about because it has happened to me. Even today, I read that same contract and think, 'What have I signed?'. Had I known the meaning of some clauses, I would not have undersigned them .... It has not been a matter of imposition, but of ignorance [on our part]. I'm referring to top bands, to all Cuban bands, not just to my case. Most record companies, I don't know if they've made an agreement, but they came with the same type of contract. When I talk of recording contracts I'm referring also to music publishers. They took advantage of the fact that we did not know a series of laws, and [now] we can't do anything about it. Now we have a bit of consulting .... But there are bands who are less important, or who find it difficult to get a recording contract.... Then a record executive from some country turns up, and proposes an immoral, amoral, or let's say improper (*indecoroso*) contract. If the band have no other chance, they are forced to accept the offer, not because they undervalue themselves or don't realize they are being exploited, but because of financial reasons, in order to keep alive the idea behind their work.... People accept that in order to solve their problems. It is the result of the period and of the difficult situation we're living in.
>
> (interview with the author, 1999)

Cuban bands have faced exploitation in the field of live music as well. Bands touring abroad have been stranded by bogus promoters, while others have found themselves in trouble with local musician's unions because of their extremely low fees. In the late 1990s, in fact, European promoters were able to hire 15-piece top bands for as little as $1000, or even less. In Italy and Spain, lesser-known groups have been hired for months as house bands by clubs and restaurants for a pittance. Under conditions of extreme necessity, musicians justified exploitation arguing that something was better than nothing. As one member of Los Van Van told a journalist, '[e]ven if we get $40 a day, it's better than what we get back home .... In Cuba we get nothing' (Cantor 1997).[13]

Cuban singer Osvaldo Chacón, now based in London, has pointed at another indirect but significant aspect related to the particular economy of Cuban music. In most of the West, Latin dance bands are not stable bands, but ad hoc outfits that constantly change their format and rehearse very little, hiring the musicians available at short notice. Cuban dance bands, on the contrary, are far more stable and, as they make most of their money abroad, have much more time to rehearse at home. This fact, together with the high technical level of musicians, represents one of the artistic strengths of Cuban MB. But from the point of view of Latin musicians who live in the West, the offer of Cuban bands at extremely low prices on the international circuit undercuts their fees and constitutes a form of unfair competition by third world workers (Chacón, interview with the author, 1998). This, paradoxically, also affects Cuban musicians who live and work permanently abroad.

Facing the market: audiences

Before the 1990s, in the professional activity of musicians, live performances played not only a central economic function, but also an important symbolic role. Live shows were considered by the media and the industry as a fundamental popularity test, an occasion to appraise the ability of musicians to communicate with their audiences. The combination of this type of aesthetics with the particular economy of Cuban music, where technology is expensive and cheap skilled labour abounds, has enabled contemporary MB groups to retain big-band formats which have long since disappeared in Western popular music.

During the *período especial*, live shows and big bands have remained central to the aesthetics of MB, but in a significantly different context. While practical difficulties such as lack of venues, lack of transport and power blackouts have drastically limited the access of local audiences to music performances, the re-conversion of the economy to tourism has diverted the activity of dance bands from gigs for locals towards dollar-only clubs and foreign tours. In a country where music and dance are so central to everyday life the boom of *salsa cubana* has thus produced a paradox. Adding to the chronic scarcity of venues and the negative

---

13 The undercutting of fees by Cuban bands is not only related to the present crisis. In the past, Cuban bands touring abroad, after giving a few concerts at the contracted official fees, often went on playing for much cheaper fees. Such a practice, which enabled musicians to retain most of these foreign earnings, was known as 'burning' (*quemar*) the places, and led to the discrediting of Cuban bands with many Latin American promoters (Díaz Ayala 1999).

image of Afro-Cuban popular culture, the dual economy has created a music circuit where the most important dance bands play mainly for tourists. Meanwhile, young *habaneros* spend boring nights sitting on the wall of the sea promenade: unless they are involved in some *bisne* (black market), they have no money to pay for a decent outfit and the entrance to a dollar-only dance club, which may cost them as much as 20 dollars.

According to the results of a survey published by a Cuban magazine in 1991, more than 90 per cent of Cubans between 13 and 30 years of age enjoyed dancing (Carrobello et al. 1991). In spite of this, the *habaneros* of the *período especial* have little opportunity to practise dance in public places. Among the few places where they can pay in pesos to watch their idols are La Tropical, a few social clubs (*círculos sociales*) and the occasional concerts held, for free or nominal fees, in theatres such as the Nacional and Karl Marx, or in open spaces such as the Anfiteatro de Marianao or La Piragua. But, in general, the expansion of tourism and the success of Cuban MB abroad have created an impossible competition for *círculos* and local councils, which cannot compete with tourist venues in hiring top bands. Local audiences have thus complained about their exclusion from tourist clubs, the long absence of popular artists on tour abroad, the difficulties in public transportation and the excessive centralization of gigs (Cruz Jorge 1997).[14]

The marginalization of local audiences is related not only to the economic difficulties of the *período especial*, but also to pre-existing problems such as the social stigma attached to Afro-Cuban music and some bizarre economic policies. As a Cuban journalist has written, 'some manifestations of dance suffer from the underestimation of certain social strata .... "There go the coarse people [*la gente chusma*]", some now say, referring to the dance nights of La Tropical' (Carrobello et al. 1991). Discussing the problem of popular entertainment in Havana, a black journalist recalled how the authorities in the late 1980s hindered his organization of dancing events at a local level when 'there was a closure of the main dancing areas, and that same activity [dancing] became something banned, forbidden, as if it were a highly dangerous crime' (Perez 1999).[15]

---

[14] Talking to a Cuban journalist in 1997, Cortés said that from a concert in Cuba he earned twice what he earned from a gig in Paris, expenses deducted (López 1997). Because of such a paradox, sometimes gigs are more expensive in Cuba than abroad. In May 1999, the price for a gig by La Charanga Habanera in Havana was higher than for their concert in Italy earlier that year. In 1999, one informant commented that singer Paulito FG was able to make a substantial part of his earnings by charging Cuban promoters, under-the-counter, high fees for his local performances.

[15] In fact, fights and stabbings are not uncommon during music and dance shows in the barrios and at La Tropical, which, both indoors and outdoors, is heavily patrolled by police. During Cubadisco 2002, held at the fortress of El Morro, there were rumours of one person being killed.

According to him, the authorities' worries about dance events, and the use of recorded music as a substitute for live bands, eventually resulted in the disintegration of many bands, with dozens of musicians becoming unemployed and even stopping making music altogether. The replacement of live performances with recorded music – already observed in the period 1985–90 by Daniel, who wrote that in nightclubs 'disc jockeys are the norm, although live bands do appear on occasion' (1995: 97) – is another curious Cuban phenomenon, attributed by some to misguided policies adopted by Cuban tourism companies, which generally manage discothèques (Vázquez, interview with the author, 1999). In the heated discussion following Perez's speech, Afro-Cuban journalist Nancy Robinson erupted,

> I am one of those journalists who are not afraid of the word *popular*, *bailable*, *marginal*, because there you have the people who stay late and get up early. I'm one of them.... There are people who are afraid of the word 'popular'. Popular is *chusma* [rough], is *marginal*, is the *nichedumbre* [mass of black people]. Let's go to the hot heart of the matter: 'I'm not going to go there, there are Blacks (*negros*) ...'. It's the fear and the negative publicity they do about *bailables*.... There is a movement against dancing, it's a movement against the *nichedumbre* .... There are people who fear dancing, even colleagues who can't talk of *timba* or *rumba* because they've never been to a *bembé* [Afro-Cuban religious party].... It's a social prejudice: 'I'm not going to *La Piragua* because that is for everybody, builders, drunkards as well'.
>
> (Perez 1999)

In the 1990s, the extremely thorny and politically sensitive issue of popular entertainment in Cuba, already discussed in Chapter 1, was complicated further by the rise of the dual economy and the irruption of tourism. To the old prejudices against MB were added the fact that tourist dance clubs had sometimes become centres for prostitution. In 1997, a local music executive warned me that those places were 'socially contaminated', explaining that 'you find a lot of prostitutes at those shows, which are very important because dance music enables them to "show off their merchandise"' (Faya, interview with the author, 1997). The situation posed a series of problems, both practical and symbolic. For foreigners, these venues became obvious pick-up places; for the local youth, an occasion to try and approach tourists; for the authorities, a place for illegal activities promoted by a marginal subculture that created an image detrimental to tourism, and sometimes put foreigners at risk.[16] From the late 1990s on, the Cuban authorities reacted to the situation with police raids and the closure of several dance clubs (see Chapter 8).

---

[16] In the late 1990s, there were various cases of tourists robbed by *jineteras*, and even a few cases of murder of foreigners related to prostitution.

After the eventual reopening of most dance clubs, however, prostitution around these places reappeared, albeit in a less visible fashion. As long as nightlife and dance culture remain an important part of the tourist appeal of the island, the elimination of prostitution remains highly unlikely.

The limited access of ordinary Cubans to records and live performances, and the scarcity of printed information (the only newspaper circulating today in Cuba is *Granma*, the organ of the Cuban Communist Party) have given the broadcasting media an even more important role than before the *período especial*. As an essential promotional channel for bands and the main source of musical information for fans, radio performs a crucial gatekeeping function. But because radio exposure requires the presence of a recording, which people without earnings in dollars can hardly afford, the crisis has put lesser-known musicians into a kind of vicious circle. In that sense, the economy of music in Cuba has become similar to that in capitalist countries: no airtime, no commercial success.

Most of the music heard on local radio is of the type that in the West would be defined as 'commercial', with a mix of Cuban and international popular music. In real economic terms, however, the only Cuban commercial radio is Radio Taíno, which broadcasts MB and commercial adverts and produces the enormously popular programme 'De cinco a siete' ('5 to 7'). Like the press, all radio and TV stations are owned and controlled by the state, and (with the possible exception of Radio Taíno) are its only non-self-financing companies, a fact that bears witness to the grip of the government on the media, and to their strategic importance (Acosta 1999).

The lack of reliable data on music consumption represents a problem for researchers. In the absence of any kind of measurement of music tastes and/or consumption, one may wonder how media and music industry policies are established, and how the popularity and 'value' of artists on the island are gauged. A view frequently heard in Cuba is that

> [m]aybe in the rest of the world an artist's success is measured by the number of records he sells . . . . Here in Cuba that's not the most important parameter. Here the popularity of an artist is defined by his popularity with the dancer. . . . And generally, that kind of public does not buy records.
> (Music producer Cari Diez, in Cantor 1997)

The statement makes some sense, because sales charts are far from representing an *objective* measurement of popularity (Hamm 1982), and because in Cuba record sales are scarcely significant. On the island, at any rate, people do buy tapes and listen to the radio, so this might form the basis for some reliable statistics. Cuban music magazines sometimes publish music charts, but do not explain how data are collected (presumably through a panel of music 'experts'). The argument quoted above, therefore, remains circular, because it does not take into account the role of the media, how they select the music they broadcast and how they influence the popularity and the economic rating of artists.[17]

The impact of the US embargo

> Cuban music has never been blockaded. Those who have been blockaded, for many years and still today, are Cuban musicians who live in Cuba.
>
> Juan Formell (quoted in Padura Fuentes 1997a)

In Cuba, the issue of the US embargo, or *bloqueo* (blockade), is evoked in virtually all political statements, and projects its shadow on any discussion concerning music. The embargo is often blamed by musicians and music executives for the difficulties and relatively poor international sales of Cuban music. Such an explanation is not totally convincing. Until the early 1990s, when the embargo had already been in place for years, Cuban music had virtually no market outside the island. Today, with US measures against trade with Cuba tightened by the Helms-Burton law (1996), the music made on the island occupies a far more relevant place on the international market. The fact that during the 1990s its export significantly grew suggests that US trade laws have not succeeded in blockading Cuban music, and that the local music industry has improved its efficiency.

US laws prevent US companies from advancing money to Cuban residents (and thus from signing Cuban musicians), but not actually from making deals via third parties. According to the US Treasury Department, this practice is commonly employed, and explains why on the island tourists can buy Coca Cola and Kodak films: they are not produced in the USA (Cantor 1997). Similar deals have been made, for example, by Universal through its Mexican subsidiary and by Atlantic (part of the Time-Warner conglomerate) via the label Caliente.[18] Investment in Cuba, therefore, is technically possible, and has repeatedly tempted the global entertainment industry (J. Ballester, in Muñoz 2001).

---

[17] In 1997, Caribe assigned its artists prizes for their record sales in Cuba, stated as follows: El Médico, 42 000 copies (*Para mi Gente*), Van Van 30 000 (*Lo ultimo en vivo*) and 20 000 (*Ay dios, ampárame!*) (Vicent 1997). Compared with the figures on the estimated sales of Cuban dance music abroad, reported above, these figures seemed highly dubious.

[18] Havana Caliente has released albums by Adalberto Alvarez and Van Van, the latter of which won a Grammy in 2000. Universal Music Mexico in 1998 signed a distribution deal with Magic Music, and EMI Spain has done the same with Caribe. In 1999 in Havana there were also rumours of a possible deal between Sony and Egrem, but this did not come to anything.

In practice, however, the giants of international music have teetered between interest and a wait-and-see attitude, backing away from any serious investment because of the potential risks posed by the embargo law's sanctions. Music transnationals have made a few steps in the release of licensed material, but have steered clear of the financial and promotional effort they put behind other Latin American stars in the mid to late 1990s. To be sure, US companies are not very happy about the embargo, and have repeatedly argued about its effectiveness and role in allowing new economic actors to step in (see, for example, Henderson 1997). In the words of the owner of one US record company, 'The embargo has handed the American market for Cuban music to European companies' (Ned Sublette, quoted in Cantor 1998a).

Cuban musicians, for their part, appear rather sceptical on the role and commitment of the global music majors. After making a CD in 1997, distributed by EMI Spain, Cortés commented bitterly,

> EMI is not interested, not interested at all. EMI is buying air. Capitol is buying air. Warner too, say, Sony, everybody. The law of the embargo does not allow big transnationals to do business with Cuba. They are buying a piece of air. 'Who knows, if one day the government would fall...'. [They do it] to put a foot in the door.
>
> (Cortés, interview with the author, 2000)

The problem of Cuban recorded music, thus, is not that of being materially unable to reach the USA, but the fact that its sales in that country (and elsewhere) are affected by poor promotion and distribution. Sales of Cuban music in the USA are disappointing because they are made mainly through small specialist shops, which, in total, usually sell no more than a few thousands copies. Many US Latin radio stations, moreover, are controlled by Cuban-Americans, and do not broadcast music made in Cuba, nor advertise concerts by Cuban bands. The legal stalemate between the two countries has also favoured cases of video and audio piracy of Cuban music in the USA and made it practically impossible for the Cuban music industry to fight them in court (Cantor 1998a).

Cuban musicians touring abroad have faced similar problems. At first, the embargo pushed dance bands towards markets such as Europe, Latin America and Japan. In the second half of the 1990s, the legal loophole provided by the Berman Amendment encouraged them to tour the USA as well: according to US government sources, between 1994 and 1999 the number of Cuban artists visiting the country for the purpose of work increased from 55 to 763 (Arocha 2000). But the work of Cuban artists in the USA is still subject to severe limitations. Because they are considered employees of the Cuban government, they cannot officially enter the USA but must apply for a waiver to get a visa. Since the Amendment authorizes only cultural exchange, they can receive money only in the form of per diem and reimbursement costs. Music concerts, therefore, can take place only in non-commercial circuits such as jazz festivals or universities, and cannot be adequately promoted.

One might argue passionately about which music is more 'cultural' (is recreational music 'uncultured'?) but, in practice, the limitations imposed by the Amendment tend to favour performances by folk ensembles or *Buena Vista*-like projects rather than by commercial dance bands. The embargo laws, thus, do not actually forbid Cuban musicians from playing in the USA, but make it extremely complicated for them and for their North American promoters. To such a legal framework add local restrictive interpretations of the law, notably in Miami, where a vocal fringe of anti-Castro hardliners has been able, to this day, to exert substantial political and cultural pressures.

Popular music and censorship

As the increasingly challenging attitudes of timba musicians show, compared to previous years, the early 1990s in Cuba represented a period of ideological softening and greater institutional tolerance towards the arts and expressive forms. The limited development of a civil society and of a market economy in Cuba, however, did not necessarily imply a free circulation of ideas and opinions, and the end of attempts at political control of artistic expression. Resounding episodes such as the censorship of La Charanga Habanera in 1997 (see Chapter 8) urge us to consider the various mechanisms that the Cuban authorities can deploy to rein in cultural production.

One of the preconditions for political control, in a way, is precisely the lack of popularity polls and the unaccountability of the media to the public, which may act as powerful instruments of manipulation not only of public taste, but also of artistic activity. As music writer Helio Orovio has suggested,

> mass-media, which are not of the mass (*masívos*) but are controlled by a minority, try to direct taste, in Cuba as in the rest of the world. If they were controlled by the masses, they would have real opinion polls, surveys, but that is not the case.
>
> (interview with the author, 1999)

As Orovio points out, such a problem is not exclusive to the Cuban music industry, but in Cuba it is particularly dramatic because of the pervasive role of the state and its ample institutional margins for interference. The lack of data on popularity, moreover, exposes the media to practices of nepotism and corruption, repeatedly hinted at to me by musicians.

Occasionally, allegations on payola have emerged in public, referring to artists who were said to have paid to be on the air or to appear on magazine covers.[19] Such episodes suggest that the problem of arbitrary behaviour and manipulative practices in the media, already denounced by Acosta in the 1980s, still waits to be solved and, if anything, may have become worse with the new economic inequalities and higher financial stakes of the *período especial*.

Referring specifically to the institutional control of the content of MB, bandleader Giraldo Piloto has declared,

> our album *Juego de manos* has been censored. It contained thirteen tunes, and the regulators of the radio ... have banned ten of them. Three of them have been accepted because I have had discussions at all levels, and were accepted as a concession. [That has happened] Because a guy said that we were singing of unfaithful couples, of sex, and radio did not promote that vision.
>
> (interview with the author, 1999)

Since many MB musicians have raised the issue of censorship during my interviews, I asked Piloto to be more specific on the meaning of the word. He made it clear that, in Cuba, singing a 'problematic' song in public, in theory, is not forbidden. What happens, rather, is that the media, by banning specific songs and marginalizing certain artists on the airwaves, pressurize musicians into self-censorship.

> You can sing [a song], but they do not broadcast it on radio or TV. If you cannot promote your band on radio or TV, people cannot hear and learn the tunes. In most places, people pay the entrance to clubs when they know the band and the songs, and this has seriously affected us. If people cannot hear our music on radio or TV, how can they possibly know what Klimax are doing? ... It is a hopeless task.... If the song does not get media rotation, it does not stick.
>
> (ibid.)

Such use of censorship was defended in 1997 by Alicia Perea, the then director of the Instituto Cubano de la Música, the top institution of Cuban music:

> We believe in freedom of creation.... No one can prohibit that someone write a song. But the promotion of that song and the repetition of the song in the media – it's a function of the media to control that.... the media have a big role in deciding at what time and how often something is played. You can't deal with cultural problems in an uncultured way.
>
> (Cantor 1997)

---

[19] At a seminar held at Cubadisco 99, composer César Portillo de la Luz commented on the enduring presence of a singer on Cuban radio despite his waning popularity, and reported of a well-known TV programme which had been terminated because of a 'trafficking in sale of [air]time: artists who could afford to pay were always on the air' (Havana, May 1999).

Even accepting that there must be institutions deciding what is good and bad in music, there remains the problem of the totally opaque criteria they adopt, and of the enormous margins for arbitrariness that such a mechanism lends them. In practical terms, Cuban musicians try to avoid problems by adopting self-censorship, which thus becomes the most effective means of institutional control. Talking about the polemics on MB lyrics in the late 1990s, for example, Juan Carlos Alfonso, composer and leader of dance band Dan Den said: 'I've always been careful with my texts. Some bands have the tendency to go too far with their lyrics, to adapt their music to the coros closer to the street (*coros más de barrio*)' (interview with the author, 1998). From another perspective, controversial *trovador* Pedro Luís Ferrer has lamented musicians' lack of control over their access to music performances:

> I've had no troubles with the creative issues . . . . The problem is that, in order to make a concert in a corner of my house, I have to ask permission from the authorities. Where do you expose your work? And with whose permission? That is the problem with our freedom to create.
>
> (Foehr 2001: 55)

All the same, the 1997 straightforward ban on La Charanga, in a sense, represented more an exception than a rule (see Chapter 8). Music censorship in Cuba does not generally take the form of a direct veto on artists, which might be difficult to enforce with musicians signed to foreign record labels, and can produce negative publicity. Institutions, rather, prefer to operate indirectly, by pressurizing musicians into self-censorship, manipulating the media in order to affect artists' public exposure and economic rating, controlling the artists' access to state-managed clubs and facilities, and restricting their freedom of movement through the issuing of visas and travel permits. This may happen because of inscrutable decisions taken by music agencies, which all ultimately report to Artex (in a strange anomaly, artistic agencies – without which Cuban musicians cannot work – also control the issuing of exit visas) (Ishikawa 2001). In other fields of cultural production, successful but controversial films have disappeared from cinemas soon after their premiere, and books announced by publishers have never made it to the shops (Davies 1996; Cantor 1999c).

Cuban law also gives the government ample bureaucratic and financial means to influence and pressurize foreign companies (such as record labels) operating in Cuba. Investment laws require such companies to operate through a local, state-controlled firm, buy their supplies from Cuban state companies and hire workers via Cuban institutions. Fiscal laws leave wide discretionary margins on the tax regime applied by the state to foreign investors (Larsen 1998). Despite the mild process of economic liberalization, therefore, the 'Cuban government remains in control over the investment process and can dictate arbitrarily when the investment is to end' (Travieso-Díaz 1997: 110).

Conclusions

In the early 1990s, the Cuban government acknowledged music as an important economic asset, opening it to foreign investment and introducing legal changes in the activity of professional musicians that granted them greater economic freedom. Since then, the presence of foreign record companies has helped Cuban musicians to re-enter the international market, giving them an exposure never previously achieved after 1959.

The irruption of the market economy has posed a series of dilemmas for both musicians and audiences in Cuba. In the case of musicians, it has accentuated the divide between commercial and non-commercial artists, leaving a great number of them un- or under-employed, and exposed to exploitative practices. By diverting most of the performing activity of dance bands towards foreign tours and tourist clubs, the new economy of music has objectively discriminated against local audiences. To such economic marginalization can be added old prejudices towards Afro-Cuban dance music and the new social stigmas attached to MB.

Compared to previous decades, the 1990s showed a far more tolerant attitude on the part of the Cuban authorities on artistic matters. But it would be wrong to assume that the economic reforms of the *período especial* have produced in Cuba an irreversible progression towards freedom of expression. To this day, the media and key areas of the music industry have remained firmly under the grip of the Cuban government, who can exert control on cultural production and limit freedom of expression in popular music through forms of economic and political pressure, and, in some cases, explicit censorship.[20]

Although it is difficult to assess thoroughly the impact of the US embargo on Cuban music, it is clear that the US trade blockade has prevented the full involvement of transnational record companies in Cuban music, deterring them with the threat of economic sanctions, and has handed the local music market to European independent record companies. This has resulted in poor international promotion and distribution of Cuban recorded music, a fact that, despite a few notable

---

[20] In April 2003, Gorky Carrasco, a member of the controversial rock band Porno Para Ricardo, was arrested amid vague accusations of drug trafficking, and later sentenced to four years (*Freemuse* press release, <www.freemuse.org>).

exceptions, has considerably limited its commercial possibilities on the international market.

The embargo, at the same time, has not materially prevented Cuban music from reaching the international arena, nor Cuban musicians from touring abroad, including, increasingly, in the USA. As Latin Americans are becoming the biggest ethnic minority in the USA, it seems logical that Cuban musicians should try to penetrate the rich North American market. But this remains an extremely difficult task, because the international opportunities for Cuban music, as for the rest of the Cuban economy, appear heavily conditioned by Miami politics.

With its one-million-plus Cuban population and physical closeness to the island, the city represents for Cuban musicians their most natural foreign audience, and the most difficult place to play. For years, political pressures and terrorist tactics have kept Cuban bands away from Miami. In the 1990s the intransigence of the Cuban-American community started to waver. Since Issac Delgado performed there, top names of Cuban MB such as NG, Los Van Van and Manolín have played in Miami, sometimes amid political rows. After the riots during the performance of Van Van in October 1999, polemics surrounding the presence of Cuban bands in Miami led to the cancellation of the Midem Latino and to the Latin Grammy Awards being moved to Los Angeles. Nevertheless, the limited but growing presence of Cuban artists in the USA seems to have helped to bridge political differences or, at least, to show that US audiences are, by and large, more interested in bridging than exacerbating the divide.

Part II
Matters of Style

Chapter 4

Timba as a Genre and a Musical Style

Timba has already its '*way*', its manner of being made, which
makes its sound distinctive: mainly its complex percussion, its
combination of percussion with bass, its aggressive, difficult,
intricate piano tumbaos, its virtuoso passages of the horns, and,
especially, its truly popular lyrics.
José Luís Cortés (interview with the author, 2000)

Timba can be described and analysed from different perspectives. From
one point of view, it can be seen simply as the name of a new style of
music that emerged in Cuba in the 1990s. From another perspective, it
can be regarded as a social phenomenon and an artistic movement that
manifests itself through a multiplicity of signs. In both cases, timba
appears as an expression of Cuban popular culture that largely feeds on a
dialogue with the life and problems of Cuban urban Blacks. This chapter
and the next one discuss issues of musical style, content and meaning in
timba songs, and look at their connection with a particular black youth
subculture that emerged during the *período especial*.

This chapter sets off by tracing the origins and the emergence of the
word 'timba', showing how the term has long been in circulation in
Afro-Cuban popular language. Here, I formulate some hypotheses on the
meaning of the word, and in particular in relation to its African origins.
I then examine the use of the term by contemporary MB musicians, and
look at how they explain and use it to describe a specific style of
contemporary dance music. Contrary to words like 'salsa', the term has
not emerged as the result of a record company's marketing strategy, but
from a conscious effort by Cuban musicians to try to differentiate their
music from other styles and to forge a common front against growing
institutional criticism.[1]

I then examine the characteristics of timba as a musical style, looking
at issues of structure, format, organization of the instrumental parts and
improvisation. Here, I present a description of the most salient musical
aspects of timba and provide notated excerpts taken from well-known

---

[1] The term 'salsa' was adopted as a music label in the early 1970s in New York after its
adoption by US Latin record company Fania. For hypotheses on the origins of the term
'salsa', see Blum 1978.

songs. By analysing how the new music relates to and is differentiated from previous Cuban and Latin dance styles, I show how timba has developed a distinctive sound and a particular 'work' of the rhythm section that reveal a marked influence of jazz in the instrumental parts, and of rap in the vocal approach.

The final part of the chapter discusses the issue of structure in timba songs, a much-debated question in Cuban circles in the late 1990s. Contrary to views that construct timba as a subversion of the classic formal rules of Cuban popular song, I relate its changes to the Afro-Cuban origins of timba, showing how the oft-criticized inclusion of popular catchphrases and alleged repetitiveness of songs connect to the history of black Cuban popular music, and are related to its specific function as dance music.

Besides attempting for the first time to pin down analytically the musical character of timba, this chapter shows how this music appears to defy binary stylistic oppositions such as national vs. foreign, traditional vs. modern, and local vs. global, weaving together a range of sounds that are all inscribed onto the musical expressive range of the black diaspora. In a sense, it may be argued that the musical nature of timba lies precisely in the way it draws eclectically on the whole sonic rainbow of the black Atlantic, in a sequence that opens with rumba and closes with hip-hop.

Naming the style: son, salsa and timba

What is today called timba, such as for example the music played by NG La Banda in the early 1990s, has not always been publicly known by that name. Although already in circulation among musicians, the word emerged in the public arena as a term to define a specific type of contemporary dance music only in the late 1990s (see Chapter 9). Before, that type of music could be dubbed son, *música bailable* or *salsa cubana*, for lack of better words and in an attempt to exploit its relative affinity with international salsa.[2] Even today, the use of the term 'timba' in Cuba is neither universal nor unproblematic. This is due to the fluid nature of music labels, and has to do with the way speakers contextualize and ideologically place music. It seems useful here, therefore, to try to give a short description of the meaning of these terms.

Música popular bailable, or *música bailable* (MB), is a generic term employed by Cubans to designate popular dance music, as part of the

---

[2] On the early records of NG La Banda, for example, songs were described as *balada-salsa, son, bomba-salsa* and so on.

category defined by León as *música popular elaborada* ('elaborated popular music') (León 1982). In general, the expression MB – which is widely used in the music industry for purposes of administrative classification (Robbins 1989) – may refer to any type of dance music, including older styles such as danzón or mambo, recent styles such as timba, and even foreign ones such as merengue or tango. When used in the context of present Cuban music, however, it generally means contemporary Cuban dance music. Such music in Cuba has a wide, inter-racial mass appeal, but is largely seen as the main recreational music of lower-class Blacks. Throughout its history, in fact, MB has widely drawn on Afro-Cuban folkloric styles, has been largely made by Afro-Cuban musicians and has been mostly consumed by Afro-Cuban audiences, who remain its most dedicated fans.

Son, which originated in the early twentieth century in the eastern part of Cuba and is said to represent the fusion of Spanish and African elements, is considered the Cuban national music style (León 1982).[3] Initially associated with lower-class Afro-Cubans, lowlife and margin-ality, it was first rejected by the creole bourgeoisie and then eventually co-opted as the quintessential national style. In its traditional form, son has slowly declined since the 1930s, but has been at the core of much of the MB subsequently produced in Cuba. In a way, the word in Cuba is used today with two meanings. In a proper sense, it refers to the historical style, recently revived by traditionalist products such as *Buena Vista Social Club*. In a wider sense, the word is also used as a name for modern *música bailable* (singers of dance music are in fact often called *soneros*).

Salsa is the name given to a type of dance music born in late 1960s–early 1970s in the Latin, mainly Puerto Rican barrio of East Harlem, New York. Throughout its more than thirty years of existence, this music has been the object of countless controversies on its origins and on the extent of the Cuban contribution to it. Today, musicians and scholars generally agree that salsa essentially developed from the structure of Cuban son, but has incorporated eclectic influences ranging from US soul and rock to Caribbean and Brazilian music, eventually becoming a pan-Latin style (Manuel 1988; Gerard and Sheller 1989). Today salsa is produced and consumed in virtually all the countries of Hispanic Latin America, and particularly in those facing the Caribbean Sea.

Contrary to what many people think, therefore, salsa is not a Cuban invention, but an elaboration made by Puerto Rican musicians resident in New York on a Cuban musical model. As such, salsa remained virtually inaccessible to the general Cuban public until the early 1980s,

---

[3] For a discussion of the genesis and the stylistic characters of son, see Robbins 1990 and Moore 1997.

when the style enjoyed a veritable boom and started to be imitated by local dance bands (see Chapter 1). After initial institutional hostility, the label has eventually been accepted in Cuba as a suitable term for *música bailable* produced in the early 1990s, when local musicians and foreign entrepreneurs tried to remark its comparative closeness to international salsa. In the late 1990s, then, MB musicians decided that a different name was needed to promote their specific brand of dance music, and to avoid identification with foreign salsa. Through a series of concerts, interviews and articles in the press, they publicly launched the word 'timba' (see Chapter 9).

As we can see, MB has been and still is labelled by Cubans in a variety of ways. The often interchangeable usage of music terms such as salsa and timba, for example, explains why a quintessential *timbero* like Manolín has been nicknamed 'the doctor of salsa', and why the music of Adalberto Alvarez has been identified at different times as son, salsa and occasionally timba. Sometimes, the term timba has even been used in retroactive fashion, such as when Juan Formell claimed that timba is all the dance music made in Cuba since 1959 (Martori 1998).

Conversely, after the recent international boom of 'traditional' Cuban music, some dance bands have started to dub their own music as son, choosing to underline continuity, rather than rupture, with the music of the past (see Chapter 9). The presence of multiple words to define contemporary dance music in Cuba has generated a great deal of confusion in foreign writers and commentators. Not all of them seem to be aware of the existence of the term timba, which does not appear in Manuel et al. (1995) or in Díaz Ayala (1999), and is barely mentioned in some of the most recent books on salsa (Steward 1999). In Cuba, the word timba is now widely used and understood, but it does not seem to have caught popular imagination to the extent of becoming a universally accepted term, a fact that is perhaps related to the difficulties in imposing the style on the international arena.

Hypotheses on the origins of the term

The term 'timba' exists both in the Spanish language and in Afro-Cuban slang, and can be related to different origins, uses and meanings. In the Spanish lexicon, timba has basically two meanings: a) a form of gambling, b) belly (in Cuba and Central America). Its phonetic closeness to words such as *tumba*, *tumbador* and *rumba*, however, suggests a connection with words of African origin, especially from Central Africa, a region from where a considerable number of black slaves were brought to Cuba (Castellanos and Castellanos 1987).

In his *Glosario de Afronegrismos*, published in 1924, the scholar of Afro-Cuban folklore Fernando Ortíz reports the term timba as the name for a type of gambling, and as part of the expression 'tener timba', meaning to be able to do something difficult or meritorious. He also reports the phonetically similar word *timbeque* with the meaning of an 'improper dance, typical of black people', and also 'uproar, scandal, turmoil' (Ortíz 1990). The word timba might also be related to *tumba*, a word of Kikongo origin meaning 'drum' (cf. Spanish *tambor*, French *tambour* and Italian *tamburo*, all generic terms for 'drum'). According to Ortíz, *tumba* is an 'African drum widely used in Eastern Cuba – Afro-Cuban dance popular in that region' (ibid.). As linguist Armin Schwegler suggests, the term timba 'is almost certainly Kikongo, meaning "drum" in America ... but originally meaning "trunk of tree" + "to beat", thus *drum* .... In this sense it is found in the African use in Palenque, Colombia'.[4]

In his later work on Afro-Cuban musical instruments, Ortíz also reports: '*Tambo*, earlier, and today *tumba*, mean "ceremony or celebration of initiation" in certain sects of Kongo origin.... today tumba is used mainly in Oriente, signifying a type of African drum, the act of playing it and a dance' (1952–5, IV: 144). In the past tumba defined several types of Afro-Cuban drums such as *tumba francesa* and *tumba de monte*, but today is generally used as short for *tumbadora* (from here come a series of related words such as *tumbador* and *tumbao*), that is a single-headed barrel drum usually called conga out of Cuba, typical of rumba and today widespread in dance music, salsa and Latin jazz.[5]

'On the other hand', writes Ortíz, '*túmbo, túmbu, túmbe, tímba* mean 'belly' in various Bantu areas, possibly referring to the 'belly dance' or 'ombligada' ... Cuban *timbeque* might derive from those terms' (1952–5, IV: 115).[6] Schwegler, as well, points out that in Cuba the word timba has another non-musical meaning, also of Kikongo origin: 'to be stiff, erect

---

[4] Personal communication, December 1998. Quotations are taken from Schwegler 1999 and 2000b.

[5] The root *timb-*, indeed, appears in a series of names of Latin American membranophones. *Timbales*, for example, are a set of two single-headed, open metal drums mounted on a stand and played with sticks (in Cuba they are often called *pailas*). *Timbal* is sometimes also a generic name for 'drum' in Eastern Cuba, and for a small Congo drum used in Haiti (Leymarie 1996; Elí Rodriguez, Casanova Oliva et al. 1997). *Timba* is the name of a single-headed, conical Brazilian drum, approx. 90 cm high, 'the sound, drumming technique and rhythm patterns [of which] ... are similar to those of the *djembé*' (from the catalogue of Redondo Percussion, Maastricht/Holland). *Timbale* is also Portuguese for kettledrum.

[6] Note also the similarity of the word *timbeque* to modern *tembleque*, one of the dance movements performed by women in Cuba at timba concerts.

... especially in an obscene sense', a word possibly related to *n*timba, 'lasciviousness, sensual disposition (man and woman); quality of ability to generate; to be erect (obscene)' (1999: 199), and, by association, 'to love, to make love' (2000a: 161).

The use of the term timba in popular language and songs points to a close semantic relation between the words timba and rumba. Discussing the origins of rumba, León relates the word to 'a series of terms of Afroamerican origin like *tumba*, *macumba*, *tambo*, and others meaning collective partying, with the general meaning of group, meeting' (1974: 140). This seems to suggest an identity of words such as tumba, timba and rumba, meaning both drum and the occasion where drumming and dancing takes place. The hypothesis seems to be corroborated by folklorist Rogelio Martínez-Furé, who 'suggests that *mba*, the root of the word rumba, now refers to dance and is found throughout the Caribbean and Latin America. According to him, it represents similar festive dance events and has similar accents in the dancing, e.g., on flirtation, chase of the female, or bumping the pelvis area' (Daniel 1995: 168, n. 7; italics mine).[7] This might confirm a semantic connection between words such as rumba and timba and names of other Afro-Latin American dances like Cuban *mambo*, Puerto Rican *bomba*, Colombian *cumbia*, Brazilian *samba*, Argentinian and Uruguaian *candombe* and Peruvian *malambo*.

Timba, rumba and modern dance music

The word timba occurs frequently in old Cuban songs. 'Timba' is the title of a mambo by D. Perez Prado, and appears in that of an old *guaracha* called 'Timba timbero'.[8] In many songs, the words timba and *tumba* are associated with rumba. That is the case with 'Sobre una tumba una rumba' by Ignacio Piñeiro (Orovio 1994: 156), of a piece interpreted by *conguero* Chano Pozo called 'Timbero la timba es mía', and of Miguelito Cuní's 'Guaguancó a los rumberos'. In the latter song, Cuní sings: 'I remember those *rumberos* / I remember those *timberos* / who in my Cuba sang guaguancó.' In several rumbas, in fact, the terms timba and *timbero* are used as synonyms of rumba and *rumbero*. This is

---

[7] Daniel (1995: 64) traces back the African antecedent of Cuban rumba mainly to Central African areas: 'particularly, the BaKongo, Lunda, and Luba of Zaire [now Congo] have been known historically to share dances that focus on a gradual closeness of male and female dancers and the touching of bellies or thighs'. This may in turn relate to the *ombligada*. This hypothesis would suggest a connection between timba and rumba both in linguistic terms (referring both to the *tumbadora* drum and to movement of the belly) and in the actual dance movements.

[8] A. Orejuela and H. Orovio, personal communications, Havana, May 1999.

how Faustino Drake celebrated the death of the rumbero Malanga in his famous composition 'Llora timbero':[9]

> I hear a voice calling me:
> Arenilleo,
> I hear a voice telling me:
> Malanga has died.
> Unión de Reyes cries
> for her greatest *timbero*

(ibid.: 145–6)

I have posed the question of the meaning of the term timba to several musicians. While none of them seemed to be sure about the origin of the word, all stated that the term had long been circulating in popular parlance and in musical jargon. The word, for example, had been used in the 1960s and 1970s by Cuban bands with names such as Cotán y su Timba-Rock (D'Rivera 1999) and Johnny Sayas y la timba caliente (Frometa, interview with the author, 2000). As a synonym for rumba, it appears both in contemporary rumbas and in dance music songs.[10] Asked in an interview if the word had a meaning besides that of the contemporary musical style, José Luís Cortés made the gesture of playing a drum with his hand and replied: 'Yes, *timberos* are those who play rumba' (interview with the author, 2000).

In musical jargon, to say that a musician 'tiene timba' (has got timba) means something like 'tiene sabor', that is, plays with swing. According to one informant, the expression has been in use for years, together with others like 'tiene bomba' and 'tiene yunfa', to mean that a musician plays with feeling (Vázquez, interview with the author, 1999).[11] Some musicians told me that 'timba' means heart, strength, energy, while others have identified the term with the quasi-orgasmic rhythmic climax of the second part of dance songs.[12] As a former member of the timba band Bamboleo, singer Osvaldo Chacón, says, 'It's like the climax, the

---

[9] Malanga (José Rosario Oviedo, 1885–1923), a master in the style of rumba called *columbia*, was born in Union de Reyes, a village in the Matanzas area. The song has also been recorded by Arsenio Rodríguez (now on the CD album *Cuba*, Fremeaux, Paris) and, more recently, by the all-star Cuban ensemble Estrellas del Areíto under the title 'Llora timbero' (*Estrellas del Areíto*, Egrem, 1979; re-released on CD by World Circuit, 1998).

[10] See, for example, the tracks 'Yo soy descendiente de los timberos' and 'Oye mi china', recorded by Afro-Cuban rumba ensemble Clave y Guaguancó (*Songs & Dances*, Egrem, 1990), and Van Van's songs 'De la Habana a Matanzas' (on the CD *Ay dios amparame!*, Caribe, 1995) and 'Te pone la cabeza mala' (on the CD *Te pone la cabeza mala*, Caribe, 1997).

[11] This usage is not far from the expression 'tener timba' referred to by Ortíz.

[12] Viart, personal communication, Turin, July 1997; Lombillo, personal communication, Havana, May 1999.

peak, when for example the young woman gets mad, gets into the fire, for me this is the essence of timba' (interview with the author, 1998).

Writing about mambo, a Cuban scholar once defined it as an 'ordered musical anarchy' (O. Urfé, quoted in Martínez Acosta 1988). Such a definition fits perfectly with the description of what happens in the second part of timba songs, where the narration stops, coros and vocal improvisations make their irruption, and the musical discourse reaches it emotional climax with the insertion of instrumental riffs and breaks. That apparent anarchy is visible as well on the dance floor, where couples split and women start to dance on their own.

In an article published in 1989, James Robbins made probably the first written reference to the use of the term as a name for a specific style of Cuban dance music. The article, based on interviews with musicians conducted in Cuba in the period 1987–8, did not mention bands or songs, but clearly indicated that in the late 1980s the terms was used by musicians in relation to *música bailable*, and not, as previously, to urban folkloric rumba. Discussing the taxonomies of Cuban music, Robbins wrote,

> *Son*, while multifaceted with regional variants, can be prescriptive; *salsa* and *timba*, both of which are considered descendants of *son*, are less so. *Salsa* is generally taken to include *son* and other non-Cuban genres and thus is raised to a higher taxonomic level; *timba* is modernized *son* in which musicians are expected to play idiosyncratically with less reliance on fixed patterns.
>
> (1989: 385)

In conclusion, to establish a univocal meaning for the word 'timba' seems a difficult and perhaps pointless task, because the term in Cuba has multiple meanings and uses.[13] On a musical level, however, the phonetic closeness of words like timba and tumba seems to illuminate their semantic connection, a fact reinforced by their interchangeable usage in the context of Afro-Cuban rumba. As a music and a dance, timba is clearly and unmistakeably Afro-Cuban not only because musicians and audiences are overwhelmingly black, but also because at a specific musical level timba is permeated by rumba rhythms and themes, by Afro-Cuban slang and references to life in the black neighbourhood. It is probably fair to say that timba re-interprets in modern times the rebel, anarchic and challenging spirit of rumba.

As with the names of other African-American styles such as jazz, rock 'n' roll and funk, the term timba originates on the street, carries at the level of its very name sexual connotations and has eventually passed

---

[13] Other possible origins suggested for the usage of the term are expressions such as *pan con timba* (bread with *timba*, a kind of guayaba jelly), the barrio of La Timba (a black neighbourhood near Plaza de la Revolución in Havana) and the English word *timber*, allegedly printed on wooden boxes used by *rumberos* (Coloquio at the Cubadisco Music Fair, Havana, May 1999).

from musicians' slang into the mainstream discourse. Although the word has entered public usage, however, it remains somehow musically and politically controversial because of its association with marginal subcultures. Why, then, do I adopt the term in this book? For at least two reasons. The first one is factual: the term timba is now commonly used by both MB musicians and their audiences. The second reason is that the word timba provides a far more specific term than salsa, son or *música bailable*. Contrary to those words, it clearly identifies a type of music, an attitude and a subculture that are new and specific to the Cuba of the *período especial*. As El Tosco has graphically put it, 'I prefer to call Cuban salsa timba, in order to stress that it is quite black and comes from the barrio' (Manrique 1998a).

A new musical style

As I mentioned in Chapter 2, NG La Banda are often credited in Cuba as the inventors of timba. With their sound, Afro-Cuban aesthetics and controversial lyrics, they have provided a blueprint for 1990s MB bands, creating, according to Formell, 'a structure which the younger musicians have also adopted' (Castañeda 1998b). What Cortés has done, in reality, is to assemble elements there were already present in Cuban music and give a danceable, commercial form to ideas that had emerged in the 1970s in the experimental *descargas* (jam sessions) of art schools. According to pianist Lazaríto Valdés, leader of Bamboleo,

> timba is from art schools. They used to call it ferocious timba (*timba feroz*). For instance, you'd have five congas playing a guaguancó rhythm, with a little more fills and choruses with jazzy phrasing and something a little more advanced than son and those kinds of things ... The music wasn't called timba but they used the word to mean flavour. ... I think [it started] before 1980, around then. More or less when Irakere was started. ... [Timba] was very violent because the horns had a lot of phrases and the polyrhythms were very strong, it was more of a jazz. When people started listening to salsa in Cuba, it softened that music up a bit.
>
> (Delgado 2000)

Valdés's quote mentions all the fundamental ingredients of timba, that is, rumba, jazz and salsa. To people who first listen to them, timba songs present an intricate sound texture, a distinctive density, on which the voices place their coros and 'truly popular lyrics'.[14] In order to make

---

[14] I have used the Cuban term 'coro', rather than 'chorus', because that word in English carries different meanings. In jazz and popular music, for example, the term may suggest the presence of a verse-refrain song structure, which in Cuban popular music is not always the case.

sense of the density of timba, in the following sections I examine the complex interplay of resemblances and differences, of borrowings and innovations that make timba into such an innovative music style.

Instrumentation and sound

Cuban dance music is generally categorized under specific instrumental formats (Acosta 1983; Orovio 1992). Contrary to most dance music produced in Cuba during the 1960s and 1970s – which was dominated either by the flute-and-violins *charangas* (however modified) or to a minor extent by trumpet-led *conjuntos* – timba's most immediate model of sound and format is the Cuban jazz band. This particular type of jazz big band was born between the 1930s and the 1940s with the insertion of Cuban percussion and playing techniques in swing bands, and played a repertoire fusing US jazz and dance music with local popular music. The format was employed during the 1950s to great effect and success by orchestras such as those of Dámaso Pérez Prado and Benny Moré.

After the revolution, jazz bands went into decline as dance orchestras and reappeared as concert bands, first with the Orquesta Cubana de Música Moderna, and then with jazz-fusion band Irakere (see Chapter 1). The latter group was largely responsible for bringing the sound of the Cuban jazz band back to the dance floor. In its original version, the band employed a format that featured piano/keyboard, electric bass, drum kit, electric guitar, two saxes (alto and tenor), two trumpets, flute, two percussionists and one singer. Irakere represented the model for NG La Banda, which, in its original format, included piano, keyboard, bass, drum kit, two trumpets, alto sax, flute, two percussionists (congas and bongó) and two singers, a total of 12 people. The members of the band also occasionally played other Cuban percussion instruments.

This instrumental format, whose sound is focused on horns and percussion, came to dominate the scene of MB in the 1990s, when it was adopted by all timba bands. On a stable core consisting of piano, keyboard, bass, horn section, drums/timbales, congas and hand-held percussion such as cowbell and güiro, timba bands have adopted minor format variations in the type of instruments and number of personnel (now generally close to 15 elements).[15] These variations generally concern

---

[15] In 1999, La Charanga Habanera featured 13 people, with four singers, piano, keyboard, bass, three trumpets (occasionally alto sax), congas and two percussionists (one playing a combination of timbales, snare, cymbals, bass drum and woodblocks, and the other one playing bongó, cowbell and guiro). On their 2001 European tour, NG had grown to 15 people, augmented by one singer, one tenor sax and one guiro player. In Havana in 2003, however, they had shrunk to nine people.

the number of singers, the composition of the horn section and the way the percussion is organized. The adoption of trombones, for example, signals the attempt of some bands to move close to the sound and market of international salsa.[16]

In general, in modern Cuban music electronic technology plays a far more marginal role than in the popular music of the rest of the Western world. This fact is due to both the particular aesthetics and the atypical economy of Cuban dance music. Much Cuban popular music is not conceived in terms of sound reinforcement, and traditional formats such as *conjuntos* can easily do without PA systems. To this can be added the fact that electronic equipment is extremely expensive in Cuba. Timba bands, on the contrary, do make use of electronic sound technology, in the form of electro-acoustic and electronic instruments, sound amplification and occasionally drum machine and sequenced instrumental parts. In timba, PA systems play an important role in producing a typically powerful sound where, without amplification, voices could not be heard. The use of electronic technology contributes to timba's aggressive undertones and, as in other third world countries, stands as a symbol of modernity and economic power.[17]

As in much popular dance music of Hispanic Latin America, the timba sound has horns in the foreground. The wind section can consist of two trumpets, alto sax and flute (as in early NG), three trumpets and an alto sax (as in La Charanga Habanera), or even two trumpets, two saxes and two trombones (I. Delgado's band). Horns, though, do not carry the same weight in all timba bands. In groups such as NG La Banda, they play a decidedly enhanced role with virtuoso parts and solos, representing a stylistic mark that is crucial to the construction of the modern and artistically authentic image of the band. In most bands, on the contrary, horns simply contribute to the overall sound texture, coming to the fore in introductions and *mambos* (instrumental sections). La Charanga Habanera, for example, have excellent musicians, but

---

[16] Trombones, for example, were used by Issac Delgado's and Manolíto Simonet's bands. Other individual format variations were the use of electric guitar (Paulíto FG), flute (NG, Manolíto), electric violin and cello (Charanga Habanera, Manolíto). One exception to the large big-band format of timba described above is represented by bands such as La Barriada, an eight person outfit that has stripped the sound of timba to its bones (piano/keyboard, bass, drum kit, conga, two trumpets, tenor sax, singer). By having its drummer working on a texture that simulates the sound of other percussion instruments (such as timbales, bongó and claves), its players alternating in playing and singing, and one keyboard switching between piano and synthesizer, La Barriada effectively reproduces the sound of a far larger band.

[17] PA systems are very expensive in Cuba and only top bands can afford them. Their ownership represents both a symbol of prestige and a means of exerting control over lesser known bands and artists.

make a music that appears far more focused on singers and presents a sound with an artificial, pop quality which makes large use of reverberation, synthesizer timbres and even drum machines.

The sound of timba bears a certain resemblance to salsa, to the point that, in the early 1990s, timba was often called *salsa cubana*. In fact, timba and salsa share loose similarities in instrumentation and structure, which are due to their common origin in Cuban son, and to the popularity of salsa in Cuba in the 1980s. In terms of both format and style, however, they present some crucial differences. Salsa has left more or less intact the rhythm section of son, is dominated by the sound of trombones and does not employ drum kit, electric bass or a second keyboard (Acosta 1997). Timba, on the other hand, is placed along a continuum of modernization of the rhythm section of Cuban MB, which has led to the inclusion of rhythms and instruments from the Afro-Cuban folkloric tradition, and from rock and jazz. The result is a more prominent percussive sound and a rhythmic texture that is far more complex than in salsa.

Both styles reveal marked jazz influences, which come from different directions. In salsa, they mostly come from swing, and show modern jazz influences only occasionally (for example, in the modal piano style of Eddie Palmieri). While also using the concept of the horn section, timba looks at much more contemporary models, such as US funk and jazz fusion, as produced by bands and artists such as Weather Report, Chick Corea, Earth Wind & Fire and Blood, Sweat & Tears. In terms of singing, contemporary salsa leans towards sentimental ballads sung by individual singers, while timba is dominated by collective singing and an aggressive, rap-inflected vocal delivery. The two styles, finally, radically diverge in terms of geo-cultural references. Salsa is today an internationalized music style for a pan-Latin audience, often produced by pan-Latin bands. Timba is firmly rooted in Cuba in terms of musical references, language, content and dance style.

As in salsa and big-band jazz, in timba arrangers play an important function in the creation of an instantly recognizable sound. In that role, names of arrangers have emerged such as J.L. Cortés, Juan Ceruto, Giraldo Piloto and Ivan 'Melón' Gonzáles. As in jazz and salsa, arrangers do not write down all instrumental parts, but usually only the horn passages (introduction, mambos, riffs) and particular patterns or effects, leaving the musicians who play piano, bass and synthesizer free to interpret the chord changes. Timba arrangers' attempts to find a distinctive voice, however, have often been counterbalanced by a certain tendency to imitate the sound of the most successful bands. In the late 1990s, various Cuban musicians and music fans had complained to me that most timba bands had ended up sounding very much the same, becoming recognizable only by their singers.

Identifying structure

Formally, timba evolves from a structure that is different from that of the verse/refrain song or ballad common to most Anglo-European pop. Its general model is found in both 'classic' son and rumba. Here, we have a bipartite structure with a shorter, quieter first narrative section or *tema* (*largo* in son and *canto* in rumba), followed by a longer, more upbeat part called *montuno* or *estribillo* (sometimes *capetillo* in rumba) (Crook 1982; Robbins 1990b). Such a bipartite model is common to much Cuban dance music. In the general economy of timba songs, these two sections, which are usually connected by a short instrumental bridge, do not carry the same weight. The longer and more energetic montuno represents the climax of the song, the part that listeners and dancers enjoy best, and the section that, in fact, some people call timba.

As a highly eclectic style that makes room for romantic sections, rapped refrains and jazz horn solos, from the formal point of view timba has increasingly moved away from the simple bipartite structure of previous dance music towards a somewhat more fragmented organization. Such a shift has mostly been based on the expansion of the second part, which is typically filled with coros (one of the trademarks of timba), stops, instrumental phrases and breaks. Here the interweaving of staccato horn riffs, syncopated piano and bass figurations, and percussive ostinatos raises the tension and creates the typical sense of urgency and 'organized chaos' of timba. Together with the extremely fast tempo, these factors often make it difficult for dancers to dance to the songs in the traditional, salsa-like *casino* style.

Going into more detail, I want to look at the terms used by popular musicians to identify the different sections of the song. *Introducción* is the instrumental introduction, with horns usually in the foreground. *Tema* (also *melodía* or *cuerpo del número*, 'song's body') is the melodic, narrative first section sung by the lead singer. *Puente* is the instrumental bridge. *Coro* or *estribillo* is the choral refrain that alternates in call-and-response with the verses sung by the singer in the second section.[18] *Mambo* is the instrumental solo played by the horn section in the second part.[19] The general organization of timba songs can be broadly described as follows:

introducción // tema ‖ puente ‖ coro I / *mambo* I // *c.* II / *m.* II // *c.* III / *m.* III//etc// [*coda*]

---

[18] In fact, the term 'estribillo' sometimes identifies the entire second part of songs.

[19] Cuban musicians also identify various other parts, such as, for example, the *champola*, a particular type of short mambo where horns play diverging melodic lines.

The first section of the song usually presents a tema (literally, 'theme') in a ballad style, often reminiscent of salsa in narrative, topic and tempo (although it may use as well elements of son, rap or soul), and dealing with subjects such as love and male–female relationship. The second section, which I call here montuno, represents a musical and narrative break. Here, the story stops, giving way to an alternation of coros and solo verses (*guías*) commenting on the subject of the tema, and adding contextual elements that open spaces for new interpretations. This type of general structure is found in many early songs of NG La Banda, and around the mid-1990s became a sort of timba formula.[20]

The refrains of the montuno are of paramount importance in the musical and textual economy of the song. Coros – of which there may be three or four (and many more during live performances) – represent the real focus of the song, the hook that catches the attention of listeners. Many songs start with an almost abrupt quotation of the first coro, placing it before the instrumental introduction, and using it as a signal and a promise of more to come. This procedure was first adopted by Cortés, and was motivated by a desire to get dancing those young people who might otherwise not start dancing until the montuno (Cortés, in *Mamá, yo quiero saber*, 1999). As singer Carlos Manuel Pruneda explains,

> I place a lot of weight on the chorus and the response ... as my audience want to dance and get into it quickly unlike older 'son' music, which has slower introductions. We drive hard, we cut to the fast section quickly. That's how the band and I test a song – when the dancing gets crazy, it's working. The new generation loves it.[21]

In the montuno, coros alternate with mambos, instrumental sections that offer virtuoso-oriented bands an occasion to show off their musicianship. The first mambo is usually longer and has the character of an instrumental interlude, while the subsequent ones tend to be shorter and overlap with coros. The final mambo of a timba song, in fact, may consist of little more than a horn riff closely alternating with the last coro. The shortening of the temporal gap between the coro and the instrumental riff has the effect of creating a sense of accumulation and collapse of structure, something vaguely reminiscent of the technique of final *stretto* in fugue, where the parts enter in close succession without allowing for the complete exposition of the theme. The song may end with the last coro fading out, or with an instrumental coda, usually derived from the introduction.

---

[20] Not all timba songs conform to such a model. Indeed, various songs by NG present a different form of organization. 'El trágico' and 'La bruja', for example (see Chapter 7), maintain the general bipartite form, but in the first section employ a verse-chorus structure. 'Los Sitios entero', on the other hand, employs an unusual tripartite structure ABA (see Chapter 6).

[21] 'Carlos Manuel y Su Clan', interview published on <timba.com>, 2001.

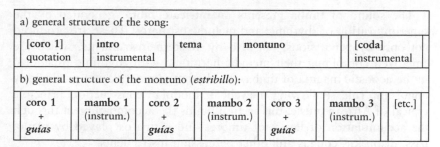

a) general structure of the song:

[coro 1] quotation	intro instrumental	tema	montuno	[coda] instrumental

b) general structure of the montuno (*estribillo*):

coro 1 + *guías*	mambo 1 (instrum.)	coro 2 + *guías*	mambo 2 (instrum.)	coro 3 + *guías*	mambo 3 (instrum.)	[etc.]

Example 4.1 Block diagrams of the structure of timba songs and of the montuno section

The typical structure of a timba song may be succinctly represented as shown in Example 4.1.

Organization of the rhythm section

This section focuses on aspects of organization of the rhythm section and instrumental style and phrasing that constitute relevant features of timba as a musical style. I use here examples taken from songs by the two single most important timba bands, NG La Banda and La Charanga Habanera. All the tunes contain lyrics that touch on contents that are crucial to timba. 'Los Sitios entero' (NG) is an ode to a marginal, Afro-Cuban *rumbero* neighbourhood of Havana. 'Papá Changó' (NG) is dedicated to santería deity Changó, the Cuban equivalent of the Yoruba god Shangó. 'El temba' (Charanga Habanera) is a not-too veiled reference to the widespread phenomenon of *jineterismo*. The content and contexts of the songs are discussed in detail in Chapters 6 and 8.[22]

Making sense of how the various instrumental parts dovetail in the dense rhythmic and timbric texture of timba has required a combination of watching live performances, listening to records and conversing with musicians. Among these, for his invaluable help with the transcriptions and the technical clarifications, I wish to acknowledge here Cuban composer and arranger Raúl Frometa, who has experienced modern MB first-hand by playing for some years with Orquesta Revé. All the notated examples below, taken from commercial recordings, provide comparisons with previous Cuban and Latin dance styles and must be understood as forms of descriptive notation for analytic purpose, and not as performance scores.

---

[22] 'Papá Changó' is taken from the CD *En directo desde el patio de mi casa*, 1995; 'Los Sitios entero', from the LP *No se puede tapar el sol*, 1990; 'El temba', from the CD *Pa' que se entere la Habana*, 1996.

The sound of timba presents an intricate fabric generated by the superimposition of rhythmic and melodic ostinatos. These are produced not only by percussions, but also by Western instruments, which are employed combining their melodic-harmonic with rhythmic functions. In the acoustic magma of timba, the rhythm section plays a particularly important role. Following a cyclical, modular construction principle typical of African music, this section builds the accompaniment through the accumulation of layers of timbres and ostinatos played by piano, bass, drum kit, congas and other percussion instruments.

Harmonically, the interaction between the melodic movement of the bass, the chords played by the synthesizer and the fast piano rhythmic arpeggiatos (*tumbaos*) employing passage notes and chromaticisms produces an ever-shifting fabric, with results more varied, open and dissonant than those generated by the relatively static use of bass and piano in son and salsa. Timba, in fact, makes wide use of jazz-derived harmonies in the form of secondary 7ths and other dissonant, unresolved chords.

As in other Caribbean styles, in Cuban music the bass represents the sound that grounds the feet of the dancers to the music. Cuban music of the past has developed a characteristic way of bass-playing called *bajo anticipado* ('anticipated bass'), which derives from the technique used in son by the double bass (and earlier by the *marímbula*). That is an ostinato that combines rhythmic and harmonic functions, anticipating the rhythmic stress and the harmony of the following bar. The resulting rhythmic-harmonic displacement is one of the typical features of Cuban popular music, and sets it apart from several other Caribbean and Western dance styles, where the bass tends to play symmetrically (accentuating beats 1–3, or 2–4) and stresses the harmony of the bar. Example 4.2a, taken from a 1930s son, shows how the bass, in the second and fourth bar (dominant harmony), anticipates the harmony of the following bar (tonic). Such style of playing has largely passed to salsa, where musicians typically interpret chord changes between tonic and dominant, as shown in Example 4.2b.

Under the influence of different aesthetic canons, technological restraints and the emergence of a generation of conservatoire-trained players, the development of bass playing in modern Cuban MB has taken

Example 4.2a   Anticipated bass in son in the early 1930s (from Manuel 1985: 254)

Example 4.2b Anticipated bass in salsa (adapted from Gerard and Sheller 1989)

quite another direction. Towards the end of the 1960s, Cuban dance bands started producing bass lines that sounded remarkably different from the anticipated bass of traditional *conjuntos*. Incorporating influences from international music, bands such as Van Van and Ritmo Oriental featured syncopated, percussive bass lines derived from US soul or from jazz and blues walking bass.[23] During the 1970s, Irakere's virtuoso bass player Carlos del Puerto elaborated an agile, percussive style of playing that made use of effects such as sustained notes, glissandos and slaps, and combined the technique of anticipation with jazz and funk lines.[24] This could happen because in Cuba the electrification of the bass has not passed through the adoption of pick-ups or the 'baby bass', an instrument with a technique similar to the double bass, but of the bass guitar. The style spearheaded by del Puerto has strongly influenced timba, producing lines that are different from both the bajo anticipado of son and salsa, and Caribbean styles such as merengue, where the bass stresses, march-like, the strong beat.

Example 4.3 reports the transcription of a fragment of the bass part in NG La Banda's 'Los Sitios entero'. As we can observe, the bass performs a rhythmic ostinato function anticipating the harmony of the following bar (as in bars 76–81), but goes far beyond that, playing melodically and making use of wide octave jumps (bars 69, 73, 85), arpeggiatos (bars 73 and 85) and chromatic passages (bars 72 and 73). We should note, also, the virtuoso sequence of semiquavers in the bridge (bars 97–100), which, played in unison with the horn section, leads to the central part of the song. Such playing requires a high level of musicianship, and introduces rhythmic displacements that can make timba particularly difficult to dance to. In fact, the extent of melodic lines and syncopation used by some bass players in timba has been such that they have been accused by other musicians of playing as if they were soloing, eventually disorienting dancers.

According to a Cuban author, in Cuban dance music 'the fundamental work of the pianist ... consists in playing *tumbaos*. He certainly plays

---

[23] See, for example, songs like 'Yuya Martínez' by Los Van Van (1969) or 'La Chica Mamey' by Ritmo Oriental (1975).

[24] According to D'Rivera (1999), such use of the technical possibilities offered by electro-acoustic bass was first suggested by Irakere's guitarist Carlos Emilio Morales.

Example 4.3 Bass line in José Luís Cortés's 'Los Sitios entero' (bars 65–101). From the album *No se puede tapar el sol*, NG La Banda (Egrem, 1990)

chords as well, but not as frequently as he plays *tumbaos*, the most suitable medium to provide the cadence and rhythms for dancing' (Sardiñas 1996). In much Cuban popular music the piano, besides providing a harmonic guide, performs an essential rhythmic function by playing a sequence of arpeggiato chords called *tumbao*. This sequence follows a syncopated ostinato pattern usually two- or four-bars long. The piano tumbao, which descends from son, derives from the adaptation of *tres* patterns.[25] The son tumbao, which employs diatonic arpeggios played in octaves by both hands and stresses the first beat every two bars (Example 4.4), has been widely adopted in salsa piano playing. The tumbao may be used by pianists sparsely and alternated with chords, or played throughout the whole piece.

Timba pianists have adopted for their instrument the same dynamizing principle, but tend to play tumbaos which are faster, more irregular, percussive and syncopated, and make use of passage notes, dissonances and chromaticisms that show a remarkable jazz influence. According to many musicians (for example, Betancourt, interview with the author, 1999), the use of such angular, asymmetrical tumbaos was spearheaded by Peruchín (R. Argudín Justíz), the first pianist of NG. Another style that has largely influenced contemporary timba pianists has been that of César 'Pupi' Pedroso, who has played with Van Van for many years. The complex rhythmic-harmonic interaction produced by the piano tumbao greatly contributes to creating the sense of urgency typical of the montunos of timba. In the song 'El temba', the piano virtually repeats throughout the whole montuno the same four-bar cyclical tumbao (Example 4.5). Not all timba pianists play the same tumbao with both hands. Pianists of the younger generation such as Tirso Duarte, who has worked with La Charanga Habanera, and Ivan 'Melón' González, who has worked as an arranger with Issac Delgado, for example, used to play different parts with their hands, introducing melodic elements in the tumbao and filling the texture with a rich polyrhythm.

Example 4.4 Traditional Cuban piano tumbao (adapted from Manuel 1988: 35)

---

[25] The *tres* is a three double-stringed guitar, typical of son. Out of Cuba, the piano tumbao is often called *montuno* or *guajeo* (*vamp* in English). A further confusion is generated by the fact that, in Cuba, 'tumbao' also describes a fixed accompanying pattern played by bass or congas.

Example 4.5   Piano tumbao from David Calzado's 'El temba' (montuno
section). From the CD *Pa' que se entere la Habana*, La Charanga
Habanera (Magic Music, 1996)

Another characteristic feature of timba is the adoption of a second
keyboard. This adds density to the general sound by producing a
harmonic layer made of chords (*colchón*, literally 'mattress'), generating
effects such as strings, synthesized bass and percussion, or stressing
particular accents of the horn section. In some cases, the second keyboard
is used to play a *contratumbao* (counter-tumbao), that is, an additional
rhythmic-harmonic pattern complementing the tumbao of the piano, as
in the work of Juan Carlos González, previously with La Charanga.

As in all Afro-Caribbean music, in timba percussion has a fundamental
role. Besides the parts played by bass and piano, all the rhythmic skeleton
of timba is constructed by an intricate web of ostinatos performed by a
variety of percussion instruments. Here the main rhythmic guide is
provided by a time-line called *clave*, a short asymmetric ostinato
produced by two wooden sticks or a woodblock. The pattern, which
represents the rhythmic foundation of much Cuban dance music, is
played throughout the whole piece and sometimes can be barely heard.
At other times, it cannot be heard at all, but is nonetheless considered to
be implied in the music (any Cuban musician is able to identify and tap
it). In dance music, the most commonly used patterns are the son and
rumba *guaguancó* clave, related to the two genres.

As illustrated in Example 4.6, both patterns can be used either in the
3 + 2 or 2 + 3 form. Canonically, the two forms cannot be mixed, and the
piece must keep the clave pattern from start to end. In timba, however,
one can often hear inversions of clave, sometimes more than once in the

Example 4.6 Son and rumba guaguancó clave (standard/reversed)

course of the same composition. At first sight, the difference between the rumba and son clave looks minimal, simply consisting, in the rumba clave (3 + 2 form), in a 1/8th displacement of the third stroke in the first bar. Because to Cuban ears rumba is not only the folkloric style for voice and percussion, but any popular song based on the rumba clave, however, the simple displacement of that one accent produces a rhythmically propulsive pattern that for Cuban listeners is of enormous relevance. The frequent adoption of the rumba guaguancó clave in timba, therefore, represents the institutionalization of the presence of rumba as the core, the propulsive principle of MB songs. For Afro-Cuban bands and their audiences, such reference constitutes a crucial identity marker: in that pattern, all the spirit of rumba vibrates, constructing a red thread that connects timba to the music of old *conjuntos* such as that of Arsenio Rodríguez and groups such as Irakere and Ritmo Oriental. As a foreign researcher reports, 'dark-skinned Cubans and other Cubans of varying backgrounds playfully and excitedly dance to the rumba clave when it intersperses a popular song' (Daniel 1995: 62).

The sense of closeness to rumba is also manifest in the use of conga drums or *tumbadoras*, which in dance music are essentially employed to give fluidity to the accompaniment by producing a rhythmic layer called by musicians *marcha* ('march'). This often happens without the listener being able to hear the whole drum pattern (again called *tumbao*, a word most obviously related to *tumbadora*), but only the two open tones played on the last beat (in a 4/4 bar). Solo drumming is infrequent in timba: but the use of sets of two, three and even four congas (generally played by one percussionist), together with the clave and *cáscara* patterns, produces a polyrhythm reminiscent of rumba (where each instrument would be played by an individual musician). *Cáscara* ('shell') is another rhythmic element taken from rumba and consists of a two-bar ostinato played with the sticks on the shell of the timbales. Other ostinatos are played by cowbell, maracas and güiro (a scraped gourd), providing continuity to the music discourse and filling in the timbric space. With its penetrating sound, the cowbell also performs an important guiding role. Finally, the Cuban percussion section features a bongó, the little double drum typical of son, whose sound is sometimes simulated by woodblocks.

Such an impressive array of Cuban percussion is complemented by the drum kit, the presence of which is characteristic of timba (the instrument is absent from both traditional *conjuntos* and *charangas* and salsa ensembles). Such a presence clearly descends from jazz bands and from the experimentations with rock made by modernist dance bands during the 1970s. Some timba bands adopt the drum kit as such, leaving the Cuban percussion to other musicians. Other bands employ variable combinations of drum kit augmented with timbales, woodblock, cowbell and so on.

In contrast to rock or classic jazz, however, in timba the drum kit is not employed to provide a steady rhythmic guide, but to intensify certain sections and passages, especially with bass drum, snare and hi-hat. Toms and cymbals tend to be utilized sparsely, as in the closure of phrases. As a consequence, in timba the bass drum is not used to produce the constant 1–2, 1–2 pulsation found in Caribbean styles such as merengue, *soca* or *zouk*, but, for example, to mark, together with the snare, the transition from the tema to the montuno. Jazz-oriented timba bands such as NG and Klimax, however, tend to make more extensive and virtuoso use of the instrument.

Horns are one of the most typical marks of contemporary Cuban MB. In traditional *conjuntos* and in salsa, they generally play tunes and phrases with a marked melodic character and relatively long rhythmic values. In timba, the phrasing of horns tends to be fast, syncopated and sometimes staccato. In the case of bands such as NG, phrasing is evidently inspired by jazz and funk. Example 4.7, a transcription of the mambo of 'Los Sitios entero', played in unison by two trumpets and two saxes on a part originally conceived for solo flute, illustrates why NG's horn section has been nicknamed 'the frightening horns'.

Another particular aspect of the treatment of horns in timba – when compared to older styles of MB, where they generally play parallel, harmonized parts – is that they often play in unison, sometimes harmonizing on the last note of the phrase. This gives them a more compact, powerful and agile sound. More weight can also be added to the horns mass sound by a bass part played in unison, as in the introduction of 'Papá Changó' (bars 9–16), strongly reminiscent of 1970s funk (Example 4.8).[26]

---

[26] Here, only trumpet I plays the whole ascending chromatic scale in bars 13–14. Trumpet II, saxophones and bass play twice the same scale (in other words, bar 14 is identical to bar 13).

Example 4.7   Horns solo (mambo) in José Luís Cortés's 'Los Sitios entero' (bars 202–17). From the album *No se puede tapar el sol*, NG La Banda (Egrem, 1990)

The transition to the montuno is often announced by a typical timba formula: percussion (with the exception of clave) stops, the piano tumbao enters, the bass drum pulsates off beat and the bass produces a percussive, descending glissando.[27] Such a bridging section – called *apoyo* (support) or *presión* (pressure) – is generally 8-bars long, and prepares the first exposition of the coro (or even accompanies it, as in 'El temba'). As the coro starts, the pulsation of the bass drum stops, percussion (congas and cowbell) re-enters and the bass starts its regular tumbao. The effect can be used again in the course of the song, in order to create variety in the accompaniment and produce a rhythmically intensifying effect (Example 4.9).[28]

The role of improvization

Because African and black American music are often stereotyped as largely spontaneous forms, many Western listeners tend to think of

---

[27] Such glissando, called by some musicians *bomba* ('pump' or 'bomb'), is produced by hitting the strings with the wrist of the right hand and then sliding it towards the neck of the instrument, while the left hand keeps the strings muted. According to Frometa, this technique was introduced in Cuba by Carlos del Puerto after he saw Jaco Pastorius using it with Weather Report in Havana in 1979.

[28] In 'Papá Changó', for example, the effect is used four times: at the beginning of the song (quotation of first coro), as a bridge to the first coro, and in the course of both the second and third coros.

Example 4.8   José Luís Cortés's 'Papá Changó'. Introduction, horns and bass (bars 1–20). From the CD *En directo desde el patio de mi casa*, NG La Banda (Caribe, 1995)

Cuban music as an expression that gives ample space to improvization. In fact, timba, and more in generally Cuban MB, give instrumental improvization only a limited role. This is not surprising when one considers that a complex machine such as a 15-piece band of *música bailable* requires a high degree of preventative organization.

Example 4.9 'Papá Changó', apoyo and coro I, bars 1–16 (José Luís Cortés)

Example 4.9   (continued)

Example 4.9   (concluded)

Timba instrumentalists enjoy a moderate degree of musical freedom in the creation of the accompaniment, for example in the way piano and bass interpret the *cifrado* (chords) and create their own tumbaos, or in the parts played by percussion instruments such as drum kit and timbales. In live concerts the band-leader may give individual musicians a little more autonomy when presenting them, jazz-fashion, at the end of the show, allowing for occasional solo breaks with improvised passages. As Manolíto Simonet explains,

> The song is fully composed and assembled, but there is always space for improvisation ... in the creation of the *sabor* [swing] of the piece. For example, the drummer adjusts [*acómoda*, literally 'accommodate'] when he prepares for the first *mambo* .... One tells him to make a preparation of eight bars, and inside those eight bars he improvises .... *Coros* follow the layout, are already [pre-]assembled, but not what the solo singer says ... the singer improvises a series of things that are not on the record. That happens all the time, every day is different.
>
> (interview with the author, 1999)

As Manolíto points out, live shows allow for improvisation by lead singers as well. These place their impromptu interventions in the montuno in the responses to the coros, where they may come up with topical comments and solicit participation from the audience. Vannia Borges, former singer with Bamboleo, makes a distinction between *guías* ('guides') and *improvisaciónes*. Guías are responses to the coro that sound as if they are improvised, but are actually prepared in advance (they usually follow the guías heard on records). Improvisaciónes, on the contrary, are a singer's responses to the coro that vary in relation to the context, and are usually placed in the last part of the montuno (Delgado 2000).

The leader of Bamboleo, pianist and composer Lazaríto Valdés, explains how his band works out songs' variations during their live shows:

> My [song] follows a fixed arrangement until the first or second *mambo*. From the second *mambo* on, it depends on how the audience reacts. If it's an audience that likes the tune, I'll toss out another *mambo* that of course is already pre-rehearsed. Or we invert the order of the *mambos*, we do a break, we keep the tumbao playing by itself, some polyrhythmic stuff is done, some effects, all pre-rehearsed, are done.
> Q: So the variations themselves are all pre-rehearsed and you can tell the musicians to try this option or that option?
> Exactly. Every tune has its... its routine, okay? But ... it depends on how the public is reacting at that moment.
>
> (ibid.)

In other words, timba songs articulate into a series of sections which are, up to a certain point, modular and interchangeable, and must be memorized by musicians. Using conventional signs, these modules can be recalled, repeated, skipped or swapped, thus modifying not only the piece's length, but also the profile of its musical discourse.

The rhythm section requires a separate discussion. A fundamental aspect of the rhythmic organization of timba is represented by the use of *bloques* ('blocks'). These are essentially like jazz breaks, but are written down and usually played by the whole band in certain passages of the song, and generally used to connect different sections of the piece (J.C. González, interview with the author, 2002). In a salsa piece such effects are few, but in a timba song they abound, and are all memorized by musicians. While generally played by the whole band, *bloques* can sometimes be played only by the rhythm section. As K. Moore notes, the use of bloques and the amount of improvisation depend on the type of organization adopted for the rhythm section, and are crucial in characterizing the band's individual sound. Groups like Manolíto or Klimax, for example, leave in their bloques a certain amount of space for improvisation. Other bands like La Charanga Habanera tend rather to follow a fixed structure. Groups such as Bamboleo, finally, employ 'generic' bloques, that can be called and used at will during live shows in different pieces (Moore 2001).

The narrow space for instrumental solo improvisation in timba evidently does not depend on Cuban musicians' technical limitations. Rather, it responds to the specific codes of dance music, which, in order to be danced, requires a high degree of predictability and formal redundancy. That explains why, contrary to what some people think, the use of improvisation can sometimes be problematic with Cuban audiences, but easier with foreign ones. This underlines a conflict between creative aspirations and commercial function that permeates, in different degrees, all timba.

> I can tell you that the majority of musicians like to play jazz, to make concert music, because this is a music that enables us to develop most, it's the type of music with which we can pour out all we have inside ...
> Q: Do you think that making dance music can be a limitation?
> Yes, of course!
> Q: How much space is there for improvisation in MB?
> The space that the bandleader or the singer might conceive, and the one allowed by MB, which has its codes, everywhere. If today you play at La Tropical, and you are a standard band – not one of the most famous ones – and start playing a trumpet solo, no matter how good it might be, at a certain stage people leave .... We have played in 13 different European countries, and noticed that at the end of the concert ... people expect a demonstration [of the ability] of every musician.... The Cuban who goes to one of those dancehalls wants to dance, does not go to listen to the solo by this or that chap. In Europe, it is different.
>
> (Piloto, interview with the author, 1999)

The black roots of timba

As a style of music played by young musicians (but not bandleaders!) for a largely young audience, and breaking with many aspects of previous Cuban music, timba has solicited a great number of criticisms in Cuba. Many of these have focused on timba's challenging content and subcultural leanings, and will be discussed in the following chapters. From a musical point of view, the most frequent criticisms have been targeted at the unusual, fragmentary and extended structure of contemporary dance songs, sometimes described as a subversion of musical canons. In particular, criticisms have focused on the quantity and the repetitiousness of coros, perceived as factors that have a disintegrating role on the form of the song. According to some critics, moreover, these 'excesses' represent a serious obstacle to the diffusion of timba abroad. As one of them comments,

> [i]n salsa there used to be a trend called *salsa erótica* or *salsa romántica*, which nevertheless had a message. In Cuba it was very different: people are much more interested in the coros, the *estribillos*, [which are] most of the time grotesque, of bad taste .... It's total euphoria, ... people dance until they can't take it. A song can last two hours, one hour ... before, we used to follow a precise form, introduction, development, finale, they taught us that at school.
> Q: Isn't that like the montuno in son, which you can extend as much as you like?
> Yes, you can, but at a certain point it becomes boring, repetitive. No one making that type of music out of Cuba does anything like that, they are not [i.e., would not be] successful, you need to follow the timing of a song and of a record. I know bands in Cuba who have done gigs with five songs, improvising coros after coros.
>
> (Crespo, interview with the author, 1998)

It is like writing a song that consists almost entirely of its refrain, and little else. As producer J. Betancourt says,

> For some years now, Cuban bands have been giving a crucial importance to the estribillo, because that is the phrase that sticks. That is just the opposite of what you studied at school, writing a nice introduction, a development of the theme, estribillo, the mambos, final section, coda .... All that in today's Cuban MB has been totally revolutionized. Most groups try to start songs with the coro that sticks better. And that does not just happen live, but also on records, breaking all the international codes of song-making. This makes more difficult our presence in international popular music .... What Cuban dancers wait for is the coro, which is what motivates them. Dancing has changed, therefore music has changed. Maybe you play an introduction, a theme, and so on: the audience stands there, still, listen but don't dance, waiting for the coro. Therefore some composers decided to start songs with the estribillo, knowing that dancers do not want to waste their time. So the story has become very short, and

then you have three, four, five, six estribillos, and as many as five
mambos.
Q: Who started such fashion? Was it El Médico?
I think before him it was the Orquesta Revé, who did that all the time.
After them, [came] Manolín, Paulito FG, La Charanga Habanera. [It]
Never [happened] with NG, Adalberto, Van Van, they have kept the old
codes. This does not mean they don't do that live, because, if one does it,
the other ones have to do it as well. But not on records.

(Betancourt, interview with the author, 1999)

In effect, timba songs are often extremely long. In their recorded form,
they can last seven, eight and even nine minutes, far more than the
average international pop song. That length may easily double on live
performances, thanks to the *ad libitum* expansion of the montuno. In
some songs by El Médico, in fact, the montuno is six times longer than
the tema, which lasts less than a minute. Such an expansion of the
second part indicates a modification of the musical structure, with the
tema moving towards the background and the song mainly identifying
with the montuno, producing a shift of attention from the narrative to
the emotive, participative part. As one local music executive put it,
'the montuno section, the call-and-response part ... has developed a
lot, it's more danceable, does not need to be understood, it's more for
leisure, it's a kind of hedonistic music' (Faya, interview with the
author, 1997).

The tastes of audiences mentioned by the executive were not abstract
tastes. They were those of young people patronizing Havana nightclubs
in the mid- and late 1990s. The expansion of the montuno – the part
that best supports the participation of the audience through dance, sing-
along coros, vocal improvisations and other actions such as inviting
people to dance on stage – has therefore reflected the adaptation of
MB to the tourism-driven economy, where dance music has become a
showcase for the celebration of the sensuality of the *mulata* (see
Chapter 7).

Despite its supposedly musically subversive and disintegrating effect,
however, the tendency to expand the montuno and shorten or drop the
narrative part also has a historical justification, representing a return to –
or the resilience of – an older structural order of Afro-Cuban popular
music. It has often been written, for example, that traditional son
consists of a classic bipartite form of largo and montuno (Manuel et al.
1995). In reality, that is not true for early son, described by Grenet as
nothing but 'the repetition of an *estribillo* consisting of not more than
four bars originally called *montuno*, sung in chorus, and a contrasting
tune for solo voice usually not longer than eight [bars]' (1939, quoted in
Orovio 1992: 456–7). As eminent Afro-Cuban composer Miguel
Matamoros once stated, 'early *sones* were made of nothing more than

two or three words, and people spent the whole night repeating them, like that son that says "*Caimán, caimán, caimán, donde está el caimán?*" (cayman, cayman, cayman, where is the cayman?) (quoted in Robbins 1990a).

The same point is made by León (1974) and Alén Rodríguez (1994). Gómez Cairo (1995) observes how, in early *sones*, rural people danced to extremely long montunos (as son was then called) made of the reiteration of the same estribillo, with an antiphonal structure that enabled people to respond in chorus. The bipartite 'classic' structure of son originated later, in the 1920s, as the result of a process of adaptation to dominant Eurocentric aesthetic canons (Moore 1997). In such an evolution, son incorporated a narrative section closer to Hispanic *canción*, producing forms such as the *bolero-son* made famous by Matamoros, in a process that might well have been emphasized by the recording medium.[29] Alongside the elegant bipartite form canonized by the recordings of groups such as the Sexteto Habanero, therefore, live performances by son dance bands (because son was first and foremost MB) have probably continued to be based on extended montunos. Witness to such a tendency is the work of Afro-Cuban *conjuntos* such as that of Arsenio Rodríguez, who played a type of son that often totally lacked the narrative part and consisted entirely of the montuno section (therefore called *son montuno*).

The comparison of the structural characters of timba with early son appears here particularly illuminating, because musical criticisms of timba have often been based on its alleged distance from the standards of musical Cubanness as embodied by traditional son, and on its tendency to incorporate foreign stylistic elements. In reality, many of the elements blamed on timba were already present in early son: reiteration, absence of narrative development, antiphonal alternation chorus–solo singer, vocal improvisation, musician–audience interaction. The length of timba songs in live performances, and the sometimes daring content of their improvisations, thus, seem to suggest a persisting resistance to dominant aesthetic canons that connects present forms of MB to Afro-Cuban dance music of the past.

---

[29] On the role of recording in the stabilization of son, see Giro 1995b: 223. On early records, which presented severe limitations in terms of length and acoustic quality, reiterations with decontextualized vocal improvisations tended to sound like meaningless repetitions, while solo voices were easier to record. The introduction of a narrative section, thus, added variety and responded to the tastes of the dominant classes. Although the discussion of this aspect would need further historical research, it seems reasonable to presume that a remarkable discrepancy has existed throughout the twentieth century between Cuban popular music recorded and live, and between performances for different audiences, in a way not dissimilar from early blues and jazz (Tirro 1977).

'El temba': analytical overview

In this section, I take a closer look at the musical construction of 'El temba' by David Calzado, as performed by La Charanga Habanera. The song, released in 1996, follows in its general structure the diagram presented in Example 4.1a, and exemplifies the timba formula that emerged around the mid-1990s. The piece is about six minutes long and is broadly divided into two parts. It opens with a quotation of the first coro, followed by an instrumental introduction. It then presents a melodic tema of about 1'15", followed by an iterative montuno of about 4'. The time rate between the first and the second part is 1 : 3.

The melody of the narrative part, in G major and consisting of 60 bars, follows the Anglo-American song form AABA. While the steady course of the piano and bass tumbaos and the rhythmic ostinatos of the percussion keep the song rooted in the tradition of Cuban MB, the jazzy harmonization and the punctuation of the vocal theme with short, harmonized horns phrases confer on this part of the song a character of sophisticated ballad. (Example 4.10 features only the AAB part. The repetition of A goes from bar 1 to 12.) The tune of the first coro, by contrast, is rather simple and consists of a 4-bar long, strongly syllabic melody constructed on a five-note segment of scale (I–V). This slogan-like coro is made of two sub-segments with an echoing pattern (Example 4.11). The first coro alternates with the responses of the lead singer (guías) and is repeated four times, after which a new repetition of the coro gives way to the instrumental mambo. (A transcription of the lyrics of the first coro and guías is provided below.)

(coro) Un temba pa' que te mantenga pa' que tu goces, pa' que tu tengas

(coro) A *temba* who pays your upkeep so that you can enjoy yourself, you can have things

(solo) Oye Nene, yo te aconsejo que te busques un temba, pero que tenga

(solo) Listen Nene, I suggest you find yourself a *temba*, but one with money

Búscate un temba que te mantenga pa' que tu goces, pa' que tu tengas

Find yourself a *temba* who pays your upkeep / so that you can enjoy yourself, you can have things

Oye, pa' que te mantenga, pa' que goces y te lleve pa' la tiendas, pa' la tiendas

Listen, so he can pay your upkeep so that you can enjoy yourself, and be taken around shopping

Búscate un temba que te mantenga pa' que tu goces, pa' que tu tengas

Find yourself a *temba* who pays your upkeep / so that you can enjoy yourself, you can have things

Example 4.10   'El temba' (David Calzado), *tema:* vocal melody. From the CD
Pa'que se entere la Habana, La Charanga Habanera (Magic
Music, 1996)

Bu - sca - te un tem - ba que te man - ten -

- ga   pa' que tu   go - ces pa' que tu ten - gas

Example 4.11 'El temba', first coro (C1)

Un temba que te cuide dia y noche, hasta que te compre un coche	A *temba* who could look after you night and day/ until he buys you a car
Búscate un temba que te mantenga pa' que tu goces, pa' que tu tengas	Find yourself a *temba* who pays your upkeep / so that you can enjoy yourself, you can have things
Asì, que te mantenga, que subministre porqué no tengas, y que te llene de prendas	So, who can keep you, who supplies you / because you have not, and who can give you a lot of clothing
Búscate un temba que te mantenga pa' que tu goces, pa' que tu tengas	Find yourself a *temba* who pays your upkeep / so that you can enjoy yourself, you can have things

The coro has an equally simple and repetitive harmonic structure, consisting of a 4-bar sequence of chords repeated throughout the whole montuno (Example 4.12). The sequence C/B7/Em/D can be interpreted as a variant of the flamenco harmonic descending progression (in this case, Em/D/C/B7). Rather than beginning on bar 1, this progression starts on bar 3, creating, through the non-coincidence between harmonic and melodic sequence, a sort of rolling, chasing movement of melody and harmony. The first coro (4 bars) is musically and textually longer than subsequent coros (2 bars – see Example 4.13).

In the montuno, the bass, which in the tema of 'El temba' plays, salsa-like, a syncopated line anticipating the harmony of the next bar, supports the coro with a steady pattern, which has a mirror rhythmic structure similar to the coro (Example 4.14). The song presents a series of percussion ostinatos played by clave, guiro, maracas, timbales and cowbell. The clave adopted here is the son clave, in its reversed form. The rhythm section marks the start of the montuno with an *apoyo* pattern which accompanies the exposition of the coro. Supported only by clave and guiro ostinatos, the piano exposes its tumbao, while the bass drum (so far, the drum kit has been heard only at the beginning of the song) plays a pattern partially coinciding with the clave. Here, bass

Example 4.12   'El temba', first coro (C1) with harmonic sequence (piano)

Example 4.13   'El temba', coro C1" (shortened variation of C1)

Example 4.14   'El temba', bass pattern (montuno section)

and congas stop, producing the impression of a temporary suspension of the musical discourse (Example 4.15). Note that in the example, on the lower staff, lower notes represent congas' closed tones, higher ones open tones.

Looking at the overall structure of the montuno (Example 4.16) one notices how, in the first part, the coro is followed by the guías and the

Example 4.15 'El temba': vocal melody, harmony and percussion in the
opening of the montuno section

Example 4.15   (continued)

Example 4.15   (continued)

Example 4.15   (concluded)

Coro 1 4 bars un temba pa' que te mantenga, pa' que tu goces, pa' que tu tengas	*guía 1* 4 b.	**C1** 4 b. Búscate un temba que te mantenga, pa' que tu goces, pa' que tu tengas	*g1* 4 b.	**C1** 4 b.	*g1* 4 b.	**C1** 4 b.	*g1* 4 b.	**C1** 4 b.
Mambo1 8 b.	**M1** 8 b. repeats							
Coro 1 4 b. un temba pa' que te mantenga, pa' que tu goces, pa' que tu tengas	**Mambo2** 4 b.	**C1** 4 b. Búscate un temba que te mantenga, pa' que tu goces, pa' que tu tengas	**M2** 4 b.	**C1** 4 b.	**M2** 4 b.			
Coro 1' 4 b. no te equivoque con el temba, temba, pa' que tu goces pa' que tu aprendas	*coro* 4 b. que pase de los 30 y no lleggue a los 50, ehi!, pa' que te de' la cuenta	**C1'** 4 b.	*coro* 4 b.	**C1'** 4 b.	*coro* 4 b.	**C1'** 4 b.	*coro* 4 b.	
Coro 1' 4 b. no te equivoque con el temba, temba, pa' que tu goces pa' que tu aprendas	*guía 2* 2 b.	**C1''** 2 b. pa' que tu goces, pa' que tu aprendas	*g2* 2 b.	**C1''** 2 b.	*g2* 2 b.	**C1''** 2 b.	*g2* 2 b.	**C1''** 2 b.
Coro 2 2 b. pa' que tengas, lo que tenías que tener	*coro1* 2 b. pa' que tu goces, pa' que tu aprendas	**C2** 2 b.	*c1* 2 b.	**C2** 2 b.	*c1* 2 b.	**C2** 2 b.	*c1* 2 b.	
Mambo3 2 b.	**Coro 2** 2 b. pa' que tengas, lo que tenías que tener	**M3'** 2 b.	**C3** 2 b. un papirriqui con wanikiki	**M3** 2 b.	**C2** 2 b. pa' que tengas, lo que tenías que tener	**M3'** 2 b.	**C3** 2 b. un papirriqui con wanikiki	Repeat 3 times

Example 4.16   'El temba', block diagram of the montuno section

first mambo in a well-spaced sequence. As the montuno progresses towards its end, the repetitions of the apoyo pattern and the speeding up in the turnover of the sections heighten the tension, with guías rapidly alternating and overlapping with rapped coros, mambos and instrumental riffs. We have, thus, coros like C1', a variation of the first coro C1, followed by another choral reply *c*, and C2 followed by *c1*. The diagram shows how the montuno progresses from a regular and symmetrical structure to an asymmetrical one. In terms of lyrics, all the coros (except C3) are generated by variations of C1, in a process of repetition essential to imprint the catchwords of the song in the listener's mind.

Chapter 5

Voices, Words, Bodies: Content, Meaning and Timba Subculture

Pure mathematics,
this is what you are:
pure mathematics

You, you, you, calculating mind ...
Multiply yourself by zero and vanish!
You, I don't want to see you!
Manolíto y su Trabuco[1]

Contemporary Cuban MB is set apart from previous Cuban music and much Latin dance music not only because of its particular sound, form, rhythmic organization and instrumental phrasing, but also because of the role it gives to the voice. In popular music, voice is a vehicle for lyrical content and a means for conveying the individual mark of expression. In timba, the function of the popular song as a form of intimate communication between the singer and his/her listeners is complemented, and partially contradicted, by the presence of coros, the choral refrains that constitute the emotive focus of its compositions. In the first part of this chapter, I examine the role of coros, showing how their vocal style, particularly influenced by rap, constructs the discourse of timba songs in interaction with content and language.

Being a type of dance music, timba is frequently represented – sometimes even by its own makers – through the vocabulary of 'tropical music', and described as sensual, exotic and festive. On a closer examination of content, language and narrative strategies, however, timba songs reveal important references to topical issues. No matter how rhythmic and entertaining they are, dance songs contain forms of social commentary that are meaningful for their audiences and are greatly responsible for the popularity of the style. Examining the way timba songs construct their meaning, I suggest that the composers of contemporary MB have developed a strategy of ambiguity which allows for multiple and even contradictory inter-pretations, and makes them appeal to the widest possible audience while avoiding censorship.

---

[1] 'Amor matemático' by Ricardo Amaury Fernández, from the CD *Marcando la distancia*, 1998.

Another typical aspect of timba lies in its relationship with popular culture, and notably with US black popular culture. This is not only perceptible on a musical level, but is visible in the Afro-Cuban street language on which timba draws to create its catchphrases, and in the visual style of timba musicians and audiences, who do not make a mystery of their predilection for the symbols and styles of African-Americans. In this sense, Cuban timba does not represent simply a musical style or phenomenon, but also the focus for a distinctive youth subculture identified by a set of behaviours and visual signs. In the final part of this chapter I look at how timba audiences have developed ways of dancing and dressing that set them apart from the older generation and relate, at the same time, to past Afro-Cuban popular culture and modern international hip-hop styles.

Situating the voice: coros and vocal style

Coros are one of the trademarks of timba and represent, in the oratorical economy of the song, the voice of the people. Simple and anthemic, they express concisely the feeling of the 'street' through the use of popular expressions called *dicharachos*, which often re-enter colloquial language very much in the way catchphrases in TV adverts are incorporated into the language of Western youth. For young Cubans, for example, coros such as 'búscate un temba que te mantenga / pa' que tu goces pa' que tu tengas' possess a tremendous figurative force, which comes from their use of slang expressions like *temba*, alliteration and rapped vocal delivery. Such extensive use of coros, now a feature common to practically all contemporary MB, was spearheaded by Elio Revé, the now defunct leader of a band that has functioned as an incubator for many important names of contemporary Cuban dance music.[2] As a former member of the band remarks, the Orquesta Revé emphasized the centrality of street culture as the breeding-ground for the coros of *música popular*, playing a pivotal role in the development of timba:

> [The Orquesta Revé] were people with a low [cultural] level, but have modernized dance music .... The Revé had a power that killed you, their musical level was not so high, but the energy, the *coros* .... Revé used to say: 'The refrain can't be long. It must contain the five vowels, aeiou. If it contains those vowels, it's a hit.' It must be short because it sticks better. Or you must make the first one longer, and the second shorter.... Before everything else, people listen to the refrain, and once assimilated that, listen to the rest of the story.

---

2 Among the important musicians who have passed through the Orquesta Revé are Juan Formell, Paulíto FG and Juan Carlos Alfonso.

... [for example] El Tosco is a musician from the street, not a musician who stays at home, home and work. When he's not working, he goes at 3 o'clock in the morning to the Café Cantante [a famous club in Havana], and meets the people from the street, those who make you successful, and listens to any coarse word that might inspire him. At the right moment, he uses that word, which gives him a tremendous boost. The same is true for La Charanga Habanera, [there's] a lot of street [in their songs] '*Búscate un temba que te mantenga*' ...
Q: What about older people?
They criticize it, but the youth who live on the street love it .... [Those coros] immediately make you successful. You need to come really from the street.

(Frometa, interview with the author, 2000)

The adoption of popular catchphrases in the construction of dance songs, therefore, is not an invention of timba. As the work of Van Van shows, the strategy was already common in dance music made well before the 1990s. In the early 1980s, composer Leo Brouwer complained that MB composers 'start from a badly-constructed *dicharacho*, and with that they build a *montuno*' (Tabares 1996). But in timba coros have become enormously important, coming to the fore and multiplying in their number. As Lazaríto Valdés explains, the coro is the compositional core of timba songs:

Composers give you the lyrics with a coro, which you study to see whether it's going to be a hit with the people or not, whether it's a social coro, a political coro, a coro about everyday life in Cuba, an international coro, a coro about love, whatever. You listen to the coro and put a suitable tumbao to it. After ... you do the introduction of the song ... then the cuerpo, you put horns onto the cuerpo, and then you start creating some effects so the tune does not get confused with other ones, and there you have the whole structure.

(Delgado 2000)

As I mentioned in Chapter 4, coros have become so typical of contemporary MB that timba has been described by its detractors as an endless sequence of meaningless refrains. According to one musician, in timba, 'there are many, too many *coros*, very repetitive, lyrics are meaningless, many dicharachos, popular expressions.... Today in Cuba there are millions of dicharachos, every band has dozens of them' (Crespo, interview with the author, 1998). The most obvious example of a similar use of coros can be observed in the formulaic shift of timba around the mid-1990s with singers such as Manolín, whose songs had temas lasting less that a minute and coro-filled montunos lasting more than seven.[3] Despite such excesses, as discussed, the presence of coros represents an element of strong continuity with Afro-Cuban musical traditions, rather then a subversion of them.

---

[3] For example, in 'A pagar allá', on the CD *Una aventura loca*, 1994.

In conceptual terms, for listeners the refrains are the real focus of the song. But because they are placed at the end of the linear narrative structure, coros enable timba composers to claim that they represent the people's comments on the narrative of the tema. That strategy, in a sense, allows the author of the text to disappear and people to 'speak for themselves' (a claim further substantiated by the fact that the public often sing coros along with the band). In such a confusion of roles, listeners may end up asking themselves who says what: is it the band employing popular expressions, or the people taking up the coros invented by the band? Such ambiguity gives composers the opportunity, up to a certain point, to make controversial assertions without taking responsibility for them.

It is important to remember here that the tema comes chronologically first and is the part most obviously exposed to attacks from the censors. Potentially problematic statements, therefore, are usually placed not in the first part of the song, but in the coros and guías of the montuno. Hidden among refrains and mambos, during live performances, improvisaciónes may add crucial contextual information and twist the apparent meaning of the tema.

'El temba' is a good example of this kind of communication strategy. The tune starts as a conventional ballad, but in the montuno shifts its focus from love to a praise of materialism. The song never mentions prostitution, but contains references to female venality and sugar daddies that leave young Cubans with few doubts about its real meaning. In spite of that, the ambiguous architecture of the piece has enabled its composer David Calzado to claim, against growing criticisms from the Cuban press, that his song did not encourage but actually criticized materialism (Manrique 1996a).

The contrast between the two sections of timba songs is also articulated by different styles of vocal delivery. In the first part of the song the vocal style is generally close to salsa or soul-tinged ballads. In the second part, the solo singer frequently adopts modes of delivery derived from the voice portamento in rumba which intertwine and contrast with the coros, often more spoken than sung. The incorporation of the verbal modes of North American rap and Jamaican ragga, also, represents an element of substantial novelty in timba when compared with previous Cuban MB and conventional salsa. Such impact of rap on the coros of timba can be heard both in the 'sophisticated' approach of El Médico, where half-spoken delivery is allegedly used to support a less-than-perfect vocal technique, and in the aggressive-sounding coros of La Charanga Habanera or Bamboleo.

Contrary to much *rap en español*, however, straightforward spoken declamation in Cuban dance songs is not used throughout the whole piece, but employed as an effect and integrated into a Cubanized framework. One obvious example is represented, in many montunos, by the contrast created by the semi-spoken coros and the guías sung by the lead singer. In other cases, rap-inflected parts are used as introductions, as in NG's 'Echale limón' or in Adalberto Alvarez's '¿Y que tú quieres que te den?'.[4] In 'El cocinero', by Klimax, different singers rap the first part, while in 'Estamos en la escena' Paulíto alternates singing and speaking on a background of bass, piano and percussion, and delivers some lines in English.[5] Whatever the approach, there is no doubt that the infiltration of the vocal modes of US black music into timba has acted as a stylistic novelty and an important element of contrast, preparing the ground for the recent boom of Cuban rap (see Chapter 10).

Lyrics: content and language in timba songs

> Many people say it's vain
> others that it's coarse.
> But the Cuban
> loves Cuban music …
> This is Cuban music,
> and don't call her coarse!
> Manolito y su Trabuco[6]

Writing about French Caribbean popular music, Jocelyne Guilbault once quoted Dick Hebdige reminding us how, 'for most music lovers, music is more to do with pleasure than education' (1993: 157). That view may explain why dance music is meaningful to its audiences and why, at the same time, it is often considered intellectually irrelevant: it manifests its meanings through pleasure, and not didactically. Because of its festive character and its celebration of dance and sensuality, therefore, Cuban dance music has not escaped the curse of Caribbean music in the West.[7] Seen as a quintessential party music, it has been perceived as a genre associated with stereotypes of exoticism and tropicalism, where contents are irrelevant. Such a misunderstanding of Caribbean popular music has been frequent even among Latin American politicians and intellectuals, who have often tended to look at dance music more as a form of entertainment (and of populist propaganda) than as a culturally

---

[4] Found, respectively, on the CDs *Echale limón*, 1995 and *Adalberto Alvarez y su Son*, 1993.

[5] Found, respectively, on the CDs *Juego de manos*, 1997 and *Paulíto*, 1996.

[6] 'Llegó la música cubana', on the CD *Marcando la distancia*, 1998.

[7] One can think, for example, of routine descriptions of Latin music by Western journalists as 'hot', 'rhythmic' and 'sexy', or of the frequent use of images of tropical beaches and/or female curves in the packaging of Cuban dance music.

meaningful expression, sometimes manifesting puritanical views and even rejecting local popular music (Otero Garabís 1996).

Like many other Caribbean styles, timba escapes narrow definitions of 'engaged' music, adopting textual strategies that are markedly different from those of Western types of 'content' music. In so doing, timba produces texts that are highly relevant to its audiences, showing how dance music can be festive *and* meaningful. Their lyrics, in fact, contain themes and references that in Cuba have caused a great deal of cultural and political controversy. (One song by NG, never released on record, is actually called 'Crónica social'.)

As anywhere else, Cuban composers try to write songs that will 'stick' by addressing themes that are significant to their audiences. In some cases, these themes are markedly Afro-Cuban, such as those dealing with santería, a religious cult crucial to the definition of black identity (see Chapter 6). Other times, stories may touch on social criticism. 'Un socio (pa' mi negocio)' ('A partner for my business'), by Los Van Van, for example, is the story of someone seeking to start up a business, and was launched in 1994, when the economic reforms suddenly authorized private entrepreneurship in Havana.[8] 'Picadillo de soya', by NG, makes jokes about the low-quality soya food that the government tried to persuade Cubans to eat during the 1993–4 food crisis.[9] 'Cara de guante', again by NG, is a picaresque tale about a pretender, a man who, hiding behind multiple work and party engagements, is caught by his wife while dancing with his mistress, in a not-too-veiled reference to the double standard of members of the political elite.[10] Most often, timba songs deal with topics such as love and everyday life. But the ways these stories are told, and the sub-themes they contain, avoid generalized, universal statements, and sketch characters and situations typical of the black barrio.

These songs stand out not just for their themes, but also for their language. Marking their distance from cultivated forms of popular music, timba songs adopt slang expressions taken from Afro-Cuban street jargon such as *temba, fula, bisne* and *chen*.[11] The passage of street themes, views and expressions from marginal barrios to the national stage has played an important part in the history of Cuban popular music at least since the emergence of son, when the bond between music and black street culture has been at the heart of its rejection by the Cuban elite. It is perhaps more shocking to come across similar criticisms

---

8 On the CD *Lo último en vivo*, 1994.
9 On the CD *La bruja*, 1995.
10 On the CD *La que manda*, 1994.
11 Respectively, middle-aged man, dollar, (illegal) business and exchange.

levelled at timba at the beginning of the new millennium. But because the dominant discourse of Cuban society continues to represent Afro-Cubans as troublesome people of shameless sexual behaviour, it is not totally surprising to find that vulgarity has served as a pretext to attack MB (see Chapter 7).

Another reason for the resistance of American elites to the use of popular language is more overtly political. Throughout the Atlantic diaspora, street language has long functioned as a coded language of the marginals, impenetrable to outsiders, marking the identity of low-class Blacks as a separate social group (Averill 1997). Such use of language, which has its roots in the times of slavery, has extended to contemporary black popular culture, and is clearly visible in rap. In a way parallel to North American hip-hop, timba composers have adopted the language of the largely black audience they write for.

One of the problems in reading the meaning of timba lies in the ambiguity of its celebration of sensuality, in the difficulty of deciphering its calls to the body and sexual innuendos. As I mentioned earlier, the meaning of timba, like that of much African and Latin American music, is often stereotyped in a vision of tropical sensuality – to use Frances Aparicio's graphic expression, of 'rhythmic butts' (1998). My reading of timba aims instead to stress how this music contains, for those who can understand them, aspects that express a popular culture of resistance, and that help to build, in the context of popular music, something similar to the 'virtual time' described by John Blacking (1973), where music becomes a means of transcending reality. This power of music manifests not only in the contents of timba, but first and foremost in a festive and irreverent character that is close to the spirit of the medieval carnival, described by Bakhtin as

> a temporary liberation from the dominant truth and from the existing regime, the provisional abolition of all hierarchical relationships.... Carnival ... freed consciousness from the power of the official view of the world, enabled people to look to reality in a new way: without fear, without devotion, in a fully critical, but, at the same time, positive and non-nihilistic way, because it uncovered the material principle of the world, becoming and alternation, the invincible and eternal triumph of the new, the immortality of the people.
>
> (1979: 13, 300; my translation)

As Bakhtin suggests, authoritarian regimes have always feared popular entertainment, sensing the destructive force of laughter and the liberating power of pleasure. Through lyrics, dance and music, timba appropriates the concept of carnival, constructing a temporary liberation from scarcity, rhetoric and political control. Timba songs, through their use of slang, their everyday stories and their celebration of dance, sex and the body, reveal the subversive power of music vis-à-vis the perceived void and oppressiveness of the official discourse. The street songs of timba, therefore, emphatically reject deep meanings and articulated discourses, such as those found in the elaborated imagery of *nueva trova*. To *trovadores'* sophisticated and distanced language, timba bands oppose popular, emotionally-charged *dicharachos* which convey the immediacy of face-to-face communication.

At the same time, because timba, like carnival, is ideologically ambiguous, it cannot be seen as a politically rebellious music. Timba's promise of happiness and liberation, in fact, might quickly switch into a form of harmless escapism, which could be easily turned to political advantage. There is no doubt that the relative freedom of expression enjoyed by timba bands (and audiences) in Cuba represented an important outlet for the social pressures experienced by local society in the early-mid 1990s. In a way, the success of timba in Cuba is precisely the result of the musicians' ability to negotiate between carnival and control, to navigate their songs between escapism and liberation.

The incorporation into colloquial language of expressions taken from dance songs proves how deeply popular music resonates in everyday Cuban life. In 1997, an article in the magazine *Bohemia* lamented the spread of vulgar and slang terms and the impoverishment of the Spanish language in Cuba, stigmatizing the youth for using expressions taken from street language and popular songs. One Cuban expert declared: 'Looking after language is not only a linguistic, but also a political responsibility.'[12] The director of the Institute of Literature and Linguistics added, 'values pass through language. When they deteriorate, this has its model not only in the one who steals, but also in the one who speaks.'[13] The article appeared as a clear attempt to criminalize people who speak 'differently' and, curiously, was reported by the anti-Castroist Miami press as evidence of the decline of Cuban society under Castro. Despite opposite political interpretations, such convergence of view between Miami and Havana on the negative role of popular slang suggests a common puritanical and authoritarian conception of language.

In their use of language, topics and stories, timba composers work within rather narrow margins, imposed by the need to use a simple language, avoid censorship and try to make a break into the international market. Lyrics seek to evade control through a strategy that makes timba songs readable from many different points of view, generating different

---

[12] Quoted in 'Especialistas preocupados por el empobrecimiento del español', *EFE/Nuevo Herald*, 16 August 1997.

[13] Ibid.

meanings for different listeners. Most typically, the real topic of the song is not explicitly stated, but emerges obliquely as a sub-theme. That happens, for example, in songs related to issues of race discrimination ('Búscate un congelador' and 'Una mulata muy fina' by NG), sex tourism ('Superturistica' and 'Hagámos un chen' by La Charanga), materialism and gender relationships ('La apretadora' by NG, 'La chopimaniaca' by Van Van).

Love songs are an illuminating example of such a strategy. Many songs that start singing about romantic love, in their second part turn out to be attacks on women. I have described the strategy of gradual disclosure of meaning used in 'El temba'. Similarly, songs such as 'La chopimaniaca' ('The shopping-obsessed woman'),[14] or 'La apretadora' ('The squeezer') represent women as predatory creatures. Similar verbal aggressions, while reflecting widespread sexism in Cuba, cannot be reduced to a pure and simple expression of *machismo*, because they contain as well comments on scarcity, consumer culture and gender roles in times of crisis, constructing a mirror, reversed image of the sketches of erotic love and sophisticated nightlife celebrated by the songs of El Médico.

As I shall discuss at length in Chapter 7, the discourse of timba on women needs to be read not only in the light of the generic abuse of women by a male-dominated discourse in popular culture, but also in relation to the shift in economic power between the sexes brought about by the crisis. The connection between women, materialism and money, evoked in so many timba songs, therefore, relates not only to a macho attitude common to US black and Latin American popular music, but also to the rising status of *jineteras* in Cuban society, and to their increasing economic emancipation from male power. The *bruja* (witch) and the *superturística* (the super-touristic woman) attacked in popular songs appear as logical consequences of the behaviour of the *apretadora* or *chopimaniaca*, a woman who cannot content herself with the extremely limited economic options offered by local males and ends up looking for a suitable middle-aged, affluent foreign partner.

It would be naive to think of the ambiguity of timba lyrics as mechanistically constructed, one meaning for the censors, another for the audience. Timba songs use ambiguity in a much subtler way, generating multiple, centrifugal meanings. The same text, thus, may offer a criticism of women to frustrated Cuban men, an ode to *jineterismo* to Cuban young women, a celebration of the sensuality of the *mulata* and an incitation to seize the moment to foreign male audiences. In their apparent simplicity, lack of depth and celebrative and/or abusive mood, timba songs place themselves at the crossroads of conflicting interpretations, balancing

---

14 *Chopin* is the popular name for state-owned, dollar-only shops.

chronicle and entertainment, seeking to stay popular, comply with market pressures and avoid political difficulties.

I once asked José Luís Cortés about the reasons for the controversies caused by his lyrics. His long reply illustrates how he places MB, and his own music, in Cuban society:

> Dance music communicates in an exact code, which is that moment when people want to go and dance, enjoy themselves with their partner. This is the main aim of MB, to make people dance in that moment. It's not music for sitting down and listening.... MB is 'shake your waist' ..., a good arrangement, a good rhythm for making people dance, and forget about everybody else. [Some] People say it's vulgar ... [but] the term says precisely that, *música popular, po-pu-lar*. Its literature comes from the most humble sector of the people, individuals who get up at 5 o'clock in the morning to work at the docks, people who surely do not have a culture, a great culture.... MB originates from that type of everyday experience. It is not music of the elite, is *música popular*.
>
> ... Now, obviously, who are those criticizing it? Those who are part of the elite. What do they want? They would like that MB never existed, or would like to see an MB made for them, with affected lyrics, difficult words. No, MB is not 'I wait for you in the infinite horoscope of life', it's 'shake your waist', 'I saw you on the street, in the park, I kissed you, we went out together, had a drink, spent our time together, danced and sweated' .... This is what it is. If you change its meaning, it's not MB anymore, it's something else.
>
> ... When you get into education, they want you to lose your idiosyncrasy. But you may be educated and keep it, ... That does not mean that when you write a song you must use affected words to show the elite that you are a cultivated man .... You can leave that to Silvio Rodríguez, to Pablo [Milanés], the *trovadores* who in their songs deal with deep things. What we do is making people dance .... You may have a song mentioning whatever problem in society, but it must be seen and treated from the point of view of the people, of the popular lexicon, of how people will understand it. It's [a music] mainly targeted at that type of people, not at the elite.
>
> (interview with the author, 2000)

For Cuban audiences, at least ideally, dance music is essentially live music. Live performances provide songs with spaces for vocal improvisation, leading to improvisaciónes where singers can tune the song to a specific context and establish a dialogue with the public. Such a practice may produce controversial statements and, together with dance and body language, orientate the interpretation of songs in directions totally different from those suggested by a simple reading of the lyrics or listening to the records. The censorship of La Charanga Habanera in 1997, in fact, was justified by the Cuban authorities on the basis of the daring vocal and scenic improvisations of the band at a mass concert (see Chapter 8).

The context-sensitivity and the centrality of live performance in MB, however, may conflict with the new, expanding market for Cuban music.

Together with songs' length and rhythmic difficulties, topicality might work against the diffusion of timba abroad. By listening to timba on records, non-Cuban audiences (including Spanish-speaking ones) can easily misunderstand slang words and miss crucial statements. When it comes to writing lyrics, therefore, timba composers face the additional challenge of making songs understood by non-Cuban audiences. For that reason, perhaps, various timba bands now print their lyrics (but not their guías) on their CD booklets. As the leader of La Barriada, Juan Kemell, explained to me while on tour in the UK,

> in the lyrics, you must make a timba that is more international, and you can make a timba that is clearly Cuban so that people understand you and enjoy it ... we ... do things that we don't play over here because we know that people wouldn't understand it. For example people would perfectly understand our song 'Me estás haciendo la pala', but not its coros. ... We do not play it [here] because not even Colombians [living in London] could get its meaning, unless you explain it beforehand.
>
> (interview with the author, 1998)[15]

Given that top timba bands and singers are predominantly male, it is not surprising to find their songs' discourses revolving so much around women. Recently, however, Cuban popular music has seen the rise of female timba bands. Some of them are female-only groups such as Son Damas or Anacaona (the latter taking their name from a band that was probably the first all-female band of Latin America). These bands, together with female-fronted Bamboleo, have brought into timba an attitude of striking back at men reminiscent of female African-American and Latin rap. To songs where male singers charge women with accusations of infidelity and venality, and address them with verses like, 'now you come running on your knees, to ask me to take you for a walk ... listen! stay on your own, adventurer!',[16] the two crop-haired vocalists of Bamboleo (see Plate 13) reply with aggressive coros reminiscent of US female hip-hop, subverting the traditional submissive image of women in Cuban popular culture:

> Sorry about what?
> Hit the road daddy
> There's no turning back![17]

In a TV interview made a few years ago, Bamboleo's lead singer, Vannia Borges, dismissed the accusations of vulgarity in timba lyrics, claiming

---

[15] Colombians are the biggest Hispanic Latin American community in London. The phrase translates literally as 'you are making the shovel', but actually means 'you're helping

[16] La Charanga Habanera, 'Que te lleve otro', from the CD *Pa' que se entere la Habana*, 1996.

[17] 'Arrepentido de que? / Coje caminito derechito, papito / No hay vuelta!' Bamboleo, 'Ya no hace falta', from the CD *Ya no hace falta*, 1999 (translation from the booklet).

that the texts of MB simply reflected the social situation in Cuba. She explained that she and the other singer had rejected the traditional female *mise* with stage costumes and heavy make-up, opting instead for shaved heads and casual clothing. Because the music scene was very *machista*, with male singers always singing at women, she said, they had decided to start singing back at men.[18]

Representing the body: timba as a subculture

During the 1990s, the exponential growth of deviancy and crime in Cuba, in particular among the youth, caused worried reactions from social researchers, generating condemnations by the media and intense repressive activity from the police (see Chapter 8). What has been interpreted from the point of view of dominant culture as a decline of moral standards and a deviation from the social norm, however, from another point of view appears as a set of alternative values and behaviours shared by an ample group of young urban Cubans.

The notion of *subculture*, elaborated in the study of Western societies, can help to shed light on how styles develop as means of symbolic resistance to dominant values through certain rituals (Hebdige 1979). The concept provides a useful framework to describe the visible signs that unite timba audiences and musicians, such as language, behaviour and clothing. In this sense, sound appears as one element of a complex meaning that is constructed through a web of 'extra-musical' elements and behavioural and visual codes.[19]

As a music and a dance, timba represents a focal point and the most important catalyst for that subculture, the site for the coalescence of a style that originated in the barrio but became fully visible with the tourist boom. In its multiple references to the 'street', timba celebrates the black underworld through the characters of its stories, its music (rumba and MB are largely associated by mainstream Cuban society to those type of individuals) and its audiences. In fact, as we have seen, timba's initial boost was provided by black 'marginal' barrio youth. Today, among the local patrons that one can spot in dollar-only discotheques and clubs, are many black *jineteras*, *pingueros*, *chulos* and *macetas* (that is, female and male prostitutes, pimps and black market traffickers).

---

[18] *Global Beats in Cuba*. Documentary by Rapido TV-France, broadcast on 13 November 1998 by Channel 4, UK.

[19] Although I use here the distinction between 'musical' and 'extra-musical', I am aware of the fact that this opposition, frequently made by musicologists, is largely arbitrary, and has been variously criticized by ethnomusicologists and popular music scholars.

Black marginal subcultures are not new in the history of Cuban popular culture. During the nineteenth century, colonial *costumbrista* literature provided colourful descriptions of *negros curros* (literally, 'elegant Blacks'), free blacks who came from Southern Spain and in Havana constituted a criminal social group characterized by a particular slang, flamboyant clothing and aggressive behaviour (Ortíz 1986). According to writer C. Villaverde (1882), the *curro* was 'the young black or mulatto ... vicious bully, with no work or earnings, aggressive by inclination and practice, petty thief by profession, who grows up in the street, lives out of robberies and looks destined from birth to whip, shackles or violent death' (quoted in Ortíz 1986: 4). Curros had their female counterpart in *curras*, sometimes described as *mulatas de rumbo* (prostitutes) (ibid.).

Similar representations of urban black marginal groups, which sound shockingly similar to the current stereotype of blacks in North America, have later reappeared associated with the members of black mutual-help societies such as *ñañigos*, a widely-feared secret male brotherhood that Cuban mainstream society has long held responsible for violent crimes in Havana, and that possesses complex religious and musical rituals (see Chapter 6). The picture of the black man as an archetypical criminal characterized by ostentatious, womanizing and vicious behaviour has been frequently associated with rumba as well (Carpentier 1946; Alén Rodríquez 1999). Old rumbas such as 'El vive bien' celebrated the character of the *rumbero* as a tough man living off women and conducting a flamboyant lifestyle devoted mainly to gambling and drinking, projecting a portrait not dissimilar to that of the *malandro* depicted in old Brazilian popular songs.

This picture is remarkably close to the self-portrait of *timberos* and *jineteras* as *luchadores* ('fighters'), that is, of individuals who succeed by struggling their way through life (see Chapter 7). Such continuity, and contiguity, of marginal black street cultures is remarked by the popularity of words such as *chévere* (or *chébere*), a title of respect of *ñañigo* origin once used generically in Cuba as synonymous with *curro* and *guapo* (bully). In the modern context, the term has been adopted in the street slang of young Afro-Cubans with totally positive connotations, meaning good, brave, generous, elegant (Santiesteban 1997). Singer Issac Delgado, for example, is popularly known as 'El chévere de la salsa'.

The emergence of *despelote*

Popular dance is an area where audiences express their creativity in an omnivorous bricolage of movements and gestures. New kinds of music often solicit new forms of dancing, and these are not simply novel sets of steps, but different ways of conceiving and representing the body. As black cultural theorist Stuart Hall has observed, black musicians 'have used the body as if it was, and it often was, the only cultural capital we had. We worked on ourselves as the canvases of representation' (1992b).

During the 1990s, the boom of timba brought to the fore a new way of dancing called *despelote* (sometimes *tembleque*), a style of dancing markedly dissimilar from most previous Cuban and Afro-Caribbean popular dances. As in other Afro-Caribbean styles like salsa, merengue or zouk, the standard Cuban dance is danced in a couple and ruled by a code of romantic gallantry where the man holds the woman and leads her around the dance floor. That is true both for the more traditional dancing style of son and for *casino*, the most widespread form of popular dancing. The latter, which appears as a local version of salsa (in reality its origin), derives from the incorporation of figures and turns typical of US swing into the slower, gentler son. Another Cuban choreographic invention is the somewhat competitive *rueda de casino* ('casino's wheel' or 'roulette wheel'), a circle dance where several couples dancing *casino*-style perform complicated figures and swap partners following the calls of a dance-leader. In timba, *casino* is not absent, but is mainly danced on the tema, the part that most closely resembles salsa. In live shows one can observe how, during this part of the song, some people dance in a couple, some on their own, and others do not dance at all, just stand and watch the band.

The beginning of the montuno marks a hiatus not only in the musical and narrative discourse, but also in the choreographic expression. Here couples split and the despelote starts. This essentially consists of an individual dance mainly executed by women, who lift their arms and perform a series of steps and sexually-provocative figures based on exaggerated pelvic movements (see Plates 5 and 18). Some of these movements have a name: *la batidora* ('the blender') features rapid pelvic rotations, and the *tembleque* ('shaking') shows the whole body vibrating and trembling as if by effect of electrocution. Other movements present women rotating their arms over their heads, with open hands as if holding a big ball; bending at 90 degrees and rhythmically shaking their bottom; side-stepping, shoulders-shaking; performing a rapid movement of hands and shoulders back and forth, while rhythmically thrusting the pelvis and progressively bending their knees, legs wide apart. Sometimes, young women jump on stage performing the *batidora* to an ecstatic audience.[20]

---

[20] *Despelote* dancing can be seen in the TV documentary *Global Beats in Cuba*, or at any concert by timba bands where a young female Cuban audience is present.

In despelote men are either absent or play a fairly marginal role, totally overshadowed by the hyperactive presence of women. When not dancing on their own, the women may allow men to dance behind them and sometimes hold, but never lead them (see Plate 18). This practice appears to move in a direction almost opposite to the traditional structure of couple dancing, which privileges male domination and reinforces gender patterns (Pietrobruno 2000).

According to some informants, the term 'despelote', Spanish slang for 'chaos' and 'frenzy', was first used as a catchphrase by the bandleader Elio Revé to warm up his audiences, as in the phrase 'Tremendo despelote!'. *Tembleque*, which in a strict sense is the name of one 'figure' of despelote, derives instead from the Spanish *temblar* (to tremble),[21] but is also phonetically close to the slang *templar* (fuck), and to the Afro-Cuban term *timbeque*, cited by Ortíz as an 'improper dance, typical of black people' (1990: 407).

As an individual dance style, despelote has little to do with the canonical forms of popular dance where European-derived couple dancing had been creolized by the incorporation of movements derived from African dancing. Rather, the style appears directly related to black dance styles such as conga and rumba (in *guaguancó*, in fact, the couple never touches), and shows similarities to analogous styles that have recently emerged in Jamaican, Colombian and Brazilian popular dancing. According to Osvaldo Fournier, a black dancer and graduate in contemporary dance of ENA with experience in popular shows, despelote emerged during the 1980s and spread in the following decade:

> At the beginning, as with any dance with a strong sensual or erotic charge, it was rejected, seen in a bad light by part of the population. At the beginning of and mid-1980s, it was still very strong, and not everybody danced it. [It happened] In popular festivals – not in private houses, it wasn't permitted, nor in cabarets ... in squares, at carnivals or at places such as La Tropical, where a lot of people were there.... [It was the time of] Van Van's song 'Por encima del nivel' ['Sandunguera', 1981], it was during the 1980s, and the dance of the *sandunguera*, a woman with *sabor* [i.e. sexy] who moves well, started from that rotational movement of young women that began in the 1980s.
>
> (interview with the author, 1998)

Orovio, as well, underlines the relationship between despelote and the tradition of Afro-Cuban dances such as rumba and conga, and observes in this new style of dancing not only elements of continuity with past local culture, but also borrowings from foreign black styles, describing it as 'a sometimes brilliant mix of elements from rumba and Afro-Cuban folklore

---

[21] The practice of female dancers 'shimmying and quivering ... from head to foot' was observed in the cabaret rumba in the 1940s by Earl Leaf (quoted in Moore 1995: 175).

with rap and North American dance styles' (interview with the author, 1997). This process of creative appropriation of local folkloric and foreign pop styles by dancers, underlined by Orovio, makes a particularly interesting point, because it parallels the genesis of timba as a musical style. In Cuban music and dance, the migration of elements between folklore and the popular domain does not constitute a one-way process. While *rumberos* appropriate musical and choreographic elements from hip-hop (Daniel 1995), timba bands feature songs where musicians and members of the audience dance mixing rumba with *break-dance* steps. As one might expect, middle-aged Cubans who dance *casino*-style share reservations on despelote:

> [In timba] the rhythm is quicker, too syncopated, very, too difficult for dancing – the opposite of dance rhythms such as cha-cha-cha or mambo. It's a dance that they only do in Cuba, it's impossible to dance it out of Cuba, and it's a sports marathon! ... The despelote is not a dance, it's a ... mega-erotic movement, where the one who shakes more wins! I don't know who invented it or how it was born, but it goes well with this music [timba]. They call it despelote because it is a great despelote [mess] ... it has no established line, no steps, and everybody does what they want.
>
> (Crespo, interview with the author, 1998)

To put it in other words, the freestyle spirit of despelote (which, indeed, does have some recognizable figures) seems to reflect timba's individualist spirit and its sound as 'organized chaos'. The centrality of women in this type of dance, remarked by Fournier, has been noticed by other researchers, who have observed how, at the beginning of the 1990s, despelote was mainly practised by *jineteras* in tourist dance clubs, becoming a generalized style only in the late 1990s.[22] The central role of despelote in the economy of tourism and in the nightlife of mid-1990s Havana – where *jineteras* danced, according to a music executive, 'to show off their merchandise' – explains the extension of timba songs, where the multiple coros and improvisations of the montuno allow for *ad libitum* expansions of the most danceable part of the piece.

The decline of couple dancing and the marginal role of men in despelote – where they are either absent or dance in the shadow of their female partners – may also be seen as a metaphor for men's diminishing economic role in society, a reflection of the crisis of roles further analysed in Chapter 7. The young entrepreneurial *jineteras* who in the mid-1990s were the prime movers of Havana dance floors were also the main economic actors of the informal economy of the *período especial*. To them, going onstage and performing the despelote at the request of musicians singing sexist lyrics did not represent an act of submission, but

---

[22] Orejuela, personal communication, Havana, May 1999.

the demonstration of an equal-to-equal relationship between two interdependent economic subjects. Those excluded from such a relationship were ordinary Cuban men, who had to content themselves with the sexist abuses sung by MB bands and with the money their women might pass them.

Onstage, aside from the incursions of despelote practitioners, dance also takes place among musicians. As in most Caribbean dance bands, all those who can, dance or move rhythmically while playing. The focus of onstage dancing is most frequently on lead singers, who perform steps, mimic the lyrics and show dance routines that they teach to the audience. This typically takes place during the montuno, where singers may invite the audience to follow their movements and/or words, or where musicians of the band may be called front-stage to exhibit their dancing skills. As I have mentioned, the shows of La Charanga Habanera introduced into performances of Cuban MB new spectacular codes, following a process of spectacularization and specialization of dance music performances observed elsewhere in the Caribbean (Guilbault 1993). That has sometimes led bands to supplement the show with the presence of professional dancers.[23]

Dress and visual style

The meaning of timba is further illuminated by the dress codes adopted by its musicians and audiences. Although not rich by Western standards, successful musicians in Cuba represent an economically privileged category which has access to foreign travel and hard currency earnings, and can be easily spotted among the mass of ordinary Cubans for their expensive accessories and trendy clothing.

For timba musicians, the most immediate visual reference appears to be the style of young African-Americans (see Plate 13). The fashion of US urban Blacks has functioned for many years as a source of inspiration for the visual style of Cuban dance bands, who, during the 1970s and 1980s, could be seen sporting uniforms and hairstyles modelled on soul and funk bands. A look at the records and stage pictures of musically diverse black bands such as Los Zafiros, Ritmo Oriental, Irakere and Son 14, for example, shows tight dark suits with thin ties and straightened hair, and white bell bottom trousers with Afro hair-styles.

In the 1990s, the influence of US hip-hop transported onstage informal dress codes, breaking the protocols of Latino culture that prescribed

---

[23] At a certain stage, for example, the band of singer Carlos Manuel incorporated two dancers into their show.

coordinated, smart stage clothing (a type of formal clothing that can still be seen when dance bands play in the presence of the authorities). In a country where a pair of cheap jeans costs more than a month's wage, dance musicians can be seen sporting Tommy Hilfiger and Calvin Klein designer T-shirts, wide slacks or jeans, Nike sneakers or big boots, baseball caps, dark shades and golden accessories like watches, chains and rings.

Timba audiences, whenever possible, follow similar codes. Young black men seen in Havana cabarets wear European and US designer T-shirts and sportswear, sneakers and caps, fashionable sunglasses, golden chains. Women wear lycra leggings and trousers, jeans, miniskirts, evening dresses, golden rings and bracelets, high-heels or platform shoes. But dressing in style in fashionable nightspots is something only people with easy access to dollars can afford. Smart clothing, thus, very often marks class distinctions between *macetas* and *jineteras/os*, people with relatives abroad, children of the political elite and the rest of Cubans. They can be seen dancing at public festivals or at La Tropical wearing cheap, sometimes visibly shabby clothing, and walking around with plastic bottles filled with homemade rum. In my visits to La Tropical, the only smartly-dressed people I've met were musicians sitting in the VIP balcony, the dollar-only area of the venue, and their foreign friends.

In a country that so proudly boasts its national identity and cultural uniqueness, the extent of the penetration of US consumer culture is sometimes perplexing. In Cuba, evidently, US-inspired clothing carries strong, if ambiguous, connotations. In its most radical interpretation, the association with images of US capitalism can be read as expressing a rejection of revolutionary values. On the other hand, the pure and simple sporting of a Nike cap or pair of shoes may not necessarily mean an anti-revolutionary stance. But as a manifestation of a desire for modernity and a style associated with consumer culture, the adoption of these symbols still suggests an attitude that challenges the regime of scarcity of the *período especial*.

Sporting Western clothing, therefore, can mean a lot of different things. It can be seen as a way of dressing in style, an ostentatious sign of a new class distinction between haves and have-nots, a challenge to official rhetoric, an indication that the person is a musician, a black marketeer or a 'well-connected' young woman, and maybe all those things at the same time. For every Cuban, wearing smart clothing may represent an act of symbolic resistance to poverty, scarcity and insularity. For black Cubans, however, the adoption of the visual codes of African-Americans carries a special resonance, stressing a bond that bypasses nationality and connects them visibly to the 'imagined community' of the black diaspora.

In the past, the Cuban government has taken very seriously the ideological challenge represented by subcultural youth styles and, to this day, has not abandoned a tendency to equate non-conformist attitudes with ideological deviance (and to repress them). In 1997, for example, the police in Havana launched a campaign aimed at preventing young people from sporting clothing with US visual symbols. The ambiguity of the way visual styles work, however, has made it easy for people wearing such clothing to deny, when questioned by the authorities, anti-nationalistic stances and troublesome political associations.

The power and ambivalence of the symbols of Western consumer culture in Cuba emerge clearly when young communists can be seen wearing denims and sneakers, and their official magazine, *Somos Jovenes*, publishes cover pictures of groups of youths dressed in the most stereotypical Western fashion (see for example the January 1998 edition). It is a paradox that underlines the level of penetration of Western consumer culture, the ambiguity of its meanings and the deeply contradictory signals emanating from the Cuban media and establishment. Officially, the ideological call is all for the struggle against materialistic, capitalistic values, and against the symbols of US cultural imperialism. But the re-emergence of market mechanisms, the demonstrative effect of tourism, the enormously popular Latin American soap operas broadcast by Cuban TV and the ostentatious lifestyles of popular musicians, state bureaucrats and managers of *empresas mixtas* send quite opposite, disorienting messages to the local youth.[24]

Conclusions

The examination of the musical and visual codes of contemporary Cuban MB conducted in the last two chapters shows timba's multi-levelled association with Afro-Cuban popular and urban folkloric styles in musical structure and organization, rhythm, language and dance. Such a connection does not prevent this style from appearing as much modern and eclectic as it looks 'traditional', and makes it difficult to conceptualize it in simple terms of continuity with the past. For local audiences, timba retains a decidedly modern, cosmopolitan feel.

Together with music, the textual strategies of timba make it into a cultural expression hard to pin down and pigeonhole into established musical genres. As a form of social chronicle, timba escapes clichés of tropical and Caribbean music, but does not fit into canonical definitions

---

[24] *Empresas mixtas* ('mixed companies') are joint-ventures between foreign and state companies.

of 'engaged', political music. Timba songs construct their meaning ambiguously and inter-textually, producing lyrics that allow for multiple, context-sensitive interpretations. Such a fundamental ambiguity does not originate explicitly political messages, but becomes politically meaningful because it conveys the liberating, subverting potential of music and pleasure. It is precisely the ambivalence of timba's carnivalesque representation of the world that makes its impact more enduring and penetrating, and its political control more difficult.

Timba represents the site of visibility of an urban youth subculture hungry for consumer culture and at odds with 'correct' revolutionary values. This subculture manifests its distance from previous modes and codes through a multiplicity of signs that range from slang to dance, from the adoption of 'deviant' behaviours to that of the visual symbols of US Blacks. The variety and ambiguity of these signs parallel the musical eclecticism of timba, and embody its restless movement between past and present, local and foreign. Praising their *orichas* (African deities) on stage, *timberos* mix rumba with rap and wear santería beads alongside golden chains and baseball caps.

These subcultural symbols, signs and attitudes reveal a deep connection and resonance of timba with the black Atlantic, a culture where 'musical expression has played a role in reproducing what Zygmunt Bauman has called a distinctive "counterculture of modernity"' (Gilroy 1993: 36). 'The vitality and complexity of this musical culture', suggests Paul Gilroy, 'offers a means to get beyond the related oppositions between essentialists and pseudo-pluralists on the one hand and between totalising conceptions of tradition, modernity, and postmodernity on the other' (ibid.). The multiplicity of signs and references of timba makes it into a musical style and a social phenomenon that appears to focus on different directions, making it difficult to pin it down, describe it with the conventional language of cultural nationalism, and fit idealizing representations of third world cultures.

1 José Luís Cortés, aka El Tosco, here with a friend. The flute player, composer and leader of NG La Banda is unanimously recognized as the initiator of timba.

2 El Tosco with NG La Banda during a concert in Havana.

3 CD artwork for *La bruja* ('The Witch') by NG La Banda, with Cortés in jacket and tie (Caribe 1995). The motorbike-shaped broom is an allusion to *jineteras* who, for some time, used to hook foreigners from the back of a motorcycle.

4 Notice-board for activities at Hotel Capri, announcing 'NG La Banda and guests' in the Salon Rojo (June 1997).

5 NG La Banda doing their 'waist-shaking contest'.

6 Los Van Van's singer Pedrito Calvo checking the dance style of a member of the audience during a band's concert in Havana in 1999. He has since left the band.

7 and 8 The provocative artwork for La Charanga's mid-1990s albums: above, *Pa' que se entere La Habana*; below, *Tremendo delirio* (Magic Music 1996 and 1997).

9 Besides radio, word-of-mouth and rudimental posters are the main advertising channel for music concerts in Havana. A hand-written poster at a crossroad announces a concert by Paulíto FG at the Hotel Comodoro.

10 Cover picture from the CD *Una aventura loca* (Caribe 1994), the first album of Manolín aka *El Médico de la salsa*, who lives now in Miami.

11 Singer Paulíto FG at La Tropical.

12 The latest, 'boy band' version of La Charanga Habanera, the most spectacular timba band.

13 A picture from Bamboleo's third album (*Ya no hace falta*, Ahí Namá 1999), stressing the band's allegiance with African-American visual styles and the 'street'.

14 Pianist and composer Lazaríto Valdés, leader of Bamboleo and member of a family of distinguished popular musicians. He is the nephew of Oscar Valdés Jr., the first singer with Irakere.

15 Pianist and composer Manolíto Simonet, leader of El Trabuco.

16 Giraldo Piloto, drummer, composer and leader of Klimax.

17 An ecstatic audience during a timba concert in Havana.

18 Female dancers dancing during a concert in Havana. Male partners are either absent, or semi-hidden behind them.

19 Street classes: girls in a square of the largely Afro-Cuban suburb of Guanabacoa rehearsing some typical steps of *despelote*.

20 'Socially contaminated area': *jineteras* in a discotheque in Havana.

21 Street rumba (photo © Frédéric Vigneau 1997. Reproduced courtesy of F. Vigneau).

22 Players of *batá* sacred drums during a santería ceremony (photo © Frédéric Vigneau 1997. Reproduced courtesy of F. Vigneau).

23 Two protagonists of the Afro-Cuban cultural renaissance: Amado Dedeu (left), leader of the rumba ensemble Clave y Guaguancó, and the visual artist Salvador González (right), painter of the Afro-Cuban *murales* that cover the walls of the *Callejón de Hamel* in central Havana.

24 Detail of a mural painting by González. The writing reads: 'Envy is the worst kind of witchery'.

25 Hip hop graphics on the walls of the *Anfiteatro* of Alamar, an open-air concrete arena in the homeland of Cuban rap at the eastern periphery of Havana.

26 Cleaning the act: a leaflet for 'Rumbadelica', a potpourri of Cuban dances presented by the Conjunto Folklórico Nacional at Sadler's Wells Theatre in London, UK (February 2000). The picture below portrays a rumba.

27 Young *raperos* at the *Casa de la Cultura* in central Havana.

28 The world-famous Cuban rap band Orishas, during a show in Europe.

29 Two late heroes of *Buena Vista Social Club*, pianist Rubén González (1919–2003) (left) and singer Manuel 'Puntillita' Licea (1927–2000) (right).

30 A UK advertisement for the film *Buena Vista Social Club* by Wim Wenders (*Time Out*, September 1999).

31 Authentication campaign: '100% pure Cuban'. *Buena Vista Social Club* has provided the stamp of authenticity for other releases by UK record label World Circuit (*Songlines*, Summer 1999).

32 The elderly rumbero Ricardo 'Santa Cruz'.

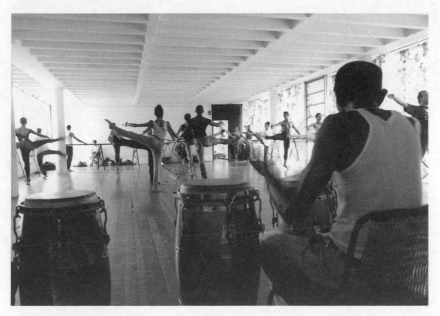

33 Dancers of modern dance train to the sound of rumba at the Teatro Nacional (Havana, July 1997).

Part III

Dangerous Connections

Chapter 6

'Oh God, protect me!':
Race, Religion and the Revolution

I am the poet of rumba
I am danzón, echo of the drum.
I am the mission of my roots,
the story of my slum.
I am the life passing by,
I am the colors on a string of beads
keeping my roots alive.
I am chilli pepper,
I am hot,
I am the step of Shangó,
step of Obbatalá,
step of Yemayá,
bravery of Oggún,
the marble of spinning-top of Elegba.
I am Obbá,
I am Siré, Siré,
I am Aberiñan and Aberisún,
I am reason in the puzzle,
the man who brought light
the Obedí the Hunter of doubt,
I am the hand of truth,
I am Arere,
I am conscience
I am Orula.
Los Van Van, 'Soy todo' (from a poem by Eloy Machado)[1]

Timba is largely made and consumed by urban black Cubans, and produces songs which make copious references to Afro-Cuban culture through music, language and topics. But timba is by no means the only type of music danced and listened to by black Cubans. It does not bear inscribed on itself any natural relationship to black ethnicity, and cannot boast an exclusive right to its representation.

The subject of the typical traits of black music has been much debated in popular music studies and cultural studies, where views assuming fixed characters of black cultural expression have been confronted by notions of entirely conventional cultural identities (see, for example, Frith 1983; Hebdige 1987; Tagg 1989; Mercer 1994). Following Stuart Hall, Gilroy

---

[1] Translation by Pérez Sarduy and Stubbs 1993.

(1993) has suggested that, while not fixed, identities do not exist in a vacuum, but are actively constructed through their shifting representations. He has stressed how references to a shared black culture and experience have been crucial to the building of the cultural identity of the black diaspora, in terms not of literal continuity of essentially 'African' signs or contents, but of traditions which have been continuously re-constructed, generating new hybrid identities.

In this chapter, I examine how timba songs have mobilized the themes of rumba and santería, two aspects of Afro-Cuban popular culture that have long remained at the margins of the revolutionary new society. Such a reference has enabled timba to stage a continuity with the past and solicit the identification of its audiences through both musical form and content. By bringing to the centre of the national arena these previously silenced themes, timba has become a vindication of the culture of black Cubans, marking the beginning of a stage of unprecedented flourishing of black expression (see Chapter 10).

In the first part of the chapter, after looking at the position of Blacks and their culture in Cuba before 1959, I examine the place of Afro-Cubans and their culture under the revolution. I discuss how, despite its material gains under the revolution, in today's Cuba the black sector of the population is still over-represented in dispossessed areas of the country, and is frequently portrayed by the dominant discourse as a troublesome social group. A similarly problematic position has been that occupied in the decades since the revolution by black expressive culture, which has either gone through selective processes of institutionalization or has been strongly marginalized.

This has particularly been the case with dance and music expressions such as rumba, a form of entertainment and social chronicle of working-class Blacks which has survived as a spontaneous form in marginal barrios. This type of rumba and its audience represent a major source of inspiration for *timberos*, and especially for bands such as NG La Banda. While avoiding explicit challenges to official discourses, NG's songs such as 'Los Sitios entero', by identifying the barrio with the US black ghetto, articulate a poetics of marginality that illuminates the critical, anti-elitist scope of their music and questions the place of Afro-Cubans in Cuban society.

Santería, the main African-derived religion, is another key marker of black identity that has become central in timba songs. In the second part of the chapter, I examine how this religious practice has powerfully re-emerged during the *período especial*, indicating not only the resilience of African religion, but also its fundamental pragmatic role.

By celebrating santería, timba bands have drawn Afro-Cuban religion from secrecy to the musical stage. This process of spectacularization is strongly related to the economy of the *período especial*, and has sometimes been criticized as an exteriorization and a loss of authenticity of Afro-Cuban culture. While pointing at a complex, contradictory relation between religion, popular culture and tourism, I argue here that the use of santería themes by black popular musicians represents an attempt to recombine past and present constructing an image of 'a deeply grounded, yet modern society' (Waterman 1990b).

In this chapter, therefore, I highlight how the cultural bricolage of timba has built its audience using elements both of continuity with local Afro-Cuban culture, through the two key identity markers of rumba and santería, and of rupture with it, with borrowings from foreign, mostly African-American diasporic cultural forms. This postmodernist strategy has been used to ground timba in the past while constructing an opposition between Afro-Cuban identity and a wider, all-embracing notion of *cubanía* that challenges representations of Cuba as a culturally and racially unified, pacified society. Far from being a revivalist and/or nostalgic operation, such a move has enabled timba to appear at the same time ancient and modern, and to project itself beyond physical and cultural national boundaries.

Afro-Cubans and their culture before 1959

Casual travellers visiting Cuba are often struck by the racial mix visible on the island, and by the looseness that appears to characterize racial relations in a country where Blacks, Whites and people of Asian descent coexist peacefully. Cuban society shows a level of integration much higher than the rest of Latin America and the USA, with their racial tensions and cities where ethnic groups are segregated within their own respective residential areas. That might induce one to think that in Cuba racial distinctions do not count. But it is not so.

No up-to-date official data exist on the number of Blacks among the Cuban population. In 1979, Casal, underlining the growth of the black population in Cuba after the revolution, estimated that in 1970 their number (including mulattos) had reached around 40 per cent of the total population, mainly distributed in the eastern part of the island and in the area of the capital city. Today, semi-official figures estimate the Black and mulatto population at around 34 per cent (Hatchwell and Calder 1995).[2] Other sources, however, stress how the definition of 'Blackness' for census purposes is highly problematic, and indicate that the percentage

---

[2] 1981 census data stated that Blacks represented 12 per cent, Mestizos 22 per cent and Whites 66 per cent.

widely oscillates between 34 per cent and 62 per cent (Monge Oviedo 1992; De la Fuente 2001).[3]

As in other post-colonial societies, the difficulties in assessing the number of Blacks in Cuba depend on the extremely subtle, subjective and mobile ways in which people make distinctions of race. On the island, for example, not all people of apparent African descent are called or consider themselves *negro* (Black). Following the minutiose categorizations produced under colonial domination, modern Cuban popular language pigeonholes people according to colour of skin, eyes and type of hair into at least twenty racial 'popular phenotypes' (Guanche Pérez 1996a). Such a language, which mixes phenotypical distinctions with social ones, may call a fair-skinned person of mixed race *adelantao* (forward) and a Black with no apparent signs of white ascent *atrasao* (backward) (Paz Pérez 1988).

In the history of Cuba, the role of Blacks has been both crucial and paradigmatic. Brought to Cuba as slaves to work in the sugar plantations and mills, in the nineteenth century Blacks have been largely responsible for the building of the wealth of the so-called 'saccarocracy' (sugar barons), and in making the Pearl of the Antilles into an economic power. Under the leadership of mulatto general Antonio Maceo, Blacks fought together with Eastern *criollos* in the ill-fated Ten Years' War against Spain (1868–78). Yet, after the abolition of slavery (1886) and independence (1898), they remained on the lower rungs of Cuban society. Mostly illiterate or with an extremely low level of education, under the Republic Afro-Cubans were concentrated in the poorest areas of the country and performed the humblest jobs. When not the victims of violent political repression, they continued to be subjected to discrimination, and to be banned from the circles of the white, *criollo* bourgeoisie (Helg 1995; De la Fuente 2001).

Despite their social and political marginalization, Blacks – who around 1840 amounted to 58.5 per cent of the entire Cuban population – have made fundamental contributions to national culture, notably in the field of music. Between mid-1800 and early 1900, they gained increasing space in both cultivated and popular music, filling the ranks of popular music ensembles and giving origin to important creole musical forms such as *habanera* and *danzón* (Carpentier 1946).

As happened later with jazz in the USA, such music and dance was tolerated, and even enjoyed by the ruling elites, but not always accepted in principle. The discussion of the role of Blacks in the forging of Cuban culture, in fact, generated a great deal of political and cultural

---

3 According to Martínez Fernández et al. 'recent estimates place the proportion of Cubans of African descent on the island at over 60 per cent' (2003, vol. I: 301).

controversy before and after independence from Spain. Involved in heated diatribes on the essence of national culture, Cuban white intellectuals and musicians generally denied the influence of Afro-Cuban culture on national music, or rejected it on the grounds of its corrupting power (Sánchez De Fuentes 1923; Martínez Furé 1990b). Polemics focused, especially, on black music and dance forms such as rumba, conga and the religious music of santería. Perceived by the middle class as 'African', barbaric forms, and variously related to immorality, crime and social upheaval, these expressions were the target of police repression and bans until the late 1930s (Díaz Ayala 1981). Controversies also hit commercial popular styles such as danzón and son, which, before being eventually accepted, were strenuously resisted by the local bourgeoisie (Robbins 1990a; Moore 1997).

The rise and international popularity of black popular styles such as commercial rumba (or *rhumba*) and son between the 1920s and the 1930s provided new openings for Afro-Cuban artists, but did not cut their ties with secular and religious black culture. Important musicians such as Ignacio Piñeiro, Arsenio Rodríguez and, later, Benny Moré wrote tunes containing references to black urban folkloric culture, and were themselves deeply immersed in the world of rumba and santería (Moore 1997). The commercial success of black popular styles in the 1930s did not put an end to discrimination against black musicians, who generally continued to be excluded from the best-paid jobs and worked in low level cabarets and theatres, clubs of ill repute, and *sociedades de color* (Valdés Cantero 1988).

The ground for the nationwide acceptance of black styles like son and commercial rumba was prepared by the emergence in the 1920s of the movement of *afrocubanismo*, which, on the model of European artistic avant-gardes of that period, aimed at incorporating elements of Afro-Cuban musical, visual and poetical expression into cultivated art. The movement drew for the first time the attention of the white elites towards black culture, making it into the object of serious investigations by white scholars such as Fernando Ortíz, Israel Castellanos and Lydia Cabrera. Within such a milieu, Ortíz brought Afro-Cuban music to the fore by organizing the first public performances of rumba and *toques de santo* (music of santería), and elaborating his notion of *transculturation*, broadly similar to that of syncretism (Ortíz 1947).

During the 1940s and 1950s, while the influence of black culture and art on cultivated production faded, interest in Afro-Cuban music expanded in the popular domain, with a 'gradual "blackening" of son- and jazz-influenced musics, that is, their fusion with stylistic components derived from marginal black music styles not yet accepted by the mainstream' (Moore 1995: 182). This period saw the boom of styles such as the mambo, the release of the first commercial recordings of the music of santería and the rise of singers such as Miguelito Valdés, Celia Cruz and Celina González, who, in different ways and at different levels, all dealt with Afro-Cuban music and themes.

Throughout the nineteenth century and the first part of the twentieth century, therefore, Afro-Cubans made a crucial contribution to Cuban national culture. Their role was all the more significant considering that Cuba, the last Latin American colony to gain independence from Spain, faced with self-rule the problem of building a national culture that could express the 'true' national spirit, differentiated from that of European colonizers. In the field of cultivated art, Afro-Cuban music has contributed to the attempts of white *afrocubanista* composers to forge a national art music. Its most important contribution to the creation of national culture, however, has manifested in the field of popular culture and music, where black popular expression has provided an answer by successfully exporting successive styles such as habanera, danzón, son, rhumba, mambo and cha-cha-cha.

Moore has noticed in Cuba the existence of a 'tension between an elite bias against African-influenced expression and a simultaneous attraction to it as a symbol of nationhood', with 'cyclical processes involving an initial rejection of syncretic Afro-Cuban culture, and later its nation-wide appropriation' (1997: 26, 25).[4] Indeed, Cuban society has generally proved to accept the cultural contribution of black expressive forms in pragmatic terms, but to deny them in principle. In the eyes of most members of the white elite, Afro-Cuban music has retained a disreputable image associated with lust, sin and crime, and has been frequently used to construct the image of Blacks as a primitive, immoral and troublesome race. Even when it has been accepted – as in the case of a dance genre like son, celebrated by *afrocubanismo* and subsequently hailed as *the* national music – black music has had its Blackness cloaked, so to speak, under the imagery and language of creole, mulatto music.

This hesitant acceptance of black cultural forms has been visible in the social and financial marginalization of Afro-Cuban musicians within the local music industry, and in the exclusion of black working-class musical expressions such as barrio rumba from the cultural mainstream. During the first half of the twentieth century, even the interest of liberal scholars in black culture remained greatly ambivalent, setting out from evolutionist ideologies that professed the superiority of Western

---

[4] This process of appropriation of low-class, marginal popular styles as national symbols by the local bourgeoisie has been frequently visible elsewhere in the Americas, for example in the USA with jazz, in Argentina with tango, in Brazil with samba and, more recently, in various Spanish-speaking countries of the Caribbean basin with salsa.

civilization and looked at Afro-Cuban culture as a manifestation of primitiveness (Moore 1994).

After the revolution

At the dawn of the revolution, Blacks in Cuba represented the lower strata of society, and suffered from forms of institutionalized and de facto discrimination that combined racial and class factors.[5] They had little access to education, were over-represented in lower income jobs, and were banned from upper-class white institutions. In Havana, they appeared concentrated in poor neighbourhoods such as 'dilapidated areas in the central city (Los Sitios, Jesús Maria, Atarés), the less desirable working class districts of Marianao and La Lisa, plus the shanty towns such as "Llega y Pon"' (Casal 1979:22).

Soon after taking power in January 1959, Fidel Castro acknowledged the contribution of Blacks to the liberation struggle and to Cuban national identity, identifying the elimination of racial discrimination as one of the priorities of the revolution (Castro 1959). The new government essentially viewed the racial problem as an effect of class divisions, and tackled it through legal, economic and educational measures (De la Fuente 2001). It abolished discriminatory rules and launched radical re-distributive measures which tended to favour Afro-Cubans as the lower strata of the population, giving them access to better work and housing conditions and a free health system. Vast literacy campaigns, together with the introduction of free education and the building of new schools, raised the level of scholarship and created the conditions for higher social mobility (Domínguez 1993). In his 'Second Declaration of Havana' (1962), Castro stated that racial discrimination had been suppressed in Cuba. Associations of black intellectuals and politicians were dissolved, and the discussion on race, seen by the government as a divisive issue, disappeared from public debate (De la Fuente 2001).[6]

Despite Blacks' unquestionable gains under the new government, however, the reality of race relations in Cuba remained less optimistic. In

---

[5] In contrast to countries such as the USA or South Africa, in general the Cuban 'normative and legal system, was clearly opposed to segregation or discrimination at all levels' (Casal 1979: 17). Racial discrimination, in particular, was explicitly forbidden by the 1940 Cuban Constitution. This legislation, however, did not eliminate widespread discriminatory practices.

[6] According to De la Fuente, during the 1960s the revolutionary government adopted a surprisingly cautious and gradualist approach on racial issues, generally avoiding confrontational stances.

her sympathetic account of race relations in Cuba, Casal (1979) acknowledged that, in the 1970s, racial prejudice was still widespread, and Afro-Cubans were under-represented in top governmental and military jobs. From 1986 on, various resolutions of the congresses of the Cuban Communist Party have raised the problem of discrimination and called for affirmative action in favour of Blacks (De la Fuente 2001).

The scarcity of Afro-Cubans in high-level institutional and managerial jobs – and their abundance in sports, entertainment and menial jobs – has often been remarked by national and foreign commentators (for example, Hatchwell and Calder 1995). Even today, Blacks appear as the vast majority in rundown areas of the capital city such as Habana Vieja, Centro Habana and Regla but are virtually absent in comfortable residential areas such as El Vedado and Miramar, where foreign businessmen and top government officials live and work. As one Cuban black intellectual comments,

> The country can today boast of great achievements among blacks, but they tend to be concentrated in sports, music, medicine and the armed forces, probably in that order. But why, despite the mass housing programs, do blacks continue to predominate in older, poor neighborhoods? Why, in the context of generalised petty crime and corruption, are there more blacks in the country's jails? Why are blacks prominent in 'folklore for the tourists' and tourist hustling? ... Why, despite the evident interracial mix of the country, are black skin and black-white relationships considered socially undesirable?
>
> (Pérez Sarduy and Stubbs 1993: 11)

The reply to such rhetoric questions lies in the fact that revolutionary policies, despite their attempt to build an ethnically-integrated nation through economic and social reforms, have not succeeded in wiping out forms of racial prejudice that were deeply rooted in Cuban society, and have continued to reproduce themselves since 1959. In contemporary Cuba, black Cubans have the same rights as their white fellow citizens, but tend to live in poorer areas, to be less educated and have less financial means than their fair-skinned counterparts. Blacks form the majority of the prison population, and are perceived by police as the archetypical criminals (De la Fuente 2001).

These prejudices are not simply residual views of a small minority, and are frequently shared and reinforced by the mass media. In the 1980s, popular women's magazines did not publish pictures of mixed couples, and in the 1990s TV soap operas continued to stereotype Blacks in negative roles (Smith 1995; Fernández 1996; Holgado Fernández 2000). Generally silenced in the public arena, the issue of race often emerges in private. While I was in Cuba, for example, people often hinted at racial discrimination during our conversations, not in words, but by rubbing their forefinger on the opposite forearm, indicating the colour of the skin. Another sure sign of the persistence of prejudice at a deep level in society is the white taboo of interracial marriages between black males and white females (Alvarado Ramos 1996).

These thin but deeply-cutting lines that separate Cuban citizens sometimes become apparent to tourists, who notice that in hotels and other areas of the tourist industry whites usually hold management positions, while Blacks abound in jobs such as janitor, cleaner and car-park attendant. In Havana and other tourist destinations, policemen (themselves mostly black) frequently harass mixed couples, on the assumption that the black person is a hooker, and the white a foreigner. Working on data published on Cuban research conducted around the mid-1990s, De la Fuente and Glasco concluded that in Cuba 'blackness is still identified with negative stereotypes such as antisocial behaviour and lack of family values and morality' (1997: 62).[7]

Black culture between marginality and folklorization

In parallel with its radical social and economic programme, the revolution acknowledged Afro-Cubans as a fundamental component of the Cuban nation, and their culture as an important element of the new national cultural identity, which could help to counterbalance the identification with Hispanic culture prevailing in Republican times. The first years of the revolution saw a vigorous political debate on the issue of race and black culture (De la Fuente 2001). Black intellectuals organized a national congress of the abakuá secret society in 1960, and black writer Nicolás Guillén, whose work had almost entirely centred on Afro-Cuban themes and language, was celebrated as the poet of the revolution.

The government supported black culture and sponsored research on Afro-Cuban folklore by setting up the National Institute of Ethnology and Folklore (1961) and publications such as *Actas del Folklore* and *Etnología y Folklore*, by financing amateur musical and dance activities through Casas de cultura (local cultural centres), and by contributing to the creation of national ensembles such as Danza Nacional de Cuba and then especially the Conjunto Folklórico Nacional, the most prestigious ensemble of Afro-Cuban music and dance, which took black folkloric

---

[7] De la Fuente and Glasco referred to research conducted by Alvarado Ramos in Havana in 1995. In the last few years, the issue of race has started to emerge in the public forum in Cuba, at least among intellectuals. For a recent discussion, see the series of articles that appeared in *Temas* no. 7, 1996 (Alvarado Ramos, Caño Secade, Guanche Pérez; Martín Fernández, Perera Pérez and Díaz Pérez; Pérez Alvares) and Pérez Sarduy 1996.

dances and music to an extremely high professional level (see Plate 26) (Daniel 1995; Hagedorn 2001).[8]

The new public role acknowledged to Afro-Cubans and the relative space acquired by their arts, however, did not imply an institutional acceptance *in toto* of black culture, which faced various problems of a political and ideological nature. The foundation and activity of the Conjunto Folklórico, for example, was initially resisted by some quarters, and took place at a stage when, in the words of one contemporary Cuban journalist, 'Afrocuban cults were considered as *brujería* (witchcraft), and atheism forced people to hide altars in their closets' ('Folklore: Sabado de la rumba', 2001).[9]

As Moore has remarked, '[i]ronically, support for black street culture on stage and in the academy came during a period of official intolerance towards Afro-Cuban religion practiced at home' (Moore 1997; 224). Writing in 1979, folklorist Rogelio Martínez Furé, one of the founders of the Conjunto Folklórico, spelt out the conditions for the acceptance of Afro-Cuban culture at that time.

> Folklore can be stimulated in its development in an intelligent and scientific way, little by little by eliminating *negative* folklore (superstitions, unsubstantiated taboos, idealistic beliefs in supernatural forces, faith-healing, xenophobia, etc) while enriching *positive* folklore (all that which helps the harmonious development of society, ... and all the flourishing art forms of popular religious beliefs whose cultural value transcends their idealist content and can be imbued with a new, revolutionary social function – music, dance, visual art, oral tradition, etc.).
>
> (Martínez Furé 1993: 112)[10]

The quote makes clear that Afro-Cuban culture could be made acceptable only by discarding its 'negative' components, and by picking up the elements that could be fruitfully mobilized to revolutionary purposes. That process of selection, of course, made Afro-Cuban culture and its expressive forms, so intimately tied to spiritual and religious beliefs, into something entirely different. Attempts at developing the 'progressive attitude' described by Martínez Furé, therefore, transformed dialogic practices such as music and dance into folkloristic artefacts and reified

---

[8] Daniel has suggested that rumba was chosen by the revolution as a symbol of social equality. As she herself admits, however, such a view of rumba is patently not shared by all Cubans.

[9] Hagedorn offers a detailed account of the genesis of the Conjunto Folklórico and the tensions behind its establishment, describing its role in presenting Afro-Cuban culture and particularly santeria in a 'folkloric, aestheticized version of itself' (2001: 7).

[10] Moore has suggested that 'the article does not reflect Martínez Furé's own views ... [as it] was written during a period of intense intellectual repression by the government' (1997: 273, n.10). Such a disclaimer, in any case, does not change the official line towards folklore at the time.

artistic products. The incorporation of Afro-Cuban music and dance into folkloric ensembles produced a de-contextualization and professionalization of black subcultural expressions. Brought from the streets of the barrio to theatre stages, they became spectacularized events and were 'embalmed alive' (Benítez Rojo 1984).[11]

Institutional support for research in the field of Afro-Cuban culture has followed similar lines. Since the 1960s, Cuban anthropologists and musicologists have produced a significant body of research on Afro-Cuban culture focused on folklore, but have given little attention to contemporary black popular culture (for example, León 1974; Alén Rodríguez 1994). Their approach has shown a remarkable continuity with the work of pre-revolutionary scholars such as Ortíz, whose line of investigation on Afro-Cuban culture, at a close view, manifests strong conceptual ambiguities on racial issues (Duany 1988; Brandon 1993). During the 1960s and 1970s, moreover, the Cuban authorities strongly discouraged the study of Afro-Cuban subjects at university (Moore 1997). As I pointed out in Chapter 1, even music teaching, while generously financed and promoted by the state, was subordinated to conceptions and curricula that postulated the supremacy of cultivated Western music and wished to stamp out the influence of popular styles.

Official black cultural Cuban policies, therefore, especially during the first two decades of the revolution, revealed a latent conflict between intentions and practices, which often contradicted the representation of Blacks as a new political and cultural subject sketched by the speeches of Fidel Castro. While the government's social and economic reforms sought to improve the conditions of Blacks and make them 'progress' through education, its cultural policies apparently did not give a high priority to Afro-Cuban expressive practices, discriminating them in favour of cultivated culture. When they did, those policies tended to mobilize aspects of black culture selectively, leading to their spectacularization and decontextualization, or to the marginalization of cultural practices deemed ideologically unacceptable. Purged of their spiritual and material connections with the life of the black community, Afro-Cuban music and dance were folklorized, secularized and made into pieces of repertoire for professional artists.

The genuine effort made by the revolution to improve the life of the lower classes, while bringing significant material advances to Blacks, prioritized national unity over racial distinctions, thus denying them a

---

[11] On the issue of folklorization, Vélez (2000) has observed how most post-revolutionary Afro-Cuban ensembles were linked to only one tradition, or to no tradition, but were performing *all* different traditions.

public space *as* Afro-Cubans. Official support for their arts was marked by attempts to purify and control a culture of marginality and resistance that, throughout Cuban history, has often proved difficult to reconcile with dominant conceptions of social order and morality.

Rumba in the symbolic geography of Havana

In 1989, NG La Banda recorded a song written by José Luís Cortés and called 'Los Sitios entero', named after a popular area of Central Havana called Los Sitios.[12] Following a practice common in popular song, where names of urban places provide a sense of belonging and identification, Cuban songs of the past often contained names of places in Havana, references to urban spaces which evaded realistic descriptions and articulated a mythological cartography of the city.[13] Contrary to many old Cuban songs, 'Los Sitios' did not sing an ode to places of conventional urban prettiness, but to tough Havana barrios, celebrating by extension their people.

> (coro) I was born in Havana
> I'm *habanero*
> Jesús Maria, Belén
> and the whole of Los Sitios.
>
> (solo) When I walk through Los Sitios
> I feel happy
> my people are partying
> man, that's the truth.
>
> ... I am an authentic habanero
> because I was born in Los Sitios.[14]

Performed by Afro-Cuban singer Issac Delgado and virtually all-black NG, the song tells of 'my people' having a rumba. Without making any explicit reference to Afro-Cubans, 'Los Sitios' evokes an area that to Cuban listeners is unmistakably black. At first sight, this celebration of

---

[12] Now in the collection *Toda Cuba baila con... NG La Banda*, Max Music, 1998. There is a previous song dedicated to Los Sitios, called 'Los Sitios asere'. A version of the piece can be heard in *A toda Cuba le gusta*, a CD by the Afro-Cuban All Stars (1997) which describes Los Sitios as a neighbourhood 'known for its *rumberos* and its popular fiestas during the 40s and 50s'. The title of the song by NG also carries a reference to a well-known work by Nicolás Guillén called *El son entero*.

[13] One might argue that popular music is mainly about constructing a sense of place, an imaginary space for identification (Stokes 1994).

[14] Nací en La Habana/ soy habanero / Jesús Maria, Belén / y Los Sitios entero / Cuando paso por Los Sitios / yo siento felicidad / mi gente está guarachando / caballero, es la verdad / ... habanero soy de cepa / porqué en Los Sitios nací, nací.'

Blackness in a country where dark-skinned people are everywhere seems quite obvious. But the reference to this dilapidated area of Central Havana fulfils a wider purpose, that of questioning the space of Blacks in Cuban society. The relevance of such a geographic reference would become clear a few years later, when, in 1994, the area became the theatre of violent anti-government riots (see Chapter 8).

The reference to rumba contained in 'Los Sitios', far from being a casual allusion, is crucial to the economy of the song, and to the whole artistic conception of Cortés. Rumba – the name of a dance, a music and a type of party – is a secular form of entertainment that emerged in the nineteenth century among Afro-Cubans living in the urban slums and *solares* (tenement houses) of Havana and Matanzas. Based on voice and percussions, it shows, in its choreography and sound, a remarkable African 'feel'.[15] Both because of its sexually allusive dance style and because of its lyrics representing a 'social chronicle of the dispossessed', rumba has long been at odds with dominant Cuban culture. Described in the nineteenth century as 'immoral, licentious, savage, and primitive', it has remained largely frowned upon by the white elites throughout the twentieth century (Acosta 1990b: 54 and 69).[16]

After the revolution, the work of ensembles such as the Conjunto Folklórico Nacional transported rumba on theatre stages, turning it into something of an official icon for Afro-Cuban culture. In the process, rumba has gone through a series of musical and choreographic modifications, becoming shorter, quicker in rhythm, more rigid in structure and increasingly focused, as a dance, on factors such as virtuosity and eclecticism (Daniel 1995). Alongside its folklorized versions, however, rumba has survived as a spontaneous form in popular neighbourhoods of the cities of Matanzas and Havana, where it continues to take place in improvised parties held in the streets and houses of barrios such as Belén, Atarés, Jesús Maria, Los Sitios and Cayo Hueso (see Plate 21). Street rumba, which has no fixed place or time, has little to do with the professional, polished performances of the Conjunto, and has remained associated by mainstream Cuban society with low-class Blacks, marginality and crime.[17] According to Cuban musicologist O. Alén Rodríguez, that form of 'authentic' rumba 'originates in a very

---

[15] In reality, rumba is an original Cuban synthesis and not a folkloric vestige (León 1974).

[16] In social terms, the origins of rumba were similar to those of son, which originated in the eastern part of Cuba.

[17] Folklorized rumba performances such as in the Sábado de la Rumba (the 'Rumba Saturday' of the Conjunto Folclórico), on the contrary, take place within a set space and frame of time, but have themselves encountered hostility from the population of the area (Moore 1997).

specific and marginal sector of the Cuban population .... Rumba calls for violence, machismo, bully behaviour, anarchism, and brings with it the law of the stronger, more macho man' (1999: 316).

This is the type of rumba to which NG's songs refer. By identifying Los Sitios with rumba, Cortés celebrates as 'an authentic neighbourhood', home to the real *cubanía*, a black, working-class area that in the imagination of white *habaneros* is tinged with an aura of danger and street-toughness. In order to give more persuasiveness to his discourse, Cortés expresses his allegiance to that world not only by referring to rumba with lyrics, but also, literally, by incorporating it into his song. This is done first by adopting the guaguancó clave and a rumba chorus, and then by including a segment of real rumba in the body of the song. It is worth examining in more detail the construction of the piece.

'Los Sitios entero' adopts a symmetrical structure ABA', different from the more common bipartite structure of timba songs. This somewhat unusual form contains two similar sections A and A', and a contrasting part B in between. The introduction of the song presents the horn section playing in unison against an ostinato produced by a syncopated piano tumbao and a descending bass progression, occasionally doubled by tubular bells. This start, in a minor key, conveys an ominous feeling of urban jungle, evoking images of the black ghetto somewhere between 1970s US blaxploitation movies and the Western film sound-tracks of Ennio Morricone. The first section (A) is represented by a call-and-response between a choral refrain (text above) and verses sung by the lead singer, who extols the pride and virtues of being born in Los Sitios.

Section B marks an immediate, sharp contrast with the previous section. After a short, virtuoso instrumental bridge, the backing band stop and their electric sound gives way to an acoustic ambience, where Delgado sings accompanied only by rumba percussions (congas, claves and *catá*). This part stages the beginning of a rumba guaguancó, complete with its initial vocalization, called *diana* or *laleo*. The contrast is stressed by the modal vocal melody based on a heptatonic scale, in opposition to the tonal harmony and chromaticisms heard in section A.

The last part of the song (A'), finally, sees a return to the overall sound and the modern feel of the first section. The full band accompanies the lead singer in montuno-fashion guías sung against the repetitions of the coro, and, after an extremely fast, jazz-influenced horns mambo (see Example 4.7, p. 119) and two more repetitions of the coro, ends with a coda derived from the bridge.

Looking closely at the architecture of the song, one can notice how its three sections represent different stages of a musical discourse which becomes a quasi-political statement through a rhetorical process that might be described as thesis, antithesis and synthesis. The first section suggests the world of the US black ghetto. Through its quotation of an acoustic rumba, the second part brings to life the streets of the barrio. The last section, by integrating *rumbero* singing with funk accompaniment and instrumental riffs, stages the final reconciliation of two sides of the black diaspora. While the first two sections establish the existence of separate realities, the third one finally identifies them.

Examples such as 'Los Sitios' indicate how timba, and particularly the music of José Luís Cortés, is not only a constant attempt to reconcile Afro-Cuban music with North American funk and jazz fusion, but can also be read as a metaphor expressing a dialogic stance that rejects (at least musically) the opposition Cuba/USA. The musical and rhetorical device employed in 'Los Sitios' calls to mind older songs, such as 'De la rumba al chachachá' ('From rumba to cha-cha-cha') by Benny Moré, where, through the juxtaposition of rumba and then contemporary cha-cha-cha, the singer provided a 'metacommentary on ... the still pervasive biases against the traditional rumba' (Moore 1995: 183). After fifty years the perception of rumba in Cuban society, apparently, hasn't changed a great deal.

The alliance with the world of the street is a common theme in popular styles, where musicians are frequently associated, or choose to associate themselves, with marginal people and lifestyles. In fact, their perceived closeness to the street and to the underworld is often at the core of the ideology of authenticity that makes popular music, literally, into the 'music of the people'. Whether motivated by biographic, aesthetical or political reasons, such an association feeds the street-credibility of popular musicians as anti-bourgeois heroes. In the case of Cortés, this alliance is functional to the construction of his public image as a member of the black community. Against his artistic and political detractors, El Tosco uses his personal story as a natural explanation for his music: his barrio origins are what make his songs authentic, a reflection of his people and their life:

> I was born a black kid (*nací negrito*) with my feet on the soil; in a marginal barrio where during the morning you used to be woken up by the uproar of rows. Because Pato Macho stabbed some bloke in the belly, so and so made herself santo [i.e. got initiated into santería], another guy got arrested because he stole a bunch of bananas .... A barrio of natural musicians.
>
> (López 1997)

Cortés's evocation of the world of rumba in 'Los Sitios' was neither occasional nor opportunistic. His music production contains a quantity of references to the everyday life of Afro-Cubans (for example, in pieces like 'El trágico', again opened by a rumba).[18] His more than nominal commitment to the barrio has been visible as well in his activity with NG, when, at the start of their career, they created a scandal in Havana with their tour of the city's barrios, where they still play today to notoriously turbulent audiences. Cortés's knowledge of the world of the barrio – because he comes from there, has lived there and has there his musical constituency – and his ability to manipulate a 'folk' ideology of community explain the persuasive power of his songs, and the phenomenal success of his music at the opening of the 1990s. By evoking that world as authentic, his songs represented an implicit stance against a part of society from which many Blacks felt excluded, and a statement against a world of grandiose words that many young Cubans saw as completely detached from reality.

Such a reading of the music of NG indicates why, despite El Tosco's and other *timberos*' claims to social realism, an interpretation of timba based on simplistic reflection theories can be misleading. In popular songs, the use of realistic elements is always functional to the construction of an audience that might confirm the authenticity of the artist, of a space for the production of a common identity and a sense of community (Redhead and Street 1989). Rather than innocently 'mirroring a reality', therefore, the references to barrio life contained in Cortés's songs, and in timba in general, must be seen as part of a strategy where composers associate themselves with what the barrio represents to the Cuban elite – a world of toughness, machismo, danger and crime populated by lower-class Blacks – and challenge the racism and the cultural conceit they perceive in Cuban society.

As Cortés once said to a journalist, 'Nobody says it, but there is racism. If a white man goes with a black woman that's all right, but the opposite, dear, is not tolerated. Once I appeared on television with a white woman, and people nagged me for quite a while. The rule is: everybody with their own ("*cada oveja en su pareja*")' (Manrique 1998a). A recent song by NG, entitled 'Una mulata muy fina', gives an idea of how the music of Cortés plays with ambiguity, making an apparently innocent song into a quasi-political statement. After a Bach-esque piano introduction, the song mocks over a cumbia rhythm a 'very fine *mulata*', who only listens to classical music and doesn't like Latin music.[19] Some comments expressed in an interview make clear who are the targets of El Tosco's irony:

---

[18] On the CD *Echale limón*, 1995.

[19] The song has never been published on record, and contains as well a sexist reference to the popular expression 'ser loca por la música clásica' ('to be mad for classical music'), which has nothing to do with music, but refers to a woman who shows a strong interest in men.

The elite don't dance .... When they have a free moment, they listen to Bach or Mozart or a good jazz record or a nice recording of popular music. But they're not the people who say 'I'm going dancing', and get on a bus and ride an hour to see you play.... Eighty percent of Cubans understand my songs and they accept them. Twenty percent don't: those who have the power to censor me.

(Cantor 1997)

This anti-elitist spirit, and the image of Cortés as a 'poet of the people' (Cantor 1998b), have been central to his music and ideology, and strategic to the construction of the musical identity of NG. Long torn between the dance floor and the concert hall, the music of the band expresses a multifaceted mix of populism and creative ambitions that echoes a tendency that emerged in the Cuban visual arts in the mid-1980s. A movement with a festive, anti-elitist nature, this trend responded with eclectic appropriations to the excessive seriousness of previous art, echoing a process of reworking of cultural traditions and creation of new hybrid identities visible across the Atlantic diaspora (Mosquera 1999).

Dance music and santería

> Cuban, defend well your religion,
> which is your reason for existence
> Los Van Van[20]

Timba has also driven its roots into the life of black Cubans by incorporating multiple references to santería. Indeed, the establishment of explicit ties with Afro-Cuban religion was one of the elements that ensured the success of the new style at the beginning of the 1990s, a decade during which popular interest in santería boomed. In 1990, NG recorded a version of 'Que viva Changó' by Celina González, a piece dedicated to Changó, god of thunder and force corresponding to the Catholic Santa Barbara.[21] Soon after, Adalberto Alvarez y su Son delivered '¿Y que tú quieres que te den?', probably the most popular tribute of MB to santería. In the space of few months, every dance band recorded their ode to the Afro-Cuban deities.

References to santería themes were not new in the history of Cuban music, and can be found in the early *sones* of Ignacio Piñeiro and the Sexteto Habanero, in the music of Arsenio Rodríguez and in the recordings made by Merceditas Valdés and Celia Cruz in the early 1950s. The 1990s boom of dance songs about santería, however, was unprecedented in the years following the revolution, and took to the fore a previously

---

[20] 'Soy Todo', from the CD *¡Ay Diós, ampárame!*, 1995.
[21] On the album *En la calle*, 1990.

marginalized aspect of Afro-Cuban culture. The phenomenon was made possible by a relaxation in the attitude of the state towards religion, and witnessed the re-emergence of an underground thread in the history of the black diaspora, where African-derived religions have been crucial as both strategies of everyday survival and cornerstones of black identity.

In the early 1990s, virtually all top Cuban dance bands produced their own song concerning santería. Among these were 'Papá Elegguá' by Orquesta Revé, 'Viejo Lázaro' by Dan Den ('Old Lazarus', dedicated to Saint Lazarus or Babalú Ayé) and 'Extraños ateos' by La Charanga Habanera ('Strange atheists'). In some cases, such as in '¿Y que tú quieres qu te den?' or in 'Papá Elegguá', the songs contained quotations of santería chants, sung in the Yoruba language, or rhythmic figurations reproducing patterns used in ritual drumming. Most often, they simply referred to it through their lyrics.

Alvarez's '¿Y que tú quieres que te den?' ('And what would you like them to give you?') opens with a lengthy introduction, where a chant to Ochún, goddess of rivers and love, is accompanied by a preluding piano and sounds of water, and then by ritual formulas of salutation between babalaos. At the start of the song proper, the lead singer chants 'They came from Africa / and stayed with us / all those warriors / and they became part of my culture',[22] and then lists some of the main *orichas* (the santería deities), such as Obatalá, Ochún, Changó and Yemayá. By stating that 'the ceremony is about to start', the song evokes a ritual in a *casa de santo* (house-temple dedicated to the religion of santería), ritually opened by Elegguá (or Elegba), the path-opener *oricha*. The song is essentially a son, but presents some atypical traits, such as a long rapped part:

The house is now full
no one can fit in
people ask themselves
what Elegguá will say....
People come,
people go,
and everybody asks for
what is useful for them.
I will ask for the good
for my mum
and peace for my family.
That people all over the world
behave well and put an end to war.
Some people say they do not believe
and the day after go and consult [a diviner].
Do not worry

---

22 'Desde Africa vinieron / y entre nosostros quedaron / todos aquellos guerreros / y a mi cultura pasaron.' From the CD *Adalberto Alvarez y su Son*, Artcolor, 1993.

ask for yourself
do not ask for bad things
or you will regret it.[23]

The song contains all the typical indicators of santería – its African origin, the name of the *orichas* and the reference to the ceremony in the *casa*. It also goes so far as to stigmatize people who deny santería in public and practise it in private, an attitude historically associated with the white middle class, who often consulted Afro-Cuban magic-divination in secret (Pedraza 1998). In the contemporary context, the criticism can be seen as directed towards orthodox Marxists who declare themselves atheists in public, and, more generally, against the hypocrisy and *doble moral* (double standards) of Cuban society.

Significantly, the song does not say much on what the singer wants from the *orichas*, but refers to people who ask for 'bad things', that is, who seek to use magic against their enemies. As in Africa, this practice is considered to be widespread and motivated by envy, a much-feared cause of illness and misfortune. The theme is frequent in the songs written by *timberos* who, having reached a position of tremendous power and wealth, frequently ask their *orichas* for protection against their enemies. In his introduction to 'Papá Changó', for example, Cortés tells his *oricha* 'do not let them destroy me / on the street there are many envious people'.[24] In the subsequent *coro*, referring to people who go around 'dispensing witchcraft', NG sing

people are envious of those who progress, Daddy Changó,
for this reason I ask you to give me firmness, Daddy Changó,
give me the light, my father, give me the light
lead me with your powers, give me that light[25]

A well-known follower of santería, Cortés appears in public almost invariably dressed in red, the colour of Changó. During their concerts, his band perform various songs with Afro-Cuban religious themes, such as the popular 'Santa palabra' ('Holy word'), where they recommend to people,

no, no, no, do not hide the beads nor the saints
because of fear of what people will say

---

23 'La casa está repleta / ya no caben más / y todos se preguntan que dirá Elegguá /... La gente sale / la gente viene / y todos piden / lo que les conviene / Voy a pedir lo bueno para mi mamá / y para mi familia la tranquilidad / Que todo el mundo / en esta tierra / se porte bien / y se acabe la guerra / Hay gente que te dicen que no creen en na' / y van a consultarse por la madruga' / No tengas penas / pides pa' tí / no pidas cosas malas / que te vas a arrepentir.'

24 'No dejes que me destruyan, Papá Changó / Hay muchos envidiosos en la calle.' From the CD *En directo desde el patio de mi casa*, 1995.

25 'La gente tiene envidia de los que progresan, Papá Changó / por eso yo te pido que me des firmeza, Papá Changó / dame la luz, mi padre, dame la luz / guíame con tus fuerzas, dame esa luz.'

look, because the saints will free you from evil
and give you many good things[26]

Religion in Cuba after 1959

Before the 1990s, although not formally forbidden, religious practices in
Cuba were actively discouraged in the name of materialism and Marxist
principles. In the 1960s and 1970s, the government repressed the activity
of various Protestant denominations and particularly of the Catholic
Church, perceived (probably correctly) as an anti-revolutionary force.
Until 1991, people who practised religion publicly were excluded from
membership of the Cuban Communist Party.

The attitude of the revolutionary leadership towards Afro-Cuban
religions has been more ambivalent. As in the case of culture, where the
authorities acknowledged the role of Blacks by selectively supporting
their artistic practices, their attitude towards Afro-Cuban religions has
oscillated 'between conflict and political agreement' (Melgar Bao 1994:
173). Blacks featured prominently among those fighting the guerrilla war
against Batista, and were often devout followers of santería. During the
first stage of the revolution, political leaders appeared in public
associated with Afro-Cuban imagery. In a famous episode, during one
of Fidel Castro's early speeches, a white dove flew on the shoulder of the
Comandante, making him appear to the practitioners of African religion
as an individual blessed by the *orichas* (ibid.).

Despite such episodes, black religious practices have often faced
institutional resistance, at best being tolerated by the authorities. To
quote again Martínez Furé, 'beliefs in supernatural forces' were excluded
from the politically acceptable cultural forms. In the words of senior
anthropologist I. Barreal, 'all elements that appear to have a religious
function or a superstitious base ... must unfailingly be discarded'
(quoted in Duany 1988: 254, n. 9).

The uneasiness of the revolution with Afro-Cuban cults had various
ideological and political motivations. In part, it reflected old prejudices
of the ruling class and intellectual elite, which were present, as a subtext,
even in the body of work of Fernando Ortíz. The institutional
ambivalence towards popular religion also echoed socialist policies in
Eastern Europe, where folkloric cultures were judged in terms of
political functionality, and religious practices discouraged or banned.
Most importantly, the hostility towards black religion reflected the

---

[26] 'No, no, no, no escondas los collares ni los santos / por temor al que digan / oye, porqué
los santos lo malo te quitan / y muchas cosas buenas que te dan.' Santería believers often wear
necklaces or bracelets with beads, the colour of which correspond to different saints.

state's fears of marginal cultures, seen either as ideologies that could foster individualism, anti-social behaviour and crime, or as practices that could conceal anti-revolutionary activities. According to Brandon, political reasons motivated the investigations into black religious sects made by the Instituto Nacional Cubano de Etnología y Folclór in the early 1960s, a period when 'armed guerrilla bands of Afro-Cuban religious devotees ... resisted and rebelled against the government and came into direct conflict with the revolution' (1993: 102).

Afro-Cuban religions lack the centralized, hierarchical organization of institutionalized religions such as Catholicism, but have revealed, in time, a remarkable resilience and power of control over their associates. Prior to the revolution, for example, the members of the male secret religious brotherhood *abakuá*, which had a strong following among stevedores and tobacco workers in the poor neighbourhoods of Havana, Matanzas and Cárdenas, fought Spanish colonization and took part in political campaigns (Pedraza 1998). The brotherhood, which still controls the work of stevedores in Havana, has been frequently portrayed by the Cuban authorities as a dangerous organization, with its affiliates (*abanekues* or *ñáñigos*) blamed, as in the early twentieth century, for violent crimes in Havana (Salas 1979a; Fogel and Rosenthal 1994).

The long history of repression of African-derived religions in Cuba, first under Spanish colonization and then under the bourgeois Republic, explains the tradition of secrecy and resistance that has enabled these practices to survive and even flourish underground.[27] After 1959, Afro-Cuban religious expressions were allowed a limited public space as folklorized forms on stage, but in real life, while not explicitly banned, were frequently persecuted by the Cuban authorities, especially between the mid-1960s and the late 1970s. In some cases believers had to ask the authorities for permission to perform their ceremonies, while in other cases they were stopped by the police and had their ritual objects and instruments confiscated (Vélez 2000).

These actions, together with official condemnations of religion and superstition, in the same period led many practitioners to hide or reject in public their own beliefs (Fernández Robaina 1997). In fact, Afro-Cuban religious practices 'were considered charming and exotic remnants of a pre-Revolutionary past' (Hagedorn 2001: 147) that were being superseded by the secularization process carried out by the revolution. 'By the mid-1960s it was clear that the religions of African origin were not

---

[27] Brandon (1993) has noted how, before the revolution, in some documented cases the practice of the Afro-Cuban cults of santería and *palo monte* had been on the wane. The resilience and the 1990s expansion of santería, therefore, suggests that repression and stigmatization not only have been ineffective, but have actually boosted participation in these cults.

perceived as progressive cultural forms but were in fact deemed to be obstacles to the construction of socialism and the formation of the "new man"' (De la Fuente, 2001: 290). Singers Celina González (b. 1929) and Merceditas Valdés (1928–1996) have both been deeply involved with santería as individuals and artists. Respectively, the so-called queen of *música campesina* (peasant music) and an interpreter of Yoruba-derived songs, they have both testified how their music with Afro-Cuban religious content faced institutional marginalization until the 1980s (Miller 1995). The official attitude towards religion, according to Valdés, changed after the publication of *Fidel y la religión*, a book in which Castro made conciliatory moves towards the Catholic Church, and particularly in the direction of Latin American 'theology of liberation' (Castro 1987).[28]

The *orichas* and the revolution

Santería, or *regla de Ocha*, is the most widespread Afro-Cuban religion in Cuba. Far from being an African relic, it represents a living practice that engages the great majority of the Cuban population and can be considered as the true national religion of the island. Like many African religions, it is esoteric (that is, it requires initiation), non-hierarchical and extremely flexible, and derives its influence not only from historical and spiritual grounds, but also from its ability to respond to practical problems.

Santería originates from the Yoruba people brought over from West Africa as slaves, and represents one of the so-called 'syncretic religions', belief systems of African origin that, in the African diaspora, have merged with the dominant religion (one of these being Brazilian *candomblé*, which presents strong affinities with santería).[29] This fusion with elements of European Catholicism explains why santería, although firmly based on African cosmogony, is so named and employs Catholic titles for its deities (each *oricha* is also called *santo*, and bears the name of a Catholic saint). In the last forty years, santería has acquired international status, gaining a growing following not only among Cuban-Americans, but also among black and white North Americans, Latin Americans and Europeans, and establishing contacts with related religions in Africa.[30]

---

[28] The growing institutional acceptance of African religion was also related to the increasing involvement of Cuba in Africa during the 1970s and the 1980s.

[29] The concept of cultural syncretism has been developed by US anthropologist M. Herskovits.

[30] On the Internet, it is possible to find US websites such as OrishaNet and Folkcuba.com, based around *botánicas* (santería stores), in California and New Jersey, respectively. On the internationalization of santería, see Murphy 1988, Brandon 1993 and Canizares 1994.

Under the revolution, santería has not experienced the systematic repression of organized religions like Catholicism, which in Cuba openly challenged official ideology, or of those such as Pentecostals and Jehovah's Witnesses, who were deemed contrary to the state's interests. Santería did not play a political oppositional role and in fact was and is practised by many Cubans who are loyal to the revolution. In a way, since 1959, santería has sought to build an autonomous role away from the political and public sphere, continuing to play, together with expressive activities such as music and dance, a role that has strengthened the identity of Afro-Cubans as a distinct social group. According to some scholars, because of their non-organized nature, Afro-Cuban religions have been unable to represent a site of ideological resistance to the revolution, reflecting 'the persistence of cultural and psychological patterns of survival' (Pedraza 1998: 29).[31] In the context of an atheist state such as Cuba after 1959, however, it is difficult to deny that the sheer practice of these religions has represented an act of mute resistance to the established order. Santería may not have defied official ideology *ideologically*, but it has done so pragmatically through its practices of secrecy and its strategies for survival.

Fidel Castro's new approach to religion in the late 1980s prepared the ground for a U-turn by the Cuban authorities on matters of religion in the following decade. After its Fourth Congress in 1991, the Cuban Communist Party resolved to admit believers into the organization. In 1992, an amendment to the Constitution prohibited religious discrimination.[32] The formal acceptance of religion allowed santería to move into the public arena, and announced the beginning of a period of extraordinary religious flourishing, which encompassed Catholicism and Protestant denominations as well, and culminated with the Pope's visit to Cuba in January 1998 (Ramírez Calzadilla and Pérez Cruz 1997). The change in official attitudes towards black religion was also signalled by the appearance of a substantial number of books on the issue. In 1987, Cuban publishers reprinted *El Monte*, a sort of 'bible' of santería written by expatriate scholar Lydia Cabrera, a former student of Ortíz. In 1990, Natalia Bolívar Aróstegui's *Los Orichas en Cuba* sold out in a few days.

The explosion of popular interest in religion during the 1990s cannot be explained simply by the lifting of legal restrictions, but must be related to the material and spiritual difficulties of the crisis. In the space

---

[31] Pedraza observes, for example, the limited size of membership in *casas de santo* and the individualistic nature of *babalaos* (priests), whose attempts to consolidate under organized structures have failed both in Cuba and in Miami.

[32] For a detailed reconstruction of the relation between the revolution and religion in Cuba, see Pedraza 1998.

of a few months, disoriented Cubans entering the *período especial* learned that the Soviet Union had ceased to be the model of socialism, and saw many of the social conquests of the revolution wane. The crisis unleashed immense material and psychological uncertainties: hunger and shortages of all types, malnutrition and illness, inflation and unemployment, loss of status and self-esteem, the breakdown of families, emigration, crime and prostitution, all accompanied by the loss of power and moral authority of the state. Religion thus inherited the mission of providing comfort and hope to people in times of crisis, helping them to keep afloat and struggle on.

In the anomic context of early 1990s Cuba, the phenomenal boom of santería can be explained by its pragmatic and multi-faceted nature. As a 'task-oriented and present-oriented system' (M.C. Sandoval quoted in Pedraza 1998: 38, n. 5) this practice represents an attempt to find solutions to existential dilemmas, illnesses and everyday problems, providing individuals with spiritual assistance and a range of services. Besides being a spiritual guide, the *babalao* (or *babalawo*, the santería 'priest') is also a person who practises magic, divination, popular medicine and psychological aid, and introduces his followers to a solidarity network of fellow 'god-children'. As established values and gains were being rapidly swept away by the crisis, santería became an important stabilizing factor.

Marketing black culture

... and as if this were not enough
now in my band I've got two *babalaos*
Los Van Van[33]

If we are someday able to welcome 10 million tourists, there is no
reason to lose our national identity and culture. On the contrary,
we would perhaps have an opportunity to strengthen our national
identity and our cultural – and why not say it – our political
influence as well. It is true what was said, that it is necessary that
our visitors not meet or have contact with marginal elements as
had happened on many occasions, but that they meet with the
masses, the best of our country.

Fidel Castro (1993)

The emergence of santería themes in timba has represented a reaffirmation not only of the role of Afro-Cuban culture as a fundamental component of Cuban cultural identity, but also of its growing marketability. The quite literal move of santería from underground onto the

---

[33] 'Llegó Van Van', on the CD *LLegó Van Van*, 1999.

public stage has exteriorized previously private and secret practices and beliefs, taking black religion into a new, mass-mediated and secularized dimension.

Let us consider, for example, the case of Los Van Van. During the 1990s, the band's recordings increasingly featured songs about santería and on Afro-Cuban themes, never present in their previous work.[34] In 1995, Juan Formell put to music 'Soy todo' ('I am all that'), a poem written by Afro-Cuban popular poet Eloy Machado, which represents a sort of manifesto of santería.[35] Through Van Van's version, the text has acquired enormous public resonance. At concerts, young Afro-Cuban singer Mayito Rivera, performing the second part of the song, addresses the *orichas* on his knees, suggesting an identification of Van Van with santería and Afro-Cuban music.

> I am the *batá* drums, the *clave*, the *quinto* and the *tres-dos*
> I am Van Van, I am Cuba
> ... I've got a friend who is a *santero*, and another who is *abakuá*
> they are better men and friends than many who are nothing
> ... Cuban, defend well your religion,
> which is your reason for existence[36]

Van Van's Grammy-winning album *LLegó Van Van*, released in 1999, has moved further down the same line, showing, on its cover, Afro-Cuban mural artwork by painter Salvador González (see Plates 23 and 24). The CD opens with a song where the coro states 'Van Van are *Lucumí* Blacks, watch out!',[37] and features one song especially dealing with the *abakuá* secret religious brotherhood. 'Appapas del Calabar', personally sung by Formell, is both a description and a celebration of the religion. Its coro 'Ékue, Ékue, chabiaka Mokóngo Ma' chévere', is taken directly from an *abakuá* initiation chant, and refers to the African-derived *fundamento* (sacred law) which has made Cuba into a sacred land (Miller 2000). Van Van have not been alone in bringing santería to the stage. During a recent concert in Italy, before performing 'Santa palabra' with NG, José Luís Cortés informed the audience that Cuban *babalaos* had sent a special blessing to Italians. Singing the coro, he staged a pantomime of ritual

---

[34] See in particular their albums ¡*Ay diós, amparame!* (1995) and *Llegó Van Van* (1999).

[35] The poem is quoted in full at the beginning of this chapter. In a documentary, Formell stated that the song initially did not please the political authorities (*Los Van Van. Empezó la Fiesta*, directed by L. Mazure and A. Vega, 2002).

[36] 'Soy los tambores batá, soy la clave, soy el quinto y el tres-dos / Yo soy Van Van, yo soy Cuba / ... Y tengo un amigo santero y otro que es abakuá, / son más hombres y más amigos que muchos que no son na' / cubano, defiende bien tu religión / que esa es tu razón de ser' (*batá* are the three ritual drums of santería; *quinto* and *tres-dos* are two drums employed in rumba).

[37] 'Van Van son negros Lucumí, cuida'o / ten cuida'o' ('Llegó Van Van'). *Lucumí* means Yoruba.

purification, miming the lyrics and asking the audience to follow his gestures.

> Cleanse yourself
> get rid of bad things
> throw them behind you
> clean yourself, my brother[38]

This trend towards the spectacularization of Afro-Cuban culture also reflects another aspect of the santería boom. In the context of the crisis, religion has become a lucrative business, with more and more people being initiated into santería and clever *babalaos* extracting hundreds and thousands of dollars from fellow Cubans and foreigners. This connection between santería and tourism has not only been made via informal channels. In an attempt to make Afro-Cuban culture marketable, the state has increasingly become the promoter of santería tourism, ironically dubbed by Cubans *ocha-tur*. Establishment-sponsored *babalaos* have been allowed to contact foreigners through cultural institutions such as the Museum of Guanabacoa and to earn as much as US$ 4000 for a single initiation.

The phenomenon of *diplo-babalaos* (as popular language has dubbed those who initiate foreigners into the mysteries of Afro-Cuban religions in exchange for dollars) dates back to the 1980s. Besides obvious economic reasons, its growth in parallel with the institutional opening up to religion reveals, arguably, an attempt to co-opt and institutionalize Afro-Cuban religions for reasons of political control, in order to gain the backing of the poor and to weaken the influence of the Catholic Church (Pedraza 1998).[39] At the beginning of 1990s, the shift in official attitudes became manifest in the appearance of a profusion of articles, books and TV programmes on santería, which suddenly brought the theme into the public arena. In the same period the Museum of Guanabacoa, which contains an important ethnographic collection of Afro-Cuban religious objects, was inaugurated. According to some sources, the interference of the state in religious matters did not please all the *babalaos* and caused notable frictions between practitioners (Argyriadis 1999).

Today, it is not unusual to see the exotic appeal of santería exploited for commercial aims. One advert found in a Cuban magazine, for example, advertises a brand of *aguardiente* called *Santero*. Another one reveals that the unique taste of rum Mulata is due to the 'legend of

---

[38] 'Despójate / quítate lo malo / échalo pa' 'trás / límpiate mi hermano.' On the CD *Cabaret Estelar*, Egrem, 1992.

[39] The term *diplo-babalaos* comes from *diplo-tiendas*. Prior to the legalization of the dollar, these were dollar-only stores where foreigners such as diplomats could buy imported goods.

Ochún, known in Cuba as the Lucumí Venus of the yoruba mythology'.[40] In the view of some foreign commentators, the Afro-Cuban appeal has also been exploited to promote sex tourism to Cuba: 'In order to bewilder foreigners, the government is putting into the arena "traditional" Afro-Cuban rituals and religious art, "traditional" Afro-Cuban music, and, of course, Afro-Cuban women' (Fusco 1997: 58). Various scholars researching the cultural impact of tourism in the Caribbean have noticed how the commercial exploitation of Afro-Cuban culture, to which the same Conjunto Folklórico is presently contributing with shows and courses, has paralleled both pre-revolutionary tourist policies and similar 'heritage' trends visible elsewhere in the Caribbean (Pattullo 1996).

> The current tourist bureaucracy exploits Cuban culture for profit, as did its predecessors. After two decades in which the government downplayed ethnic distinctions for ideological reasons, it once again emphasizes Cuba's African and Indian heritage, and, like other tourist destinations, capitalizes on folklore – authentic or manufactured – as entertainment.
>
> (Schwartz 1997: 208)

The trend of the commercialization of Afro-Cuban culture has also met considerable criticism at home. Referring to santería, ethnologist Jesús Guanche Pérez (1996b) has contrasted the present commercial exploitation of black religion with its former role as a popular medium of resistance, and senior ethnomusicologist María Teresa Linares has bitterly commented, 'it's a very impoverished religion, because many people today practice it as a commercial activity' (interview with the author, 1997).

The theme has surfaced as well in the work of young Cuban writers, who have not missed the occasion to draw abrasive portraits of tourists' encounters with Afro-Cuban culture. In *Los sietes pecados nacionales*, 'The Seven National Sins', Yoss (J.M. Sánchez Gómez) tells the story of the rise and fall of a black woman who launches a family-run restaurant (*paladar*) in Havana called Los Orishas. At the peak of her popularity, the woman decorates the *paladar* with colonial furniture, prepares a 'pizza Oshún' and offers the counselling services of a *babalao*, 'obviously at prices accessible only to foreigners with anthropological fixations'. The author wryly comments, 'long life to syncretism!'

> And the widening in the range of services is not limited to catering: besides the *babalao*, on the second floor there is a photographer ... who, for a modest sum, takes shots of smiling tourists before tempting dishes and accompanied by equally tempting *mulatas*. To those who are really into it, he even hires out Oshún, Changó, Elegguá and other *orishas*' attires (the initial puristic protests of the *babalao* ended after he was offered a fair percentage on the rental). For those unlucky foreigners who arrive on their own, the photographer places at their disposal a select group of dark-

---

[40] Respectively, in *Tropicana Internacional* (no. 1, p. 7) and *Salsa Cubana* (no. 1, p. 39).

skinned female models, who happily agree to pose in super-close-fitting shorts and mini-skirts embracing the usual Italian or Canadian ... and who sometimes leave the restaurant with them (obviously, the clever photographer gets a percentage on that as well).

(Yoss 1999: 78–9; my translation)

A year later, Yoss's fantasies have become real. Although not a paladar, Orishas has became the not-too-modest name for a rap outfit formed by four Cubans in Paris (see Plate 28). The group have recorded two extremely successful albums distributed by EMI, which contain various songs referring to santería.[41]

The boom of songs about santería and the growing interest of foreigners in black religion have posited a dilemma. Are Afro-Cuban culture and religion being corrupted by the money brought in by tourism? Or should they adapt pragmatically to the new social and economic situation, where they have become commercial catchwords and might be manipulated by the state and the tourist industry? It is difficult to deny that santería themes have greatly helped timba to expand its music constituency, both at home and abroad. In that case, the purist, essentialist argument would claim that santería, as a form of authentic folkloric culture, should keep away from the spectacularization of popular culture, in order to avoid being corrupted by commercialization.

Yet from another perspective, timba and santería can be regarded as two poles of the same continuum of Afro-Cuban popular culture, where they might be respectively described as the 'modern' and the 'traditional' ends. They represent two aspects of black contemporary culture that originate in the same social stratum, and, in the 1990s, benefited from each other. In timba songs, santería is not a pose adopted by cultural outsiders, but a discourse between musicians and their largely Afro-Cuban audience. The vast majority of popular musicians are devout followers of the religion, and various MB bandleaders, such as Adalberto Alvarez and Lazaríto Valdés, are in fact *babalaos* (Miller 1995; personal communication).

Karin Barber (1997) has observed how eclecticism and adaptability characterize many contemporary West African cultures and religions. These aspects have proved crucial in the Atlantic diaspora, where the birth of religions like santería represents the process of adaptation of African culture to adverse conditions. As in Africa, these practices have not been confined to the domain of spirituality, but have intertwined with everyday survival strategies.[42] This 'dynamic function', as art critic

---

[41] *A lo cubano*, 2000; *Emigrante*, 2002.

[42] Even before the período especial, santería had an important social and economic dimension, functioning as an underground community network and a channel to get hard-to-find animals needed for ritual sacrifices (Brandon 1993).

Gerardo Mosquera has called it, has little to do with passive notions of preservation of African culture and literal authenticity, but underlines the historical centrality of anti-essentialist processes of adaptation and eclectic appropriation:

> with Catholicism pushing at the door, the Africans simply opened it and Catholicism fell out the other side. Without prejudices or complexes, the Africans included it in a collage structure alongside their own religion (in Cuba every *santero* considers himself also a Catholic, and in addition he may be a Palero, an Abakuá, and a Freemason, without contradictions, in a system of coexisting fragments).
>
> (Mosquera, in Lindsay 1996: 227)[43]

Conclusions

In a country where Blacks represent a large sector of the population, predominate in the poorest areas and appear as a target for widespread prejudice, there is no doubt that the celebration of black expression by timba has had a crucial role in reaffirming the centrality of Afro-Cubans in the formation of Cuban national identity. Seen by many white Cubans with embarrassment and suspicion, the sounds and themes of timba represent a vindication of black working-class culture over its long exclusion from the cultural mainstream, in opposition to a notion of *cubanía* which celebrates the creole nature of the nation but accepts with difficulty the cultural expressions of its dark-skinned citizens. By dealing with those issues in non-folkloristic and sometimes controversial terms, timba songs have broken the silence surrounding the issue of race, raising difficult questions on the persistence of racial prejudice and inequality in contemporary Cuba.

The correlation between the revival of African-derived cultural expression and a process of questioning of the socially subordinated role of Blacks, obviously, is not just a Cuban phenomenon, and parallels contemporary trends visible elsewhere in the Caribbean and the Americas. In contrast to visions that tend to postulate an authentic African culture corrupted by commercialization, I have argued that timba and folkloric culture represent two polarities of the same cultural continuum. While not exempt from attempts at manipulation, contemporary black popular culture in Cuba has proved resistant to efforts at institutional control, and able to provide a ground for dialogue between Cubans, and between them and foreigners. What at first sight may be seen as a form of commercialization, therefore, from a non-essentialist perspective may take on quite a different meaning, and

---

[43] See also Vélez 2000.

be read as a cultural practice that becomes meaningful not because of its literal closeness to a model and an origin, but simply because Cuban audiences identify and accept the existence of a continuity between timba and black religious and cultural traditions. In this respect, it might be worth recalling that both rumba and santería, while often perceived and represented as originating in a mythologically distant past, are relatively recent elaborations that have undergone continuous transformations and adaptations to historical circumstances (Argyriadis 1999).

The deployment of the rhythms, melodies and themes of rumba and santería by timberos, thus, can be understood not as a nostalgic and/or exotic phenomenon, but as an attempt to assert black identity by grounding themselves in the past, and to incorporate street culture and religion into their vision of (post-)modernity. As Waterman has observed, when discussing popular music in Nigeria, 'Yoruba modernity ... has had to focus retrospectively, fix ideologically, and contour aesthetically a master tradition in terms of which its own pragmatic and up-to-date identity makes sense and appears inevitable' (1990b: 377). In its appropriation of the past, Nigerian *jù-jú* music has reinforced and reinvented 'the image of ... a kind of cosmopolitan electronic kingdom' (ibid: 376). That is precisely what timberos attempt to do, by reinventing a past that stretches to the point of being able to incorporate the present. To put it in the colourful language of El Tosco: 'people say Changó is the most super-stereophonic saint of the Yoruba religion. Let's check it out!'.[44]

The real question, therefore, does not lie in the opposition between commercialized and non-commercialized black popular culture, but in looking at whether expressions such as santería and timba can escape the pervasive commodification of Afro-Cuban culture and are compatible with the aims of the tourist industry. Witnessing the successful attempt at selling tourists not just beaches but also art and performance, in the last few years music and dance have become an integral part of the tourist marketing of Cuba. Within such a framework, timba and santería have made an impact on local economy, generated international interest, and promoted contacts between foreigners and Cubans. For the same reason, they have sometimes come into ideological and economic conflict with the state's wish to control all aspects of public life.[45] In that sense, both

---

[44] From the introduction to the song 'Papá Changó', in the CD *En directo desde el patio de mi casa*, 1995.

[45] In some cases, indeed, the 'improper' contacts developed around black music and religion have been repressed. In 1999, for example, the director of one of Matanza's folkloric group was fined $1,000 for hosting a foreigner without an official permission (*Afrocubaweb* site, 8/6/1999 <http://www.afrocubaweb.com>).

aspects of Afro-Cuban popular culture may pose serious dilemmas to tourism, an industry which needs glamour and predictability, and not social conflict. Although they might be used to play the card of exoticism and/or authenticity, they can never be totally safe.

Chapter 7

'You are a witch with no feelings': Sex Tourism, Gender and the Representation of Women in Timba Songs

The *mulata* Celestina
Got frightened by the sea
'Cause once she went swimming
and a *guabina* bit her.
Come in, come in, *guabina*
From the door on the back
Old Cuban *guaracha*[1]

Do not call me coarse,
what I am is an awesome Cuban
NG La Banda, 'Crónica social'[2]

Around the mid-1990s, the popularity of timba and of its challenging attitudes began to worry the Cuban authorities. Preoccupations emerged with growing frequency in the local press, where journalists started criticizing MB by accusing it of being vulgar and offensive to women. One target of the accusations, in particular, was a song by NG called 'La bruja' ('The witch'), which raised the issue of sex tourism and prostitution, a taboo topic that would be addressed by the authorities only at a later stage and, at least initially, with much recalcitrance.

The debate on the alleged vulgarity of the lyrics of dance songs was not new in the history of Cuban popular music. As in many other popular styles, it stemmed from a conflict between low and high culture which in Cuba informs much of the dominant discourse on Afro-Cuban popular culture. The representation of women in timba songs, in reality, did not appear to differ radically from that found in many *sones* of Cuban popular music of the past, celebrated today as classics of national culture. Rather, it seemed to conform to a wider male view of the subordinated role of women that is deep-seated in Cuban society. Such a

---

[1] 'La mulata Celestina / le ha cojido miedo al mar / porqué una vez fue a nadar / y la mordió una guabina / Entra, entra guabina / por la puerta de la cocina' (guabina is a tasty river fish). From 'La guabina', old Cuban *guaracha* reported by León 1974.

[2] 'No me llames chabacano / lo que soy es tremendo cubano.'

vision informs the enduring myth of the Cuban *mulata* as a sexual object, a common theme in Cuban popular music, but also a reference abundantly exploited by the tourism industry. The criticisms of timba, in fact, seem to have targeted the vulgarity of songs' lyrics in order to hit timba's perceived contiguity with sex tourism and the illegal economy, and the negative image of Cuba that might result from that connection.

For this reason, in this chapter I devote much space to the phenomenon of *jineterismo*, a type of informal prostitution that grew up around tourist areas in the 1990s and was particularly visible in dance clubs. What emerges is the ambiguous attitude initially adopted by the authorities towards the phenomenon and the complacent role of the tourism industry. My discussion underlines as well *jineterismo*'s ambivalent and many-sided nature, which makes this practice into a phenomenon that expresses aspects of both sexual exploitation and social defiance.[3]

Looking at the connections between timba and *jineterismo*, it appears clear that MB played a pivotal, albeit indirect role in the boom of sex tourism in Cuba. By the middle of the decade, Havana dance clubs had become sites for the staging of the sensuality of the *mulata* for male tourist audiences, with timba bands launching waist-shaking contests and inciting *jineteras* to strip off. In this context, timba songs offered texts that oscillated between social commentary and praise of their audiences, and that could be read from different angles as joyful celebration of the *mulata*, odes to *jineterismo*, misogynists attacks on women and expressions of the frustration of Cuban males, offering a representation of gender politics that was in marked contrast with the idealized pictures of gender relations emanating from Cuban institutions.

The return of sex tourism in Cuba

During the 1990s, the number of tourists travelling to Cuba rocketed. Foreign visitors, who had numbered a few thousand during the 1970s, totalled 750 000 in 1995 and 1.2 million in 1997 (Cawthorne 1998; Schwartz 1997). In 1994, for the first time, earnings from tourism surpassed the revenues generated by sugar cane, the traditional main export of Cuba, making the tourist industry into the new economic engine of the island.

---

[3] On sex tourism and prostitution in Cuba, see Díaz, Fernández and Caram 1996, Díaz Canals and González Olmedo 1997, O'Connell Davidson 1996, Rundle 2001 and Trumbull 2001.

In parallel with the presence of tourists, the visibility of prostitution grew around the main tourist areas of Havana and Varadero (the most important Cuban sea resort), showing how the boom of travel to Cuba was in no small part related to sex tourism (O'Connell Davidson 1996; Schwartz 1997).[4] It was a phenomenon considered extinct in the early years of socialist Cuba, and one that was not even foreseen by the Cuban penal code. The war on vice, in fact, had been one of the moral pillars of the revolution, which after the fall of the Batista regime had put considerable effort into dismantling the flourishing sex industry that had earned Cuba the nickname of 'brothel of the Caribbean' (Elizalde 1996a).

Facing the return of prostitution to Cuba, it is easy to imagine the shock felt by Cubans who still remembered Havana in the 1950s.[5] While airplanes unloaded hundreds of male tourists anxious to spend their dollars, sexy and smartly dressed young ladies appeared in the capital city along the Quinta Avenida, a wide avenue crossing the areas of Miramar and Playa, where luxury hotels, foreign embassies and headquarters of international companies are situated. The phenomenon, then, extended to the whole Malecón, where, at the time when people returned home from work, one could see young women hitch-hiking at traffic lights. They could be requesting an innocent lift, but if the car was driven by a foreigner, it might bring some extra benefits. At a certain stage, following police harassment, *jineteras* started to solicit tourists from the backs of motorcycles, driven by friends. The presence of young women looking for tourists grew exponentially in front of the entrances of the hotels in El Vedado, in the colonial cafés in Old Havana, in cabarets, clubs and even at the airport, where they often bade farewell to their last fiancée and welcomed the newly arrived.[6]

Caught between the scarcity of the *período especial* and the new plenty created by tourism, many Cubans seemed to kneel to the power of the dollar. In 1995, the beaches and streets of Varadero were full with young women and men hustling foreign tourists. In theory, tourists could not bring these people into their hotel rooms. But the problem could be solved with a tip to the janitor, who, on request, might put the guest in contact with the 'right people' in the business.

---

[4] I employ here the expression 'sex tourism' in the broad sense of 'activities of individuals who, whether or not they set out with this intention, use their economic power to attain powers of sexual command over local women' (O'Connell Davidson 1998: 75).

[5] Alarming as it may be for a country like Cuba, the size of the phenomenon was and largely is irrelevant compared to that in other classic destinations of sex tourism like Thailand, Brazil or the Dominican Republic.

[6] Those who think it an exaggeration may consult the travel tips contained in sex tourist websites such as a WorldSexGuide.

In many foreign countries, Cuba started to become synonymous with hot, cheap sex. The problem was raised at an international conference on tourism, where Fidel Castro declared, 'We don't want the image of a country of gambling, drugs, and prostitution: we want the image of a country with a high cultural level, a healthy country both morally and physically, an organized country that looks after the environment.'[7] Much to his dislike, however, the phenomenon expanded and found increasing resonance abroad, where the Western press started publishing articles on the issue.[8] In 1995, an Italian guide for sex travellers defined the island as 'an authentic paradise for "red light" tourists' (Morello and Taliento 1995).

The scandal of 'La bruja'

The expansion of sex tourism and prostitution disconcerted many Cubans, who interpreted it as evidence of the loss of authority by the state and of the decline in its ability to provide for citizens' needs. Because the phenomenon, quite literally, lived on the street, and was most obviously connected with nightlife and tourist leisure, it did not go unnoticed by timba musicians, who became involved in it both as social commentators and as professionals of the entertainment industry.

The years of the sudden boom of sex tourism to Cuba were the golden period of NG La Banda, who were the talk of the town and dominated the capital city's nightlife. The task of dealing with the issue, therefore, fell on El Tosco, who, faithful to his role as a social chronicler, composed a song entitled 'La bruja'. Between 1993 and 1994, the tune resonated through the dance clubs of Havana and circulated clandestinely among fans, but did not appear on record and was not broadcast by local radio stations. According to the intricate discography of NG, which includes dozens of albums, the song was first released on record in Japan, where the band was extremely popular. In Cuba, it appeared on CD only in 1995, in the wake of popularity and polemics.[9]

In the song, the *bruja*, or witch – a term that in Cuban has more or less the same meaning as in English, that of a wicked female – was a woman with no time for her Cuban lover, who looked for her desperately, because she was too busy cultivating other interests:

---

[7] *Cuba Business*, London, September 1994. Quoted in Pattullo 1996.

[8] For example, 'Sex Tourism arrives in Cuba', *The Ottawa Citizen*, 13 March 1993.

[9] On the CD *La bruja*, 1995. The artwork of the CD shows in the background a young attractive woman riding a broom that is actually made of a combination of a broomstick and a motorbike (an obvious reference to the then common practice of using motorbikes in solicitation) (see Plate 3).

I go out bored and annoyed
desperately looking for you
only to meet myself,
tired and lonely. [...]

You think you're the best
you think you're an artist
because you go by *turitaxi*
through Buena Vista
looking for something impossible
because you miss me too.

You exchanged my love
for cheap amusements.
The price of spirit
cannot be auctioned
This is why I'm comparing you
to a witch.

The disillusioned lover eventually vented his anger in the coro:

A witch, this is what you are
a witch with no feelings
you are a witch.

(solo) A crazy woman this is what you are
a [sexually] frenzied person, out of your head

You are a witch
a witch with no feelings
you are a witch.[10]

The song makes a reference to *turitaxis* (dollar-only taxis used by foreigners), but it does not mention prostitutes, *jineteras* or tourists. In its lyrics, there is virtually nothing reminiscent of the often explicit language of Western pop and rock, or the misogynist showers of words contained in much North American rap. Nevertheless, 'La bruja' caused a moral scandal in Cuba: it was banned by radio and met with the solemn condemnation of the Federación de Mujeres Cubanas (Federation of Cuban Women, or FMC), a powerful quasi-governmental organization.[11]

---

[10] 'Salgo de la casa aburrido, irritado / a buscar tu silueta desesperado / me encuentro a mí mismo / solo y cansado / ... / Tu te crees la mejor / tu te crees una artista / porqué vas en turitaxi / por Buena Vista / buscando lo imposible / porqué a ti te falto yo también / Tu cambiaste mi amor / por diversiones baratas / El precio del espiritu / no se subasta / por eso te comparo yo / con una bruja / (coro) Tu lo que eres es una bruja / una bruja sin sentimientos / tu eres una bruja / (Tu lo que eres es una loca / una arrebatà / una desquiciá) / Tu eres una bruja / una bruja sin sentimientos / tu eres una bruja.'

[11] While formally an NGO, the FMC in practice maintains strong ties with the Cuban Communist Party. All NGOs operating in Cuba are approved and monitored by the state (Puerta 1996).

With that song, Cortés dared to bring for the first time into the public arena a problem that was apparent to all Cubans, but virtually non-existent in the media and in official political discourse. This explains the institutional outrage caused by 'La bruja' in the mid-1990s, by a tune that to our ears sounds mild and even reticent. More seriously still, Cortés raised the issue not with an elaborate argument addressed to an articulate audience, but with a song of *música bailable* that had the maximum popular resonance, thus touching a problem which should not have been raised, or that should have been raised in a different form.

There were other aspects of the song that did not please the Cuban establishment. In its musical form, for example, the coro sounded more like a celebration than a condemnation, showing how the verbal disapproval of the woman was more apparent than real. And, every Cuban knew that NG were dominant in the scene of dance music and tourist discos, where their main Cuban audiences were represented precisely by *jineteras*. All these reasons contributed to the uproar in the political and intellectual elite, who interpreted the song both as a celebration of a culture and a profession that in Cuba was supposed to have been wiped out for good by the revolution and as an implicit allusion to the failure of Cuban socialism.

Listening to the song, reissued a few years ago in a Hemisphere compilation,[12] one of the first things one notices is that the tune is almost entirely sung by Cortés. His is the voice lamenting the woman's desertion, as well as the one blaming the *bruja* in the guías (according to El Tosco, the song was inspired by a real event). During live performance, the text might be changed, becoming more explicit, spicy and/or challenging, for example by transforming an expression such as *sin sentimientos* (with no feelings) into *sin sentimiento* (with no brain). The parts that best lend themselves to variations and improvisations were obviously the guías. As a Cuban scholar once told me, during a live concert in Cuba Cortés substituted *arrebatá* and *desquiciá* ('sexually frenzied' and 'out of your head') with words such as *profesora* and *intelectual* ('professor' and 'intellectual'). 'That was really too much!', commented the scholar. This illustrates how Cortés was able, without using particularly strong words, to mock the system by showing scarce respect for the sacred values of the revolution (in this case education and culture).

As El Tosco commented in an interview a few years ago, the institutional attack on timba in the late 1990s started as a reaction to his most controversial song. '"La bruja" has been the beginning of all that . . .

---

12 *The Best of NG La Banda*, Hemisphere 1999. The version of the song on this album, however, is not the most popular, which instead is found on the CD *La bruja*, Caribe, 1995.

[sic] that nobody had the courage to open the eyes to the girl; that she should not give the c... [sic] for 20 dollars. Thus I wrote a song. To this day, Silvio [Rodríguez] has written "Las flores de la Quinta Avenida", which, obviously, can be understood only by people at university, and not by those in the barrio' (Sarusky 1999; the missing words are censored in the original).

To be sure, Cortés is not the only Cuban musician who has dealt with the theme of prostitution. The issue is implicit in many dance songs of the period, such as 'Te conosco mascaríta' by El Médico, 'El temba' by La Charanga, and 'Amor matemático' by Manolíto y su Trabuco, and has also emerged in the work of cultivated *trovadores*. Silvio Rodríguez, a singer-songwriter who is today a member of the Cuban Parliament and a wealthy music entrepreneur, devoted to the topic his elliptical 'Flores nocturnas' (the one to which Cortés refers).[13] The direct and controversial Pedro Luís Ferrer wrote the more explicit 'Marucha la jinetera', which has never been released in Cuba. Ferrer's song tells the story of a woman who has been abused by her father, raped and sent to prison, and who 'in her cross has more tears than smiles'.[14]

The news of the boom of prostitution on the island found immediate resonance among the Miami Cuban community too, where media hostile to the Cuban government found yet another argument for their anti-Castro campaign. Towards the end of 1995, Radio Martí started blasting across the Florida Straits 'La jinetera', a song written by Cuban-American singer Willie Chirino.[15] The song opens with a picture familiar to all *habaneros*, that of a young woman in a miniskirt walking along the Malecón, waiting for a foreign man. Before launching, in its second part, into an anti-Castro tirade (Chirino is a vocal anti-Castroist), the song offers a description of *jineterismo* which plausibly reflects Cuban data (for example Elizalde, interview with the author, 1997; Gutiérrez 1997). What is interesting, however, is the musical and textual angle adopted by Chirino, which markedly contrasts with the way Cortés and other *timberos* addressed the same issue.

Musically, 'La jinetera' is a soft salsa ballad accompanied by guitar and synthesizer, with a minimal presence of horns, percussion and choruses. Completely focused on Chirino's voice, the song has a nostalgic character and underlines the singer's publicized condition as an exile, reflecting that of most of its Miami audience. The song talks of the woman in the third person, without the explicit presence of a narrating 'I', and describes the young woman as a single mother living with her

---

[13] From the CD *Rodríguez*, Fonomusic, 1994.
[14] From the CD *100% Cubano*, Ceyba Music, 2000.
[15] From the CD *Asere*, Sony, 1995.

baby daughter in a small peripheral flat, crying over the memory of her lover who has escaped to the USA.

Looking at the various elements of the song – the musical treatment, the adoption of an 'objective' perspective, the pitiful portrait of the woman, the use of gentle language with vaguely religious metaphors (the characters are called Eve and Adam) – it emerges how the piece by the anti-Castroist *salsero* is much closer to the stylistic conventions of Cuban *trovadores*, and to their representation of the prostitute as a victim, than to the carnivalesque spirit of *timberos*. Nothing is more distant from the pathetic portrait of the *jinetera* drawn by Chirino and Ferrer than the direct, almost brutal narrative of 'La bruja', where the narrator sends the woman to hell. This is possible because in Cortés's song the person in question is not an abstract, remote character, but a type of individual that the narrator seems to know well.

Ironically, the song and the promotional video for 'La jinetera', banned in Cuba, also provoked considerable controversy in Miami. The video of the song, where the image of Chirino was superimposed on live material filmed covertly in Havana, showed the singer driving a vintage car and flirting with a prostitute. This clip of Chirino, who plays a prominent role in the intricate politics of the Cuban exiled community, was criticized for being ambiguous and promoting sex tourism to Cuba. After such sharp criticisms, Chirino decided to shelve the video and modify it. While the song was well received by popular audiences in Cuba (despite its ban, it can sometimes be heard on the street and in bars), it drew a poor reception in Florida, where it became the object of protests by middle-aged Cuban-American women on local radio stations (Ackerman 1996).

'Dale cintura, mulata!': Queens of Havana nights

To outsiders, in any case, more than through the oblique references contained in timba songs, the relationship between *jineterismo* and music became tangible on the crowded dance floors of Cuban clubs. In the mid-1990s, places in Havana such as the Havana Club, the Palacio de la Salsa and La Cecilia, or the discotheque of the Hotel Internacional in Varadero, became important meeting places for foreigners and young Cubans. Dance clubs represented for tourists the most obvious pick-up sites, and the platforms for the staging of a show of tropical sensuality to the sound of timba. For their part, young Afro-Cubans flocked to the dance clubs firmly intending to employ their subcultural capital – their physical appearance, visual style, knowledge of music and dance – in order to *hacerse el extranjero*, that is, to find a suitable foreign partner.

Here is the vivid description of one Havana disco, circa 1995, made by an Italian journalist,

> Inside, the sight is astonishing. Dozens and dozens of young women – during the lows of tourism the rate can be two *jineteras* to every tourist – dance, shake, try to look sexy, cast provocative and not exactly mysterious glances, approach without much restraint the greenest tourist .... They touch, graze, persuade. To use a sophisticated metaphor, it's a real brothel, a whorehouse, where Italians of every age are the most active and well-connected, but where you can find the usual 50-year-old German man with a girl of 18, or the Japanese man who has gone mad after a short, too-young-looking black girl.
>
> (Evangelisti: 1999: 65)

As a music executive explained to me, many Cuban dance clubs of the time were 'socially contaminated areas' (see Plate 20). According to him,

> What is called 'Cuban salsa' has been linked very much to the Cuban tourism industry. And to that industry are also related all sorts of new lifestyles. Like a problem we didn't have ten years ago, which is prostitution. You find a lot of prostitutes linked to these shows of dance music. That is very important for them because ... dance music enables them to 'show off their merchandise', so that people [among the audience] who are on their own can say, 'that's the right woman to be with'. They sell their product using music.
>
> (Faya, interview with the author, 1997)

It was around this period that, in clubs such as the Palacio de la Salsa (defined by the Italian sex travel guide as a 'disco for classy picker-ups'), NG staged their *subasta de la cintura* (literally, 'the waist's auction', that is, the waist-shaking contest) (see Plate 5). During the montuno, the band invited young women to come on stage and show off their ability as dancers, inciting the audience to throw money to the woman performing the most convincing pelvic rotation. In the context of the scarcity of those years, when for most *habaneros* a few dollars represented an enormous amount of money, the novelty multiplied the presence of young women and attracted hordes of foreign men. In an interview conducted a few years later, a Cuban journalist interrogated Cortés on the matter, asking him to justify his conduct.

> (F. López): Let's talk of the topic that prompted this interview. At a round table a few months ago ... I said that some bandleaders, starting with El Tosco, were promoting an image of nouveaux riches, of successful men. [That success] In your case, is sustained not only by the privilege of reaching with your work a higher-than-average standard of living, but also by other gestures of waste or adoration of the dollar, such as putting a price, in that currency, on the dance of our women. What do you think as a protagonist? What can you say in your defence, in the face of an image that is on the street, [and has been] growing like an avalanche, long before the press coined it?

(Cortés): ... certainly there was a lamentable night at the Palacio [de la Salsa] .... I had drunk a bit too much and started to do the *subasta de la cintura*, which is something I have been doing since the beginning of mixed companies [joint ventures between state-owned and foreign companies, mainly in the field of tourism]. I used to auction the caps of Havanautos, the T-shirts of Havana Club [two state-owned companies] .... That was the time of competitions. Competitions on the radio and all over the place. I invented the competition of the waist-shaking of the Cuban woman. When it comes to walking, her sex appeal is not a mystery, the Cuban woman dances while she walks .... What I never did was to allow women to strip on stage, something that was quite fashionable at the time.

(López): To cut it short, did people give money or not in those *concursos*?

(Cortés): Yes, I gave money. That night a young woman started to shake her waist, but that reached a stage when it became a violent show. People were standing at their tables. I let myself go. Now, thinking about that, I realize that all that can be of damage to culture.... That woman from Camagüey gave a hell of a shake. When she stopped, I said: 'Have this cap, ... and $10 to come back to the Palacio de la Salsa.' That money was for the entrance fee. Foreigners started shouting that's crap, give more. And they started to throw money on stage. Other times I had avoided that. When I picked up the money, the total was $490. All that for shaking her waist.

(Lopez 1997)

In reality, the practice of inviting women onstage to show off their sex appeal was not an invention of Cortés, but a consolidated custom in Cuban MB. Van Van, for example, had been doing it for years before the *período especial* (see Plate 6). The transplantation of that practice into tourist-only clubs during the 1990s, however, gave it a totally different connotation, showing the symbolic and economic connection between dance music and sex tourism.

As remarked by Cortés, during the boom of timba other bands devised similar inventions to attract their audiences. La Charanga Habanera, for example, launched a song called 'Quítate el disfraz' ('Take your disguise off'), to which young women danced and took their shirts off (Orozco 1995).[16] In the context of Cuban tourist dance clubs in the mid-1990s, the celebration of the sensuality of the *mulata*, thus, took on a very specific meaning, that of an invitation to foreign males to make their choice among the female crowd. It is in such a context that one can understand the sense of songs such as NG's 'La Cachimba', where, while the coro sings 'chew the lollipop', the choreography prescribes women to do the *cintura* with their thumb in their mouth.[17]

---

[16] The song is on the CD *Hey, You, Loca!*, Magic Music, 1994.
[17] From the CD *La Cachimba*, Caribe, 1995.

In the same period, El Médico crooned his tema 'Si te vas conmigo' ('If you come with me'):[18]

> I'd love to have you on my side
> so that I could feel you
> checking your naked body
> your endless curves[19]

then, moving into a lengthy montuno, the song presents its first coro:

> Please decide whether
> you will come with me
>
> (solo) I only want you to decide
> who is the man who is going to love you[20]

Eventually, when the woman does not seem to be persuaded,

> (solo) if the girl does not want to dance
> (coro) Therefore, take her with you
> if the girl does not want to enjoy herself
> Therefore, take her with you
> 'cause she does not want to understand what I'm saying
> Therefore, take her with you
> I ask you, please, take her with you, my friend
> Therefore, take her with you
> Take her with you, take her with you
> Therefore, take her with you[21]

The song is a perfect example of the way timba songs of the time constructed their context-sensitive, ambiguous messages. Performed in tourist clubs, Manolín's tune had its apparent meaning of a complaint by a disillusioned lover turned into an ode to the sensuality of Cuban women, and eventually into an incitation to men to pick up the woman they fancied.

In the mid-1990s, playing in tourist clubs had become so central to the activity of dance bands that the topic of *jineterismo* started to filter through to the songs of older bands as well. Oscillating between gallantry and sexism, Van Van recorded songs such as 'La fruta' ('The fruit'), which told the story of a juicy papaya seen at the market (an obvious reference to women). Its coro goes: 'Come on take it, it's a national product, come on take it .... Look, Havana is full with them

---

[18] From the CD *Una aventura loca*, 1994.

[19] 'Quisiera tenerte a mi lado / para así poderte sentir / contactando tu cuerpo desnudo / las curvas que no tienen fin.'

[20] 'Decides, por favor / si te vas conmigo / Yo solo quiero que decidas tu, mujer / quien es el hombre que te va querer.'

[21] 'Y si la niña no quiere bailar / (coro) entonces llevatela! / si la niña no quiere gozar / entonces llevatela! / Porqué no quiere entender lo que digo / entonces llevatela! / Te pido por favor, llevatela, mi amigo / entonces llevatela! / Llevatela, llevatela / entonces llevatela!'

.... They're special.... But, look mate, he who touches it has to take it! (coro) If you bite it you must take it all!'[22] The song did not even mention women, but left Cubans with few doubts about its real meaning.

A vulgar music? The image of woman in Cuban popular songs

The polemics and moral reproach fuelled by 'La bruja' played an important role in the change of attitude of the Cuban authorities towards MB. In the second half of the 1990s, it became difficult for the Cuban establishment to turn a blind eye to the social consequences of tourism, and the areas of tolerance that had favoured the development of dance culture progressively disappeared. In March 1995, the Sixth Congress of the FMC addressed the issue of prostitution and sex tourism, and decided to press the government to ban sex workers from hotels and introduce changes into penal legislation. In March 1996, the issue was discussed by the Central Committee of the Cuban Communist Party (Schwartz 1997).

Dance music, which was such an integral part of tourists' nights in Havana, became a journalistic case, and had its legitimacy questioned by the press. One article, for example, had a headline reading, 'Are they killing Cuban music?' and showed a caricature of El Médico and David Calzado in the act of axing down the tree of Cuban music (Pérez 1997). The hostility of journalists focused mostly on the lyrics of MB, attacking it for its alleged vulgarity (*chabacanería*) (for example Elizalde 1996b; Tabares 1996). As a Cuban researcher still wrote in 1999, '[t]he quality of the lyrics of contemporary *música bailable* ... represents one of today's most controversial topics' (Casanellas Cué 1999a).

The moral preoccupations and the controversies concerning the lyrics of popular songs are neither new nor exclusive to timba, but as old as Cuban popular music. In the early 1920s, for example, son was rejected by the white middle class on the grounds of its alleged vulgarity and the sexual innuendos contained in its lyrics. Many pieces by classic authors and singers such as Ignacio Piñeiro, Ñico Saquito, Arsenio Rodríguez and Benny Moré portrayed women as idealized-and-despised objects of male desire, making copious use of picaresque language, double meanings and salacious expressions. After the revolution, similar accusations against the texts of popular music continued to be levelled particularly against dance music, well before the explosion of timba. In the 1980s, for example, a Cuban journalist extolling the virtues of a dance band

---

22 'Dale llévatela / es un producto nacional / dale llévatela / ... oyen, La Habana está llena / ... son especiales / / ... Cuidado compay, el quien que la toca se la tiene que llevar / (coro) Si la picas te las llevas entera!' From the CD *¡Ay dios amparame!*, Caribe, 1995.

commented that their songs lacked 'the vulgarities ... found in many *conjuntos* and Cuban bands because of a mistaken concept of *cubanía*' (Padrón 1987). In the late 1980s, one musicologist criticized the systematic confusion made by the writers of MB lyrics 'between what is playful and what is vulgar' (Martínez 1989). During the same period, according to Medin, Cuban experts considered Cuban songs 'poorly written, in bad taste, and unduly prone to undesirable tones of machismo' (Medin 1990: 126).

One possible argument in response to similar accusations is that the reasons for the success of popular music lie precisely in its contrast, in terms of themes, language and attitudes, with the world of culture with a capital 'C'. In Cuba, such a contrast is articulated by dance music, in particular through its incorporation of slang and popular expressions into the songs' coros. As discussed in Chapter 5, the adoption of street language by timba reflects a common trait of the music of the black diaspora and underlines how popular slang can be used to build a counter-hegemonic discourse, marking a line of separation between the discourse of the street and that of the political and cultural establishment.

Cuban bandleaders and progressive music writers have defended the lyrics of MB claiming that they represent a form of social realism, seen as part of a tradition of social commentary and topical song common to other types of Caribbean music, from calypso to reggae, from zouk to salsa (Orozco 1995; Acosta 1997). Music critic Rafael Lam (1996), for example, has described the songs of NG as a form of social chronicle, and Leonardo Acosta (1998) has defined the accusations against timba lyrics as part of a 'litany of insults against Afro-Cuban things reiterated with inquisitorial zeal since the "time of the Spanish"'. As usual, Cortés has provided a lapidary comment: 'I do not impose my texts: it is the street which dictates them' (Robinson Calvet 1996).

The polemic on the language of timba songs had mainly to do with their representation of Cuban women. As Susan McClary (1991) has suggested, music can be gendered on many different levels, from its stories and the public image of its performers to its musical structures. In the case of Cuban MB, for example, one might think of dancing or of the sexual reading of the meaning of the word 'timba' (see Chapter 4). The most immediately evident way to construct gender in popular music, however, is probably through songs' lyrics. In her text-based feminist reading of salsa, Frances Aparicio has shown how that music has inherited from Cuban son and bolero a victimizing representation of men and a corresponding image of women as objects of desire and contempt. Articulated through the dualism of the virgin/whore, this image is widespread in Afro-Caribbean and African-American music, and surfaces as well in the texts of contemporary Cuban MB.

The discourse on women of timba songs – which so many times start out as love songs and end up as invectives against women, portraying them as venal and unfaithful – shows strong parallels with contemporary rap and Latin American popular music where a 'central form of violence against women is the very basic speech act of name-calling, of insults and vituperative language, which we may deem as discursive terrorism or violence through words ... [that represents women as] traitors, dishonest, pretentious ... and as *bandoleras* [bandit women]' (Aparicio 1998: 161).

The text of 'La bruja' falls into a similar trend of verbal aggression to women, but with some important differences. In the first place, the song's offensive terms – words such as *loca* (crazy) and *arrebatá* (sexually frenzied) – are contained not in the text proper, but in the guías of the coro. This follows a common strategy of timba, which seeks to evade the attention of censors by hiding the most controversial comments in the montuno. Together with terms such as *bruja*, these expressions may be unkind to women, but do not appear particularly vulgar – at least, not considering the general level of misogyny in Cuban and Latin American popular music.

The song, in a sense, does not strike so much for its vulgarity, as for its ambiguity. Initially, the lyrics draw an almost pathetic portrait of the Cuban man. What happened? Was it because the woman has exchanged his love for 'cheap amusements'? A literal interpretation on the line of conventional engaged song would read 'La bruja' as a not particularly original piece of criticism of materialist values. The song, moreover, does not talk of prostitutes or *jineteras*. Why did it sound so offensive, then?

The fact is that the 'real' meaning of songs such as 'La bruja' or the pieces by El Médico – that is, the meaning perceived by timba audiences – emerges not from the verbal text alone, considered as an abstract entity, but from its relation to its actual audiences. These songs were not generic attacks on Cuban women for their easiness or venality (although they might also be read in that way), but on local women who turned down local men for foreigners. As in 'El temba', that situation was never stated, but rather suggested through allusions disseminated in the text. These feeble traces (the *turitaxi*, the 'cheap amusements') took on a much clearer meaning when the band performed in the presence of an audience almost entirely composed of tourists and *jineteras*. The song, thus, referred to them in an intentionally oblique way, adopting an attitude oscillating between misogyny, carnival and social criticism. Such ambiguity explains the reason for the enormous popularity of the song at the time, and clarifies why a negative term such as 'bruja' has acquired in popular language affectionate connotations (Casanellas Cué 1999a).

The ambiguity of the song, which was devised to allow it to be presented to its possible detractors as a criticism of materialism, has been acknowledged, in a way, by the very same Cortés. In my interview, El Tosco accepted the politically controversial nature of 'La bruja', but claimed that the problems originated from a misunderstanding, because his text had been originally intended as a defence of the dignity of Cuban women.

> Q: Your song 'La Bruja' has been criticized. What is it about?
> It talks about prostitution.
> Q: Have you had problems with that song?
> I had problems with the FMC, but not, now that is ... I don't give a shit about that. In short, the song has been very successful. Despite censorship and bans, people bought it, learned it, and I still play it and people still like it .... The song was not suitable, with all that was happening at the time with the problem of prostitution, a song dealing with that topic was obviously not well received by officials, or by somebody in the government. This is what happened, and they attacked my song. But the song tells the opposite, it defends the Cuban woman, in order for her not to be a prostitute. And it is a true story, not a fiction, and this is why the song worked and still works.
>
> (interview with the author, 2000)

Cortés's claim, in any case, does not contradict the ambiguity of his discursive strategy, and cannot hide the fact that 'La bruja' is a dance song which has as its main audience the very object of its verbal abuse, the young *mulatas* packing Havana dance floors. Portrayed as objects of male lust, women were addressed by lyrics that could as well be interpreted as celebrative. For its audiences, 'La bruja' was thus able to articulate different and conflicting points of view. While it voiced the frustrated male's view, it sang an ode to the reified body of the *mulata*, eventually emerging on the dance floor as a de facto celebration of the *jinetera*.

> Timba underlined the role of the jinetera marginal woman ... [who] became the gauge to measure the success of popular music. The tourist who arrives here holds the Cuban woman as a reference point, and says: 'Where are we going to waste our dollars?' To La Cecilia, because NG is there, they put her on stage, sing to her, and make her dance .... They [*jineteras*] were those who led European men to those places: what could musicians do? They were those who provided them .... That was one of the reasons why timba sang so much to the jineteras. Moreover, jineteras went with Spanish promoters and record producers, Italians, French, and knew El Tosco, David Calzado, Juan Formell.
>
> (Orejuela, interview with the author, 1999)

Another important aspect of 'La bruja' lies in the fact that its attack on women does not simply reflect a *machista* view, but articulates a shift of power between genders. Comments one young *jinetera*:

> Before, it was the man who went out to look for money, no matter how big the risk of being arrested: he did some business, stole, worked out

something, but not anymore. That was around 1990, around 1980. Now
the woman is the one who leads.

(Holgado Fernández 2000: 248)

In its abusive stance towards women, therefore, timba also expressed a
reaction to their rising power and to the economically subordinate role of
men in the Cuban society of the 1990s. It was an attitude, again, close to
contemporary salsa and African-American rap, where the character of

goldiggers who use their sexuality to take black men's meager earnings are
common prototypes of the black woman, giving the dismantling of the
black male as the main family provider.... [In salsa] the bandolera
construct functions as a symbol or icon that allows men to reconcile these
shifts in economics and the deflation and undermining of the traditional
Hispanic values of masculinity.

(Aparicio 1998: 164)

It is evident that the attacks on timba songs by the media and the FMC
were not simply motivated by the supposedly vulgar content of their
lyrics, but by the fact that such lyrics, in the musical and social practice
where they were being used, alluded to sex tourism and called into
question the role of the establishment. In a double sense, they appeared
to deny the achievements of the revolution and undermine its moral
authority by suggesting that the phenomenon was somehow tolerated
and/or exploited by the authorities. Timba dealt with the topic by
avoiding moralistic stances and adopting a carnivalesque attitude that
could contextually be read as a celebration of *jineterismo*. Timba songs
such as 'La bruja', therefore, were condemned not so much because they
offended Cuban women, but because they celebrated them as *jineteras*,
implicitly pointing at the failures of the revolution. As the president of
the FMC once said, 'When in the early years of the revolution the people
learned that scourges such as gambling and prostitution had been
eliminated in Cuba ... the revolution's prestige increased enormously'
(Malapanis 1996).

Women and gender roles under the revolution

A discussion of popular songs' representation of women calls into
question the position of women in Cuban society. Compared to the rest
of Latin America, women in post-1959 Cuba have found remarkable
space and recognition, with more education, health care and
opportunities in terms of work, and less dependence on men (Shnookal
1991; Molyneux 1996; Craske 1999). Revolutionary policies seem to
have been less successful in modifying gender roles and challenging
machismo in fundamental ways. In that sense, despite their material

progress, women in Cuba still appear notably subjected to male power. As the leader of the FMC Vilma Espín put it just before the beginning of the *período especial,*

> in many working families, women still bear the full responsibility for the education and formation of their children, as well as the organization of the household and household chores. This gives rise to the extremely unfair 'double work shift' that exhausts women. Within the family itself, changes in roles and relations seem to take place at a slow pace.
> (quoted in Shnookal 1991: 66–8)[23]

How does the construction of gender differences and roles differ in socialist Cuba from other Latin American countries? Connell has suggested that institutions, taken in their wider sense, manifest particular 'gender regimes', that is, the 'state of play in gender relations' (1994: 30). In the Cuban case, the adoption of this type of analysis reveals that institutions such as the state, education and the family are largely male-dominated.[24] While women, emancipated in theory, are burdened by traditional female duties, men appear to play a major role in public life. Such a male dominant role, in a sense, has been institutionalized by revolutionary language, where the model for Che Guevara's 'new man' is represented, in Fidel Castro's words, by a 'man's man' (Lumsden 1996: 119). The various attempts made by women in the past to challenge male power have met with limited success, colliding with the machismo that informs both Cuban society and revolutionary ideology (Smith and Padula 1996).[25] Even the FMC, which has repeatedly tried to raise the issue of gender roles, is itself a quasi-feminist organization sponsored by a 'patriarchal state' (Connell 1994).[26] Subordinated to the general directives of the political leadership – and an emanation of the Castro family (Vilma Espín was once the wife of Fidel's brother Raúl) – the Federation ritually hails the Comandante as 'the father of all Cubans, and guide to all Cuban women' (Molyneux 1996: 18).[27]

---

[23] Vilma Espín has also complained about the fact that many working women are single mothers as well.

[24] The 'gender regime' of Cuban institutions is also revealed by state legislation on sex and gender. Smith and Padula (1996), for example, underline how sex education programmes for young people are centred on models such as the nuclear family, heterosexuality and reproduction, and generally avoid the discussion of controversial issues such as rape, sexual abuse and domestic violence. While not actively persecuted as in the past, homosexuality still represents in Cuba a controversial, seemingly embarrassing issue (Lumsden 1996).

[25] Women have rarely held top political posts in Cuba, and, until 1985, did not feature in the Politburo.

[26] The FMC rejects the use of the word 'feminism'.

[27] In its internal debates, the FMC reveals a great deal of discussion and variety of opinions, but in its overall public function it has essentially remained a top-down

Cuban women, therefore, are often caught in a situation that requires contradictory loyalties, such as engaging with men in the struggle for the construction of the revolution, conforming to male aesthetic canons, behaving as honourable mothers and wives, working, and running the economy of the household. During the *período especial* the situation has worsened, because women have been expelled en masse from the job market and have found themselves burdened with the responsibility of finding food and other essentials on the black market (Molyneux 1996; Holgado Fernández 2000). Such a conflation of patriarchal institutional attitudes and worsening of material conditions has led one feminist to describe Cuban society as 'highly gendered' (Craske 1999), and a Cuban female historian to dub it 'phallocentric' (E. Hernández, quoted in Smith and Padula 1996: 181).

Popular culture can often give us a picture of gender stereotypes and relations that is far more realistic than declarations of intent. For example, the most popular TV programmes on the island, by far, are Latin-American soap operas ridden with racial and sexual clichés.[28] As one Cuban woman protests,

> those soaps that come over here and people devour are incredibly, incredibly *machistas* .... There, the man is always the hero, and the woman always waits for him .... Therefore those soaps have achieved a tremendous popularity in Cuba. The country gets paralysed.... You realise that audiences need them, they watch them and ask for them. I think that people over here love when in a soap, for example, a man beats up a woman, they enjoy it.
>
> (Holgado Fernández 2000: 201)

Popular songs offer countless similar representations of gender relationships. 'El trágico' by NG,[29] for example, draws a sketch of the troubles of the Afro-Cuban man oppressed by his angry, perpetually complaining woman. A variation on the theme of the victim-like complaint of men about women, the song – which opens with a rumba section that firmly situates the story in the barrio – resonates with the frustration of the male who has lost his control over women.

Besides expressing the general *machista* attitude of Cuban society, popular songs articulate the powerful sexual myth of the *mulata*, a term

---

organization that discourages grass-roots feminism, and is employed to mobilize women in defence of the revolution, with a de facto acceptance of a subordinate role of women which one might be tempted to describe as a politically-engaged version of *marianismo*, that is, the Latin American female corollary to *machismo*, 'where the ideal of woman-hood is self-abnegating motherhood' (Craske 1999: 12).

[28] The immense popularity of the *novelas* (soaps) in Cuba has even been immortalized in a famous song by Adalberto Alvarez, 'A la hora de la telenovela'.

[29] On the CD *Cabaret Estelar*, 1992.

that in Cuban colloquial language defines Afro-Cuban women with a wide range of complexion. At least since the appearance of Cirilo Villaverde's novel *Cecilia Valdés* in the nineteenth century, the representation of this female character in Cuba has been tied to illicit sex and male self-destruction. Stereotyped in the icon of the sensual *mulata*, the celebration of the beauty and sexiness of Cuban women has been constant in all Cuban popular music of the twentieth century, from early son to Los Van Van.

In the 1990s, however, the image of the sexy *mulata* also played an important part in the promotion of tourism to Cuba. In March 1991, the US magazine *Playboy* published a long reportage from Cuba entitled 'Cuba libre' ('Free Cuba'), with images of naked young local women in tourist resorts (the '3s' equation: sun, sea and sex) (Cohen 1991). The article was officially authorized and organized through the Cuban ambassador in France, INIT and the state firm Cubanacán (Domínguez 1997). During the 1990s, Cuban state companies often used this face of Cuba to promote tourism to the island, printing posters that showed feminine hips and read 'Cuba. Come and be tempted', or 'Cuba is waiting for you' (Oppenheimer 1992; Fogel and Rosenthal 1994). Evident in many publications issued by the Ministry of Tourism until the mid-1990s, the exploitation of the image of the *mulata* is celebrated as well in the Las Vegas-style music-and-dance tourist shows of Cabaret Tropicana, which are focused on exhibitions of long-legged, scantily dressed black women that have not changed much since the time of Batista.[30] As a Spanish female anthropologist has observed, 'black or mulatto women are the instruments used by governmental propaganda to promote tourism on the island. Their buttocks and explosive curves are the ideal advert to attract masculine hordes looking for the sexual myth of the *mulata*' (Holgado Fernández 2000: 202).[31]

Jineterismo between escape and survival

> The crisis was destroying everything. We spent some time suffering from hunger and being fucked up, until I got fed up with so much poverty and

---

[30] I personally find it difficult to share with Peter Manuel his view of Tropicana shows as a 'joyously kitsch' testimony of musical pluralism in Cuba (Manuel 1990b). While I am not sure that these shows hint at a postmodernist cultivation of kitsch on Cuban soil, I see them as yet another proof of the endurance of sexism in Cuban society at large, and in particular in the tourism and entertainment industry.

[31] According to a document issued by the FMC, 'part of the present tourist and commercial adverts employ women as simple object of advertisement with aims and interests similar to those of lowest-quality advertising in capitalist countries.... the stereotype of the *rumbera* and sensual mulata is enduring, and sometimes does not bear any relation with the product object of the advert' (*Memorias del VI Congreso de la FMC*, 1995).

took a decision. One night I faced Luisa and told her: 'Look, enough of
going around crossed arms and starving. On the Malecón to *jinetear*!' And
that was a right decision. That *mulata* can earn as much as 300 dollars a
week. Enough. To hell with poverty.

P.J. Gutiérrez (1998: 123)

The re-emergence of prostitution in Cuba has been one of the most
visible and controversial consequences of the 1990s crisis and of the
economic re-conversion to tourism.[32] But if the phenomenon has been
and is evident to every Cuban and foreign visitor to the island, its
interpretation remains complex and contentious, since the causes,
circumstances, modalities and personal motivations of this activity vary
enormously. For example, while so far I have used the terms
'prostitution' and *jineterismo* interchangeably, it is important to make
some analytic distinctions. In the West, prostitution describes a specific,
professional and formalized activity. By contrast, in Cuba the term
jineterismo indicates a type of informal prostitution generally practised
individually by young people of both sexes, which can be described as a
type of 'non-contractual sexual relationship', that 'tends to proceed as if
it were a flirtation rather than a business negotiation. Prostitutes flatter
tourists and affect a genuine interest in them ... [T]he two parties often
embark upon a fairly open-ended exchange ... which is based on a very
general, implicit understanding that some form of payment will be made'
(O'Connell Davidson 1998: 77–8).

The vast do-it-yourself dimension of *jineterismo* signals some marked
differences with prostitution as practised not only in the West, but also in
many developing countries. First, women or men often do not work for a
criminal organization (although there are individual pimps and networks
of taxi drivers, landlords, hotel janitors, barmen and club managers who
co-operate with prostitutes, and sometimes financially exploit them).
Second, while in the West prostitution generally means the provision of
specific sexual services in exchange for a certain sum of money, the
nature of the economic arrangement between the *jinetera/o* and the client
is often vague. Most often, *jineterismo* takes on the appearance of a

---

[32] Non-organized, individual prostitution, apparently, had never totally disappeared
from Cuba. According to Salas, in 1970 Lewis found that in one Havana neighbourhood
'prostitution, drug trafficking, and other illegal activities were rampant even though they
almost had been eliminated a few years earlier' (1979b: 102). Practised with foreigners in
exchange for foreign currency, it grew discreetly around beach resorts in the 1980s, when
Cuba made its first openings to foreign tourism (Habel 1991; Elizalde 1996a). A form of
home-targeted, 'masked' prostitution was seen in the 1970s phenomenon known as
titimanía, where young, pretty women became the mistresses, and sometimes the new
wives, of older, well-off men, usually members of the party or the army *nomenklatura* (Díaz
Canals and González Olmedo 1997). The phenomenon prompted a famous song by Van
Van.

relationship between the foreigner and the local which may last for the whole of the foreigner's stay in the country, with locals acting as escorts and playing the role of legitimate partners. Accordingly, they would expect to be driven around, taken to restaurants and clubs, and receive presents from their partners. Sometimes, the casual encounter may evolve into a serious, institutionalized relationship: Cubans introduce their families to their foreign fiancés, and these will send presents and money, return periodically to Cuba, and perhaps marry the Cuban and take them to their country. The escape route represented by *jineterismo*, therefore, is more than purely financial or symbolic, because it can offer young Cubans a way to marriage and life abroad. Having made these distinctions clear, I maintain that *jineterismo* still falls under a definition of prostitution as

> an institution which allows certain powers of command over one person's body to be exercised by another [and] which is founded upon the existence of economic and political conditions that compel people to act in ways in which they would not otherwise choose to act.... They become prostitutes because the economic, political and social circumstances in which they live make it either the best or the only means of subsisting, or they are people who are forced into prostitution by a third party.
>
> (ibid.: 7, 4–5)

Various declarations by Cuban political leaders at the beginning of the 1990s indicated a good deal of official ambiguity and leniency towards the phenomenon. Once it emerged in the local press, around the middle of the decade, the issue of *jineterismo* was initially minimized and justified on the grounds of its exceptionality and difference from prostitution. *Juventud Rebelde* (19 May 1996), for example, published an article by Mauro Casagrandi, an Italian who has lived in Cuba for many years, who argued that, contrary to professional prostitutes in the West,

> [t]he Cuban jinetera belongs to another universe. She behaves in totally different ways and does not present herself as a simple provider of a sexual service, but of a complete human relationship with her counterpart.... [T]he jinetera has a soul (given to her by the Revolution, she likes it or not). She's a person, not a thing. She is free and practices jineterismo because of that freedom.
>
> (reprinted in Elizalde 1996a: 77–85)

In other words, Casagrandi claimed, the *jinetera* chose her job because she liked it and was sexually liberated. The second interpretation of the phenomenon, which prevailed in the late 1990s, tended instead to equal jineterismo and prostitution, identifying a connection with materialism, social deviance and crime (for example Elizalde 1996a). Such an interpretation did not relate the phenomenon to material scarcity, but rather to the wrong choices and materialistic values of the young generation. According to the leader of the FMC, the quick growth of the economy and tourism had caused 'a relaxation of moral customs, a pursuit of Western lifestyles and systems to get easy money, such as prostitution' (V. Espin, quoted in Masci 1998).

Both interpretations contained elements of truth, but denied that prostitution was tied to the situation of extreme scarcity in which ordinary Cubans live, and contrasted with the reports of several foreign and local observers. In 1996, a European researcher found impoverished young women from the inner part of the country prostituting themselves in Varadero for as little as two dollars. Pointing at the race factor, she observed how apparently 'there were more Black than "mixed" or white *jiniteras* and *jiniteros* [sic]' (O'Connell Davidson 1996: 45–6). Wrong choices, also, did not explain why professionals, doctors, engineers, university graduates and teachers practised *jineterismo*, as declared in 1997 by a police officer to the magazine *Bohemia* (Gutiérrez 1997). Apparently, El Tosco's provocations were not totally unfounded.

The moralizing, if belated, condemnation of *jineterismo* by the Cuban media sharply contrasts with the apparent lack of stigmatization from the population, who accept it as a fact of life. Many ordinary Cubans seem to take for granted that lone foreigners in Cuba will look around for a suitable sexual partner. It is not a mystery either that in Cuban society *jineteras* have become positive role models, and an important economic resource for their families and peers. In the words of a policeman, they 'are the ones who solve material problems in their homes; sometimes they help when there is party in the CDR. They do not feel repudiated by their neighbours. On the contrary, in the neighbourhood they are treated like personalities ... [and] often defended by their parents' (ibid.).[33] Several Cuban authors underline how most of these young people do not see themselves as prostitutes.[34] Many of them occasionally engage in sexual relationships with tourists out of curiosity, and with the hope of getting presents or a little money to buy things they need.

One major motivation for forging a relationship with a foreigner is the desire to leave Cuba (Elizalde, interview with the author, 1997). Because ordinary citizens cannot travel out of Cuba unless they get an invitation from people resident abroad, it is those people who usually pay for the expensive bureaucratic procedures to get a passport, an exit visa and a plane ticket. The ambiguity of the phenomenon is reinforced

---

[33] The CDR (Comité de Defensa de la Revolución, 'Committy for the Defence of the Revolution'), are community-based groups acting as the party's civilian political information network.

[34] According to an FMC unpublished report, women 'make a distinction between *jinetear* – "enjoying oneself, visiting places, getting to know another world" and *prostituir*' (Forrest 1999: 201).

by the fact that the verb *jinetear* does not mean to prostitute oneself but to ride a horse, that is to exploit somebody financially. This attitude suggests an active rather than a passive role, 'close to the awareness of the fighter (*luchador*), of a person who is trying to solve his/her economic difficulties' (ibid.). It is an individualistic stance towards life common among timba musicians: as Cortés once told a Cuban journalist, 'a *luchador*, this is what I am' (Robinson Calvert 1996).

Jineterismo is a practice that most obviously involves young people, and, as such, expresses a desire for liberation not only from material scarcity, but also from boredom and the lack of space for individual expression and existential choices: '[m]any Cubans now feel that their "needs", as defined by the state, are not the only needs that are important to them' (Forrest 1999: 194). Since well-being does not mean mere survival or lack of disease, *jineterismo* can therefore be seen as a rebellious act against those needs as defined by the state and the regime of indefinite austerity imposed on its citizens, a reaction against the conditions of frustration, powerlessness and lack of perspectives experienced by the young, and particularly by young women in contemporary Cuba. Female *jineterismo*, furthermore, can also be interpreted as an act of defiance against the social code of submission imposed on women. 'Those women are not forced into prostitution by absolute poverty, but, as one member of the FMC says, "because they don't want to ride the bus, they want shoes of many colors, and they want to use the sanitary napkins they sell at the dollar stores"' (Paternostro 2000). What are the other perspectives? Comments one young *jinetera*:

> What would I do with a Cuban boyfriend on a Saturday night? ... Waiting two hours for a bus and then going home, in a flat with no privacy? Those people might be old and vulgar, but at least when I'm with them I am in a pleasant place with air conditioning, I listen to some good music and enjoy a real drink. That helps me to forget about their bad breath and their enormous belly.
>
> (Fusco 1997: 62)

The positive self-perception of *jineteras/os* parallels phenomena in the English Caribbean such as that of the Jamaican 'beachboys', a closeness underlined by the use of similar mock bureaucratic language (the Jamaican 'Foreign Service' has become in Cuba the Grupo de apoyo al turismo internacional or GITA, 'support group for international tourism') (see, respectively, Pattullo 1996 and Lumsden 1996). 'For the beachboy', Pattullo remarks, 'each "client" represents more than a means of survival and triumph over the racial/class system of his island. It also represents temporary access to the First World' (1996: 89).

An even more complicated and politically sensitive question concerns the attitude of the Cuban establishment towards the phenomenon, especially in its initial stage. The analysis of factors such as the subordinated role of women in Cuban society, the paternalism of the ruling elite, and the exploitation of the image of the *mulata* by the tourist industry indicates that the authorities did not rule out sex tourism when they launched Cuba as a mass destination for international travel in the early 1990s. Since '[t]ourist development in poor countries has often been directly or indirectly linked to prostitution' (O'Connell Davidson 1998: 75), it is fair to say that *jineterismo* has probably been considered by the Cuban government as an evil necessary to the expansion of the tourism industry. As the economic strategist of the government Carlos Lage declared in 1993, prostitution is 'the social price we pay for development' (quoted in Molyneux 1996). Declarations by Fidel Castro in the same period confirmed the initial institutional leniency on the issue. In an interview on Cuban television in 1992, for example, he stated that local prostitutes were 'the healthiest in the world' (Holgado Fernández 2000: 250).[35]

As a Cuban journalist who has written extensively on the phenomenon once told me, between hotels and prostitution there was, at least initially, a functional relationship: 'at first, here they thought that this was necessary to get more hard currency' (Elizalde, interview with the author, 1997). That explains why the managers of tourist resorts turned a blind eye to *jineterismo*. It is difficult to believe that, in a tightly controlled society such as Cuba, the authorities were not aware of the scale of the *dolce vita* in the tourist areas of Havana and Varadero in the early and mid-1990s. As one foreign researcher has commented, many people on the island consider prostitution as 'the very basis of the tourist industry in Cuba' (Forrest 1999: 192, n. 1).[36] This has been confirmed by many travellers, tour operators and travel agents. In May 1999, a Cuban musician resident abroad, in Cuba on a visit to his family, commented on the recent police raids on music clubs and the clampdown on prostitution: 'it looks as if they want to put an end to tourism in Cuba'.

The beginning of a slow recovery of the Cuban economy in 1995 marked the end of tolerance towards the phenomenon. With the growth

---

[35] In his July 1992 speech to the National Assembly (ANPP), Castro declared: 'There is no cleaner, purer tourism than Cuba's tourism .... There are no women forced to sell themselves to a man, to a foreigner, to a tourist. Those who do so do it on their own, voluntarily, and without any need for it. We can say that they are highly educated *jineteras* and quite healthy, because we are the country with the lowest number of AIDS cases' (Castro 1992). The part referring to prostitution was omitted in the article on the speech published by *Granma* on 13 July 1992.

[36] On sex tourism to Cuba, see Morello and Taliento 1995 and Evangelisti 1999. In 1999, one Italian travel agent explained to me that the reduction in Italian tourism to Cuba was due to the repression of prostitution.

of tourism, the need to lure foreign males to Cuba with images of *mulatas* became less pressing, and the government realized the destabilizing potential of prostitution. The ostentatious lifestyle of *jineteras/os* stood out as a celebration of materialistic values and a model of social indiscipline, accentuated the resentment of that part of the population excluded from the benefits of tourism, and undermined efforts made by the government to persuade its citizens to withstand scarcity and make continuous sacrifices. The damage caused by *jineterismo* could also be more than merely symbolic. The tremendous economic power created by the dual economy enabled *jineteras* to bribe hotel workers, managers and even the police (Elizalde, interview with the author, 1997; Castro 1999). Once banned from hotels, they led tourists to alternative, private forms of transportation, catering and accommodation, siphoning off hard currency from the state-controlled sectors of the economy (O'Connell Davidson 1996; Elizalde, interview with the author, 1997).

The (belated) reaction of the authorities to the problem was initially mostly repressive and moralistic. Rather than harassing tourists, the police stopped women, took them into custody, gave them a fine and sent them back home (many of them came from villages in the interior of the country). When arrested for the third time, *jineteras* were interned in 'rehabilitation centres' or sent to jail.[37] The official moral attitude has been generally that of stigmatizing and blaming women. According to two British female scholars who undertook research in Cuba in 1996 on behalf of an international organization against the sexual exploitation of children, 'the "party line" on prostitutes currently adopted by the *Federacion de Mujeres Cubanas* ... is so similar to that adopted by right-wing Western politicians about their own poor, homeless and sexually exploited that it almost beggars belief' (O'Connell Davidson and Sanchez Taylor 1996).

The connection of prostitution with crime, furthermore, has posed to the Cuban authorities both a police and a PR problem. Cases of tourists narcotized and robbed, and even of assault and murder related to sex tourism, produced bad press for Cuban tourism in the West. Such negative images of Cuba could damage tourism and represent a weapon in the hands of anti-Castro propagandists. In order to fight the phenomenon, between 1996 and 1997 the government introduced modifications to the penal code, heavily taxed private enterprise (but not that in the hands of foreign firms), cracked down on complacent hotel managers and launched periodic 'clean-up' operations on the streets of Havana and Varadero.

---

[37] Vicent (1999) reports the existence of a 'Centre for reception, classification and processing of prostitutes of the City of Havana' (Centro de recepción, clasificación y procesamiento de prostitutas de la Ciudad de La Habana).

Today, the attitude of Cuban female activists has partially changed. They are paying more attention to the phenomenon and have organized a number of working groups on the problem. As a result of pressure from them and from international organizations, the Cuban government has been persuaded to reconsider the type of tourism it promotes abroad. As a European journalist has cynically observed, however, the economic problems caused by the decline of tourism brought by the repression of prostitution have been brilliantly solved 'thanks to the restoration of great parts of Old Havana, by the pulling effect of the music celebrated by Wim Wenders's movie *Buena Vista Social Club*, and by the opening of new hotels in different areas' (Oldrini 2002). With the enormous financial differential between the normal and the dollarized economy still in place, the phenomenon is unlikely to disappear. Today, perhaps, it is less visible in the tourist areas of Havana, because prostitutes keep a lower profile and use beepers and mobile phones. But according to some sources the phenomenon has now spread to other cities, and to the neighbourhoods where Cubans live (Soler 2003).

Conclusions

In their attitude to women, timba songs are consistent with the sexually allusive language and misogynist stance found in much previous Cuban popular music, and articulate a view of the subordinated, complementary role of women that appears widespread in Cuban society. By representing women as sexual objects through the metaphor of the *mulata* as a *fruta sabrosa* – a 'juicy fruit', at the same time rich, sexy and hot – timba songs share with other Caribbean styles 'figurations of black women and mulattas as food to be consumed and continue to articulate ambivalent feelings of both desire and disavowal of the mulatta through the synecdoche of her rhythmic butt' (Aparicio 1998: xvii).

To reduce the lyrics of timba songs to a pure and simple expression of machismo, however, can be misleading. While expressing the male desire for domination, in fact, these songs reveal much about the actual frustrations of the Cuban man. As in the case of salsa, the multiple readings offered to their audiences by such songs suggest how

> music as a cultural text always ... moves beyond its written signs and, like the act of reading, ... can never be listened to twice in the same manner. To judge salsa music only from the point of view of gender politics, that is, to reject it as *musica machista* (sexist music) is to ignore the complex semiotic directions that any musical text may travel and thus embody.
>
> (ibid.: 190)

Timba songs on women, and against women, therefore, contain both elements of misogyny and celebration of the body of the *mulata* that could be subverted by their female audiences. Justified as an attack on the sexism of timba songs, the accusations levelled at MB by the Cuban press and the FMC in the second half of the 1990s were actually mainly directed to its references to *jinetera* culture, which appeared to offend the morality of the political elite.

'The polemics on texts', a Cuban author writes, 'have attacked, most of all, those songs with a message that is inappropriate from the social or the political point of view' (Casanellas Cué 1999a). By nominating, celebrating and empowering *jineteras*, these songs implicitly questioned the nature of tourism to Cuba and revealed the changing dynamics of gender relations, articulating a discourse on the inversion of economic roles, on male powerlessness and on the rising influence of *jineteras* in the Cuban society of the 1990s. To all young Cubans, *hacerse el extranjero* offered an escape route from scarcity and boredom, an access to a dream of luxury and sophistication that was denied by the *período especial*. To young women, *jineterismo* also offered a temporary route of escape from male domination. By becoming the new breadwinners, the young queens of Havana nights rejected both the state's paternalism and male control, turning the verbal attack of *timberos* on its head.

Chapter 8

'Find yourself a sugar-daddy who pays your upkeep': the Challenge of *música bailable*

These hard times, in which we must face, on our own, the task of achieving what we have dreamed, in heroic resistance, allow us to claim that a new people have emerged, a people who are also represented by a group of modest, austere and upright cadres who judge themselves, increasingly, by the results of their work, and who deserve the respect of the nation.
Document of preparation to the 5th Congress of the Communist Party of Cuba, 1997[1]

How am I going to give you
What you crave for?
'El temba', La Charanga Habanera

In the second half of the 1990s, the signs of the end of the relative tolerance of the authorities announced by the polemics on 'La bruja' rapidly became real. While the police launched repressive raids against prostitution, the press increased its attacks on MB musicians. They were now not only blamed for the lyrics of their songs, but also accused of betraying the spirit of Cuban music, and compared to speculators who had grown rich by trafficking with tourists. Previously encouraged by the state with generous economic incentives, *timberos* were now portrayed as individuals devoted to the cult of success and money, proto-capitalists representing a seminal form of new bourgeoisie.

Young *habaneros*, at any rate, continued to identify with their songs and adopt their popular *dicharachos*. These Cubans looked profoundly different from the youth of previous generations. They seemed deaf to the calls to heroism and austerity, and anxious to embrace individualism and consumer values.

Dance music played a pivotal role in the life of these young *habaneros*, who saw in contacts with foreigners an escape route (real or imaginary) from their existential stalemate. In tourist clubs, timba created a space where self-gratification and plenty were substituted for rhetoric and scarcity, and where young Cubans tried to subvert, albeit

---

[1] *Granma Internacional*, 30 April 1997.

temporarily, the power relationship between foreigners and locals that is at the core of tourism in the third world. In the second half of the decade the leading role of dance musicians as social commentators passed on to La Charanga Habanera. The success of this band launched a shockwave across older Cuban generations and the political leadership, who considered many of the group's songs and attitudes simply unacceptable. In 1997, the Cuban authorities decided they had taken enough and imposed on La Charanga, then at the height of their popularity, a ban from live shows, vetoing as well the broadcasting of their songs on radio and TV.

Youth in Havana: dire life and consumer dreams

> The tastes and preoccupations of most of Cuba's youth are
> diametrically opposed to the more conservative values of the
> generation that initially made the revolution. Willy-nilly, young
> Cubans respond not to exhortations to emulate Che Guevara but
> to the powerful mass global culture that has molded their personal
> tastes.... Not everyone ... can wear 'designer' clothes, but an
> impressive number of young Cubans will do anything to wear
> brand-name foreign clothes.
>
> (I. Lumsden, 1996: 122–3)

At the beginning of the 1990s, 40 per cent of the Cuban population was under 30 years of age (Fernández 1993) and the Cuban authorities started to look with growing concern at the behaviour and signs of disaffection manifested by this part of the population.

The problematic behaviour of the youth was not a new issue in post-revolutionary Cuba. During the 1970s, the country had experienced youth deviance on a remarkable scale, with 50 per cent of all crimes committed by minors, and juvenile delinquency concentrated among lower-class, urban, low-educated males (Salas 1979a and b). Institutional concern had been raised by the youth's apparent indifference to socialist values, visible in the adoption of Western symbols and behaviours. As the Cuban magazine *Bohemia* reported in 1977, a 'limited number of the young ... are attracted by the lifestyle and the "advances" of consumer society; minority groups take on extravagant appearance and ostenta-tious attitudes ... others maintain correspondence or other types of relationships with foreigners' (quoted in Fernández 1993: 197). Many youth of the time were arrested and punished for simply dressing in a non-conformist way and sporting long hair.

The tendency of the youth to collide with dominant socialist values manifested during the following decade as well, when a 'certain political demobilization – indeed, a certain cynicism' became apparent among the generation born after the revolution (Habel 1991: 69). During the 1980s, school truancy, juvenile delinquency and trafficking with tourists grew in Havana, and the media lamented the problem of the 'idle youth' and 'anti-social petty crimes'. On occasions, incidents with the police were reported involving groups of young people at sporting events and music concerts (ibid.).[2] In 1989, 65.9 per cent of all crimes were committed by Cubans under 30 years of age (Fogel and Rosenthal 1994).[3]

With the advent of the *período especial*, the situation observed in the 1980s grew considerably worse. Compared to previous generations, the youth of the 1990s had more expectations, but far less support from the state, now forced to divert its resources towards the preservation of minimal services and the necessities of tourism, and unable to guarantee its young citizens a profitable job corresponding to the hopes created by education. With the crisis, social mobility virtually disappeared (Eckstein 1997). Such lack of prospects fed the growing scepticism and cynicism of contemporary Cuban youth. Growing up to take state welfare for granted, the current generation resented the fact that things had been taken away from them by the crisis and the imperatives of tourism, and increasingly avoided work, a central value in socialist societies (Domínguez Gareía 1996).

In a country whose official national identity is so emphatically constructed in opposition to capitalism, youth culture reveals a passionate love for symbols of Western mass culture. From the Hollywood films old and new that fill Cuban cinemas and television channels, to sport and clothing, Cubans seem to love everything North American. As Lumsden observes, 'although Cubans cling to Spanish and African influences in their traditional and popular cultures, they lean to the United States when it comes to modern culture' (1996: 16). The origins of such influence are simultaneously remote and close, in Cuba's past as a US protectorate, in the island's physical and electronic proximity to its powerful neighbour and, most of all, in the growing presence of foreigners. As a bittersweet story circulating in the mid-1990s records, a young Cuban boy, asked what he wanted to do when he grew up, replied that he wanted to become a tourist.

Starting in the 1990s, contacts between Cubans and foreigners have acquired a systematic dimension, making the tourist, at the same time, into an economic resource, a channel of communication and a role

---

[2] In April 1991, for example, 1000 heavy-metal fans rioted with the police in Havana (Oppenheimer 1992).
[3] This suggests that juvenile delinquency in Cuba is not just a product of the present crisis.

model. Compared to previous decades, foreigners are now present in Cuba in large numbers, often entertain intense contacts with the population and sometimes return repeatedly to the island. Contact with Miami-based relatives has become another important channel of communication. Once dubbed *gusanos* and *traidores* ('worms' and 'traitors'), in the pragmatic language of the 1990s the exiles have been turned into *traedólares* ('bringers of dollars'). Remittances from abroad are today essential to the Cuban economy and in 1997 amounted to an estimated \$800m.[4] The phenomenon of Cuban families living on remittances from the USA has been duly registered by Van Van in their song 'El cheque'.[5]

In the mid-1990s, Cuban research on young *habaneros* identified three main groups: a vanguard loyal to revolutionary values; a 'wait-and-see' cluster of people who worked but look positively at consumer culture; and a group of individuals whose most common aspiration was to have 'a good house with every comfort, plenty of food and drinks, to live well with a high living standard, plenty of equipment and a car' (Domínguez García 1996: 45). Some of them took part in illegal or antisocial activities such as prostitution, theft from state companies, black marketeering and trafficking in foreign currency, and they frequently aspired to leave Cuba, possibly through marriage to a foreigner. The success of these individuals, concluded the research, produced a powerful demonstrative effect, inducing other people to follow their example and leading to a further weakening of traditional moral values.

Money, material goods, designer clothes, entertainment, sometimes drugs – the landscape of desires of young *habaneros* appears to be colonized by consumer dreams not so different from those of their Western counterparts. It would be easy to describe their lifestyle as escapist and self-indulgent, and to define them as a 'rapacious, cynical and unhappy generation' (Soler 2003). But the embracing of Western values and consumer icons by the timba subculture can also be read as a form of ritual resistance against dominant discourses, that gives such icons new, subversive meanings. Contrary to the interpretations dominating Cuban official discourse, and visible in the polemics concerning sex tourism, the increasingly deviant behaviour manifested by Cuban youth since the 1990s – although in different ways and degrees – cannot simply be explained in moralistic and/or utilitarian terms (loss of moral values, quest for material well-being), but must be seen as a

---

[4] 'Exiles' Cash helps Cuban Economy', *Associated Press*, 28 November 1997. According to other sources, remittances represent today the main source of hard currency for the Cuban economy.

[5] On the CD *LLegó Van Van*, 1999.

tactic to escape boredom, acquire social status and challenge dominant social values.[6]

The 1990s have also seen an alarming growth in the consumption of alcohol and drugs. According to *Granma* (11 August 2000), in the last few years the age of people starting to consume alcohol has considerably lowered. Cocaine, or *pica pica*, can now be bought in Cuba at extremely low prices and its use is widespread not only among foreigners but also among Cubans (including, increasingly, musicians). In 1999, Fidel Castro himself stated that drugs had been found in places such as 'discos, youth centres, night-clubs and areas of the Malecón in Havana' (Castro 1999). The growing popularity of drugs has greatly worried the police and the medical authorities of the island, once known for its extremely low level of consumption.[7] Drugs and alcohol, at any rate, represent a less terrifying way of escape from reality than other forms of deviant behaviour practised by sectors of the Cuban youth. In the late 1980s, young, mainly white *frikis* or *roqueros* ('freaks' or 'rockers') injected themselves with HIV-infected blood. The phenomenon, which involved hundreds of people then opposed by the authorities because of their association with heavy-metal music, represented a form of extreme subversion of the slogan 'socialism or death' (Prout 1999).[8]

The connection made by Cuban researchers between youth, consumer culture, social indiscipline and crime reflected the level of alarm raised by youth behaviour in governmental circles, and emerged in many articles published in the second half of the 1990s (for example, Cala and Montes de Oca 1996; Elizalde 1996a). Such concerns were justified not only by the apparent spread of materialistic values and criminal behaviour among young people, but also by the presence of the youth in anti-government demonstrations. Between 1993 and 1994, young people were at the forefront of violent street riots in the area of Regla and in Central Havana, which eventually led to the emigration of 35 000 *balseros*. During these incidents, extremely rare in post-1959 Cuba, rioters

---

[6] At the beginning of 1997, the Miami press reported the increasing irritation of the Cuban authorities with young Cubans who sported T-shirts and caps carrying US symbols. Questioned by a reporter, one young Cuban explained: 'we do this because we are already sick of so much empty talk (*muela*) against imperialism' (Sánchez 1997). A few months later, the police intervened in Havana fining people caught wearing this type of clothing (Garve 1997). The usage of these symbols did not constitute political dissidence and lent itself to diverging interpretations, but it represented a clear sign of symbolic resistance to official ideology, whose political meaning was greatly amplified by the authorities' over-reaction.

[7] In 2003, the authorities for the first time officially acknowledged the drug problem in Cuba (*Gaceta Oficial de la Republica de Cuba*, 21 January 2003).

[8] Prout's article is based on the documentary *Socialism or Death*, covertly made in 1995 by B. Norborg for Swedish Television.

destroyed various state-owned stores selling in hard currency, asking for freedom and political changes (De la Fuente and Glasco 1997). According to a commentator, it was unclear to what extent the riots were 'a reaction to the scarcity of material goods, political repression, human rights abuses, and a loss of civil liberties' (Segre et al. 1997: 242).

More worryingly, the riots took place in areas largely populated by Blacks. Since they have traditionally been seen as the sector of the population most loyal to the revolution, the riots were considered a signal of the extremely high level of the crisis of legitimacy suffered by the government during the early years of the *período especial*. Successive research revealed that 'young blacks no longer perceive the restoration of capitalism as a major reverse', and shared those views with white youths, thus suggesting that age, more than race, was the key factor in determining the level of support for the revolution (De la Fuente and Glasco 1997: 69).

While both black and white young Cubans show attitudes indicating disaffection and defiance of the system (Milán 1999), their strategies of adaptation to the crisis have been different. Compared to their white counterparts, young Afro-Cubans stand on a lower rung on the social scale, are less educated, have fewer jobs requiring qualifications and fewer chances to receive money from abroad. For this reason, they most often appear to resort to street-hustling. As both empirical evidence and reports by foreign researchers suggest (for example, O'Connell Davidson 1996; Forrest 1999), many *macetas*, *jineteras/os* and other actors of the illegal economy are black.[9] Combined with persisting prejudices portraying Blacks as troublemakers, such a state of affairs has made young Afro-Cubans caught on the streets with tourists into a major target of police repression.

'El temba': Confronting the official discourse

For Cubans, the early 1990s represented a deeply traumatizing time, but also a period of great changes and hopes. The ideological relaxation and the end of Marxist orthodoxy made artists and intellectuals increasingly critical, producing a reflection on the identity and future of Cuba in literature, theatre and the visual arts.[10] During this period, a series of state-funded, biting films appeared in Cuban cinemas – such as *Alicia en*

---

[9] With a low education, a flashy lifestyle and a social status exclusively based on economic success, *macetas* represented 'the ostentatious new rich of Cuba', the role models for the 1990s (Segre et al. 1997: 176). For a portrait of the *maceta*, see Adams 1994.

[10] On literature, see Behar 1995 and Yáñez 1998; on theatre, see Leonard 1997; on the visual arts, see Poupeye 1998 and Zeitlin 1999.

el pueblo de Maravillas (Díaz Torres, 1991), *Fresa y chocolate* and *Guantanamera* (Gutiérrez Alea, 1993 and 1996) – which were internationally praised and received a record attendance at home. In the same period, several artists and intellectuals left the island and went to live abroad. Not all of them headed for Miami: some chose to live in *semi-exilio* ('half-exile') and keep their ties with the motherland, settling in Mexico, New York or Europe. In Cuba, the necessities of the economy led to a higher degree of autonomy for the professional associations of artists, who, like musicians, enjoyed more freedom to travel and sell their work abroad (Dilla 1999).[11]

Another mark of the relaxation of restrictions of the time was the launching of the Fundación Pablo Milanés (FPM). This independent cultural foundation, established in 1993 by *trovador* Pablo Milanés, embarked on a series of projects devoted to artists who were not able to get official support. Among its multi-faceted activities, the Foundation promoted young musical talents, set up a record company and created a publishing house. Unfortunately, according to the leading *trovador* Silvio Rodríguez, the Foundation 'had such a degree of autonomy that it eventually collided with the institutions' (quoted in Manrique 1996b). In 1996, the FPM was unilaterally terminated by the Cuban government, who confiscated its properties and transferred all its projects and belongings to state-controlled entities (Puerta 1996).

This episode indicated that the higher degree of expressive and economic freedom enjoyed by the arts of the early 1990s should not necessarily be interpreted as a sign of appreciation of their critical function by the authorities. On various occasions, these censored and attempted to direct artistic expression. After four days of record attendance in Havana in June 1991, for example, the film *Alicia en el pueblo de Maravillas* was withdrawn and replaced with *Alien II* (Davies 1996). As critic Gerardo Mosquera has observed, in the Cuban arts the critical sense has been able to expand '"ritually" protected behind a greater tropological density and a cynical attitude' (1999: 29). In other words, critical positions were tolerated when not expressed in explicit terms. According to the art critic, the 'clever ruse of playing a double game with what is prohibited is one of the important critical tools of the art of the 1990s' (ibid.).[12]

Within the arts, music – and specifically *música bailable* – occupies a special position in Cuba, one that is at the same time more marginal and more important. Marginal, because dance music is largely seen by the

---

11 With the increasing success of Cuban visual arts on the international market, in the mid-1990s visual artists resident in Cuba were eventually authorized to retain earnings in foreign currency (Poupeye 1998).

12 On the official attitude towards the arts, see Cantor 1999d.

Cuban cultural establishment, as it generally is in the West, more as a form of entertainment than an art, as an expression that lacks the intellectual and cultural lustre of concert music such as jazz, classical music or intellectual singer-songwriting. At the same time more important, though, because in Cuba dance songs enjoy a level of mass response that has no match in other, more elitist and controllable forms such as literature, the visual arts or theatre.

Precisely because of their popular appeal and the way they communicate, popular songs have thus represented the main and most effective vehicle for the 'double game' described by Mosquera. In the second half of the 1990s, the role of the new champions of musical provocation passed on to La Charanga Habanera, who outdid the popularity of NG La Banda and El Médico. Constructing a markedly modern image which made use of musical and visual elements of clear US derivation, the band built a phenomenal following among young black *habaneros*, interpreting the ostentatious and cynical attitudes of the timba subculture. Asked once by a foreign journalist what he thought of Che Guevara, the young singer of the band shrugged his shoulders and said, 'I can't think anything .... He was dead when I was born' (Paternostro 1999).[13]

In 1996, the band released on a Spanish label a song called 'El temba', whose musical form I have analysed in detail in Chapter 4.[14] In the first, ballad-like section, the narrator praises his woman lamenting that he has no financial means to satisfy her 'queen's dreams'. What she really needs to fulfil her dreams, he concludes, is a *temba*, Afro-Cuban slang for a man aged between 30 and 50, that is, a sugar daddy. In the enormously popular estribillo, La Charanga rap

> Find yourself a *temba* who could keep you
> so that you can enjoy yourself, you can have things

The text allows for various readings, to the point that Calzado has sometimes claimed that it does 'not represent an invitation to take life in an interested way' (Manrique 1996a). But its portrait of women as venal and frivolous and its anthemic coros, make the song into a clear allusion to sex tourism, concisely expressed by its final coro,

> [a *temba*]
> so that you can have
> what you had to have
> a *papirriqui* [a well-off man]
> with *wanikiki* [money]

---

[13] According to one writer, such a position is common to most young artists. In his view, the youngest literary generation 'are utterly indifferent to [socialist] ideology, and turn their backs as soon as they feel its presence' (interview by D. Manera, Yoss 1999).

[14] From the CD *Pa' que se entere La Habana*, 1996.

Like 'La bruja', 'El temba' never refers explicitly to prostitution, but the text is disseminated with hints that young Cuban listeners cannot miss. Music itself, in a way, acted here as a semantic indicator, because in Cuba everybody knew the function of dance music in tourist clubs. The artwork for the album, as well, left few doubts about the intentions of La Charanga, showing a $100 banknote, and the name and title of the CD printed on the green bill (see Plate 7). On the album booklet, cartoon-like drawings illustrated the lyrics of 'El temba' in four successive steps: a big, naked *mulata*; a young slim black man with empty pockets; a bald, old, fat, cigar-smoking white man; finally, the elegant *mulata* with peroxide hair, smoking through a long cigarette holder.

In its energetic ode to love as Cuba's main form of 'convertible currency' (Garcia 1997), 'El temba' also contains one daring literary reference, which opens up yet another reading. The final lines of the song,

> so that you can have
> what you had to have

are a parody of 'Tengo' ('I have'), a poem written by the Afro-Cuban poet Nicolás Guillén. A representative of the Minorista group in the 1920s, an avant-garde movement seeking to reconcile modernism with the aesthetics of *afrocubanismo*, Guillén has been celebrated as the black poet of the revolution, the author of 'milestones of constant militancy' (Medin 1990). His poem 'Tengo', written in an iterative form and plain language, is an ode to the achievements of Blacks under the revolution, 'yesterday Juan with nothing, today Juan with everything': freedom, end of discrimination, dignity, education, work, food. The poem ends with the lines,

> I have, Yes now I have
> a place to work
> and to earn
> what I to eat must have.
> I have, just wait and see,
> I have what I had to have.[15]

By transforming the last line of 'Tengo' into 'so that you can have / what you had to have', Calzado states that what really counts is an older man with a lot of money (note as well the phonetic closeness of *temba* and *tengo*). This final statement contained in the last lines of the montuno surely represents the most subversive aspect of the song, where La Charanga cast doubts on the achievements of Blacks under the

---

[15] 'Tengo que ya tengo / donde trabajar / y ganar / lo que me tengo que comer. / Tengo, vamos a ver, / tengo lo que tenía que tener'. Guillén 1964 (English translation by R. Carr, 1974).

revolution. Ironically, Calzado did so by taking to its extreme consequences the process of inclusion of Afro-Cuban street language into mainstream culture started by Guillén in the 1930s.

The subversiveness of 'El temba' becomes even more striking when one takes a closer look at Guillén's poem and compares its statements with the situation of Cuba under the *período especial*.

> I have, let's see,
> that being black
> no one can stop me
> at the door of a dancehall or a bar.
> Or at the entrance of a hotel
> shout me that there is no bed[16]

Today Cubans are not allowed into hotels for foreign tourists. This form of discrimination applies particularly to Afro-Cubans, who, being black, are the most easily spotted by security people and the police. On the assumption that they are practising *jineterismo*, Cubans cannot book a hotel room with foreigners, not even if they arc a legitimate couple (unless they can produce evidence of being married).

> I have, let's see
> that there is no rural policeman
> who can grab me and put me in jail[17]

From 1997 on, in tourist areas of the country the police have routinely stopped Cubans seen with foreigners on the streets. Because they are commonly perceived as hustlers, *jineteros/as* and criminals, Afro-Cubans are the ones most frequently harassed. As one European female scholar recalls, the 'permanent warning I heard from my white Cuban friends before going out was: "Be careful with black people"' (Holgado Fernández 2000: 215).

> I have the land, and the sea as well,
> no country,
> no highlife,
> no tennis and no yacht,
> but beach after beach and wave after wave,
> blue open democratic giant:
> in short, the sea.[18]

---

16 'Tengo, vamos a ver, / que siendo un negro / nadie me puede detener / a la puerta de un dancing o de un bar. / O bien en la carpeta de un hotel / gritarme que no hay pieza.'

17 'Tengo, vamos a ver, / que no hay guardia rural / que me agarre y me encierre en un cuartel.'

18 'Tengo que como tengo la tierra tengo el mar, / no country, / no jailáif, / no tenis y no yacht, / sino de playa en playa y ola en ola, / gigante azul abierto democrático: / en fin, el mar.'

The *período especial* and tourist development have produced the phenomenon that Cubans call 'apartheid tourism', that is, the denial of access for locals to areas of the country reserved for foreign tourists (Benjamin 1990a: 21). Ordinary Cubans have no access to places such as Marina Hemingway in Havana or beach resorts such as Cayo Coco, unless they work or reside there. Nor can the 'democratic giant' be a great economic resource for ordinary Cubans. As most fish is reserved for tourism, state-owned restaurants and export, fishing for personal consumption and private commerce is forbidden (although widely practised).

One can only speculate on why Calzado decided to make such an uncomfortable reference in his song, a fact that would most certainly put him into collision with the authorities. One reason, probably, was related to the marketing of his own music. Released about a year after the Malecón riots, 'El temba', arguably, represented a way of winning over the sympathies of a wide sector of young black marginal audiences. On the wave of the rising strength of timba in the mid-1990s and of the incredible appeal of his band, Calzado decided to push harder, and eventually fell victim to his own hubris.

Various other songs released during that period by La Charanga dealt with the issue of tourism, which on the island was and is extremely controversial, because many Cubans feel they are being treated as second-class citizens. 'Superturistica', from the same album, has a structure and a theme similar to 'El temba'. It starts like a conventional *salsa romántica*, only to reveal that the beautiful black woman met on the street exclusively travels by *turitaxi* and goes to dollar-only discotheques. Dealing with the theme jocularly, and not as a general, abstract topic (tourism), the song adopts a strategy quite different from that of *trovadores* such as Pedro Luís Ferrer, who wrote the famous song 'Cien por cien cubano' ('100% Cuban').[19]

This song, never released on record in Cuba, is a clever piece of critique on the exclusion caused by tourism, and a bitter, ironic and articulated reflection on things Cubans have lost. A comparison between this song and those of La Charanga reveals, once again, the abysmal

---

[19] Since my Cuba is / hundred per cent Cuban / tomorrow I will book / the best hotel in Havana. / Then I will go to Varadero / and rent a house there / with the money / I've made from the *zafra* (sugar harvest). / Since my Cuba is / hundred per cent Cuban / tomorrow I will hire / a boat in Barlovento. / I want to spend the whole day / fishing lobsters / enjoying in full / the beauty of my coasts / ... /Since my Cuba is / hundred per cent Cuban / tomorrow I will buy / a ticket at the airport. / I want to travel South / to see poverty / and to come back as / a hundred per cent Cuban / to my country.' From the CD *100% Cuban*, Ceyba Music, 2000 (Spain). Another famous song dealing with the effects of tourism in Cuba is 'Tropicollage' by Carlos Varela.

distance between timba and trova, and their respective audiences. Accompanied by acoustic guitar, with its indirect commentary on the socially dividing effects of the reforms, Ferrer's song sounds like a nostalgic call to the lost egalitarianism of Cuban society. By contrast, the tunes of La Charanga addressed their audiences in street-slang and to the rhythm of dance music, voicing coros which conveyed collective opinions that appeared to put on the same level love, sex and money. 'Hagámos un chen' ('Lets make a business'), on the album *Tremendo Delirio* (1997), was dedicated to 'to all the tourists who visit Cuba'.

The rise and fall of La Charanga Habanera

> Q: Why were you forbidden from playing two years ago?
> Calzado: It was a great concert. As a live concert it was a tremendous success, but from the point of view of television it represented a difficult precedent because there was a lot of eroticism, a lot of *cubanía*, and many people over 50 who watched it thought it was too strong. There has been a lot of controversy.
> Q: What do you mean by eroticism?
> In the sense of scenic movement, the waist (*cintura*). And as a consequence, it has caused a great offence to the moral of some Cubans ... that has [left people] confused, and thus they suspended us from playing.
> Q: Aren't those movements quite common in the way people dance to timba?
> Yes, but one thing is to watch it live, another one on TV staying at home. That has created the difficulties.
> David Calzado (interview with the author, 1999)

The year 1997 saw in Cuba a great deal of musical activism. In March, the launch of the first edition of the Cubadisco Music Fair in Havana was accompanied by a record-breaking 100-hour music-and-dance marathon at La Tropical. The 'Son más largo del mundo' ('The world's longest *son*' – note the avoidance of terms such as salsa or timba) featured 72 bands and almost 2000 musicians, who played without a break for five days and nights to a total dancing crowd estimated at around 60 000 people. The event featured all the top timba bands and was sponsored by Magic Music, the record label of La Charanga Habanera. In the same year Eurotropical, another Spanish label, started operating in Cuba and Caribe Productions announced a distribution deal with EMI Spain, the first record major to be directly involved in the Cuban market (Llewellyn 1997).

By then, La Charanga Habanera had reached the peak of popularity among Cuban dance music bands. In July 1997, they were invited by the

Communist Youth's Union to give an outdoor concert for the 14th World Festival of Youth and Students, a major official event attracting to Cuba tens of thousands of young people from all over the world. The concert took place on 29 July at La Piragua, on the sea promenade of Havana, before 100 000 foreign and local young people, and in the presence of several international TV crews.

La Charanga made a grandiose landing from a helicopter, something previously unseen for a pop band in Cuba. During the concert, they performed several of their most popular tunes, full with sexual innuendos and allusions to materialism and sex tourism. Then they sang 'Usa condon [sic]', a song about unprotected sex, during which young singer Michel Maza performed his pelvic routines, took off his shirt and gestured as if to take off his trousers. Inciting the audience to skip the security barriers, he proceeded to sing a coro referring to drugs: 'Que levante la mano al que le guste la bolá / al que le guste la bola / la bolaíta que vuelve loco / la bolaíta que te pone rico' (that is, 'put up your hands those who like the stuff', i.e. coke) – to enthusiastic cheers from the audience.

The concert was broadcast on TV later the same day, and produced cries of moral scandal. On 31 July, an article in the magazine *Juventud Rebelde* defined La Charanga Habanera as the 'kings of vulgarity' (Perera Robbio 1997). The author complained about their 'violent pelvic movements', and lamented the rudeness of a song where the singer had manifested his desire for 'a pretty woman, then a lot of money to support her, and the chance to eat "first-quality meat"' (thus alluding to the virtual disappearance of meat from the average Cuban's diet). Referring to the performance, another article published later lamented the 'very serious lack of restraint in their stage projection, which had been emphasized by the TV broadcast and had been rejected by the people' (Rojas Gutiérrez 1998: 3).

A week after the event, the organ of the Cuban Communist Party *Granma* wrote that the audience had been 'profoundly offended' by the band's show (4 August 1997). A few days later, the same paper reported the declarations of a spokesperson of the Instituto Cubano de la Música (Cuban Institute of Music, or ICM), who stated that the band 'had tarnished the remarkable presence of our culture' during the festival, and that the Cuban audience had rightly felt 'deeply offended' (*Granma* 9 August 1997). For that reason, he added, the ICM had decided 'to suspend the national and international scheduling [of La Charanga] for a six-month period, so that the band could evaluate their artistic projection and image' (ibid.). On the same page, the management of the Institute of Cuban Radio and Television (ICRT) acknowledged the 'unpleasant situation' created by the broadcasting of the concert, and announced that those responsible for this 'censurable representation' had been disciplined. Since 'the artistic projection of the named musical band, as well as a good part of their repertoire, contradict the principles of our programming policy', continued the ICRT, their music was to be banned for six months from radio and TV (ibid.).

However self-evident they may have seemed to the censors, the accusations against La Charanga Habanera expressed by the press were actually rather generic, and appeared absolutely disproportionate to the seriousness of the repressive action. The articles in the Cuban press made no mention of the band's arrival by helicopter without the permission of the military authorities, nor of the 'green mango' song allegedly referring to Fidel Castro, which was instead quoted by various foreign sources (Lafranchi 1997).[20] At the same time, when compared to the explicitness of many Cuban folkloric and popular dances, and to the consolidated practices in the dance clubs of the time, the moral scandal expressed by the press about La Charanga's dance performance appeared quite surprising. The problem, the articles seemed to imply, was not so much in the performance itself, but in its broadcasting, where TV audiences who had never been to La Tropical had enjoyed all the visual and aural details. As in the case of Afro-Cuban dances of the nineteenth century, early jazz and the rockings of Elvis Presley, pelvic movements seem to become a problem when they enter the visual range of philistines.

In Cuba, television has been described as 'the main ideological and propagandistic instrument of the State and the Party'; it is the most conservative of all media and makes very few live broadcasts (Acosta 1999: 81). The modalities of the screening of the concert, therefore, cast serious doubts on the casualness of the event, suggesting that the incident might well have been conceived as a manoeuvre against La Charanga. After the event, the magazine *El Caimán Barbudo*, then conducting a virulent campaign against timba, published an interview with Francis Cabezas, the Spanish manager of La Charanga's record company. From that issue, we learn that the director of the magazine and leader of a youth association close to the PCC, Fernando Rojas Gutiérrez, was the same person responsible for the organization of the performance of La Charanga at the festival. In other words, the man orchestrating the attack on timba from the pages of *El Caimán Barbudo* was the same person who had invited the band to play at the mass concert. In the

---

[20] Lafranchi's article suggested that the reason for the ban could have been a song called 'El Mango', never released on record. The lyrics, allegedly, made allusions to Fidel Castro with verses like 'Hey green mango, now that you're ripe, why have you still not fallen?', which hinted at the army fatigues often worn by Castro. The song, however, was *not* performed at the festival.

interview, the interviewer-as-cultural commissar went so far as to say to Cabezas that 'some people say that your head has not fallen off because of your position as a foreign entrepreneur, because, if you had been a Cuban, it would have been broken into pieces' (Borges and Triana 1997).[21] Cabezas replied to the accusations by defending the performance of his band, and blaming Cuban TV for its bad use of the shots of the concert. According to him, the images were nothing new for Cuban audiences. He also stated that, before the performance, Calzado had received assurances that the show was to be edited in his presence, and broadcast five days after the concert.

A changing climate

The censorship of La Charanga was part of a wider and complex picture of changes taking place in Cuba in the second half of the 1990s. Beginning in 1995, the reforms and the expansion of the Cuban tourist industry started to show their effects, producing a slow recovery and stabilization of the economy (Monreal 1999).[22] This process offered a breath of fresh air to Cuban state finances, and new arguments to the PCC hardliners, who did not agree on market reforms and considered them only as a crisis measure. Inside the PCC, innovators who pushed for further economic liberalization were fronted by those criticizing the social costs of the reforms (Schwab 1999). In 1996, the Central Committee of the PCC discussed the ideological impact of the economic policies, and the Western press reported rumours of purges of officials considered too sympathetic to the market economy (Schwartz 1997; 'Getting Ready for Helms-Burton Law', 1996). In 1997, the Minister of Tourism, Osmany Cienfuegos, was removed from office.

The Cuban press, meanwhile, attacked social indiscipline, prostitution and crime, relating these to the expansion of the informal economy produced by the reforms. Commenting on the police 'cleaning up' of Varadero, a journalist observed that the situation there was causing an 'international scandal', adding, 'we must protect not only the main tourist area of Cuba, but also giant and vital investments that we can't afford to lose' (Elizalde 1996a: 67). In one of his speeches, Fidel Castro

---

[21] The article appeared in the same issue as the interview with J.L. Cortés discussed in Chapter 7 (López 1997). In the following years, Magic Music literally disappeared from Cuba.

[22] Between the early 1990s and 1999, the number of hotel rooms increased from 2000 to 29 000, and that of airlines flying to the island from three to 47. Foreign visitors increased from 340 000 in 1990 to 1.4 million in 1998 (Segre et al. 1997; *Caribbean & Central America Report*, 19 January 1999).

(1999) echoed this statement, observing that 'crime is the best fifth column for those who bet on the failure of the political and economic models of Cuba'. Between 1996 and 1997, the government established new fiscal and legal measures aimed at fighting crime and reining in the informal economy. In 1997, it modified the penal code introducing new sections that targeted crimes such as administrative graft, tax evasion and prostitution. Almost at the same time, the police carried out repeated raids against vice.

The situation was not made any easier by international events. In February 1996, after the shooting down of two anti-Castroist, unarmed airplanes flying over Cuban territory, the US senate passed the Helms-Burton law, aimed at further tightening the economic blockade against Cuba. This extremely controversial law – which has since not been fully enforced by the US government and has been disputed by various states and the European Union – nonetheless constituted a major deterrent for new potential investors in Cuba. On the internal front, other worrying events have made the tension escalate. In July 1997, just before the beginning of the Festival of Youth, bombs exploded in some Havana hotels. A few days later, Cuban police arrested four dissidents who had openly criticized the document for the preparation of the Fifth Congress of the PCC. The four were subsequently condemned under the accusation of 'sedition' (Amnesty International 2000).[23] The government also began to put into place new regulations against political dissent, which would remarkably widen its power to define anti-revolutionary activities.[24]

The resolutions of the PCC Congress in October 1997 suggested that the repressive wave was part of a process of political restoration. Among other things, the document confirmed the central role of foreign investment and tourism in Cuba, but denied further economic liberalization ('Cuban Party Congress ...', 1997). The Congress rejected the proposed privatization of state enterprises and ruled out the expansion of the self-employed sector, which, from that moment on, declined rapidly. As for tourism, it made clear that the new policies should promote traditional and new forms of tourism such as nautical, sporting, cultural, health and eco-tourism, stating that in Cuba there was no place for the 'alienating vices of other societies' like drugs or sex tourism, nor for 'irrational and imitative consumerism' ('Economic Resolution of the Fifth

---

[23] Three of them have since been released after serving half their sentence. The fourth prisoner was released in May 2002, shortly before the end of his term and a week before the visit of Jimmy Carter to Havana.

[24] The 'Law for the Protection of National Independence and the Economy', approved in 1999, targeted people who pass sensitive information to the USA, virtually equating the communication of information that might cause economic damage to Cuba to counter-revolutionary activity (Lapper and Fletcher 1999).

Congress ...', 1997). The following year, Carlos Lage declared that, 'without renouncing the attractions of sun and sea, culture must become the great mark of Cuba as a tourist destination' (Garcia and Pérez Mok 2001). In early 1998, President Castro emphasized Cuba's commitment to socialism, indicating that the economic reforms of the early 1990s were not intended to be part of a process of political transition. On the same occasion, he violently criticized the Cuban film *Guantanamera*, directed by the late Gutiérrez Alea, repeating his criticisms shortly afterwards at a meeting with intellectuals, where he attacked cultural liberalization ('Cuba: Ideology Shake Up ...', 1998).

End of the party?

In the early 1990s, as we have seen, Cuban MB benefited from an unprecedented level of institutional sponsorship. Enthusiastically promoted by musical empresas, it reached a significant presence on radio and TV and came to dominate the scene of the state-managed clubs (Godfried 2000), acquiring a central role in tourist entertainment. For a relatively long period, the importance of MB and the level of its mass popularity went unmatched by other forms of musical expression, allowing increasingly challenging attitudes by musicians, and over-shadowing timba's *liaisons dangereuses*. As late as 1996, the then Foreign Secretary Roberto Robaina personally congratulated El Médico, who saw with amazement some of his tunes used as soundtracks for political spots broadcast by the Cuban television.

In the second half of the 1990s, political changes and economic recovery produced a reaction to the 'degenerations' allegedly brought by the introduction of market economy, inducing, among other things, a radical re-orientation in the attitudes of the Cuban authorities towards dance music. From 1996 on, this led to increased repression against vice by the police, and to an attack to the most controversial symbols of the 'excesses' caused by the economic reforms. After the polemics unleashed by 'La bruja' and the campaign against the vulgarity of MB led by the FMC, dance music was attacked on the grounds of its commercialism and its ties with the informal economy. Timba musicians were now not only put under fire for their sympathies for the marginal world, but also accused of being newly rich and proto-capitalists.

In a sense those accusations were true, because the economic transformations of the *período especial* had made MB musicians into entrepreneurs who managed artistic, organizational and financial matters. For that reason, it was very easy, for critics, to put them on the same plan as *cuentapropistas*, a category of self-employed workers which appeared in the early 1990s. Initially intended as a simple response to the crisis, individual entrepreneurship and informal economy boomed in the mid-1990s (especially in the areas related to tourism) and had profound consequences on the development of civil society (León 1997), but remained exposed to unpredictable oscillations between tolerance and repression.[25] The very success of those entrepreneurs thus made them the object of widespread criticism. Equated to *macetas* (street-hustlers), they were accused of illicit enrichment, branded as 'politically and ideologically unstable' (Vilariño 1997: 151), and pictured as a seminal neo-capitalist class and a potentially anti-revolutionary force (Elizalde 1996).

The parallels drawn by the Cuban media between self-employed workers and musicians indicate how the criticisms levelled at timberos by the Cuban press in the late 1990s were not only dictated by moral motivations, but also by political reasons. During the first stage of the crisis, their real finest hour, MB musicians had been important wheels in the machinery of the tourist industry (Godfried 2000). With a vast popular following and an extraordinary material and symbolic power, they now represented a sector out of control: Calzado's band were overtly defying revolutionary ideology with their songs, and El Tosco complained about having to pay taxes (Manrique 1998a).

The police raids that took place after the Charanga incident gave an almost mortal blow to the economy of MB. From August 1997 on, the police raided various tourist nightspots in the capital city. The first operation targeted a dance club called El Periquitón, a well-known, clandestine gay club in the outskirts of Havana. According to an officer who took part in the raid, among the people identified at the club were 'prostitutes, pimps, some underage minors and several foreigners' (Fletcher 1997). Among these were French fashion designer Jean-Paul Gaultier, Swedish actress Bibi Andersson and Spanish film director Pedro Almodóvar, accompanied by high-profile Cubans such as the director of the Cuban Film Institute (Corzo 1997). A similar raid took place a week later in Playas del Este, a major tourist area some 30 km east of Havana.

The final offensive took place in the following year, when the police repeatedly raided the most popular discos and nightclubs of the capital

---

[25] The small family restaurants called *paladares*, for example, were legalized in 1993, were raided by the police in early 1994, resurged around mid-1990s, and came again under attack towards the end of 1997. At the beginning of the new millennium, virtually all the paladares once flourishing in the tourist areas of Havana had disappeared. From the Cuban point of view, thus, the possible benefits of family-run tourist services seemed counterbalanced by fears that '[d]ecentralizing economic decision-making does, at least for Communist Party hard-liners, run the risk of the liberalization of political life and creating a new space for civil society' (Segre et al. 1997: 242).

city. During an action named Operativo Lacra ('Operation vice'), policemen forcibly entered El Palacio de la Salsa of the Hotel Riviera in the Vedado neighbourhood, the Café Cantante near the Teatro Nacional and the famous Havana Club of the Hotel Comodoro. All three were shut down by the police. The Palacio remained closed 'for refurbishment' until further notice, while other discos attached to hotels eventually reopened, limiting access to hotel customers only (Evangelisti: 1999). On the streets, the police intensified routine checks on Cubans seen hanging around with tourists.

The ban on La Charanga marked a key moment for the whole timba movement, culminating in La Charanga's public act of self-criticism and contrition. In a press statement released after the ban, Calzado described the performance at the festival as 'unfortunate'. 'We profoundly regret that our public performance created a disagreeable image, because that was not our intention', he declared. 'We have reached the conclusion that it is our responsibility to keep an eye on the quality of the improvisations, gestures and other details which occur on stage' ('Cuba bans salsa group ...', 1997). In an interview, he added, '[t]his period ... has been a lesson to the members of La Charanga, and I think it will be useful as well to all the artists who are part of the movement of bands which have given MB the place it deserves' (P.H. 1997).

As a reward for their good behaviour, the band were released from the last month of their ban. In December, they resumed their performing activity giving concerts for labour unions, workers of the sugar industry and the Lenin School (a college attended by the children of the political elite). On that occasion, *Granma* reported, the band appeared in public after having reassessed, 'with self-critical spirit and the assistance of the Cuban Institute of Music, the characteristics of their artistic project, with an emphasis on the review of their previous repertoire and the conception of new proposals' (ibid.). The tensions caused by the ban were at the root of the split and total remodelling of La Charanga in 1998, when all but two members of the band left Calzado to set up a new band called La Charanga Forever.[26]

Even José Luís Cortés, sensing the storm approaching, adopted a far more cautious attitude than usual. In spring 1998, on the occasion of the release of his new album *Veneno*, he declared to a US journalist that 'he intended the album to be less aggressive than the usual NG disc', and added, 'It's a more Caribbean sound ... we're going back to our roots: the sound of the beach, the sun, and the palm trees' (Cantor 1998c). In another interview made on the same occasion, El Tosco was reported as saying that Cuban music must 'reflect the enjoyment (*gozadera*) of Cuba,

---

[26] The split was also due to disagreement over financial matters.

and not the tensions of the *período especial*' (Manrique 1998a). Compared to his challenging attitudes of a few years before, these conciliatory statements left the reader speechless, and showed the leader of NG on the edge of self-censorship.

Nowhere has the stormy relationship between MB and Cuban institutions in the late 1990s been more visible than in the vicissitudes of Manolín, probably the artist most hated by the detractors of timba. While the repressive wave was in full swing in 1997, El Médico released his third album, which contained a song entitled 'Mami ... ya tengo amigos en Miami' ('Baby ... I've already got friends in Miami'), where the singer exhorted Cubans to reconciliation.[27] While on tour in Florida in October 1998, he announced to a Miami journalist his intention to stay in the USA with his family for 'artistic reasons'. A few days later, he changed his mind and returned to Cuba, while wife, daughter and part of the band stayed in Miami. On his arrival in Cuba, Manolín found himself without a group and faced media ostracization, gradually disappearing from the public view. He moved to Mexico, then to San Francisco, then went back to Cuba, where he resumed working. In April 2001, *Granma* attacked him for his 'extra-musical fancies', accusing him of depicting, with his new song 'El puente' ('The bridge'), 'a rose-coloured road between Miami and Havana'. A month later, El Mèdico entered the USA clandestinely and asked for political refugee status. He has settled in Miami.[28]

Conclusions

The ban on La Charanga Habanera in summer 1997 represented the most visible episode of a confrontation between the government and Cuban society, a signal that the period of relative tolerance and freedom enjoyed by artists in music, film, theatre, the visual arts and literature was coming to an end. As those who benefited from the widest visibility, the broadest mass following and the highest earnings in the field of intellectual production, MB musicians were those who received the most exemplary punishment.

In the mid-1990s, challenging attitudes had become widespread among the youth of the *período especial*, who had reacted to scarcity and control by embracing Western attitudes, and manifesting growing levels

---

[27] The full title is 'Que le llegue mi mano (Mami ... ya tengo amigos en Miami)'; from the CD *De buena fé*, 1997.

[28] On the Manolín affair, see Cardona 1998 and 1999, Levin 1998a, Fraser Delgado 2000, and Cancio Isla 2001. On the singer's defection, see 'El cantante Manolín pide asilo en Atlanta', *El Nuevo Herald*, 19 May 2001.

of deviancy that ranged from refusing to work to consumption of drugs and alcohol, crime and even violent rebellion. La Charanga Habanera came to embody perfectly the distance of that youth from the values of the generations who had made the revolution, and, with songs such as 'El temba', they produced quasi-political statements that appeared to defy the ideological milestones and the moral authority of the revolutionary leadership. In the climate of restoration of the late 1990s, La Charanga's provocative attitudes made them into the ideal target for an institutional reaction.

The censorship of La Charanga represented an unprecedented repressive measure, a warning that the political establishment was taking music very seriously and was determined to put an end to the provocations of timba. The ban took place amidst a series of police actions aimed at repressing political dissidence and cleaning up Havana from prostitution and crime, just few months away from the 5th Congress of the Communist Party and the long-planned visit of the Pope. Significantly, the censorship of La Charanga took the form of restrictions imposed by musical and broadcasting regulators and affecting the band's economic interests, and not of a judicial repression that would have called directly into question the role of the government.

The outright veto on La Charanga represented an exemplary case, conceived to remind musicians, their audiences and the 'modest and austere cadres' of the PCC what the system could do if it decided to flex its muscles. But it was also an extraordinary acknowledgment of the power of popular music, and of the panic that music is able to generate in political systems that seek to control every aspect of public life.

Chapter 9

Marketing Nostalgia: the Rise of *Buena Vista Social Club*

People want to go somewhere and stay at home, to travel in their armchair. That's fine. Journey with us now for an hour or so and that's enough.

Ry Cooder (Williamson 1999b)

People think because of Ry Cooder and Buena Vista that Cuban music became better known. That may be true, but it set us back 40 years. Now we are fighting against the mythological vision of the old Cuba, the Cuba of the Tropicana Club and old cars.

X Alfonso, Cuban rocker and rapper (Thigpen 2002)

As I discussed in the previous chapter, what happened to La Charanga Habanera in August 1997 was the signal of a dramatic wind of change in Cuba. In this chapter, I look at how the offensive on timba musicians found a powerful, if unexpected ally in the extraordinary international success of the album *Buena Vista Social Club*. Here, I examine the story of the making of *Buena Vista* and discuss its nature as a revivalist project developed for the global market, with the participation of musicians who hardly ever perform in Cuba. Through its old-fashioned sounds and its celebration of elderly musicians, the album constructed a nostalgic representation of Cuban culture that fits flawlessly into the neo-colonial image of the island promoted by the tourist industry at the turn of the millennium.

With reference to MB, I emphasize how the international success of the album has provided the detractors of timba with a formidable tool, enabling them to construct a rhetorical opposition between 'traditional' son, as represented by *Buena Vista*, and contemporary Cuban dance music. I then examine how MB musicians have reacted to the backlash and the marginalization of dance music produced by the revivalist trend by realigning themselves under the new label of 'timba'. When in 1998 the leader of Los Van Van, Juan Formell, launched this term into the public – a term that had been in circulation among musicians and fans for years – he claimed that timba was 'the new generation of music [made] after the 1959 Revolution' (Martori 1998). With this strategic move, the leaders of Cuban dance music bands intended to challenge the equation between *Buena Vista* and national music, signalling their intention to fight their marginalization by the international record industry, and the cultural nationalist accusations which tried to position timba as a style foreign to the essence of Cuban culture.

The incredible level of controversy caused among Cuban musicians by the success of *Buena Vista* is registered here through extracts from interviews with two key actors of the rival factions, musicians José Luís Cortés and Juan de Marcos González. The violent tone of their polemics, to be sure, echoes their conflicting egos and artistic rivalries, but reflects also a timba vs. *Buena Vista* musical and political polarization which, while never explicitly articulated by the Cuban cultural establishment, was blatant in the musical environment of Havana at the close of the 1990s.

The contentious statements reported here convey a sense of the not-so-obvious shift of alliance between Cuban cultural producers and political institutions at the end of the decade. In the final part of the chapter, then, I widen my perspective and relate the boom of *Buena Vista* to the ideology of world music, looking at how the album has refocused and redefined the meaning of Cuban music for international audiences. While this has ostensibly created a novel global awareness about Cuban music, I argue that it has also contributed to reinforcing stereotyped representations eventually contributing to overshadow the activity of many contemporary Cuban musicians.

The 'rediscovery' of Cuban music

The success of the album *Buena Vista Social Club* represents one of the most singular and unpredictable musical phenomena of the last decade. Recorded in 1996 in Havana by a group of elderly Cuban musicians and produced by an independent world music label, the record has gone on to sell, to date, more than five million copies worldwide.[1] The album was originally conceived as a recording project, but has subsequently given birth to a real touring band, lent its title to an Oscar-nominated documentary, won a Grammy and acted as a brand name for a string of cognate bands and records. When I say 'brand name', I do not mean it in a purely metaphorical sense: 'Buena Vista Social Club' is today a registered trademark (®).

The album and the film have been hailed by the North American and European press as events of historical significance. In the words of one European journalist, 'living legends of Cuban music [have been]

---

[1] Figures reported by the World Circuit website, April 2002, <http://www.worldcircuit.co.uk/bvsc/framesetdisc.html>.

rediscovered by American Ry Cooder, who rescued them from oblivion and put them, under the name of *Buena Vista Social Club*, back into the history of music' (Tagliafico 1999). In the UK, the advert for the film reported the enthusiastic opinions of the British press: 'The album opened your ears – The film will touch your soul' (*The Times*), 'a warm, relaxed and colourful presentation of inspirational music makers' (*Time Out*), 'Moving and uplifting' (*Guardian*) (see Plate 30). At the end of 1999, the Anglophone press had published nearly 1000 articles on *Buena Vista* and proclaimed a 'Latin invasion' and a 'Cuban musical revolution' (Milward 1998; Boehlert 1999; Valdés-Rodríguez 1999).

For global audiences, the album has redefined the meaning of Cuban music. The promotional build-up of *Buena Vista* generated a picture of an island imbued with nostalgia, and of a city of grand, run-down buildings, industrial archaeology and exceptionally-gifted octogenarians. The talent of German director Wim Wenders, in particular, has produced a documentary of great persuasiveness, conferring on his vision of Cuba and its people a dimension that is at the same time intimate and epic.

Both the album and the film *Buena Vista*, however, have constructed an image that appears remote from the life of contemporary Cubans and the sound of today's Cuban music. While claiming to be bringing to light the true local music, they have presented the sounds of an era corresponding, more or less, to that of Woody Herman and Nat 'King' Cole. Many Cubans, indeed, know the songs of the album, which are ingrained in Cuban popular culture. But *Buena Vista* is a product for export: all the various bands who have toured the world under its star symbol play at home only occasionally, and mainly to foreign audiences. Even the Havana Social Club that gave its name to this colossal operation of branding has long since disappeared.

The album not only drew unprecedented attention to Cuban music, but also brought to the foreground world music, becoming a quasi-political symbol. *Buena Vista*, in fact, has led the 'music of the world' to its first real global crossover, showing how music that was not sung in English and was not part of dominant popular styles could be more than a niche genre, and make a break into the mainstream global music market. In so doing, it has made its music and artists into cultural and political icons. Its elderly musicians have become symbols of the resilience of Cuba, the David against the arrogance of the US Goliath, winning Cuba political sympathies worldwide.

The resonance of the album in the West, and in particular in the USA, has been such that *Buena Vista* has been seen as capable of bringing about changes in the international relationship between the USA and Cuba. In the late 1990s, the band gave a concert for diplomats at the UN headquarters in New York, and the film has been screened in the presence of the UN General Secretary Kofi Annan. According to a major international NGO, today 'Americans are more open than ever to Cuba .... What some have called the "Buena Vista Social Club syndrome" ... is a desire by many Americans to learn about Cuba, to visit Cuba, and one day, to trade goods with Cuba' (Oxfam America 2000).

The *Buena Vista* effect has been registered as well on the other side of the Florida Straits. According to a Cuban political analyst, in the last few years 'the image of Cuba in the US has been "thawing" .... Since 1998, achievements with a high impact on US public opinion – the visit of the Pope, the Elián trial, the phenomenon of *Buena Vista Social Club* – have generated a less monochromatic and sordid image of life in Cuba' (Hernández 2001). While the USA has continued to impose limitations on its citizens' travel and trade with the island, the resonance of *Buena Vista* has fed the forbidden fruit syndrome, enhancing Westerners' desire to visit the island of tropical communism before too late. Curiously, that (symbolical) blockade-breaking effect has been produced by an album that recreates the sound of Cuban music of the 1940s and 1950s, and is entirely focused on pre-revolutionary artists and repertoires.

The invention of *Buena Vista Social Club*

The most phenomenal success in Cuban music was created by chance. In March 1996 Nick Gold, the owner and manager of a small independent British record label called World Circuit, travelled to Havana to produce two albums. The first one was a project by Cuban *tres* player and leader of the revivalist band Sierra Maestra Juan de Marcos González, called the Afro-Cuban All Stars. The second one was intended as a collaboration between US guitarist Ry Cooder and Cuban and West African musicians. Just before starting the recording, the production team learned that the Africans could not make it to Cuba. They decided to arrange a different session with some of the musicians from the previous project, singer Compay Segundo and other elderly singers and musicians recruited in the Cuban capital. The album was to be produced by Cooder, known for his evocative film soundtracks and collaborations with non-Western musicians.

The *Buena Vista* session put together Cuban artists of different generations and backgrounds who had never previously played together. Compay Segundo (b. Francisco Repilado, 1907–2003) was a *trovador* and *tresero* (singer and player of *tres*), a former member of the duo Los Compadres, specializing in *canciones* (songs) and *sones*. Classically-trained pianist Rubén González (1919–2003) had played with the *conjunto* of Arsenio Rodríguez, the Riverside jazz band, and later with the Orquesta America of Enrique Jorrín, the inventor of cha-cha-cha. Ibrahím Ferrer (b. 1927) had been a singer with Pacho Alonso and Los Bocucos, a band that in the 1960s enjoyed a certain popularity with a new rhythm called *pilón*. Omara Portuondo (b. 1930) had been, between the 1950s and 1960s, part of vocal quartet Las D'Aida, specializing in *filin* and jazz-tinged *baladas*. Eliades Ochoa (b. 1946), the youngest member of the group, was a singer and guitarist specializing in traditional son, and leader of revivalist band Cuarteto Patria.

The World Circuit album was published in 1997, with a good press response but tepid initial sales (Boehlert 1999). The real boom of *Buena Vista* came two years later, with the release, in 1999, of a documentary with the same title, which generated enthusiastic reactions in the Western press (made after the album, the film actually told the story of a different record, Ferrer's solo album). The film offered a portrait of Cuban music that thrilled Western journalists, and achieved extraordinary popular success, obtaining an Oscar nomination and various film awards. In the wake of the film, the album rapidly climbed the charts. Spreading its popularity across the globe, its trademark reappeared on a series of albums and touring bands, whose musicians boasted their participation in the original recording. The *Buena Vista* concept, thus, extended as far as to include two CDs by R. González, two by the Afro-Cuban All Stars, plus the solo albums of Ibrahim Ferrer and Omara Portuondo, all marketed in the UK under the slogan '100% pure Cuban' (see Plate 31). Finally, a DVD of the film and a photographic book by the same Wenders (2000) made their appearance.[2]

An alien in Havana: the rocker as a revivalist

For Western audiences, much of the initial appeal of *Buena Vista* was certainly due to the popularity of its producer. A former rock guitarist who has played with the Rolling Stones, Cooder has carved himself a niche in the market of world music by producing a number of albums made in cooperation with non-Western musicians, such as the acclaimed *Talking Timbuktu*, recorded in 1994 with Malian guitarist Ali Farka Toure. This type of activity has earned Cooder an image as the-producer-as-music-explorer on a mission to save the endangered musics of the planet. Describing his way of working to a British journalist, he explained that he operates from home by listening to recordings of 'esoteric music' from all over the world. Then he tries to track down the musicians who

---

[2] For its *Buena Vista* products, World Circuit has produced stickers, a special CD rack and a poster of Wenders' film.

appear on the recordings ('if they are still alive') to work out with them a suitable project for a record (Williamson 1999b).

In the case of *Buena Vista*, the involvement of the US guitarist with Cuban music was mostly due to Nick Gold, with whom he had already produced Farka Toure's record in Mali. With Gold, Cooder shared a fascination for the old and bizarre and an attraction for acoustic archaeology, a moral and aesthetic attitude that led him to interpret his own work with third world musicians as an effort to save traditions. As he stated in the above interview,

> These old guys are going to disappear in a New York minute and we can't sit around moping about it. The sun is setting on these people.... Recording technology provided a storage medium for all these ideas and all this talent and it only happened from 1920 to 1965. That's the cut-off point.... Today you're not just talking records and it's no longer just a guy with a tape machine. We're going to be out on DVD and multi-cast on satellite feeds and no end of shit.
>
> (ibid.)

Cooder's postmodern quest for authenticity, attempts to preserve the past and contempt for modern technology are all elements that are central to the ideology of music revivalism. 'Revivals', writes Tamara Livingston, 'are both a reaction against and a product of modernity.' '[R]evivalists position themselves in *opposition* to aspects of the contemporary cultural mainstream ... and offer a cultural alternative in which legitimacy is grounded in reference to authenticity and historical fidelity' (1999: 81, 66). In his making of *Buena Vista*, in fact, Cooder was helped by Juan de Marcos González, who, as the leader of Sierra Maestra, had been himself previously involved in the job of saving 'Cuban traditional music' from extinction (Suárez Galván, interview with the author, 2000).

In the discourse of Cooder, the distortion produced by the low-tech equipment of the old Egrem studios in Central Havana has conferred on the sound of *Buena Vista* an archaic, pre-technological quality, a sort of acoustic authenticity mark that contrasts with the 'glassy sound' of modern US studios and 'jukebox music'. To this purpose, the US producer intentionally adopted the antiquated technique of recording with a few microphones, producing a sound that has been defined by Juan de Marcos González as 'roomy'. Through that nostalgic filter – which included not only sound but also the passé repertoire and the images of old musicians – the music of *Buena Vista* has come to represent a form of pre modern, pre-technological art emphatically opposed to today's music. Like many ageing rockers, Cooder appears to hold today's music in contempt and to perceive the sounds of the past as more real, tending to overlook the fact that it is often simply popular music made in a previous era.

Gold and Cooder's record productions, thus, have increasingly focused on the revival of obscure, retro sounds and, in the Cuban case, of artists presented to international audiences as forgotten musical heroes.[3] This has happened because the ideology of revival, with its constant calls to cultural authenticity, needs to root itself in an idealized image of the past. The anti-technological spirit articulated by the album and the producer's declarations have constructed an image of Cuban music, and society, opposed to modernity. The low-tech sound and the musicians' wrinkles have become metaphors, homologous with the cracks and faded revolutionary *murales* on the walls of Havana.

In the presence of such an operation of cultural marketing, we may ask ourselves if the dilemma posited by *Buena Vista* is one of authenticity or, rather, of *authentication*: 'who has the power to represent whom and to determine which representation is authoritative?' (Kirshenblatt-Gimblett and Bruner 1992: 304). When looked at from close up, the position of the US guitarist as cultural surfer vis-à-vis local music appears, to say the least, problematic. Like other musical projects marketed under the umbrella of world music, *Buena Vista* could be best described as a form of tourist art, a 'form of contemporary art produced locally for consumption by outsiders' and based on assumptions about the aesthetic expectations of the foreign market (Jules-Rosette 1984). In that sense, while tourism and travel represent a quest for adventure and the meeting with exotic Others, world music becomes 'sonic tourism' (Mitchell 1993) and its champion Ry Cooder the producer of a vicarious experience for armchair travellers.

The contradiction between diverging representations of local music sometimes becomes palpable in the ways that same music is contextualized and consumed by different audiences. In its repertoire, for example, the album *Buena Vista* contains various tunes that Cubans would not dance to and that have been marketed internationally as a type of music for listening to. According to an idea that conforms to an artistic view of popular music (and, conversely, of a non-artistic perception of dance music), the concerts of the *Buena Vista* bands have taken place in festivals, theatres and prestigious concert halls such as the Carnegie Hall in New York and the Royal Festival Hall in London. But because Western listeners tend to perceive Cuban music as the quintessence of dance music, they have often subverted the listening logic, ending up dancing near the stage during the concerts. This has produced a vision of Western audiences skipping around and waving

---

[3] Indeed, the whole production and image of world music labels such as World Circuit are constructed on the marketing of the 'ethnic', and particularly of the 'past ethnic', as a fashionable experience.

their arms aloft world music-fashion, in a bizarre but significant contrast to the tight dance routines visible at the Latin dance music shows patronized by 'ethnic' audiences (Perna 1999a).

The impact of *Buena Vista* in Cuba

Many of the articles on *Buena Vista* published by the European and North American press have taken for granted the narrative of discovery suggested by Wenders' film, World Circuit's press material and Cooder's interviews. The tale of Cooder as the music explorer, travelling to Cuba and rescuing artists forgotten and living in poverty has become an integral part of the rhetoric of the album. Here, some questions become necessary. What exactly was the role of Cooder in the making of the record? And who are the artists who were discovered by him?

To those who listen to the album, it soon becomes evident that the musical role played by the US guitarist in the recording is rather modest. His input is generally limited to glissandos which surface across the album and seem to signal, like notes of *theremin* in an old science fiction film, the landing of the alien on unknown musical territories. According to his A&R Juan de Marcos González, 'It's not as the movie says, that Ry came to Havana and started looking for the musicians. Ry had never listened to Cuban music, and knew nothing about it' (interview with the author, 1999). In his view, the contribution of Cooder to *Buena Vista* essentially consists of the decision to adopt the recording technique that enabled him to produce a 'vintage' sound.

> He had the idea of recording like they did in the 1940s [sic]. He is a rock 'n' roll musician, and this is how they used to record rock 'n' roll: [with] two ambient microphones ... producing a sound that resulted very attractive to Europeans. A record like *Buena Vista* has no mystery for Cubans, because in Cuba we have 150 *Buena Vista* every day. But it has a special mystery and magic for non-Cubans. The main contribution of Ry has been in the concept of sound, in the recording and in the mixing of the album. Although I am a producer and a musician myself, it would have never occurred to me to make a record with that kind of sound, with that *roomy* feeling.
>
> (ibid.)

When González stated that the sound of *Buena Vista* had no particular interest for Cubans, he did that in order to belittle the role of Cooder. But he probably, if unwillingly, told the truth. At the apogee of its international boom, the impact of *Buena Vista* in Cuba was hard to perceive. On arrival in Havana, music-conscious visitors discovered that *Buena Vista* and similar internationally successful 'traditionalist' bands did not exist in Cuba. At the end of the 1990s, the record was not heard on radios nor available in shops, and the film was not visible in any Cuban cinema. Visitors would have found, though, that 'traditional' music as played by *cuartetos*, *sextetos* and *septetos* abounded in bars and restaurants in colonial Old Havana. Even today, those who visit Cuba quickly realize that, beyond affection and national pride, for many Cubans the music of Compay Segundo and Ibrahím Ferrer has no particular significance. As a Cuba musician once told me, the now dead Compay 'was a fossil from another era' (Kemell, interview with the author, 1998).

The answer to the other question, that on the identity of the artists discovered by *Buena Vista*, is provided by the lack of familiarity with Latin American music of Western journalists and listeners. The mythology of the album is entirely constructed around the fundamental cultural misunderstanding that has made something that was perfectly known to local audiences appear as new and exotic to international audiences. Cubans well knew Omara and Compay. Moreover, the latter had already been 'rediscovered' in Spain at the beginning of the 1990s, in the course of another Cuban revival that had produced the Vieja Trova Santiaguera. In a way, that band of elderly musicians invented in Spain represented the first attempt at the marketing of Cuban music of the past, later triumphantly carried out by Gold and Cooder.

The tale of discovery of *Buena Vista* was unfair, as well, to Latin Americans, who had long been acquainted with Cuban music and could hardly consider genres such as bolero and son as new and exotic. The marketing of *Buena Vista*, in fact, appears to have totally bypassed Latin American audiences and concentrated on the 'world music' segment of the market, and a very specific cultural and ethnic consumer profile. In the words of one US Latino journalist:

> According to Monica Ricardez, Latin music buyer for the Tower Records chain in the Los Angeles area, the typical Buena Vista Social Club consumer is a Caucasian between 35 and 55 who has heard about the album through the Wenders' documentary, public radio or newspapers. This assessment was echoed by several other retail specialists.
>
> (Valdés-Rodríguez 1999)

The familiarity of Cuban listeners with *Buena Vista* type music explains why the album, aside from surprise, has not particularly impressed Cuban audiences, as even some foreign journalists have admitted (Erlich 1999). On the island, the record has been received with scepticism by music critics, amazement by the general public and absolute indifference by the youth, who mostly listen to MB, soul and rap. According to Cuban writer Leonardo Padura Fuentes (1998), the album was 'nothing more than a lucky compilation of famous tunes from the island's repertoire, well performed, but without the brilliance that many of them enjoyed in their original recording'. Music writer Helio Orovio, on his part, has remarked how the *onda retro* (revival) of Cuban music has been launched not by Cubans, but by outsiders who came to comb the island for music of the past. 'Thus', he commented, 'they have found Rubén González who had already retired and have recycled him, Pío Leyva, Ibrahím Ferrér, Raúl Planas, Laíto Sureda, old men (*viejítos*) already retired, and have recycled them all' (interview with the author, 1999).

One of the implications of the narrative of discovery of *Buena Vista* is that, before the landing of Ry Cooder in Havana, Cubans had been unable to value their own traditions and had ignored their own musical treasures. Reversing the argument, one might say that these audiences still have to come to terms with the phenomenon of music revivals so typical of consumption in the late-industrial world. The diffidence, or the indifference, of many Cubans towards the international excitement surrounding *Buena Vista* reveals their difficulty in understanding why people who were in their prime as much as forty, fifty, and even seventy years ago were suddenly being hailed as the novelty of Cuban music. How was it possible that Western audiences had been captured by such an old, un-cool type of music, which lacked the appeal, the hipness and sensuality of contemporary music?

In effect, the various *Buena Vista*-branded bands seen around the globe at the turn of the new millennium did not have a local audience, but were ad hoc groups with shifting personnel, set up for international tours. In Cuba they have played only sporadically and mainly to foreign audiences. Their musicians worked in other bands.

> Q: Do you play in Cuba as the Afro-Cuban All Stars, or as individual musicians?
> (J.d.M. González) Every musician plays with his own band.... However, we did very few performances, because I don't have time and I have a lot of international work.... until recently we had too much work and it was impossible to play in Cuba. Now we are going to start to play a bit more in Cuba, because people need to know better the essence of this work ....
> So we are going to perform in Cuba to promote the work that has been so popular in Europe and US, and we're going to be successful.
> (interview with the author, 1999)

Contortions of musical nationalism

The international success of *Buena Vista*, in any case, found in Cuba a delighted reception among the intellectual milieu opposed to the commercialism and the 'excesses' of dance music, and in the political circles who interpreted the economic reforms as a threat to the survival of the revolution. As Livingston has observed, revivalism often joins forces with nationalism. In the polarized debate of the island, the pre-modern spirit of *Buena Vista* has been co-opted into the anti-US, anti-imperialistic discourse, and employed to emphasize the national element of Cuban culture in opposition to the xenophile and 'deviant' attitudes of timba audiences and musicians.

At the end of the millennium, the political-cultural positions on matters of music, therefore, were polarized around two extremes: on one side Cuban 'traditional' music as represented by *Buena Vista*, on the other *música bailable*, the music most popular with Cubans under-40. The supporters of *Buena Vista* have put forward arguments of cultural nationalism, claiming that the album represented the rebirth of traditional music, the essence of true Cuban culture. Describing the record as a work of 'historical' relevance, the cultural magazine *El Caimán Barbudo* wrote, 'Ry Cooder's attention to Cuban music ... is of incalculable value' (Rojas Gutiérrez 1998).[4] In Juan de Marcos González's words, 'the music of contemporary Cuban youth has moved very close to US music ... national identity was disappearing' (interview with the author, 1999). The traditionalist front has advocated the identification of its positions with son, considered the national style par excellence. In the words of a local journalist, 'Buena Vista Social Club is a rising star in the broad cultural heavens and a serious warning to all those who have tried to push this people's manifestation, the Cuban Son, into oblivion' (Godfried 2000).

Various articles published by the Cuban press in the late 1990s constructed an opposition between the World Circuit album and contemporary Cuban dance music. Reporting on the filming of the *Buena Vista* documentary, one journalist wrote:

> while Wim Wenders was filming in Ibraín [sic] Ferrer's humble home, on Radio Taíno a popular ex-salsero, now called *timbero*, was talking of old and new music, of obsolete formulas and contemporary experimentation. It is unfair – he says – to try to reject dance music that today enjoys the audience's preference in Cuba. To give way to old formulas predating the boom of today's orchestras, that is: what fills (and saturates) radio and TV. It is symptomatic – he concludes – that the Grammy should be won by an album of old music with a sound that predates 1959.
>
> (Ariel 1998)

The author of the article went on to congratulate the elderly musicians of *Buena Vista*, who had been forgotten for years 'all in favour of *salsa* or *timba*, which gave the final blow to that *old*, *obsolete*, *past* music' (ibid.; italics in original). The statement served its polemic purpose, but was not upheld by historical evidence, because the blow to that type of Cuban

---

[4] The article was a riposte to an article on Cuban timba written by Spanish journalist D.A. Manrique for *El País*.

music did not come from timba at all. The decline of traditional son, in fact, had already started in the 1940s, and continued after the revolution. As musicologist A. León wrote in 1982, 'At present son is seldom heard, but has been assimilated into other genres and is present in them' (León 1982: 245). The same can be said for the jazz band tradition to which pianist Rubén González belonged, a format associated with the Batista regime and white middle-class audiences that had declined in the 1960s. If anything, a new interest in Afro-Cuban dance music, to which son belongs, had been fed by the salsa boom of the 1980s, which fuelled a dance craze among the youth after MB had been declining throughout the 1970s (see Chapter 1).

In the presence of the naïve use of concepts such as cultural identity and tradition, some specifications become necessary. Strictly speaking, despite all its promotional build up, *Buena Vista* is not an album of son, but an eclectic collection of styles and artists. Together with *sones* such as 'El cuarto de tula', its repertoire includes as well *son guajiro* ('El carretero'), bolero ('Dos Gardenias') and instrumental danzón, all styles with different origins, affiliations and audiences. Son guajiro, described as a sort of 'fake country music' (Manuel et al. 1995), is a nostalgic idealization of rural life by urban white singers. Bolero is a type of slow-tempo, romantic song with jazz-tinged harmonies and poetically-inflected lyrics, of Cuban origin but largely internationalized throughout Latin America. In its representation of a 'tradition', *Buena Vista*, thus appears as a highly heterogeneous product not only in its musicians, but first and foremost in its repertoire.

The music of *Buena Vista* is also not so nationally-made as the use of a label such as 'traditional' would lead one to presume. In its 'authentic' form rhetorically celebrated by the discourses that have accompanied the album, son is already the result of cultural hybridizations that took place in the early decades of the twentieth century. As I pointed out in Chapter 4, the first *sones* consisted of the choral repetition of a refrain alternating with a contrasting tune sung by a singer. The elegant melodies of Matamoros and Piñeiro which are today brought as the model for the tradition of Cuban son are, in reality, the result of a process of adaptation of Afro-Cuban son to the dominant taste of the 1920s and 1930s, when this incorporated a narrative part close to Spanish *canción*.

In trying to analyse the specific national weight of Cuban music, finally, we must pay attention to the impact made in Cuba by international (and especially US) music in the first half of the 20th century, and to the important position acquired by Cuban music on the international market in the same period. Several Cuban musicians took an active role in the evolution of US jazz, and jazz bands have been operating in Cuba since the 1920s (Grenet 1939).[5] All this means a prolonged foreign stylistic contribution to Cuban music, which sometimes makes it difficult, if not futile, to discriminate between what is national and what is not. Foreign influence is evident in the tradition of Cuban dance big bands, and in the style of pianists such as Rubén González, one of the stars of *Buena Vista*. As the producers of World Circuit's Cuban recordings have themselves repeatedly stressed, both *Buena Vista* and the albums of the Afro-Cuban All Stars have been attempts to recreate the 'magic sound' of Cuban music of the 1940s and 1950s (J.d.M. González, interview with the author, 1999; Arcos 2000).

The mobilization of 'traditional' son to support the Cuban cultural nationalist contention may be regarded as an attempt at constructing a theatricalization and fetishization of the past in an 'effort to simulate an origin, a founding substance' (García Canclini 1989: 117). 'Precisely because cultural heritage presents itself as alien to the debates on modernity', García Canclini writes, 'it represents the less suspect resource to secure social complicity' (ibid.: 115). He continues:

> This set of traditional goods and practices which identify ourselves as a nation or a people is valued as a gift, something we have received from the past with such a symbolic prestige that it becomes irrefutable.... Their permanence makes them imaginable as possessing an unquestionable value, and makes them into sources of collective consensus, beyond the divisions into the classes, ethnicities and groups that split society.
>
>   ibid.: 115–16

In regard to the other end of the argument, finally, it is important to stress how the accusations of xenophilia levelled by traditionalists at timba were only partially true, and for at least two reasons. First, because, as we have seen, contemporary Cuban dance music borrows widely from Afro-Cuban traditional music and culture. And second, because the most important foreign influences in timba are those of music like jazz, funk, salsa and rap, that is, styles produced by black subcultures in the Afro-American diaspora, under conditions extremely similar to those that gave rise to son. The problem with contemporary Cuban dance music, it seems, is that it does not lend itself to being easily circumscribed in geo-cultural terms or neatly identified as the representative of a tradition. In other words, its problem is that of striving to be a modern music and to resist folklorized representations, thus dissolving the image of cultural and ethnic homogeneousness, the illusion of pacification and social harmony on which *Buena Vista* stands.

---

[5] The writer Alejo Carpentier, author of a major book on Cuban music, for example, is acknowledged as the first jazz critic in Cuba (Acosta 1986).

Son vs. timba and *Buena Vista* vs. Team Cuba

Within the extremely high level of conflict and contention created by the success of *Buena Vista* among Cuban musicians, the supporters of *música bailable*, for their part, have attacked the album as a product of international marketing alien to local taste. Presenting themselves as the musical children of the revolution, MB musicians have blamed traditionalists for promoting a type of music – and, perhaps, of ideology – that was pre-revolutionary.

Many MB musicians, to say the least, have found it difficult to understand the reasons for the enormous international attention solicited by the album, and to accept the rhetorical opposition between old and modern Cuban music. According to black record producer Joaquím Betancourt, for example,

> [t]here is a very interesting phenomenon in the world, with the *onda retro*. Cuban music cannot be unaffected by that. This trend of traditional music [i.e., *Buena Vista*] is also the product of *onda retro* .... But I think it absurd to say that that is the authentic Cuban music. There is a lot of traditional music, including music made before people such as Compay Segundo or Matamoros .... You can't just say that that music is the true Cuban music: it is as authentic a Cuban music as contemporary music and other types of good music are.
>
> (interview with the author, 1999)

Several young musicians have felt that the space given to old Cuban music by Western promoters and record companies because of the *Buena Vista* effect has been unfair. In their view, the revivalist trend has privileged a type of music already past and dead, misleading international audiences. As the leader of one dance band put it,

> Cuban music hasn't stopped in the 1940s, as most people think, 'Guantanamera' and so on. Cuban music has evolved a lot .... People over here [UK] are 40 or 50 years back in relation to contemporary Cuban music. They should listen more to contemporary production, and those who are promoting Cuban traditional music should think about investing money into new things, into the development of music.
>
> (Kemell, interview with the author, 1998)

Not surprisingly, some of the harshest criticisms of *Buena Vista* have come from the leader of NG Las Banda, José Luís Cortés, who has repeatedly blamed the Western press for their support of the project. 'I do not understand why somebody who has played with The Rolling Stones [i.e. Ry Cooder] goes to Cuba and plays with musicians that are neither very good nor feature in the great records of Cuban music. The result is a mediocre and false work' (Manrique 1998a). In our interview, he expanded on the subject:

Q: In Europe the success of *Buena Vista* has promoted a different image of
Cuban music [from timba]. You have criticized the project ...
Cortés: No, I haven't criticized anything, I've told the truth. Those who
have criticized the project have been you, the journalists, who misunder-
stood the meaning of *Buena Vista* in front of the world. *Buena Vista* is a
meeting of musicians now extinct in Cuba. They are not part of the
market, they are musicians from the Republic, from the 1920s, 1930s.
Compay Segundo is 92 years old. And all [the others] are 70 years old.
They are out of date, they are relics.... you can't use this to crush the
others. I have read interviews and articles in Western papers saying that in
Cuba there is no music, and that they had to chase down these old people
because the revolution had not produced [new] musicians. In France, they
went as far as saying that *Buena Vista* is the new Cuban music, the Cuban
music that has revolutionized Europe. This is where I have argued ....
I simply said that Ry Cooder came to Cuba with a lot of imagination (and,
by the way, paying very little money), put together musicians who didn't
even have a job, and projected them very well, looked for the right type of
marketing, put money into it, marketed the record all over the world,
made a movie. Clearly, for 40 years nothing had come out of Cuba with
such a strength, [and] because the product was well marketed people
received it well. But not because it is better than what people are doing
now .... Nor [because it] is more representative of our times. Cuba has
had its own musical development, a very big one. It is this approach that
confuses those who say: 'Look, those old Cuban musicians, hell!, a big
hand for them! We must help them, they must live another thousand years
making their music!' But you cannot say that that is the only music they
make in Cuba, or the new project of Cuban music. That is a lie. That music
has already been played by Matamoros, Ñico Saquito, Ignacio Piñeiro,
Benny Moré, old people who are all dead now.... There isn't one single
original tune, they are all by dead people.

(interview with the author, 2000)

For his part, asked to comment on Cortés's criticisms, Juan de Marcos
González has given a reply that reveals the level of animosity generated
among musicians by *Buena Vista*:

Q: What do you think of the hostility to *Buena Vista* expressed by some
Cuban dance musicians, such as J. L. Cortés?
It's total nonsense. This is something that often happens with some of these
young musicians .... They find it painful to accept that the work they have
been doing throughout their life hasn't been acknowledged by anybody,
and that some oldies, who were starving until a while ago, are now
successful.... some musicians, such as Cortés, have a very good academic
background, and think that son is simple, and because it has no
complexity, think it's a lesser music, therefore inferior. I think it's an
absolutely stupid view.

(interview with the author, 1999)

At a musical level, *Buena Vista* has inspired various attempts by
traditionalist outfits old and new to ride the global retro wave. Despite
their relative success on the international circuit, these bands have not

gained much favour with local audiences. Juan de Marcos González's former band Sierra Maestra, for example, who have done pioneering work in the revival of Cuban music of the past, in practice continue to play mainly abroad. According to their present leader,

> The success of *Buena Vista* has had no repercussions in Cuba. People heard that they won a Grammy, as they heard all over the world, but young people have not yet absorbed (*interiorizado*) that fact, they have not appropriated it.... The *Buena Vista* phenomenon has been a very separate [i.e. isolated] phenomenon, perhaps because it was not a band, it was a selection of singers and individuals, and maybe for that reason it did not stick as it should have. The reality is that in Cuba with *Buena Vista* nothing has happened.
>
> (Suárez Galván, interview with the author, 2000)

Faced with the rise of *Buena Vista* on the international market on one side, and the moralization campaign on the other, MB musicians have tried to strike back by launching a novel music alliance, and a new label for their own style. In January 1998, top Cuban bandleaders and singers met with Juan Formell at La Tropical, and decided to overcome their legendary rivalries by joining forces to form an all-star band named Team Cuba. Commenting on the event, Formell declared:

> Here we are summing up 30 years of work, sacrifices, and struggling against all the prejudices, the lack of understanding and the attacks of the market.... for the music that we make today in Cuba, the time for going everywhere and singing 'La Guantanamera' or the 'Son de la loma' is part of the past; we do not deny those classics, [but] our work has as much merit as theirs, and must be known all over the world.
>
> (Henry 1998)

Under the slogan 'Somos lo que hay' ('We are what there is', one of El Mèdico's catchphrases), Team Cuba gave a concert in February 1998 in Varadero. On that occasion, the band featured Juan Formell, José Luís Cortés, Manolín 'El Médico', Paulíto FG, Issac Delgado and Adalberto Alvarez, plus singers and musicians from their respective bands, under the musical direction of Joaquím Betancourt. In May, Team Cuba gave a performance in Central Havana, featuring as well David Calzado. The concert took place in the square facing the neoclassic Capitolio, before an audience of 70 000 people and in the presence of figures of international Latin music such as US entrepreneur Ralph Mercado (Galilea 1998a).[6] Under the same name, the alliance undertook a European tour in summer 1998, with major timba concerts held in France and Spain.

---

[6] The concert was sponsored by Spanish SGAE and took place at exactly the same time as another music event sponsored by SGAE, the Havana International Guitar Festival. The cultural elite, presumably, was not at the Capitolio.

The unprecedented coalition of Team Cuba coincided with the launch of the term 'timba'. As discussed in Chapter 4, the word had been circulating underground among musicians and fans for years. Its public adoption was strategic for several reasons. It would help to avoid the negative connotations of salsa, signal the specific, national and black character of contemporary Cuban MB and gain media exposure by marking its own distance from international Latin music. As one Cuban journalist reported, Formell

> insists that Cubans are dancing differently now, and that he is promoting the use of the term 'timba' because of the new circumstances. 'There was a moment when we had to accept the word "salsa" because of the international situation. At that time we were on the defensive, but now we're on the offensive and we can say, "No, that's not what we do. We're somewhere between traditional son and salsa."' 'Is the use of this new term strategic?' 'We dance and play differently and we didn't have a name for it,' he responds, 'and yes, by combining our artistic criteria we're going to enter the market. It's a new initiative and it needs a new name, timba, a musical name like rumba or conga.'
>
> (Castañeda 1998b)

In a way, Team Cuba was almost as heterogeneous as *Buena Vista*, because it put under the same umbrella bands and artists of different generations and with rather distinct attitudes to MB. Older bands such as Los Van Van and Adalberto Alvarez y su Son, for example, found it a means of rejuvenating their own image with young audiences, and projecting themselves as the progenitors of timba. Conversely, sharing the stage with these prestigious, established names of MB represented for young musicians such as Paulíto and El Médico a chance for authentication as legitimate heirs in the lineage of Cuban popular music.

Interestingly, not all contemporary MB bands whose music stylistically falls under the rubric of timba employ such a label for their own music. Presumably because of the institutional hostility towards salsa and timba, and the rejuvenation of son induced by *Buena Vista*, some dance musicians have tactically adopted the term 'son'. In my interviews in 1999, for example, Manolíto Simonet and Giraldo Piloto (see Plates 15 and 16) respectively defined their own music as 'son cubano' and 'son progresívo' ('progressive son'). Other musicians have revealed a somewhat more ambiguous attitude: Adalberto Alvarez, who in Cuba is popularly known by the nickname 'gentleman of son' ('El caballero del son'), claims to be a *sonero* and distances himself from salsa and timba, but has taken part in the Team Cuba initiative.[7] Contemporary MB

---

7 As Cortés so concisely puts it, Alvarez has to do timba as well 'because otherwise he would starve' (Sarusky 1999). On the vacillations of Alvarez, see Pérez 1997 and Cantor 1999c.

musicians, therefore, appear to make tactical use of the term 'son'. By presenting themselves as representatives of a quintessentially national style, they seek to capture the attention of the international market and avoid ostracism on a national level.

With its resounding success, the Team Cuba event did not please the critics of timba. According to the magazine *Juventud Rebelde*, the Team did not include all the truly representative names of Cuban music and had clear 'commercial motivations' (Acosta Llerena 1998). Radio journalist Eugene Godfried, a vocal advocate of traditional son, suggested that the launching of the timba label was an attempt to preserve an economic and artistic dominant position unfairly acquired in the early years of the *período especial*.

> The promoters of Cuban Salsa were definitely taught serious lessons [by *Buena Vista*], but they remain persistent. Their urgent objective became to seek new ways and forms to try and safeguard the privileged positions they had obtained through selective preferential treatments and mechanisms granted to them by different entities within the state apparatus. Consequently, they attempted to carry out a name change for their production. No longer were they Cuban Salseros producing Cuban salsa, but now they out of the blue became 'Timberos' playing 'timba'.
>
> (Godfried 2000)

Godfried went on to explain that timba bands were 'nothing more than "crisis groups"' (ibid.). To put it concisely, in other words, he said that in the improved economic environment of the late 1990s, dance music was no longer necessary to the economy. If that was true, then, one must presume that the 'excesses' of timba, and its contiguity with the underworld in the early years of the *período especial*, were perfectly known to the Cuban establishment.

From the other side of the ideological barricade, El Tosco bluntly stated that 'the "Team Cuba" of salsa was a success, despite the fact that many Cuban entities wanted to defeat the movement of dance music in our country, and continuously tried to make it stumble' ('Nueva salsa cubana . . .', 1999). Drummer and bandleader Giraldo Piloto observed as well,

> thanks to the success of the oldies of La Vieja Trova Santiaguera, Compay Segundo, *Buena Vista Social Club*, a movement in favour of that music has developed. There are journalists who think that timba is going to end, it will not last. Timba will always remain. It would only disappear if the Cuban youth in a club were dancing to the music of *Buena Vista*, to traditional music, but that does not happen . . . . There is a double image of Cuban music.
>
> (interview with the author, 1999)

The existence of a large-scale offensive against MB was confirmed by Helio Orovio, the author of the *Dictionary of Cuban Music*.

Commenting in 1999 on a national music award given to a Cuban singer, he said:

> Now we are at a stage where they need to lessen a bit the diffusion of salsa and timba, and therefore they need to promote refined, elegant types of *canción*. The giving of the Cubadisco award to Miriam Ramos was not an innocent act: a fine, exquisite, intellectual singer with refined songs from the international repertoire accompanied by a concert pianist. Two years ago, they would have given the prize to timba made by El Médico or Paulito. Such is the fickleness of those who try to direct popular taste.
>
> (interview with the author, 1999)[8]

In the same period, the intervention of a black journalist at a music seminar in Havana expressively captured the irritation of many Cubans at the bizarre international success of the revivalist trend.

> Why Americans, foreigners must dictate my tastes? ... I don't care about the oldies: they are geriatric glories ... but I like Paulito FG. Why should they impose those old people on me? I want to hear what José Luís Cortés is doing. I like and respect Compay Segundo, 'Chan Chan', but I want to listen to Van Van, NG, Paulito.... to respect our ancestors [that's fine], but hey!, we need to live today, because it is very *sabroso*! To listen to 'Longina', but also to 'Cabeza mala'!
>
> (Pérez 1999)[9]

The final years of the 1990s, therefore, were characterized by a great deal of semiotic warfare, aimed at defining who were the depository of the authentic national expression. By allegedly rescuing Cuban 'traditional' music, *Buena Vista* enabled son to be mobilized by cultural nationalists in a process of re-articulation of Cuban identity. *Timberos* reacted by trying to establish themselves as the legitimate heirs of Cuban music, using the label 'timba' in retro-active fashion. In various interviews, Formell claimed that timba was the name of dance music made in Cuba after 1959.[10] In a somewhat contorted argument that implied that timba was the new music made under the revolution, he tried to push the cultural establishment to stand by timba, and to reject *Buena Vista* as a type of pre-revolutionary music and foreign-induced phenomenon. As David Calzado put it commenting on the success of World Circuit's

---

[8] Miriam Ramos (b. 1946) is a Cuban white singer with a varied repertoire made of traditional tunes, *nueva trova* and international songs.

[9] Pérez records N. Robinson in discussion at the Cubadisco 1999 Music Seminar, Havana, May 1999. The speaker was referring to one of Van Van's hits, 'Te pone la cabeza mala'.

[10] In his words, 'The cultivators of Cuban popular dance music after 1959 have never been *salseros* nor traditional *soneros*, but they have played a new musical rhythm they now call timba.... Timba can be defined ... as the new generation of music [produced] after the 1959 Revolution' (Martori 1998).

album, 'What bugs me is the subliminal message that what has come since the revolution is worthless' (Llewellyn 1999c).

Cuban music as world music

The most visible impact of *Buena Vista* has been that produced in the international arena, where its worldwide popularity has completely redefined the meaning of Cuban music for global listeners. Previously virtually unknown to international audiences, today the music of Cuba is inextricably tied to the images of the elderly musicians, of cigar-smoking, panama-hat wearing Compay Segundo, of crumbling Havana lashed by ocean waves. Isn't that a wonderful tourist advert? I read the publicity for a record of Cuban music recently published in Europe. Quoting the ever-present Compay, Omara and Ibrahím, the ad reiterates the old clichés of Latin music: 'a sunny, joyous, magic CD, like the environment which has given birth to its sounds'.[11]

In a way, Cooder's work on Cuban music has reconstructed the exotic stereotypes that world music had initially tried, or professed to try, to dispel. The representation of Cuban music and culture projected by the album, in effect, is far from the hybrid and postmodern image of world music hailed a decade ago by academic writers (for example Feld 1995; Goodwin and Gore 1995) and from the 'global village' rhetoric of creolization promoted by many world music festivals. One might say that *Buena Vista* has actually made a crucial contribution to the restoration of a retro mythology, aimed at inducing a sort of cult of kitsch in the Western viewer-listener – something that is cool because it is not fashionable and solicits emotional participation while it distances itself from it. Paraphrasing Walter Benjamin, it is the art of the global *flâneur*.

The success of *Buena Vista* seems to have been due to that ability to navigate between the two polarities of world music, the ethnic and the postmodern, without identifying entirely with either of them. The album does not contain folkloric music, nor a combination of this with Western pop and rock. But it presents fundamental features of both, that is, an aura of authenticity mixed with an element of novelty, which consists not in a modern fusion but in a marked reference to the past. Both the marketing of the record and the revivalist discourses of Ry Cooder constantly appeal to the *difference* embodied by Cuban sounds and artists of the past as a stamp of authenticity. Opposed to the artificiality of today's music, these discourses intentionally ignore the fact that the

---

[11] *I Viaggi di Repubblica* (supplement to *La Repubblica*, no. 258, 30 January 2003). Significantly, the advert was published in the daily's travel magazine.

repertoire of the album is nothing but old popular music, that is, something which, by definition, is produced by the industrialization of music and does not pre-exist it (Frith 1988). When Compay Segundo and Rubén González were young, Cuban music was already highly industrialized, it dominated the Latin American market and Cuba was able to export mambo and cha-cha-cha all over the world.

Shortly before the global 'discovery' of Cuban music, Deborah Pacini Hernández (1998) claimed that Cuban popular music had benefited from the expansion of world music in the 1990s, entering the world music market thanks to its 'African' character, as opposed to other, more watered-down types of Afro-Latin music such as salsa. The recent success of *Buena Vista* and of Cuban music of the past, and the correlated marginalization of timba, I argue, show exactly the opposite. While the latter has proved far too complex and controversial (too black, perhaps?) to break into a market hungry for colourful sounds and catchy tunes, the former perfectly falls into the laid-back, joyous clichés of third world 'traditional' music.

One of the arguments often put forward in discussions on *Buena Vista* is that the success of the album has led an international focus on Cuba, eventually benefiting all the music and culture of the island. The argument is plausible, but can be easily overturned. In the first place, the success of the album has not materially broken the US economic embargo, which still stands and largely keeps the international music industry away from Cuba. Furthermore, it has produced such an overexposure of Cuban music – or, better, of what the international music industry presumes Cuban music is – that it has virtually saturated the interest of Western media. This opinion is largely shared by Nick Gold, the man who masterminded the monster hit of world music (Gurza 2001).

It is clear that the criticism formulated of one album cannot be transferred in bulk to all world music, a wild and contradictory but not necessarily conservative array of artists and styles. But the importance of the Cuban case must not be underestimated – not only for its quantitative impact, but also and especially for the persuasiveness of the ideology that has fed it, and that reveals the paternalism and ambiguity often lying behind projects ostensibly favourable to local music. The paradox lies in the fact that, while placing itself as an emphatically pro-third world genre, such world music entirely founds its aesthetics and ethics on fictions of authenticity, on reduced views of the concept of 'local' and cultural identity. A territorialized music for the international market, it presupposes a world neatly divided into Third and First, periphery and centre, them and us. By constantly referring to difference, such an idea of world music ends up reproducing it, eventually becoming more a tool for marketing otherness and channelling cultural stereotypes than a means for improving the understanding of and communication with other cultures (Perna 2002b).

Apparently, the success of world music in its 'traditional' script seems to represent a victory of local styles on cultural imperialism, juxtaposing their vitality with the attempt to impose on the world a homogenized, transnational culture. This evocation of cultural imperialism repeatedly surfaces in the discourses of Cooder, Wenders and the Cuban ideologues of *Buena Vista*. In fact, that success imposes a type of music which is precisely the product of artificial divisions of the world and of false dialectic between local and global. Built on attributions of genuineness which are founded on the past, these divisions imply a concept of cultural identity that is 'highly suspect ... often nostalgic and/or reactionary' (N. Garnham, in Laing 1986). The success of *Buena Vista* has proved that difference can be not only marketable, but also highly lucrative. While transnational music corporations look with interest, in the literal sense, at artists from marginal countries, the recent case of Cuban music shows how small is not always good, and indie not necessarily better than major.

The boom of *Buena Vista* has presented a phenomenal promotional opportunity for Cuba and (perhaps) for all Cuban music. Blaming the album for its success would therefore be absurd, and unfair to its participants. But it cannot be denied that Cooder and Gold's project has produced a reduced and domesticated vision of a society that today is crossed by terrible tensions. From the film and the album, Cuba has emerged as an uncontaminated site of human purity, protected from the evils of capitalism and globalization. While one may indeed object to the cruelty (and ineffectiveness) of the US embargo on Cuba, one also wonders whether the revivalist, nostalgic picture painted by the *Buena Vista* discourse can be the best way to do justice to the vitality of Cuban contemporary culture, and to the Cuban people's legitimate aspirations to escape poverty and underdevelopment.

The *Buena Vista* affair, perhaps, exposes some unsolvable contradictions implicit in the notion of world music. Regarded as a progressive area of music marketing, by its very nature, world music cannot disentangle itself from an ambiguous mediating role between different cultures, countries and markets. Who discovers what? Who holds the right to validate local cultures? What are the aesthetical and political implications of the promotion of 'traditional' music? In our case, a sample of music of the past, supposedly authentic and superior to Westernizing contemporary music, has been co-opted into a neo-colonial representation of Cuba as a romantic, cool holiday destination. Meanwhile, 'Westernized' local music has kept on singing stories of life in the barrio that the global public has not been able, and perhaps is not even willing, to hear.

Livingston has suggested that 'revivalist ideologies tend to be constructed on certain modes of thinking and structuring of experience that are shared by middle class people in consumer-capitalist and socialist societies' (1999: 66). *Buena Vista*, in effect, signalled the convergence of the anti-consumer culture ethos of world music and the anti-capitalistic (ultimately, anti-US) ethos of the detractors of timba. Such a multi-purpose function – its nature as tourist art and its possible role in a nationalistic agenda – has been cynically suggested by Juan de Marcos González, who has been proved to know well the ideological machinery of world music:

> *Buenavista* [sic] ... has been made in order to take out of their alienation the citizens of the first world, who are totally crushed by the high technology of a developed society which creates problems that are more existential than economic.... Many people now want to smoke Cuban cigars, dance to son or salsa, come to Havana to have an affair with a *negrita* (or a *negrito*), and get drunk around Old Havana. T-shirts and posters of Che Guevara are sold in great quantity, and all [this] points at a rediscovery of our possibilities and values.... There is a present revivalist trend which perfectly fits Cuban son, which, furthermore, holds the magic of the exotic, tropical little island.
>
>   (Padrón Nodarse 1998: 34–7)

Conclusions

In the different political climate of the late 1990s, and after the ban on La Charanga Habanera and the moralization wave, the emergence of *Buena Vista* signalled a substantial cultural and musical shift, both at home and abroad. At home, it further cornered dance musicians into 'traditional' representations of local culture, which were mobilized in favour of nationalist discourses, and unleashed violent polemics between opposite musical fronts. On the international side, the success of the revivalist album rapidly deflected the seminal interest shown by the international music industry for contemporary Cuban music towards traditional music (whatever that might mean).

Produced by a foreign record company, *Buena Vista*, by creating a string of successful bands and albums, has generated substantial economic returns for Cuba. Without any doubt, however, its bigger dividends have been political. Together with the film, the album has promoted on the international arena an image of Cuban culture that is diametrically opposed to that projected by timba. Its nostalgic, gentle neo-colonial mood has contributed to creating a tourist-friendly image of

Cuba and, at the same time, has reaffirmed a nationalist, island-based, state-sanctioned notion of *cubanía*, in opposition to the diasporic, transnational cultural identities of young *timberos* and émigré Cubans.

As I discussed in the last part of the chapter, with all possible good intentions, this world music album has had a perverse effect on the rest of local music, overshadowing contemporary Cuban music production on the global stage, and winning a level of financial support never achieved by a record of Cuban MB. For the launching of the album *Buena Vista Social Club*, for example, Nonesuch invited foreign journalists to Havana for a week, all expenses paid. East/West and World Circuit have done the same for the launch of albums by Compay Segundo and the Afro-Cuban All Stars (Padrón Nodarse 1998, 34–7). While apparently helping to break the isolation of Cuban music, *Buena Vista* has thus actually cut off contemporary musicians, obscuring the social relevance of timba, its innovative character and its centrality as *the* music of contemporary young Cubans.

But the biggest paradox of *Buena Vista*, perhaps, has been the way it has been able to reconcile the tastes of the Cuban ruling elite with those of both US liberals and Miami right-wingers. Because of its international success, the album has been hailed as a stalwart of national culture in Cuba. On account of its anti-modern and exotic appeal, it has been marketed to US liberals sympathetic to Cuba's resistance against political and cultural imperialism. Thanks to its vintage sounds and artists, it has appeased the nostalgic tastes of the white, middle-class exile community in Miami.[12]

---

12 On the reaction of Cuban-American audiences in Miami to the screening of Wenders' movie, see Levine 1999.

Chapter 10

Beyond Palms, Rum and 'Che': Black Music into the New Millennium

The boom of timba in the 1990s, it appears now, coincided with a very particular stage of the recent history of Cuba. It was the moment of the island's descent into hell during the early years of the *período especial*, when the economic crisis peaked, forcing the government to introduce market reforms and generating the most dramatic moral, ideological and political crisis of the Cuban revolution. In summer 1994, while NG and El Médico entertained foreigners and *jineteras* in Havana tourist clubs, young Blacks rioted on the Malecón. For some years, the boom of timba seemed to announce new spaces for individual freedom and expression, and, to some, even the demise of Cuban socialism. As we have seen, that was not to be the case.

At the opening of the new millennium, Cuban dance music is, to say the least, at an impasse. While the historical bands of MB have guarded their positions, the new outfits that emerged in the mid-1990s have seen their chances for success considerably restrained by the international revivalist wave, which has flooded the Western music market with a deluge of *Buena Vista*-type bands.

Whatever the current fads and the future directions of its music, however, Cuba remains today a tremendous music machine. The reasons for this are both evident and complex. They have their roots in the strength of the African cultural heritage and in the colonial history of the island, and in the important place occupied by Cuba in the international music scene during the first half of the twentieth century. To this can be added the exceptionally high quality of the music made by the generations of post-revolutionary musicians, trained in the conservatoires of the island and then filtered into multiple artistic routes.

Even during the years of maximum isolation of Cuba, the island's musicians kept up to date with international changes in musical taste, constantly renewing their language. Such strength of Cuban music is perceivable not only in the quantity and quality of the local production, both cultivated and non-cultivated, but also in the great number of Cuban musicians who travel, work or live abroad, in Mexico, the USA, Canada, Latin America and, increasingly, Europe.

Without counting the number of amateur practitioners, often of excellent level, in Cuba today there are about 12 000 professional musicians, that is about one for every thousand people. Music has proved one of the main, if not *the* main, intellectual assets of the island – and even one of its paradoxes, when one considers the notorious indifference of its leader for the art of sound. During the 1970s and 1980s, young people were motivated to study music mostly by artistic ambition and desire for self-expression. Today, to aspirations so difficult to achieve have been added more down-to-earth motivations such as obtaining, through the music profession, a passport for travelling abroad and the opportunity to earn dollars. In present-day Cuba, the average musician continues to earn very little, and has a lot of time for rehearsing, experimenting and inventing (both in the musical sense, and in that of making ends meet).

The main problem of music in Cuba remains the fact that, for the musicians based on the island, as well as for ordinary Cubans, hopes for the improvement of their own material conditions come essentially from abroad, be that in the form of foreign records sales and tours or of tourist audiences at home. In terms of economic profitability, since the financial resources of the majority of Cubans are all invested in survival, the internal market for music is non-existent. If nothing else, one of the positive effects of the recent 'made in Cuba' boom has been the growth and differentiation of the offerings of Cuban music. The most extraordinary fact has been the direction of such musical expansion, almost entirely oriented towards the various filiations of Afro-Cuban music.

With the crisis of the international music industry, the new millennium has brought about notable changes in the Cuban music industry. In Cuba today there are about ten national labels and eight foreign labels in operation (Benemelis, interview with the author, 2003). Various foreign record companies (especially Spanish) that monopolized the market of MB in the mid-1990s have disappeared or ceased their operations on the island. The mid-1990s third-party deals of Cuban musicians with US record companies resulted in poorly-funded promotion and distribution. The international contracts of Issac Delgado with RMM, Paulíto FG with Nueva Fania and La Charanga Habanera with Universal Mexico, and the distribution deal of NG with EMI Spain did not produce the expected fruits, and were terminated in the late 1990s. As a result, Cuban record companies now appear firmly back in control of the record output of Cuban artists. Most *timberos* now make their records on Cuban labels, and state-owned company Artex has acquired the entire catalogue of a foreign company, which contains the crème of 1990s Cuban MB.

In the last few years, on the other hand, the output of the Cuban record industry has remarkably diversified. Compared to a few years ago, the industry has now far more varied catalogues and better-produced records, owns some excellent recording studios and has taken its first steps into the perilous waters of international music law to challenge US embargo regulations in court (see Chapter 3). The industry can count on an immense musical mine with compositions of every possible era and genre, an archive of recordings starting from the early days of the gramophone record, a pool of highly talented session musicians, an improving musical and technical infrastructure and, surprisingly, a number of musicologists employed by record companies.

At the same time, both the Cuban music industry and Cuban musicians are today probably more conscious of the objective limitations to the export of Cuban music created by the international political stalemate and the periodical crises of the international relations between Cuba and the USA. Given the 1.5 million Cubans who live in the United States, and the fact that Latin Americans are becoming the biggest ethnic minority in the country, the Cuban industry continues to consider the USA as its most natural market (Muñoz 2001). But, as in the rest of the world, the Cuban music industry's performances in the USA continue to be conditioned by poor distribution and promotion.

Timberos backed into a corner

Amidst traditionalist fads and cultural nationalistic polemics, the most important Cuban dance bands and artists have tried to defend their position, and newer bands have found it difficult to emerge on the international arena. Among the groups who became popular in the second half of the 1990s are Klimax, the avant-garde formation of timba (an offshoot of NG, they play a rhythmically and harmonically challenging type of timba), Manolíto Simonet y su Trabuco (a very danceable and catchy mix of timba and son), La Barriada (according to their own definition, 'the smallest timba big band') and, more recently, Carlos Manuel Pruneda, the author of the monster-hit 'Malo cantidad' ('Super-bad'). Already a singer with Irakere, Carlos Manuel has the *physique du rol* of the popstar, is white, and makes a timba that attempts a fusion with other Caribbean rhythms (he has had one album produced by an Anglo-American record company). The problem is that he has asked for political refugee status across the Straits, and is now in the process of launching a career as a singer and actor in the USA.

Some new formations have incorporated the term 'timba' into their name, such as Danny Losada y su Timba Cubana and Osvaldo Chacón y su Timba (the latter is one of the very few timba bands based outside Cuba, in London). La Charanga Forever are a not particularly imaginative version of their original band (La Charanga Habanera) and have gone through innumerable changes of personnel. A very interesting phenomenon is that of female timba bands, such as Anacaona, Son Damas and, most of all, Bamboleo. Under the direction of versatile jazz pianist Lazaríto Valdés (nephew of Oscar Valdés Jr., the first singer with Irakere) (see Plate 14), the two female singers of Bamboleo have opened their way into the international market with a fusion of timba, rap and jazz, surely one of most exciting products of Cuban dance music in recent years.

Despite its relative stalemate at the international level, timba remains by far the most popular style on the island, and the one able to draw the most committed and enthusiastic dancers. Through their multiple difficulties, *timberos* and other Cuban musicians seem to have learned better how to manage themselves, keeping away from unfair recording deals with self-styled record executives, and from making albums with foreign labels that might be important, but do not promote and distribute their CDs.

This is what has happened to Los Van Van. In year 2000, the historic band of Cuban MB received a Grammy for their CD *Llegó Van Van*, produced by the label Havana Caliente, a subsidiary of Atlantic. The album featured excellent recording and sumptuous artwork, but was poorly distributed in the USA (because of political pressures?) and eventually started to circulate in pirated versions. After exchanges of accusations between the band and the record company, Van Van have reissued the album on a Cuban label. Added to these problems, in the last few years have been frequent changes of personnel and signals of tensions among the band, and of a process of rejuvenation which might soon lead to the withdrawal of Juan Formell from the music scene. Meanwhile, Van Van pianist César 'Pupi' Pedroso has left the band to form his own group, presently one of Havana's favourites.

To this day, La Charanga Habanera continue to be the most popular and spectacular timba band, with an increasingly 'pop' sound and sexy choreography performed by young musicians-singers-dancers (see Plate 12). NG La Banda, by contrast, seem to have re-oriented themselves towards a mix of timba, pop and Latin jazz. Abroad, they continue to offer flamboyant concerts, opened by a long version of Chick Corea's 'Spain' and filled with old and new hits, terrific instrumental solos and the gags of El Tosco, now an experienced showman. Cortés's record output has been less convincing and no longer features dozens of records per year as in the mid-1990s. Today, he seems to be more interested in producing records by other artists and touring with his own band. But it remains a fact that many of his most controversial songs have never made it to CD. The latest news reports a novel home version of NG shrunk to nine people, with three young female singers and without a bass player (synthesized). Keeping at the top of timba is not an easy task.

The position of MB in Cuba has not been improved by recent controversial decisions from the Cuban authorities, such as banning the entrance of women not accompanied by a male partner to Havana music clubs, eliminating the direct payment of musicians in hard currency (substituted by monthly payments through *empresas*) and implementing forms of political pressure on radio stations in the context of a so-called *batalla de ideas* (ideological battle) (Brito López 1999, Linares 2003).

As a style, timba has made inroads into international Latin dance music, and its influence is now apparent in the work of various Latin musicians and producers, always watchful of the innovations radiating from Havana. Timba breaks can be heard in the albums of US Latin soul bands such as DLG, of salsa singers such as Willie Chirino and Victor Manuelle, and in the work of producers such as Sergio George and Isidro Infante. Cuban bands tour and play frequently in Europe, Latin America, Japan and the USA, and increasingly in Miami. There, young Cuban-Americans have proved more curious and open to dialogue with Cuba than their parents, who still crave 'a simple, reduced Cuban culture ... based on shared memories, similar tastes in food and music, and the notion of what Cubans "were like"' (Rieff 1994: 128).

Timberos are now aware that the possibility of a crossover of timba into the global market is not just around the corner, as they seemed to believe in the mid-1990s. The causes are multiple and cannot be blamed solely on the US embargo, institutional hostility or the *Buena Vista* effect. They lie in the difficulty of translating timba for non-Cuban audiences, even Latin American ones. In comparison to the relative easy rhythms, catchy tunes and simple dance steps of salsa (already an insurmountable obstacle for many Western dancers), timba has lyrics that are too local, with too much slang, songs that are too long, rhythms that are too complex. Talks of experimentations with 'four-minutes timba' that were circulating in 1999 among music executives have not materialized (Llewellyn 1999b). All in all, MB musicians find it difficult to break into the global market because there is no international category corresponding to timba, a style that appears to challenge all existing classifications. Timba is not cheap, easy-going tropical dance music as usually expected in the West, it is not salsa, nor jazz, nor son. It is not Afro-Cuban traditional music, nor rock, nor socially engaged song. In a way, timba is something of all this.

Timba bands, therefore, remain essentially and primarily bands who have to be listened to and seen live, because of the skill of their musicians, the charisma of their singers and their ability to communicate with the most refractory audiences. For Cuban MB musicians, nothing is more depressing than facing an audience that stands and listens. For this reason, bands devise all sorts of tricks to infect people downstage with the virus of dance and, if the concert is attended by a Cuban audience, to make them into an active part of the show. Unfortunately, sound recordings are rarely able to convey an idea of the power and the charisma of timba played in front of its own audiences.

The revivalist wave

As expected, by the turn of the millennium the boom of *Buena Vista* had flooded the West with a neo-traditional tidal wave. The invasion was initially led by the musicians who participated in the original project. Organized under various names and bands, they took the international music circuit by storm and played triumphantly in theatres and festivals around the globe. Some of them, in fact, are today the most well-paid artists in Cuba.[1] In 2002, the elderly Ferrer, Portuondo and González were decorated by Fidel Castro for 'their constant struggle in defence of the most authentic cultural values of our nation' ('Condecoran a artista de *Buena Vista* ...', 2002). After his lucky break with Ry Cooder, Compay Segundo resumed international touring with his own band at the green age of 95, in a global tour de force that probably hastened his death in July 2003.

Besides the artists who might boast their connection with *Buena Vista*, other, more or less similar occasional bands and a countless number of CD-clones have emerged. A positive note is represented by the reconstitution or reappearance on the international circuit of historical formations of Cuban son, such as the Septeto Nacional (with new musicians, as it was founded in 1927!), classic *charangas* such as the Orquesta Aragón, and bands such as the Conjunto Chapottín, heirs of the legacy of Arsenio Rodríguez. On the big international scene, excellent groups of son revival such as the Cuarteto Patria led by guitarist Elíades Ochoa and the Familia Valera Miranda have made their appearance.

Finally, bands such as Los Jóvenes Clásicos del Son and Cotó y su Eco del Caribe, who offer an acoustic fusion of son and contemporary influences, have emerged on the international music circuit. In addition, the old ensemble Sierra Maestra, the first revivalist band of Cuban music, continues to circulate from which have emerged two champions of neo-traditional music, Juan de Marcos González and the younger Jesús Alemañy. With his own project Cubanismo, trumpet player

---

[1] According to Juan de Marcos González, in 1998 the main artists of *Buena Vista* netted about $100 000 each (Cantor 1999e).

Alemañy, who lives in the UK, has invented for international audiences a sparkling instrumental sound that mixes traditional dance tunes with new compositions and jazz and creole influences. On a somewhat similar, albeit more jazz-leaning, line, brilliant flute player and arranger Orlando Valle 'Maraca' works with his own band Otra Visión.

Rap, *a lo cubano*

The big thing in Cuban music at the beginning of the new millennium has been the boom of Cuban rap. With the amazing success of Orishas's *A lo cubano*, rap has emerged from the peripheral barrios of Havana and landed on the European charts and in the reviews of *Rolling Stone*. Although for many people Cuban rap seemed to come out of the blue, in fact this style has been popular in Cuba for more than a decade, and in particular in Havana, where it accounts for at least 200 bands. The first national rap festival, held in the eastern part of the city, dates back to 1995, a year when the event attracted more than 3000 people. Since then, this self-financed festival has moved to a bare arena covered with graffiti in Alamar, a peripheral neighbourhood with a dense Afro-Cuban population (see Plate 25). Born between the concrete apartment buildings built on the model of Soviet peripheries and the dark, suffocating rooms of colonial Old Havana, Cuban rap is the product of a generation that has known only the darkest times of the revolution.

In the varied scenario of Cuban hip-hop characters have emerged such as producer Pablo Herrera, who has taught at university and speaks English and Russian. While studying the culture of US Blacks, Herrera came into contact with the first rap outfits and started to work with them, quickly becoming the main rap producer of the island. Among his productions are those with Amenaza (the early version of Orishas), Obsesión and various female outfits, plus the organization of performances and compilation CDs of Cuban rap, such as *The Cuban Hip-Hop All Stars, Vol. 1*, which contains some of the most important names of Cuban rap, such as Obsesión, Anonimo Consejo (Anonymous Opinion) and Grandes Ligas (Big Leagues).[2]

A firm supporter of the Cuban way of rapping, Herrera is concerned with keeping its integrity and street connections, and criticizes the commercial attitudes of US rappers. He is also anxious to minimize the rougher edges of local hip-hop, which could make the style look counter-revolutionary in the eyes of the authorities and condemn it to an early death (a mistake already made by Cuban rockers). Commenting on

---

[2] Papaya Records, New York, 2002.

North American rap, he says: 'That rebelliousness doesn't happen in Cuba, because the system is not hostile.... Cuban rap is very much about positive lyrics and attitudes and working with the community and the system. It's about trying to push the system to its best' (Smith 1999).

In a similar way, Ariel Fernández, a young journalist and host to the only rap programme on Cuban radio, believes that local hip hop is innovative and reflects daily life, contrary to most Cuban music that is popular abroad. Like many of the youngest *raperos*, Fernández criticizes MB as commercial. 'If you hear a salsa band, the music says, "I feel OK. I feel all right. Move your ass with a girl. Feel happy".... Typically, salsa music doesn't say anything. The salsa artists bring to the society an image, a kind of life of rich people that many Cubans don't feel ok with' (Foehr 2001: 36–7).

In reality, as we have seen, timba shows clear traces of the musical impact of rap, for example in the coros of La Charanga and in the male-bashing attitude of Bamboleo (Vannia Borges, former singer with the band, is a self-declared fan of Dr. Dre, Snoop Doggy Dogg, Wu Tang Clan and Notorious B.I.G). The misunderstandings about the meaning of Cuban salsa on the part of rappers are, quite probably, the product of a strong rivalry. In contrast to *timberos*, *raperos* are all amateurs, and earn almost nothing from their music.[3] It is thus quite understandable that they seek to give substance to their own aesthetics by presenting rap as a music more real than the music 'for tourists'. Among those sweating on the dance floor at La Tropical on Saturday evenings, at any rate, there are no 'rich people' in sight.

In the last few years, the cultural engagement of young rap promoters has been rewarded with official legitimization. In June 1999, representatives of the movement were received by Abel Prieto, the youthful-looking writer who holds the charge of Minister of Culture. After the meeting, Prieto has declared: 'We have to support our Cuban rappers because this is the next generation of Cubans and they are saying powerful things with this art' (Hoch 1999). After years of DIY, lean times and self-financing, rappers thus obtained from the Ministry audio equipment and financial and logistic help for the organization of their national festival. Rap music can now be heard not only in Alamar, but also on radio and occasionally in venues and theatres (see Plate 27). As a young musician has commented, 'Damn, for years we didn't get anything, and now we are being driven around on a bus, and given beans, *yuca*, and steak for rehearsals! They're really taking us seriously' (ibid.).

---

[3] According to some of them, Cuban rappers have received no money whatsoever from the international *and* local compilations of Cuban rap (Familia's Cuba Represent; interview with the author, 2003).

Despite the romance with the cultural authorities and the fact that rappers such as Orishas, SBS and X Alfonso are now almost an institution, many rap outfits have not given up their provocative stance. In August 2002 the Eighth National Rap Festival took place, supported by the Institute of Cuban Music and surrounded by cultural debates, with the presence of some foreign bands and the notable absence of the artists quoted above. On the first night, 18-year-old rapper Papá Humbertico went on stage with a banner reading 'denuncia social' (social denunciation), and sang songs telling stories about *jineteras* and against the police, who were a massive presence at the location. Addressing policemen, he sang:

> Listen
> Just you
> You who never let me in peace
> I'm not afraid of you,
> I'm not scared by your blue uniform
> Nor by your rank
> To me you never cease to be an ignorant
> Come on
> Here I am
> Repress what you like
> My hands with your handcuffs
> Throw me into your bloody van
> But I, I won't shut up[4]

In the course of the festival, this time attended not only by young Afro-Cubans but also by many tourists and foreign journalists, the central theme that emerged was one of racism and of the harassment of Blacks by the police. Other bands such as Alto Voltaje (High Voltage) sang coros with not-too-oblique references to the political situation:

> Another one may die in the process
> Of seeing the changes in time
> I'm sick of the routine
> When will it end?[5]

At the very last minute, the closing night of the festival, which was programmed in downtown Havana, was moved to Plaza Africa in Alamar. There, between power blackouts, a solid presence of the police and an ecstatic audience, the festival ended with spectators singing along with Hermanos de Causa (Brothers of Cause):

---

[4] 'Oye tú / contigo mismo / contigo, que en paz no me dejas un instante / no te tengo miedo / no me intimida tu vestimenta azul / ni el cargo que tengas / para mí no dejas de ser un ignorante/ adelante / estoy a tu disposición / aprieta todo lo que quieras / mis manos con tus esposas / móntame en tu jodido camión / que yo, yo no me callaré.'

[5] 'Uno más puede morir en el intento / de ver los cambios en el tiempo / de la rutina estoy cansado / ¿Hasta cuándo es esto?' (Vicent 2002).

He's always an anti-social
They slander at random
Always catching the black man red-handed[6]

Discrimination against Blacks seems to be the main theme of socially-engaged rap in Cuba, which has bravely taken the denouncement of racism into the public arena on the island. As one of the early songs of Amenaza went, 'They said black but they never counted me / they said white but the clan rejected me / they said so many things / I'm the person that nobody wanted / the black with the white / the cry of a half-breed.'[7] In 2002, another song about racism, 'Quién tiró la tiza?' ('Who threw the chalk?'), started to circulate underground and became enormously popular, to the point of soliciting a song in response.

After the festival, the Cuban authorities announced the creation of a Cuban rap agency, which meant that rappers could be treated as professionals (Díaz 2002). This shows the commitment of the Cuban authorities to this type of music, but also raises doubts about the establishment, through institutionalization, of mechanisms of artistic control. In the meanwhile, the director of musical programmes of a local radio station has been sacked for broadcasting the reply to 'La tiza', which, apparently, had been censored by the Cuban Institute of Radio and Television for problems of 'ideological deviation' (Serpa Maceira 2002). According to an independent source, after the festival, the Casa de Cultura in Alamar received from the Ministry of Culture an order to check the lyrics of rap songs before any concert. As the director of the Casa declared, 'This is a preventive measure adopted in order to avoid any act of disobedience which does not conform to our revolutionary process' (Aguiar Díaz 2002).

While there is no doubt that the themes touched on by *raperos* will not make their life any easier, one may also question the musical perspectives of the new style. What is *Cuban* in Cuban rap? Various local rappers I have interviewed have claimed that the identification in their music of an explicitly national stylistic element beyond their language and their themes is not so important. According to Herrera, 'we can say that is Cuban rap because it is made by Cubans for a Cuban audience, and they make it on the basis of a Cuban conception of reality' (Basso Ortíz 2001).

What is certain is that Cuban rappers, with the technical means at their disposal (cassettes with breaks copied from records or stolen from

---

[6] 'Siempre es un antisocial / hay calumnias al azar / agarrando siempre al negro con las manos en la masa' ('Concluye con críticas al racismo Festival de Rap de la Habana', Notimex, <YupiMsn.com> 20 August 2002).

[7] 'Dijeron negro pero a mí no me contaron / dijeron blanco pero en el clan no me aceptaron / dijeron tantas cosas / soy el ser que nadie quiso / lo negro con lo blanco / el grito de un mestizo' (Vicent 2002).

the airwaves, or, in the best cases, a personal computer) cannot compete with refined productions such as those of Orishas. With their CD *A lo cubano*, later followed by *Emigrante*, FlacoPro, Yotuél, Roldán and Ruzzo have brilliantly solved the dilemma by ingeniously inserting in the cadences of Latin rap harmonic progressions reminiscent of Cuban traditional tumbaos, and the melodic arches performed by Roldán's voice. The first Orishas album even features a piece of quasi-timba ('1.9.9.9.'), and yet another elaboration of 'Chan Chan' by Compay Segundo, transfigured in '537 C.U.B.A.' into a sort of hip-hop anthem.

Some rappers on the island appear to be exploring the multiple points of contact between hip-hop and Afro-Cuban music. The analogies between rap and rumba are countless: both are born out of black barrios, represent forms of social chronicle made with little technical means and give ample space to improvisation. Like early *rumberos*, the early Cuban rappers made up their comments on rhythms produced on wooden boxes. Like *timberos*, many of them sport baseball caps, sneakers and other symbols of hip hop fashion alongside bead necklaces and the clothing of those initiated into santería.

For its part, contemporary rumba is not immune to the influence of hip hop, sometimes visible in the incorporation of rap locution and break-dance steps. From a strictly musical point of view, the most interesting perspectives for Cuban rap seem to come from a fusion of this type, born not from a production team in a recording studio, but from a dialogic opening of the music of lower class Cubans to the musical forms of the black diaspora. It is not coincidental, perhaps, that bands such as Anonimo Consejo sing songs such as 'Guapo como Mandela' ('Brave like Mandela') and often take part in reggae festivals organized by the local rasta movement, which is itself growing. Cubatón, a more danceable and escapist version of Cuban rap inspired by reggaetón, is now becoming increasingly popular with bands such as Cubanítos.

Paradoxically, Cuban rap owes its strength to its marginality, its barrio black identity, its technological economy. Contrary to other styles of Cuban music which require a long musical training and a remarkable level of virtuosity, rap is accessible to virtually everybody. To the cultural authorities, perhaps, this makes *raperos* more congenial than enriched *timberos* (in a strict sense, also, rap is not dance music). But it also makes them more difficult to control. Their audacious strategy for carving out a public space is exemplified by the shrewd way artists such as Papá Humbertico challenged institutions during the festival. By protesting against racism and the police and reclaiming freedom of expression, *raperos* bring to light the friction points in contemporary Cuba and take part in the construction of a civil society that will not accept the label of 'counter-revolutionary', but interrogates the political leadership and asks for tangible answers.

> I love my flag
> I was born here, and here I will die
> Be sure, I have clear the concept of the Cuban revolution
> I am with this, but not with you
> ... This is for you, stupid, is for you.
> Police, police
> You're not friends of mine
> For young Cubans
> You're the worst punishment[8]

The return of Latin jazz

Another effect of the present cultural flourishing, which reveals the great variety and quality of the music produced on the Pearl of the Antilles, has been the powerful return of Afro-Cuban jazz to the international scene. For more than twenty years, Western audiences have heard the music of Irakere and that of two of its illustrious expatriate members, trumpet player Arturo Sandoval and saxophone player Paquito d'Rivera. The leader of Irakere 'Chucho' Valdés is now considered to be one of the best jazz pianists in the world. But the increasing interest in music made in Cuba has brought to the international fore other Cuban talents who play jazz, such as pianists Gonzalo Rubalcaba, Ramón Valle and Hernán López-Nussa, or saxophonist Yosvany Terry. In such a panorama, the aforementioned Alemañy and 'Maraca' occupy a special place, exploring the ties between jazz and Cuban traditional music.

As in the rest of the world, in Cuba jazz is a music for musicians and connoisseurs, not a mass phenomenon. But it has special importance, for at least two reasons. The first one is its indirect influence on much Cuban music, visible both in the neo-traditional experiments of 'Maraca' and in timba bands such as NG, Klimax and Bamboleo. The other reason is that in Cuba one perceives clearly, probably as in no other country in the world, the very thin line that separates black musical styles. Not only do *timberos* play jazz breaks on the rumba clave, but Irakere have played for years a fusion of jazz, rock and Afro-Cuban folkloric music. Even now, the band, who can be considered the most direct progenitor of timba, feature a singer and continue to play dance tunes. The boom of Cuban

---

[8] 'Amo mi bandera / aquí nací y aquí me van a enterrar / seguro puedes estar de que tengo bien claro el concepto de la revolución cubana. / Estoy con esto, pero no contigo / ... Esto es contigo, loco, esto es contigo./ Policía, policía / tú no eres mi amigo / para la juventud cubana eres el peor castigo' (Vicent 2002).

jazz, in a way, has demonstrated what a generic and slightly derogatory label such as 'Latin jazz' really means, that is, Afro-Cuban, and sometimes Afrobrasilian jazz, indicating a possible way out of the shallow waters of Latin jazz as a minor style.

During the last ten years or so, the quality of the music produced on the island has not only led to the acknowledgment of Cuban jazz by foreign audiences, but has also attracted a number of foreign artists to Cuba, especially from North America and the Caribbean. The 1997 Jazz Plaza Festival (founded in 1978) included performances from musicians such as Roy Hargrove, Steve Coleman and Puerto Rican David Sanchez, all artists who are particularly interested in the exploration of the relations between jazz and Afro-Caribbean music.

During the festival, Sanchez and Hargrove took part in jam sessions with timba ensembles such as Van Van, Klimax, Bamboleo and Issac Delgado's band. On that occasion, Sanchez made a declaration that probably represents one of the best compliments ever attributed to timba. '[O]ne of the amazing things about Cuban music now is that there's no sense of compromise in the popular music,' he said to a US journalist. 'It's the smartest pop music I've ever heard, and while it is for a dancing audience, it is really complicated and profound' (Watrous 1997). Following his participation in the festival, trumpet player Hargrove, together with Chucho Valdés and the band Crisol, produced the album *Habana*, which won a Grammy in 1998. Valdés has since received another Grammy for jazz in 2001, and a Latin Grammy in 2002. The 2002 Festival was marked by appearances from celebrities such as singer Harry Belafonte and writer Gabriel García Márquez. Among the musicians invited (although not all present) were Brazilians Egberto Gismonti, Ivan Lins and Ed Motta, guitarist Larry Coryell, Kenny Barron, Joe Lovano and Uri Caine, and Cuban pianist Gonzalo Rubalcaba, who had been absent from Cuba for ten years.

The orphans of rock

A discussion of Cuban rock, the Cinderella of the island's music, is outside the scope of the present book. Nevertheless, I would like to make a few points on a style that, although often considered alien to Cuban culture, has been present and practised in Cuba since the 1950s, and whose evolution has virtually coincided with the history of the revolution.

As discussed in Chapter 1, despite its ostracization by the government, between the 1960s and the 1970s rock was popular with Cuban youth, and was played by several dozen bands. During the 1970s, in particular, groups emerged that are still active today, such as Sintesis, who in 1987 produced one of the best albums of fusion between rock and Afro-Cuban music (*Ancestros*). Rock has had a wide-ranging influence on the evolution of other Cuban styles (to name just one band, Van Van). As a style in itself, however, it has never really been very popular. Both as a music and as a subculture, Cuban rock has cultivated an image of marginality and rebelliousness that has made it appear to the establishment as an imported, deviant and potentially counter-revolutionary phenomenon. Between the 1970s and the 1980s, thus, apart from occasional exploits such as that of Sintesis and Mezcla (another band experimenting with fusions with Afro-Cuban music), rock in Cuba has survived mostly underground, amidst many practical and political difficulties.

Between the 1980s and the 1990s, local rock widened the range of its variants with the inclusion of sub-styles such as punk and, particularly, heavy metal, and the appearance of bands such as Zeus, Agonizer, Futuro Muerto, Garage H, and then Extraño Corazón, Perfume de mujer, Bolsa Negra and VIH (that is, HIV, because all its members were HIV-positive). The name of this last band, which relates to the painful story of Aids self-injection mentioned in the previous chapter, highlights the strong nihilistic component of a part of Cuban rock culture.

Another striking aspect of Cuban rock – which is common (to say the least) to other Latin American countries – is the fact that most of those who appear to practise it and listen to it seem to be white. This characteristic signals a distinction between youth subcultures and recalls the contrast made years ago in Puerto Rico between *cócolos* and *roqueros*. *Cócolos* were young Blacks listening to salsa, while *roqueros* cultivated foreign music in English. As in Puerto Rico, in Cuba similar differences are articulated by visual style: Cuban *roqueros* wear worn-out, tight denims and black T-shirts, while salsa fans tend to lean towards hip-hop fashion. The former mostly listen to foreign music and despise MB, while the latter prefer soul and timba and consider rock fans, or *frikis*, as spoilt boys. Without pushing the discourse too far, it is clear that these styles articulate quite visible racial and class differences. Contrapositions between youth subcultures are not exclusive to the Western world.[9]

Today rock in Cuba enjoys a relatively higher level of institutional support. The local music industry has recently given it more space, publishing CDs of pop-rock bands such as Buena Fé and Moneda Dura. Some Cuban rock bands have played abroad and had some of their songs

---

[9] On distinctions between *roqueros*, *salseros* and *raperos*, see Rey 2000.

included in international compilations of *rock en español*. The style has also proved an important point of reference for relatively young, controversial *trovadores* such as Carlos Varela. In general, however, rock remains in Cuba a largely minority style, partially because of its cultivation of an alternative and sectarian image, and partially because it is obscured by other musical styles (and this despite its black roots). In Havana, one can encounter places such as the Patio de Maria, cultural circles that essentially function as rock fans' ghettos, and occasional sold out concerts in the city's theatres. But Cuban rockers are constantly looking for new spaces, lamenting the general indifference of the media and the music industry, and trying to establish contact with foreign record labels. Since most of these have an altogether different idea of Cuban music, however, we find ourselves returned to 'Go' once more and the problems faced by timba in relation to the *Buena Vista* effect, as discussed in the previous chapter.

Despite all this, it is important to remember that rock represents an important, if largely underestimated, influence on Cuban music, and on Latin music in general. Without considering the impact of Anglo-American rock, for example, it would be difficult to understand phenomena such *Tropicalismo* and much of the popular music produced in Brazil since the 1970s, as well as the music of Cuban bands such as Irakere and NG.

Towards a Havana Renaissance?

In the context of the stormy developments of Cuban MB in the first part of the 1990s, the musical adaptation of 'Soy todo' by Los Van Van represents a public statement of Cuban popular music's bond with, and debt to, Afro-Cuban popular culture. Such a trend does not concern just music, but reflects a far wider front where black popular culture has remerged from the ghettos to become visible, in some cases giving way to new forms of professional activity. It is a movement of regeneration of black culture that includes dance, poetry and the visual arts, and that I have elsewhere defined as 'Havana Renaissance', in memory of another famous black renaissance, that of Harlem in the New York of the 1920s (Perna 2001).

In the Cuban capital city, individuals such as Eloy Machado, aka El Ambia ('brother' in the abakuá language), today organize music-and-poetry performances at official institutions such as Uneac, the powerful Union of Cuban Artists and Writers. In the Callejón de Hamel, a short alley in the densely Afro-Cuban area of Cayo Hueso, artist Salvador González has painted the walls of the buildings surrounding his house with *murales* inspired by the imagery of Afro-Cuban religion (see Plates 23 and 24). On the street, every Sunday, rumba ensembles play to local people and an increasing number of foreigners. The artistic work of González, who has painted and exhibited in many countries, is now known all over the world.

To emphasize the central role of music in the Cuban black cultural renaissance, the last few years have witnessed the emergence of new bands and the re-vitalization of old Afro-Cuban ensembles, such as the Conjunto Clave y Guaguancó, founded in the 1950s, and Yoruba Andabo, revived around El Ambia at the end of the 1980s, both from Havana. The cultural and musical renaissance has extended out of the capital and in particular to Matanzas, a town east of Havana which represents a vital centre for black culture and especially for rumba. There today formations such as Afrocuba and Los Muñequitos de Mantanzas (who in the last decade have toured, taught and recorded extensively in the West) or bands of more recent foundation such as Congo Luanda operate. To this can be added the prodigious flourishing of percussion and dance courses in Europe and the USA, held by both Cuban expatriates and artists resident on the island. Every year, hundreds of foreign musicians visit Cuba to attend seminars and take percussion classes. Many of them are initiated into santería.

The explosion of international interest in Afro-Cuban culture has also touched the main institution of folkloric culture, the Conjunto Folklórico Nacional. Besides its shows and frequent tours abroad, among its activities the Conjunto now organizes *sábado de la rumba* and folklore workshops for foreigners at its headquarters in Havana. These include courses in both popular and folkloric dances such as rumba, and in music and dance tied to santería, *congo* and *arará* traditions.[10]

The progressive movement of Afro-Cuban culture from the margins to the centre of the Cuban cultural scene has been celebrated by the appearance of the album *La rumba soy yo* ('I am rumba'), which earned a Latin Grammy in 2001. Produced for a Cuban record company by Joaquím Betancourt and Cari Diez, the CD was born out of the intention of 'proving that rumba is a living genre, part of a folklore that is constantly evolving, but is not completely known' (Castañeda 2001). For this purpose, the album featured percussionists such as Tata Guïnes and Changuito, rumba bands such as Los Muñequitos de Mantanzas, Los Papines, Clave y Guaguancò and Yoruba Andabo, and timba singers such as Issac Delgado, Haila Mompié, Mayito Rivera and Aramís Galindo.

---

[10] See the Conjunto's website, <www.cubaescena.cult.cu>.

Diasporic identities: timba and the black Atlantic

For Cuba, the 1990s represented the moment not only of its most acute economic and social crisis, but also of a new and extraordinary opening up to the outside world. The decade that began under the star of MB closed under that of a multiplicity of black styles which seem to represent the true mark of the music of the island in the new millennium. In different and sometimes contrasting ways, this new music reflects and at the same time feeds a growing consciousness of the centrality of Blacks in national culture.

At the beginning of the *período especial*, the role of musical battering ram was taken up by timba, a popular style able to conjugate cosmopolitan attitudes and continuity with black traditions. As we have seen, the style then collided with institutional hostility, the obstacles created by the US embargo and its own aesthetic limitations on exportability. Finally, the expansion of timba was arrested, or greatly limited, by the global success of *Buena Vista*, which, at the end of the 1990s, refocused the interest of international audiences on a very narrow section of Cuban music. I have discussed at length in this book the negative role of this phenomenon in constructing a romanticized vision of Cuban culture and society. Here, nonetheless, I want to stress how, despite diverging aesthetics and ideological affiliations, both timba and the music of *Buena Vista* (and that of the related revival of son) are the product of musical forms originating from a largely Afro-Cuban matrix. To these styles have been added, in quick progression, the re-emergence of Cuban jazz, the exceptional flourishing of traditional ensembles for voice and percussion, and the boom of rap.

Such an explosion of black music underlines an extraordinary moment of grace for the Afro-Cuban expressive arts, and the existence of a variety of positions and antagonisms inside this cultural movement. These are revealed in the ways the different expressive forms manifest their relationship with ideas of tradition and modernity, express notions of belonging and extraneity to national culture, and compete to present themselves as genuinely representative of Cuban identity. The idea of what Cuban culture is has thus been articulated in quite different ways. For rumba and son ensembles, it has meant going back to the 'roots'. For *timberos* and jazz musicians, it has produced attempts to mediate between local past music, international influences and artistic aspirations. For the exponents of the younger generation, finally, it has meant looking directly at the music of African Americans and black Hispanics who live on the other side of the Florida Straits.

In the musical and cultural dialectic of contemporary Cuba, modernity and tradition represent important but not mutually exclusive points of reference. Modern styles such as rap and timba found themselves retrospectively and turn their eyes on rumba and santería, while, for its part, a traditional folkloric style such as rumba is now acknowledging and accepting the influence of hip-hop. All these aspects of the present black cultural renaissance in Cuba demonstrate profound ties with a past that goes far beyond the last few decades and has its roots sunk deep in the experience of slavery, where music and dance represented 'an enhanced mode of communication beyond the petty power of words – spoken or written' (Gilroy 1993: 76).

In my investigation, I have highlighted how timba, under its apparent escapism and engagement with tourist entertainment, is a culturally meaningful and politically significant form that articulates a specific Afro-Cuban urban subculture and retains a vital dialogue with Cuban society. As a form of dance music, it is central to contemporary secular Afro-Cuban identity and to the articulation of its difference to mainstream culture. By drawing Afro-Cuban religion onto music stages and mixing spirituality and materialism, timba 'keeps the roots alive', and challenges a Eurocentric, folklorizing conception that has largely informed forty years of Afro-Cuban official cultural policies.

As I stressed in the previous chapter, nationalistic rhetoric and musical rivalries in the late 1990s created in Cuba an artificial opposition of timba vs. son, where son was hailed as a reified, theatricalized model for national culture. In many ways, this is precisely the opposite of what son has been in the course of its history, that is, an open, dynamic form which 'has functioned historically as an ideological battlefield, a stylistic space mediating African, European, and other cultural influences' (Moore 1997: 111–12). Moore adds:

> Son was and continues to be a form of musical and stylistic bricolage, demonstrating the creative fusion of distinct traditions, national and international. It contains oppositional elements potentially liberating to the Afrocuban working-class community, as well as the constraints of middle-class influence, and thus illustrates the contradictions so prevalent in popular culture. It is a metaphor for the social order within which it developed, embodying and perpetuating emerging conceptions of Cuban-ness.
>
> (ibid.: 113)

While in the last few years the pendulum of the (third) world music discourse seems to have swung towards narratives of authenticity and tradition, timba, like son in the past, continues to display 'the restlessness of spirit which makes ... [the] diaspora culture vital' (Gilroy 1993: 16). It is modern, yet embraces santería and rumba. It is popular, yet is played by musicians with formidable training in classical music. It is Cuban, yet incorporates multiple foreign influences, is made by artists with a thoroughly cosmopolitan background and is circulated globally by records and touring bands, speaking to both foreign audiences and expatriated Afro-Cubans. Timba relies on orality (both primary *and* secondary, following the distinction set by Walter Ong), is performative, processual and dialogic, and employs structures that are open, and can accommodate all sorts of borrowings, quotations and impromptu insertions.

Similar postmodern characters have emerged in the popular cultures of other post-colonial societies and have been interpreted through various notions of cultural mixing such as syncretism, *métissage*, creolization and hybridity. In my introduction, I have already stressed the theoretical limitations of a concept such as syncretism. Guilbault has employed the concepts of *métissage* and *creolité* to discuss French Caribbean popular music as world music. Setting off from Homi Bhabha's influential work on post-colonial cultures, she has described world music as 'both transnational and translational' (1997: 32). According to her, 'the specificity and processes engaged in the construction of world music have the benefit of inviting us to move beyond the quest for narratives of originary and initial subjectivities, and to address new questions that acknowledge the complexity and fluidity of meanings involved in the act of constructing and rearticulating identities through music' (ibid.).

The notion of 'hybrid cultures' has been employed by Néstor García Canclini to describe the reformulations of 'traditional culture', and the collapse of distinctions between cultivated, folk and mass culture characterizing contemporary Latin American societies. Canclini has argued that postmodernist 'critique to inclusive narratives on history can help to disclose the fundamentalist pretensions of traditionalism, ethnicism and nationalism, in order to understand the authoritarian drift of liberalism and socialism' (1998: 22). His analysis appears particularly valuable here, because it shows how fully postmodern cultural practices are taking place in countries that the West largely perceives as backward and characterized by an unfinished modernity. To quote again Lipsitz, it is precisely their hybrid and fragmentary character that makes diasporic cultures those 'best prepared for cultural conflict and political contestation in a globalized world' (1994: 31).

In the case of timba, the notion of the black Atlantic elaborated by Paul Gilroy provides probably the most flexible conceptual framework for looking at this cultural expression of the black diaspora whilst avoiding the deadlock of essentialism vs. anti-essentialism. In that sense, it is revealing that Gilroy pays special attention to dance and music, considering the latter as a 'foundational element' of the black Atlantic. To underline the role of dance music and the level of emotional intensity visible in the participation of people in dance in Cuba may seem a truism, but it helps to remind us of the *necessity* of dance and music in Caribbean societies. 'The expressive cultures developed in slavery continue to preserve in artistic form needs and desires which go far beyond the mere satisfaction of material wants [and] ... reiterate the continuity of art and life' (ibid.: 57).

Gilroy's analysis, however, developed from a predominantly Anglo-US-Caribbean angle as it is, does not take into account Hispanic Afro-Caribbean culture, nor its specific history in Cuba. It is therefore important to stress here that timba, as a music style predominantly produced and consumed by Afro-Cubans, while not related to black ethnicity in any essential way, is rooted in a local black culture that shows evident African retentions in language, religion, music and dance. Within the 'multiple subject positions' (Bhabha 1994) that inform the identities of individuals in post-colonial societies, timba articulates both a sense of belonging and a need for modernity that hold a central place in the identity of contemporary Afro-Cubans.

Moreover, Cuban timba presents very specific musical traits. In contrast to hip-hop and other diasporic styles, abundantly elaborated through the recycling and re-encoding of fragments via audio technology, timba employs these old paraphernalia of music-making, that is, musical instruments: to listen to a timba concert is to hear a perfectly synchronized music machine, like a jazz big band or a symphonic orchestra. This fact ensures that, while biographically and aesthetically gravitating over the black barrio, timba musicians are perfectly at ease with the sophistications of Western art music and jazz, and able to criss-cross musical territories at will.

Dance is central to virtually all the music produced by the black Atlantic. Yet, in many discourses on music, 'dance music' remains a dismissive term. In this sense, the restless musical motion of timba conveys not only a generic creole character of Cuban culture and young black musicians' cosmopolitan and competitive drive, but also their will to confront musical categories. Timba's defiance of established conceptions, cultural as well as political, carries a challenge to distinctions between music styles deemed cultural and worthy of attention, and others merely representing entertainment for the masses and *la gente baja* (the low people).

When one looks at the artistic trajectory of musicians such as José Luís Cortés, it becomes clear that timba does not reflect any natural character of Afro-Cuban expression, but *constructs* itself in reference to Afro-Cuban urban subculture and in opposition to highbrow, elitist culture. The political situation in Cuba makes it difficult for musicians to formulate explicit comments in the way, say, a US rapper or a Jamaican toaster would be able to do. But, in a way, it compels timba musicians to give their best, mobilizing their resources of musical, verbal and body language to construct a multi-layered commentary that can cut very deeply into Cuban society.

Like rappers, *timberos* might be dismissed as nothing but proto-capitalists. But on the island their celebration of consumer culture can carry strong oppositional connotations. In the same way, their frequent calls to *cubanía* cannot be translated in the all-including language of the nation-state, and may be deemed a form of cultural activism. Their use of rumba in songs such as 'Los Sitios entero' – and, at a deeper, quasi-subliminal level, of rumba clave – is not casual or residual, a relic of Afro-Cuban culture lying at the bottom of the Cuban black musical experience. It is an attempt to mobilize the music of Cuban marginal Blacks alongside that of the US ghetto, making the identification between the two at the same time self-evident and cogent. By representing Cuban identity through black *cubanía*, *timberos* make an active cultural and political move that seeks to project unity among Afro-Cuban masses and underline their closeness to black diasporic cultures. Timba, in fact, constructs a transnational 'us' that crosses the borders of Cuba and stretches to include expatriated Cubans and wider diasporic audiences, who look at music and dance as the most powerful expressions of their own culture. This is, perhaps, the greatest political challenge presented by timba. As El Tosco said recalling his concerts in Miami,

> [The US papers wrote] 'NG stopped the traffic in Washington Street'... In the US, in the heart of the *gusanos* (worms), the Miami people, who hate Cuba. There, NG stopped the traffic, and there were even more [people] than for *Buena Vista*! [*he laughs pleased*] ... As I am the music of the *balseros* (rafters), I am from their times, the *balseros* have been to my concert to sing and dance what they've brought with them from Cuba.
>
> (interview with the author, 2000)

Is timba, therefore, to be looked at as a 'local' music? And if so, what is its relationship with 'global' culture? Timba is certainly local in terms of possessing a geographically and ethnically identifiable Cuban audience, in incorporating verbal, musical and choreographic elements of Afro-Cuban urban culture, in feeding and being fed by a distinctive youth black subculture. But it has also proved equally porous to foreign styles and, since the mid-1990s, has entered the global market via records and tours. Such a circular trajectory highlights the conceptual sterility of oppositions such as local and global, because 'once in circulation, music and other cultural forms cannot remain bonded "in" any one group and interpreted simply as an expression that speaks to or reflects the lives of that exclusive group of people' (Negus 1996: 121).

That dichotomy between 'local' and 'global' audiences can also be overcome through the notion of 'bifocality', which Rose (1994) has employed to show how US rap works both as a means of information and solidarity between black people, and as a form of communication with white people. Timba presents aspects that talk specifically to Afro-Cubans, rhythm, words, discourses and dance styles that are largely circulated through live performances and by word of mouth. Yet, at the international level, it is played and sold to, used and enjoyed by black and non-black people, some of whom do not even understand Spanish, and circulated through international Latin networks of dance clubs and festivals, radio stations and record labels. As in other diasporic styles, in timba Blackness appears as a character simultaneously inherent *and* staged, which has ultimately become part of the appeal of the music to both local and foreign audiences.

It might be argued that, given the obsession of the Cuban establishment with their US arch-enemy, the allegiance of *timberos* with a resistant subculture such as African-American hip-hop should have made them more politically acceptable. In practice, this has not been the case. The relationship of timba to the cultural imagery of capitalism makes it a too complicated and controversial form to be easily accepted into a reduced, normalized vision of Cuban identity. Through its ties with the black Atlantic, timba has reaffirmed a meaningful, modern way of being Black, and undermined overarching notions of national unity and purity. Discussing the weariness of young Miami Cubans with Cuban-American politics, David Rieff has written, 'cosmopolitanism encourages ambivalence, not fidelity' (1994: 127). The same might be said for Cubans living on the island. Cultivating their ties with wider African-American culture, *timberos* trespass the boundaries of national culture and the prescriptive, restrictive visions of Cuban identity set by nationalist ideology.

The regeneration of Afro-Cuban arts and the re-emergence of a strong black identity posit important questions to contemporary Cuban society, interrogating it on the meaning of being Cuban and on the reasons for the permanence of mechanisms of social exclusion of Blacks. They also pose difficult questions for the political leadership, because they seem to contradict ideas of national identity, ethnic homogeneousness and social pacification which for forty years have constituted the basis of revolutionary policies. If the Cuban government has on various occasions tried to mobilize Afro Cuban music and culture in its struggle to put forward a united front on national culture, the ties of the actors of the Havana Renaissance with 'marginal' subcultural groups and the music of the black diaspora, and their looking towards Cubans who live outside Cuba appear to lead in the opposite direction. While rap gains popularity and elaborates a version of national hip-hop, its own existence and transnational ties with the culture of US African-Americans challenge the territorial definition of Cuban cultural identity provided by nationalists, showing how music can tell us much about how Caribbean people 'imagine their communities, invent new traditions, narrate the nation, and deterritorialize that state through popular music' (Duany 1996: 185).[11]

---

[11] That the Afro-Cuban cultural flourishing is not a simple fad, but represents a moment of rearticulation of Cuban cultural and political identity is confirmed by various meetings organized in the last few years by black intellectuals and artists, and by the foundation in 1999 in Havana of the Cofradía de la Negritud ('Fraternity of Blackness'). While not explicitly pursuing political goals and intending to work within the framework of a racially integrated nation, the Cofradía aims to draw attention to the position of Blacks in Cuban society and to the growing inequalities of the *período especial*, representing, with the possible exception of the early years of the revolution, an unprecedented public move in post-revolutionary Cuba (De la Fuente 2001).

Bibliography

Abbreviations: journals, magazines and newspapers

BH	*Bohemia*	MC	*Música Cubana*
CB	*El Caimán Barbudo*	MH	*The Miami Herald*
CS	*Cuban Studies*	MNT	*Miami New Times*
EH	*El Nuevo Herald*	NAC	*NACLA Report on the*
ET	*Ethnomusicology*		*Americas*
EP	*El País*	PM	*Popular Music*
GI	*Granma Internacional*	RyC	*Revolución y Cultura*
GR	*Granma*	SC	*Salsa Cubana*
JR	*Juventud Rebelde*	TI	*Tropicana Internacional*
LAMR	*Latin American Music*	WoM	*World of Music*
	Review		

Note that dates in square brackets indicate unconfirmed dates of publication.

Ackerman, E. (1996) 'But will it play in Peoria?'. *MNT*, 18 January

Acosta, L. (1977) 'Las músicas afroamericanas: integración y reinterpretación'. *RyC*, **60**, 54–61

—— (1982) *Música y descolonización*. Habana: Arte y Literatura

—— (1983) *Del tambor al sintetizador*. Habana: Letras Cubanas

—— (1986) 'Machito: padre del jazz latino y de la salsa'. *RyC*, **5**, 16–23

—— (1990a) 'The Problem of Music and its Dissemination in Cuba', in Manuel 1990a, 187–213 (first published in Acosta 1983)

—— (1990b) 'The Rumba, the Guaguancó, and Tío Tom', in Manuel 1990a, 51–73

—— (1993) *Elige tú, que canto yo*. Habana: Letras Cubanas

—— (1997) 'Terminó la polemica sobre la salsa?'. *MC*, **0**, 26–9

—— (1998) 'La timba y sus antecedentes en la música bailable cubana'. *SC*, A. 2, **6**, 9–11

—— (1999) *Dal tamburo al sintetizzatore: la musica cubana e afrocubana*. Viterbo (Italy): Massari [Italian edn of Acosta 1983, updated with a new final chapter]

—— (2000) *Descarga cubana: el jazz en Cuba 1900–1950*. Habana: Unión

—— (2002) *Descarga número dos: el jazz en Cuba 1950–2000*. Habana: Unión

—— (2003) *Cubano Be, Cubano Bop: One Hundred Years of Jazz in Cuba*. Washington: Smithsonian Institution Press

Acosta Llerena, O. (1998) 'Estan todos los que son?'. *JR*, 16 August

Adams, D. (1994) 'Cuba's New Capitalists'. *Hemisphere*, Winter/Spring, 8–10

Aguiar Díaz, J.A. (2002) 'Censura contra poetas y cantantes'. *Grupo Decoro*/Cubanet 9 December, <http://www.cubanet.org/>

Alén, O., Acosta, L. Vilar G. et al. [1985] *Incidencia del rock en la juventud cubana actual*. Habana: CIDMUC Report (mimeo)

Alén Perez, A. (1988) 'Aproximación al gusto musical'. *Clave*, 9, 46–9

Alén Rodríguez, O. (1985) 'Lenguaje musical de Cuba'. *RyC*, 11, 18–23

—— (1986) *La música de las sociedades de tumba francesa en Cuba*. Habana: Casa de las Américas

—— (1994) *De lo afrocubano a la salsa: géneros musicales de Cuba*. Habana: Artex

—— (1999) Review of Y. Daniel, *Rumba*, 1995. *LAMR*, 20 (2), Fall–Winter, 313–19

—— (2000) 'Nations and Musical Traditions: Cuba', in D.A. Olsen and D.E. Sheehy, 822–39

Alvarado Ramos, J.A. (1996) 'Relaciones raciales en Cuba: Notas de investigación'. *Temas*, 7, July–September, 37–43

Amnesty International, 'Cuba', in *Annual Report 2000*, <http://www.amnesty.org/>

Analisis de la programación musical de la TV cubana (1986). Habana: CIDMUC (mimeo)

Aparicio, F. (1998) *Listening to Salsa: Gender, Latin Popular Music and Puerto Rican Cultures*. Hanover and London: Wesleyan University–University Press of New England

—— and Chávez-Silverman, S. (eds) (1997) *Tropicalization: Transcultural Representations of Latinidad*. Hanover and London: University. Press of New England

Apter, A. (1991) 'Herskovits's Heritage: Rethinking Syncretism in the African Diaspora'. *Diaspora*, 1 (3), 235–260

Arcos, B. (2000) Interview with Ry Cooder, in 'The Global Village', *Pacifica Radio*, Los Angeles, 27 June, <http://www.pbs.org/buenavista/musicians/bios/cooder_int_full_transript.html>

Ardévol, J. (1969) *Introducción a Cuba: la música*. Habana: Instituto del Libro

Arenas, R. (1993) *Before Night Falls*. London: Viking

Argyriadis, K. (1999) *La religión à La Havane*. Amsterdam: Éditions Archives Contemporaines

Ariel, S. [1998] 'Wenders sobre La Habana'. *CB*, A. 31, **285**, 16–17

Arocha, Z. (2000) 'Getting Along Culturally with Cuba'. *The Washington Post*, 24 February

Austerlitz, P. (1997) *Merengue: Dominican Music and Dominican Identity*. Philadelphia: Temple University Press

Averill, G. (1997) *A Day for the Hunter. A Day for the Prey: Popular Music and Power in Haiti*. Chicago and London: University of Chicago Press

Ayorinde, C. (2000) 'Regla de Ocha-Ifá and the Construction of Cuban Identity', in P.E. Lovejoy (ed.) *Identity in the Shadow of Slavery*. London and New York: Continuum, 72–85

Azicri, M. (2000) *Cuba Today and Tomorrow: Reinventing socialism*. Gainesville: University Press of Florida

Bakhtin, M. (1979) *L'opera di Rabelais e la cultura popolare*. Torino: Einaudi [English edn: *Rabelais and His World*. Bloomington: Indiana University Press, 1984]

Baloyra, E.A. and Morris, J.A. (eds) (1993) *Conflict and Change in Cuba*. Albuquerque: University of New Mexico Press

Barber, K. (ed.) (1997) *Readings in African Popular Culture*. Oxford: Currey

Basso Ortíz, A. (2001) '¿Por amor del arte?'. *La Jiribilla*, <http://www.lajiribilla.cu/>

Béhague, G. (1982) 'Folk and Traditional Music in Latin America: General Aspects and Research Perspectives'. *WoM*, **XXV** (2), 3–18

—— (ed.) (1994) *Music and Black Ethnicity: The Caribbean and South America*. Miami: North-South Center–University of Miami

—— (1997) Review of Gómez – Elí Rodríguez 1995, *Música latinoamericana y caribeña*. *LAMR*, **18** (1), 127–9

Behar, R. (ed.) (1995) *Bridges to Cuba / Puentes a Cuba*. Ann Arbor: University of Michigan Press

Bello, N. and Casanellas Cué (2002) 'La timba cubana'. *Clave* (segunda epoca), A. 41 (5)

Bello, R. (1990) '700.000 personas han visto a los Van Van en su gira nacional'. *GR*, 9 May, 5

Bengelsdorf, C. (1994) *The Problem of Democracy in Cuba: Between Vision and Reality*. New York and Oxford: Oxford University Press

Benítez Rojo, A. (1984) 'La cultura caribeña en Cuba: continuidad versus ruptura'. *CS*, **14**, 1–15

—— (1998) 'The Role of Music in the Emergence of Afro-Cuban Culture'. *Research in African Literatures*, **29** (1), 179–84

Benjamin, M. (1990a) 'Things Fall Apart'. *NAC* **24** (2), August, 13–22

—— (1990b) 'Soul Searching'. *NAC*, **24** (2), August, 23–31

Benmayor, R. (1981) 'La "Nueva Trova": New Cuban Song'. *LAMR*, 2 (1), Spring–Summer, 11–44

Bethell, L. (ed.) (1993) *Cuba: A Short History.* Cambridge: Cambridge University Press

Bhabha, H. (1994) *The Location of Cultures.* London: Routledge

Blacking, J. (1973) *How Musical is Man?* Seattle and London: University of Washington Press

Blum, J. (1978) 'Problems of Salsa Research'. *ET*, January, XII (1), 137–49

Boehlert, E. (1999) 'Cuban Revolution'. <Salon.com>, 20 August

Boggs, V.W. (ed.) (1992) *Salsiology: Afro-Cuban Music and the Evolution of Salsa in New York City.* Westport, Conn.: Greenwood Press

Bolívar Aróstegui, N. (1990) *Los orishas en Cuba.* Habana: Unión

Borges-Triana, J. (1997) 'Francis Cabezas: Un Manager en la Habana' *CB*, A. 30, **282**, 10–12

Brandon, G. (1993) *Santería from Africa to the New World.* Bloomington and Indianapolis: Indiana University Press

Brito López, M.A. (1999) 'Prohíben la entrada de mujeres a las discotecas en La Habana', BPIC/*Cubanet*, 29 June <http://www.cubanet.org/>

Brock, L. and Castañeda Fuentes, D. (eds) (1998) *Between Race and Empire: African-Americans and Cubans before the Cuban Revolution.* Philadelphia: Temple University Press

Broughton, S. et al. (1994) *World Music: The Rough Guide.* London: Penguin

Brouwer, L. (1989) *La musica, lo cubano y la inovación.* Habana: Letras Cubanas

Bunck, J.M. (1994) *Fidel Castro and the Quest for a Revolutionary Culture in Cuba.* University Park, PA: Penn State University Press

Buongiorno, P. (1997) 'Cuba Boom'. *Panorama* (Italy), 18 December, 24–34

Cabrera, L. (1986) *El monte: Igbo Finda, Ewe Orisha, Vititi Nfinda.* Miami: Universal

Cala, N. and Montes de Oca, E. (1996) 'Indisciplina social: el asedio de las malas costumbres'. *BH*, A. 88, **2**, 12–16

Cámara, M. (1995) 'Third Options: Beyond the Border', in Behar 1995, 217–25

Cancio Isla, V. (2001) 'Músicos en Cuba brindan su apoyo a Manolín, "el médico de la salsa"'. *MH*, 10 April

Canizares, R.J. (1994) 'Santería: from Afro-Caribbean Cult to World Religion'. *Caribbean Quarterly*, **40** (1), March, 59–63

Caño Secade, M. del C. (1996) 'Relacciones raciales, proceso de ajuste, y política social'. *Temas*, 7, July–September, 58–65

Cantor, J. (1997) 'Bring on the Cubans!'. *MNT*, 19 June

——— (1998a) 'La isla de la Musica'. *MNT*, 28 May

—— (1998b) 'The Sound of Change'. *MNT*, 16 October

—— (1998c) 'Poets of the Pueblo'. *MNT*, 5 November

—— (1999a) 'Home for the Holidays'. *MNT*, 21 January

—— (1999b) 'Cuban Music goes Commercial'. *Billboard*, 20 February

—— (1999c) 'Free Radio Miami: Adalberto Alvarez y Su Son'. *MNT*, 25 March

—— (1999d) 'Portrait of the Artist as a Communist Bureaucrat'. *MNT*, 24 June

—— 'Welcome to the Bureaucracy'. *MNT*, 24 June

Caraballo, M. (1997) 'Un Yuma en el Salón Rosado'. *TI*, 5, 19–20

Caraballo Sánchez, M. (1996) 'Un buen momento para el derecho de autor'. *TI*, 1, 59–60

Carbonell, W. (1961) *Crítica, cómo surgió la cultura nacional*. Habana: Yaka

Cardona, E. (1998) 'Médico de la Salsa "ingresa" en Miami'. *EH*, 31 October

—— (1999) 'El Médico de la Salsa ya no está "arriba de la bola"'. *EH*, 16 September

Carpentier, A. (1946) *La música en Cuba*. Habana: Letras Cubanas 1988 [English edn: *Music in Cuba*. Minneapolis: University of Minnesota Press, 2001]

Carr R. (1974) *Tengo, by Nicolás Guillén*. Detroit: Broadside Press

Carranza Valdés, H. (1997) 'Economic Changes in Cuba: Problems and Challenges', in Centeno and Font 1997, 186–200

—— et al. (1996) *Cuba: Restructuring the Economy. A Contribution to the Debate*. London: Institute of Latin American Studies

Carrobello, C., Ramón, N. and Terrero, A. (1991) 'La gente va llegando al baile' [part 1]. *BH*, A. 83, 32, 9 August, 4–9

Carrobello, C. and Terrero, A. (1991) 'El baile no tiene casa' [part 3] *BH*, A 83, 34, 23 August, 10–13

Casal, L. (1979) 'Race Relations in Contemporary Cuba', in *The Position of Blacks in Brazilian and Cuban Society*. London: Minority Rights Group 7, 11–27

Casals, R. (1998) 'Turismo, el corazón de la economia'. *GI*, 33, 2 March

Casanellas Cué, L. (1999a) 'Textos para bailar: una polémica actual?'. *SC*, A. 2, 7–8,12–15

—— (1999b) *La música bailable y su incidencia en la habla popular cubana*. Habana: CIDMUC (mimeo)

Castañeda, M. (1996) 'Battle of the Genres'. *GI*, 20 March

—— (1998a) 'Roy Hargrove with Chucho Valdés: Triad for a Grammy'. *GI*, 4 March

—— (1998b) 'Juan Formell: From Practice to Theory'. *GI*, 1 April

—— (1998c) 'A Space for Cuban Recordings'. *GI*, 12 May

———— (2000) 'Cubadisco 2000: una aventura de comunicación y encuentros'. *GI*, 5 May

———— (2001) '*Rumba Soy Yo* wins Latin Grammy', *GI*, 30 October

Castellanos, E.J. (1997) *Los Beatles en Cuba*. Habana: Unión

Castellanos, I. (1983) *Elegua quiere tambó: cosmovisión religiosa afrocubana en las canciones populares*. Cali, Colombia: Universidad del Valle

Castellanos, I.M. and J. (1994) *Cultura afrocubana, IV: letras, musica, arte*. Miami: Universal

Castellanos, J. and I. (1987) 'The Geographic, Ethnologic, and Linguistic Roots of Cuban Blacks'. *CS 17*, 95–110

Castellanos, R. (1998) 'La timba cubana en Uruguay con Los Van Van: entrevista con Juan Formell'. *En Perspectiva/ Radio El Espectador*, Uruguay, 27 October, <http://www.espectador.com/>

Castro, F. (1959) 'Discurso del 22 marzo de 1959'. *Revolución*, 23 March

———— (1961) 'Palabras a los intelectuales'. Speech at the Biblioteca Nacional José Martí, 30 June, in *Palabras a los intelectuales*. Habana: Editorial Política [reprinted in *Política Cultural de la Revolución Cubana*. Habana: Ciencias Sociales, 1977]

———— (1976) 'Informe al primer congreso del Partido Comunista de Cuba', in *Enseñanzas de la Revolución de Cuba*. Bogotá: Ed. Suramérica

———— (1987) *Fidel and Religion: Castro talks on Revolution and Religion with Frei Betto*. New York: Simon & Schuster

———— (1992) Speech to the Asamblea Nacional del Poder Popular. Havana, 12 July, broadcast by Havana Tele Rebelde [transcription and translation in Castro Speech Database, FBIS–Foreign Broadcast Information Service <http://www.lanic.utexas.edu/la/cb/cuba/ castro. html/>]

———— (1993) Speech at the closing of the Assessment Meeting of the Communist Party of Cuba, Havana Convention Centre, 7 November, broadcast by Radio Rebelde [transcription and translation in Castro Speech Database, FBIS–Foreign Broadcast Information Service, <http://www.lanic.utexas.edu/la/cb/cuba/castro.html>]

———— (1994) Varadero News Conference, broadcast by Havana Tele Rebelde, 26 May [transcription and translation in Castro Speech Database, FBIS-Foreign Broadcast Information Service <http:// www.lanic.utexas.edu/la/cb/cuba/castro.html>]

———— (1999) Speech for the 40th anniversary of National Revolutionary Police on 5 January, Havana. *GI*, 7 January

———— (2003) Speech for the inauguration as President of the Republic of Cuba, 6 March

Castro, M. (2004) 'Triumph of the Zealots', *MNT*, 29 July

Cawthorne, A. (1998) 'Tourism Boom Shakes up Cuban Society'. *Reuters* (Havana), 31 August

Centeno, M.A. and Font, M. (eds) (1997) *Toward a New Cuba? Legacies of a Revolution*. Boulder and London: Rienner

Centro de Estudios Sobra América (1992) *The Cuban Revolution into the 1990s: Cuban Perspectives*. Boulder: Westview Press

Clifford, J. (1992) 'Traveling Cultures', in L. Grossberg, C. Nelson and P.A. Treichler (eds) *Cultural Studies*, New York and London: Routledge, 17–46

Cohen, J. (1991) 'Cuba libre'. *Playboy*, **38** (3) March, 69–75

Cohen, S. (1993) 'Ethnography and Popular Music Studies'. *PM*, **12** (2), 123–38

'Condecoran a artistas de Buena Vista Social Club' (2002), *Efe/El Universal* (Mexico), 13 August

Connell, R.W. (1994) 'Gender Regimes and the Gender Order', in *The Polity Reader in Gender Studies*. Cambridge: Polity Press, 29–40

Cornelius, S. and Amira, J. (1992) *The Music of Santería: Traditional Rhythms of the Batá Drums*. C. Point, Ind.: White Cliffs Media

Corzo, C. (1997) 'Relatan cineastas pesadilla en Cuba'. *EH*, 22 September

Craske, N. (1999) *Women and Politics in Latin America*. Cambridge: Polity Press

Crook, L. (1982) 'A Musical Analysis of the Cuban Rumba'. *LAMR*, 3 (1), Spring–Summer, 93–123

Cruz Jorge, M. (1997) *Análisis de mercado de una agrupación de proyección internacional: la agrupación de Issac Delgado*. Habana: CIDMUC (mimeo)

'Cuba, nucleo original y hoy principal elaborador de 'salsa': y además, militante' (1978). *CB*, **131**, 16–17

'Cuba bans Salsa Group for 6 Months' (1997). *Associated Press* (Mexico City), 11 August

'Cuba cracks down on dissidence' (2003). *BBC News*, 19 March

'Cuba: Ideology Shake Up threatens Cultural Liberalization' (1998). *CNN Inter Press Service* (Havana), 4 March

'Cuban Party Congress reveals that Economy is faring worse than expected' (1997). *Latin American Weekly Report*, 14 October

La Cultura en Cuba socialista (1982). Habana: Letras Cubanas

D'Rivera, P. (1999) *Mi vida saxual*. San Juan de Puerto Rico: Plaza Mayor

Daniel, Y. (1995) *Rumba: Dance and Social Change in Contemporary Cuba*. Bloomington and Indianapolis: Indiana University Press

Davies, C. (1996) 'Recent Cuban Fiction Films: Identification, Interpretation, Disorder'. *Bulletin of Latin American Research*, **15** (2), 177–92

De la Fuente, A. (1998) 'Race, National Discourse, and Politics in Cuba: An Overview'. *Latin American Perspectives*, **100**, (25: 3), May, 43–69

―――― (2001) *A Nation for All: Race, Inequality, and Politics in Twentieth-Century Cuba*. Chapel Hill: University of North Carolina Press

―――― A. and Glasco, L. (1997) 'Are Blacks "Getting Out of Control"? Racial Attitudes, Revolution, and Political Transition in Cuba', in Centeno and Font 1997, 53–71

De la Hoz, P. (1987) 'El rock nuestro de cada dia'. *RyC*, 5, May, 10–14

―――― (1990) 'Comienzo y final del baile'. *GR*, 2 February

―――― (1991a) 'Mi salsa'. *GR*, 21 March

―――― (1991b) 'Rap hasta la locura'. *GR*, 20 June

―――― (1997) 'Adalberto Alvarez: en el alma de los bailadores'. *TI*, 3, 2–5

Delgado, A. (2000) 'Bamboleo: lo que se baila, lo que se usa'. Interview with Lázaro Valdés and Vannia Borges. *Descarga*, 27 August, <http://www.descarga.com/cgi-bin/db/archives>

Delgado, K.M. (2001) 'Iyesá: Afro-Cuban Music and Culture in Contemporary Cuba'. Unpublished PhD Thesis, University of California at Los Angeles

Delgado, L. (1996) 'Somos eróticos porqué somos cubanos'. *Diario 16* (Spain), 22 February

Del Pino, A. (1997) 'De frente al público: Paulíto FG'. *RyC*, A. 36, 5, 22–4

Del Puerto, C. and Vergara, S. (1994) *The True Cuban Bass*. Petaluma, Calif.: Sher Music

De Motas, M. (1996) 'Represión en La Tropical'. *APIC/Cubanet*, 23 October, <http://www.cubanet.org/>

Desipio, L. (2003) 'Cuban Miami: Seeking Identity in a Political Borderland', *Latin American Research Review*, 38 (2), 207–19

Díaz, A. L. (2002) 'Rap cubano: ¿Quién tiró la tiza?', *Grupo Decoro/Cubanet*, 4 October, <http://www.cubanet.org/>

Díaz, C. (1997) *La nueva trova*. Habana: Letras Cubanas

Díaz, E., Fernández, E. and Caram, T. (1996) *Turismo y prostitución*. Habana: FLACSO (in-house document)

Díaz Ayala, C. (1981) *Música cubana del Areíto a la Nueva Trova*. San Juan de Puerto Rico: Cubanacán

―――― (1994) *Cuba canta y baila: discografia de la música cubana*, vol. I. San Juan de Puerto Rica: Fundación Musicalia

―――― (1999) *Cuando salí de la Habana, 1898–1997: Cien años de música cubana por el mundo*. San Juan de Puerto Rico: Fundación Musicalia

Díaz Canals, T. and González Olmedo, G. (1995) 'Cultura y prostitución: una solución posible'. Habana: Universidad de la Habana, Facultad de Sociología [in *LASA* Papers 52 (1997, 167–75)

Dilla Alfonso, H. (2000) 'The Cuban Experiment: Economic Reform, Social Restructuring, and Politics'. *Latin American Perspectives*, **110** (27: 1), January, 33–44

Dilla, H. (1999) 'The Virtues and Misfortunes of Civil Society'. *NAC*, **32** (5), March–April, 30–36

Domínguez, J. (1993) 'Cuba since 1959', in Bethell 1993, 95–148

Domínguez, J.L. (1997) 'Comienza una transición hacia el autoritarismo en Cuba?'. *Encuentro de la cultura cubana*, **4/5**, Spring–Summer, 7–23

Domínguez García, M.I. (1996) *Jóvenes Cubanos: expectativas en los 90*. Habana: Ciencias Sociales

Dopico Black, G. (1989) 'The Limits of Expression: Intellectual Freedom in Postrevolutionary Cuba'. *CS*, no. 19, 107–42

Dore, E. (ed.) (1997) *Gender Politics in Latin America: Debates in Theory and Practice*. New York: Monthly Review Press

Duany, J. (1988) 'After the Revolution: The Search for Roots in Afro-Cuban Culture'. *Latin American Research Review*, **XXIII** (1), 244–55

—— (1995) 'Review of O. Alén Rodríguez 1992, *De lo afrocubano a la salsa*'. *LAMR*, **16** (1), 93–5

—— (1996) 'Rethinking the Popular: Recent Essays on Caribbean Music and Identity'. *LAMR*, **17** (2), 176–92

Dunlop, A. (1995) 'What Effect have the 1990's Economic Reforms had on Cuba's Political Institutions and Culture'. Unpublished Masters Thesis, University of London–Institute of Latin American Studies

Durán, L. (1993) Interview with J.L. Cortés, April (manuscript)

—— (1996) Interview with R. González, May (manuscript)

Eckstein, S. (1997) 'The Limits of Socialism in a Capitalist World Economy: Cuba Since the Collapse of the Soviet Bloc', in Centeno and Font 1997, 135–50

'Economic Resolution of the Fifth Congress of the Communist Party of Cuba' (1997). *GI*, 15 October

Elí Rodríguez, V. (1989) 'Apuntes sobre la creación musical actual en Cuba'. *LAMR*, **10** (2), 287–97

—— (1994) 'Cuban Music and Ethnicity: Historical Considerations', in Béhague 1994, 91–108

—— (1999) *La música entre Cuba y España: tradición e innovación*. Madrid: Fundación Autor

——, Casanova Oliva, A.V. et al. (1997) *Instrumentos de la música folclórico-popular de Cuba*. Habana: CIDMUC (2 vols)

Elizalde, R.M. (1992) 'Bailando suave'. *JR*, 5, January

—— (1996a) *Flores desechables:¿Prostitución en Cuba?*. Habana: Abril

—— (1996b) 'Látigo sobre la rencilla salsera', *JR*, 8 September, 13

—— and Perera, A. (1997) 'Turismo Sessuale'. *El Moncada* (bulletin of the Italia-Cuba Association), a. V, **1**, March, 17–18

'El rock por dentro' (1986). *RyC*, **3**, 13–19

'El rojo y el verde' [1997]. *CB*, A. 30, **280**, 4–7; 26–7

Estado actual de la Música Popular Cubana (1991). Habana: CIDMUC (mimeo)

Erlich, R. (1999) 'What do Cubans think of the "Buena Vista Social Club"?'. *San José Mercury*, 28 October

Estival, J.-P. (1996) 'Nouveaux enjeux ou continuité historique? La rumba, un example afrocubaine'. *Cahiers des Musiques Tradition-nelles*, **9**, 201–23

Evangelisti, M. (1999) *La marcia su Cuba: la nuova revolución degli italiani*. Roma: Stampa Alternativa

Evenson, D. (1990) 'Channelling Dissent'. *NAC*, **24** (2), August, 26–8

Feld, S. (1995) 'From Schizophonia to Schismogenesis', in G.E. Marcus and F.R. Myers (eds) *The Traffic in Culture: Refiguring Art and Anthropology*. Berkeley: University of California Press, 96–126

Fernández, D.J. (1993) 'Youth in Cuba: Resistance and Accommodation', in Baloyra and Morris 1993, 189–211

—— and Cámara B.M. (eds) (2000) *Cuba, the Elusive Nation: Interpretations of National Identity*. Gainesville: University Press of Florida

Fernández, N.T. (1996) 'The Color of Love: Young Interracial Couples in Cuba'. *Latin American Perspectives*, **88** (23: 1), Winter, 99–117

Fernández, O. (1995) *Strings and Hide*. Habana: José Martí

Fernández Barroso, S. (1979) 'La música en Cuba durante la etapa revolucionaria'. *Revista de la Biblioteca Nacional José Martí*, **2**, May–August, 119–31

Fernández Robaina, T. (1971) *Indice de Revistas Folklóricas Cubanas*. Habana: Biblioteca Nacional José Martí

—— (1997) *Hablen paleros y santeros*. Ciencias Sociales: Habana [first published 1994]

—— (2002) 'El tratamiento del tema negro en el rap cubano'. *La Jiribilla*, August, <http://www.lajiribilla.cu/>

Ferreira, R. (1998) 'Cuba convierte en negocio la moda de lo afrocubano'. *EH*, 16 January

Ferriol Muruaga, A., González Gutiérrez, A. et al. (1998) *Cuba: Crisis, ajuste, y situación social (1990–1996)*. Habana: Ciencias Sociales

Fitzgerald, F.T. (1994) *The Cuban Revolution in Crisis*. New York: Monthly Review Press

Fletcher, P. (1997) 'Cuban Police Close Disco After Vice Raid'. *Reuters* (Havana), 28 August

—— (1998) 'Cuban Film Chief Plays Down Bad Review from Castro'. *Reuters* (Havana), 27 February

Foehr, S. (2001) *Waking Up in Cuba*. London: Sanctuary

Fogel, J.-F. and Rosenthal, B. (1994) *Fin de siglo en la Habana*. Bogotá: Tercer Mundo

'Folklore: Sabado de la rumba' (2001). *Habana Hoy*, March, <www.afrocubaweb.com>

Forrest, D.P. (1999) 'Bichos, Maricones and Pingueros: An Ethnographic Study of Maleness and Scarcity in Contemporary Socialist Cuba'. Unpublished PhD Thesis, University of London–School of Oriental and African Studies

Fraser Delgado, C. (2000) 'The Salsa Doctor is out'. *MNT*, 14 September

Freemuse/Danish Centre for Human Rights (2002) *Second World Conference on Music and Censorship*. Copenhagen, 28–9 September

Frith, S. (1983) *Sound Effects: Youth, Leisure, and the Politics of Rock 'n' Roll*. London: Constable

—— (1988) Music for Pleasure: Essays in the Sociology of Pop. Cambridge: Polity Press

—— (ed.) (1989) *World Music, Politics and Social Change*. Manchester: Manchester University Press

—— and Goodwin, A. (eds) (1990) *On Record: Rock, Pop, & the Written Word*. London: Routledge

Fusco, C. (1997) 'Jineteras en Cuba'. *Encuentro de la cultura cubana*, 4/5, Spring–Summer, 53–63

Galilea, C. (1998a) 'La Habana enloquece con la mejor orquesta de baile en años'. *EP*, 17 May

—— (1998b) 'Las estrellas de la salsa cubana ponen a bailar a sus 5.000 espectadores en Madrid'. *EP*, 28 May

Garces, C. (1980) 'Irakere, experimentación con éxito'. *BH*, 72, 21 March, 30–1

García, A. and Pérez Mok, M. (2001) 'La importancia del turismo en el desarrollo futuro de la economía cubana en las condiciones de la globalización de la economía'. Paper presented at the XXIII International Congress of Latin American Studies Association (*LASA*), Washington DC, 6–8 September

García, C. (1997) *The Agüero Sisters*. New York: Knopf

García, M.C. (1996) *Cuban Miami in Havana Usa*. Berkeley: University of California Press

García Canclini, N. (1998) *Culture ibride*, Milano: Guerini e Associati [first published as *Culturas híbridas: Estrategías para entrar y salir de la modernidad*, Mexico City 1989]

García Meralla, E. (1997a) 'Timba Brava'. *TI*, 4, 5–7

—— (1997b) 'Música popular cubana 1963–1990. ¿Que tiene que sigue ahí?'. *Musicalia Dos*, 1, 4–7

—— (1997c) 'El boom que experimenta la música popular cubana mucho se debe a un sonido que algunos llaman timba'. *TI*, 4, 7–11

—— and Henry, T. (1998) 'Somos lo que hay: crónica de un concierto'. *SC*, A 2, 5, 20–21

—— (1998) 'El camino de NG'. *TI*, 7, 12–14

—— (2001) 'Conversando con el *Charanguero Mayor*'. *SC*, A. 5, **16**, 23–6

Garofalo, R. (1993) 'Whose World, What Beat: The Transnational Music Industry, Identity, and Cultural Imperialism'. *WoM*, 35 (2), 16–32

Garve, L. (1997) 'Multan a jóvenes por su vestimenta'. *APIC-Cubanet* (Havana), 24 June, <http://www.cubanet.org/>

Gerard, C. and Sheller, M. (1989) *Salsa: The Rhythm of Latin Music*. Tempe, Ariz.: White Cliffs Media

'Getting Ready for Helms-Burton Law' (1996). *Latin American Weekly Report*, 25 April

Gilroy, P. (1993) *The Black Atlantic: Modernity and Double Consciousness*. London: Verso

Giro, R. (ed.) (1995a) *Panorama de la música popular cubana*. Habana: Letras Cubanas

—— (1995b) 'Los motivos del son: Hitos en su sendero caribeño y Universal', in Giro 1995a, 219–30

Glasser, R. (1995) *My Music is My Flag: Puerto Rican Musicians and their New York Communities*. Berkeley: University of California Press

Godfried, E. (2000) 'Buena Vista Social Club: Critics, Self-criticism, and the Survival of Cuban Son', in *AfrocubaWeb*, November, <http://afrocubaweb.com/>

Goizueta, G. (1996) 'Caminar por la cuerda de un violín'. *TI*, **1**, 17–19

Gómez, Z. and Elí Rodríguez, V. (1989) *Haciendo música cubana*. Habana: Pueblo y Educación

—— (1995) *Música latinoamericana y caribeña*. Habana: Pueblo y Educación

Gómez Cairo, J. (1995) 'Acerca de la interacción de géneros en la música popular cubana', in Giro 1995a, 123–37

Goodwin, A. and Gore, J. (1995) 'World Beat and the Cultural Imperialism Debate', in R. Sakolsky and F. Wei-Han Ho (eds) *Sounding Off!* New York: Autonomedia, 121–31

Gramatges, H. (1997) *Presencia de la Revolución en la música cubana*. Habana: Letras Cubanas

Grenet, E. (1939) *Música popular cubana*. Habana: Secretaría de Agricultura

Grenier, L. and Guibault, J. (1997) '*Creolité* et *Francophonie* in Music: Socio-musical Repositioning Where it Matters'. *Cultural Studies*, **11** (2), 207–34

Guanche, J. (1983) *Proceso etnoculturales en Cuba*. Habana: Letras Cubanas

Guanche Pérez, J. (1993) 'La religiosidad popular en la música tradicional cubana'. *Folklore Americano*, **56**, June–December, 27–42

—— (1996a) 'Etnicidad y racialidad en la Cuba actual'. *Temas*, **7**, July–September, 51–7

—— (1996b) 'Santería cubana e identidad cultural'. *RyC*, **2**, 3–6

Guerra, R. (1989) *Teatralización del folklore*. Habana: Letras Cubanas

Guerra Sierra, M. (1997) *Agrupaciones de música popular bailable actual*. Habana, CIDMUC (mimeo)

Guilbault, J. (1997) 'Interpreting World Music: A Challenge in Theory and Practice'. *PM*, **16** (1), 31–44

—— (with G. Averill, E. Benoit and G. Rabess) (1993) *Zouk: World Music in the West Indies*. Chicago and London: University of Chicago Press

Guillén, N. (1964) *Tengo*. Santa Clara, Universidad Central de Las Villas [republ. in *Sóngoro Cosongo y otros poemas*. Madrid: Alianza Editorial, 1998]

Gurza, A. (2001) 'From Cuba with Tension'. *Los Angeles Times*, 12 July

Gutiérrez, P.J. (1997) 'Prostitución: cuantas caras tiene Eva?'. *BH*, A. 89, **26**, 10–13

—— (1998) *Trilogía sucia de La Habana*. Barcelona: Anagrama

Habel, J. (1991) *Cuba: The Revolution in Peril*. London: Verso

Hagedorn, K.J. (2001) *Divine Utterances: The Performance of Afro-Cuban Santería*. Washington: Smithsonian Institution Press

Halebsky, S. and Kirk, J.M. (eds) (1985) *Cuba: Twenty-five Years of Revolution, 1959–1984*. New York: Praeger

—— (eds) (1992) *Cuba in Transition: Crisis and Transformation*. Boulder: Westview Press

Hall, S. (1990) 'Cultural Identities and Diaspora', in J. Rutherford (ed.) *Identity*. London: Lawrence & Wishart

—— (1992a) 'New Ethnicities', in J. Donald and A. Rattansi (eds) *Race, Culture and Difference*. London: Sage [reprinted in H.A. Baker, Jr., M. Diawara and R.H. Lindeborg (eds) *Black British Cultural Studies*, Chicago and London: University of Chicago Press, 1996, 163–72] [conference paper from 1987]

—— (1992b) 'What is this 'Black' in Black Popular Culture?', in G. Dent (ed.) *Black Popular Culture*, Seattle: Bay Press, 21–33

Hamm, C. (1982) 'Some Thoughts on the Measurement of Popularity in Music', in Horn and Frith, 3–15

'Hardline Communists Prevail in Cuba' (1997). *Associated Press* (Havana), 28 August

Hatchwell, E. and Calder, S. (1995) *Cuba: A Guide to the People, Politics and Culture*. London: Latin American Bureau [2nd edn, 1999]

Hebdige, R. (1979) *Subculture: The Meaning of Style*. London: Methuen
—— (1987) *Cut 'n' Mix: Culture, Identity and Caribbean Music*. London: Comedia
Helg, A. (1995) *Our Rightful Share: The Afrocuban Struggle for Equality, 1886–1912*, Chapel Hill: University of North Carolina Press
Henderson, D.R. (1997) 'Why Our Cuba Policy is Wrong'. *Fortune*, 13 October
Henry, T. (1998) 'Timba, timberos!'. *SC*, A. 2, 5, 22–3
Hernández, C. (ed.) (1982) *Ensaysos de música latinoamericana*. Habana: Casa de las Américas
Hernández, E. (1986) *La música en persona*. Habana: Letras Cubanas
Hernández, R. (2001) 'Los árboles y el bosque: políticas cubanas post Elián'. *Foreign Affairs*, **1** (3), Fall–Winter
—— and Borges Triana, J. et al. (2002).'La música popular come espejo social'. *Temas*, **29**, April–June, 61–80
—— and Coatsworth, J.H. (2001) *Culturas encontradas: Cuba y los Estados Unidos*. La Habana: Centro Juan Marinello and Cambridge, Mass.: Centro de Estudios Latinoamericanos, Harvard University
Hernández-Reguant, A. (2000) 'Revolutionary Modernity does not sell Records: Buena Vista Social Club'. Paper presented at *Musical Intersections*/IASPM Canada Conference, Toronto, 1–4 November
Herskovits, M.J. (1958) *Acculturation: The Study of Culture Contact*. Gloucester, Mass.: Smith
Hesmondhalgh, D. (1998) 'Globalisation and Cultural Imperialism: A Case Study of the Music Industry', in R. Kiely and P. Marfleet (eds) *Globalisation and the Third World*. London: Routledge, 163–83
Hoch, D. (1999) 'Not only built 4 the Cuban Bronx'. *The Village Voice*, 29 September–5 October
Hoffmann, B. (ed.) (1995) *Cuba: abertura y reforma económica*. Caracas (Venezuela): Nueva Sociedad
Holgado Fernández, I. (2000) *¡No es fácil! Mujeres cubanas y la crisis revolucionaria*. Barcelona: Icaria
Horn, D. and Frith, S. (eds) (1982) *Popular Music Perspectives*. Papers from the First International Conference on Popular Music Research. Göteborg-Exeter: IASPM
Human Rights Watch (1999) *Cuba's Repressive Machinery: Human Rights Forty Years After the Revolution*. New York, Washington, London and Brussels, <http://www.hrw.org>
Informe central al Segundo Congreso del Partido Comunista de Cuba (1980), in N. Madan (ed), *La lucha ideologica*. Habana: Editora Política, 1982
Ishikawa, B. (2001) 'Despierta, que estás en Cuba!', in <timba.com>, 17 August

Jones, N. and Smith, V. (1998) 'Cuba', in *South America, Central America and the Caribbean* (7th edn). London: Europa, 254–75

Jules-Rosette, B. (1984) *The Messages of Tourist Art*. New York and London: Plenum Press

Katel, P. (1994) 'Choosing to Die'. *Newsweek*, 16 May

Kirshenblatt-Gimblett, B. and Bruner, E.M. (1992) 'Tourism', in R. Bauman (ed.) *Folklore, Cultural Performance, and Popular Entertainments*. New York and Oxford: Oxford University Press, 300–307

Kovaleski, S.F. (1999) 'Havana Daydreamin'. *The Washington Post*, 5 March

Lafranchi, H. (1997) 'The World Dances to a Cuban Beat'. *Christian Science Monitor*, 2 October

Laing, I. (1986) 'The Music Industry and the "Cultural Imperialism" Thesis'. *Media, Culture and Society*, 8, 331–41

Lam, R. (1996) 'NG, la garra del tigre'. *BH* (edición internacional), A. 88, **12**, 43–5

―――― (1997) 'NG, La banda que manda'. *Musicalia Dos*, **1**, January–March, 8–11

Lapper, R. (1999) 'Foreign Investment: Ambiguous Stance towards attracting Big Guns'. *The Financial Times/ Country Survey: Cuba*, 24 March

―――― and Fletcher, P. (1999) 'Return to Favour for Hard-line Approach'. *The Financial Times/ Country Survey: Cuba*, 24 March

Larsen, J. (1998) 'The Economics of Tourism in Cuba'. Unpublished Masters Thesis, University of London–Institute of Latin American Studies

'La salsa en el complejo cultural del Caribe' (1980). *CB*, **152**, August, 8–9

León, A. (1964) *Musica folclórica cubana*. Habana: Biblioteca Nacional 'José Martí'

―――― (1974) *Del canto y del tiempo*. Habana: Letras Cubanas

―――― (1982) 'Notas para un panorama de la música popular', in C. Hernández (ed.) *Ensaysos de música latinoamericana*. Habana: Casa de las Américas, 235–45 [translated as 'Notes toward a Panorama of Popular and Folk Music', in Manuel 1990a, 1–23]

―――― (1990) 'Of the Axle and the Hinge: Nationalism, Afro-Cubanism, and Music in Pre-Revolutionary Cuba', in Manuel 1990a, 267–82

León, F. (1997) 'Socialism and *Sociolismo*: Social Actors and Economic Change in 1990s Cuba', in Centeno and Font 1997, 39–51

León, J. (1997) 'Tropical Overexposure: Miami's 'Sophisticated Tropics' and the Balsero', in Aparicio and Chávez-Silverman 1997, 213–27

Leonard, C. (1997) 'La Cubanía: The Soul of Cuban Theatre in the mid-1990s'. *Latin American Theatre Review*, **30** (2), Spring, 139–52

Levin, J. (1998a) 'Médico de la salsa volverá hoy a Cuba'. *EH*, 3 November

—— (1998b) 'NG La Banda taps Primal Energy of Cuban Streets'. *MH*, 6 November

Levine, A. (1999) 'Viva "Buena Vista Social Club"', in <*Salon.com*>, 9 March

Leymarie, I. (1996) *Musique Caraïbes*. Arles: Cité de la Musique

—— (2002) *Cuban Fire: The Story of Salsa and Latin Jazz*. London and New York: Continuum

Linares, J.C. (2002) 'Aumenta la censura en las emisoras de radio cubanas'. *Cuba Verdad/Cubanet*, 2 March, <http://www.cubanet.org/>

Linares, M.T. (1974) *La música y el pueblo*. Habana: Pueblo y Educación [previously published as *La música popular*. Habana: Instituto Cubano del Libro, 1970]

—— (1998) *La música entre Cuba y Espana*. Madrid: Fundación Autor

Lindsay, A. (ed.) (1996) *Santería Aesthetics in Contemporary Latin American Arts*. Washington, DC: Smithsonian Institution

Lipsitz, G. (1994) *Dangerous Crossroads*. London and New York: Verso

Livingston, T.E. (1999) 'Music Revivals: Towards a General Theory'. *ET*, **23** (1), Winter, 66–85

Llewellyn, H. (1997) 'Acuerdo Musical'. *EP*, 2 June

—— (1999a) 'Caribe debuts Cheap Tapes'. *Billboard*, 30 January

—— (1999b) 'Cuban Timba headed for Major Global Markets'. *Billboard*, 30 January

—— (1999c) 'Timba burns in Cuba'. *Billboard*, 30 January

López, F. [1997] 'Salto entre dos: entrevista con José Luis Cortés'. *CB*, A. 30, **282**, 13–15

Loyola Fernández, J. (1997) *En ritmo de bolero: el bolero en la música bailable cubana*. Habana: Unión

Lumsden, I. (1996) *Machos, Maricones and Gays: Cuba and Homosexuality*. London: Latin American Bureau

McClary, S. (1991) *Feminine Endings: Music, Gender, and Sexuality*. Minneapolis and Oxford: University of Minnesota Press

—— and Walser, R. (1990) 'Start Making Sense! Musicology Wrestles with Rock', in S. Frith and A. Goodwin (eds) *On Record*. London: Routledge

—— and —— (1994) 'Theoryzing the Body in African-American Music'. *Black Music Research Journal*, **14** (1), Spring, 75–84

McGarrity, G.L. (1992) 'Race, Culture, and Social Change in Contemporary Cuba', in Halebsky and Kirk 1992, 193–205

Madan, N. (ed.) (1982) *La lucha ideologica*. Habana: Editora Política

Malapanis, A. (1996) 'We will defend Workers' Political Power at any Cost', *The Militant* (NY), **60** (23), 10 June

Mamá, yo quiero saber. Entrevistas a músicos cubanos (1999). Habana: Letras Cubanas

Manrique, D.A. (1996a) 'La realidad cubana, a ritmo de salsa'. *EP*, 21 February

────── (1996b) 'Creo en lo que ha hecho la revolución y quiero estar dentro para pulir los defectos'. *EP*, 19 September

────── (1998a) 'El músico José Luís Cortés refleja en su disco 'Veneno' "la gozadera de la música cubana"'. *EP*, 17 March

────── (1998b) 'El reinado de los clásicos'. *EP*, 28 April

Manuel, P. (1985) 'The Anticipated Bass in Cuban Popular Music'. *LAMR*, **6** (2), 249–61

────── (1986) 'Cuban Popular Music Literature: Progress and Polemics'. *Studies in Latin American Popular Culture*, **5**, 253–6

────── (1987) 'Marxism, Nationalism and Popular Music in Revolutionary Cuba'. *PM*, **6** (2), 161–78

────── (1988) *Popular Music of the non-Western World*. New York and Oxford: Oxford University Press

────── (1989) 'Rock Music and Cultural Ideology in Revolutionary Cuba', in Frith 1989, 161–6

────── (1990a) *Essays on Cuban Music*. Cuban and North American Perspectives. Lanham and London: University Press of America

────── (1990b) 'Musical Pluralism in Revolutionary Cuba', in Manuel 1990a, 285–311

────── (1990c) 'Salsa and the Music Industry: Corporate Control or Grassroots Expression?', in Manuel 1990a, 159–80

────── (1994) 'The Sound of the Barrio: Thirty Years of Salsa'. *NAC*, **28** (2), September–October, 22–9

────── et al. (1995) *Caribbean Currents: Caribbean Music from Rumba to Reggae*. Philadelphia: Temple University Press

Marks, M. (1992) 'Cuban Counterpoint: History of the son montuno'. Sleeve notes to the CD *Cuban Counterpoint: History of the son montuno*, Rounder 1078

Marre, J. and Charlton, H. (1985) *Beats of the Heart*. London: Pluto

Marshall, P. (1988) *Cuba libre: Breaking the Chains?*. London: Unwin

Martín, J.L. (1999) 'Thinking about Socialism: The New Cuban Social Sciences'. *NAC*, **32** (5), March–April, 37–40

Martin, L. and Morales, M. (1999) 'Cuban Music: Protests and Hype Subside'. *MH*, 24 June

Martín Fernandez, C., Perera Pérez, M. and Díaz Pérez, M. (1996) 'La vida cotidiana en Cuba: una mirada psicosocial'. *Temas*, 7, July–September, 92–8

Martínez, M. (1993) *Cubanos en la música*. Habana: Letras Cubanas
Martínez, M.A. (1980a) 'Música Popular – Paquito d' Rivera'. *RyC*, **89**, 75–6
―――― (1980b) 'Música Popular – Helio Orovio'. *RyC*, **91**, 74–5
―――― (1980c) 'Música popular: Después de la encuesta'. *RyC*, **92**, 75–7
―――― (1981) 'La salsa: Un paliativo contra la nostalgía?'. *RyC*, **109**, 8–17
―――― (1982) 'El imperio de la salsa'. *CB*, **171**, 19–20
―――― (1986) 'Chucho al piano'. *RyC*, **8**, 12–17
―――― (1988a) 'El misterio de la improvisaciòn'. *RyC*, **12**, 2–7
―――― (1988b) 'Son de Adalberto'. *RyC*, **30**, 2–7
―――― (1989) 'Zoila Gómez, musicóloga'. *RyC*, **10**, 26–9
―――― (1990) 'Leonardo Acosta: siempre seré musico'. *RyC*, **1**, 34–41
Martínez Acosta, P. (1988) 'El carácter antigenerico de la salsa caribeña'. *Música*/Casa de las Américas, **114**, 23
Martínez Fernández, L., Figueredo, D.H., Pérez, L.A. Jr. and González, L. (2003) *Encyclopaedia of Cuba*. Westport and London: Greenwood Press
Martínez Furé, R. (1979) *Diálogos imaginarios*. Habana: Arte y Literatura
―――― (1990a) 'Regarding Folklore', in Manuel 1990a, 251–65
―――― (1990b) 'Tambor', in Manuel 1990a, 27–47
―――― (1993) 'Imaginary Dialogue on folklore', in Pérez Sarduy and Stubbs 1993, 109–16
Martori, R. (1998) 'Artistas De Siete Bandas De Baile Estrenan El "Team Cuba"'. *AFP/EFE – Diario Las Américas* (Havana), 12 May
Masci, R. (1998) 'Sconfiggerò il turismo sessuale a Cuba'. *La Stampa* (Italy), 7 June
Matas, J. (1971) 'Theater and Cinematography', in Mesa-Lago 1971, 429–50
Mauleón, R. (1993) *Salsa Guidebook: For Piano & Ensemble*. Petaluma, Calif.: Sher Music
Medin, T. (1990) *Cuba: The Shaping of Revolutionary Consciousness*. Boulder: Rienner
Medrano, F. (1999) *Ni Chicha ni Limonada: Depictions of the Mulatto Woman in Cuban Tobacco Art*. Albuquerque: University of New Mexico
Mesa Lago, C. (1981) *The Economy of Socialist Cuba: A Two-decade Appraisal*. Albuquerque: University of New Mexico Press
Melgar Bao, R. (1994) 'Los "orishas" y la ciudad de la Habana en tiempo de crisis'. *Cuadernos Americanos*, **46** (Nueva Epoca), September–October, 166–84

Memorias del VI Congreso de la FMC (1995) FMC – Equipo de Servicios Traductores e Intérpretes: Habana

Mercer, K. (1994) *Welcome to the Jungle: New Positions in Black Cultural Studies*. London: Routledge

Mesa-Lago, C. (1971) *Revolutionary Change in Cuba*. Pittsburgh: University of Pittsburgh Press

—— (1974) *Cuba in the 1970s: Pragmatism and institutionalization*. Albuquerque: University of New Mexico Press

—— (ed.) (1993) *Cuba: After the Cold War*. Pittsburgh: University of Pittsburgh Press

Middleton, R. (1990) *Studying Popular Music*. Milton Keynes and Philadelphia: Open University Press

Milán, G. (1999) 'Inequality and Anomie in Cuba'. *NAC*, **32** (5), 34–5

Miller, I. (1995) 'The Singer as Priestess: Interviews with Celina González and Merceditas Valdés', in R. Sakolsky and F. Wei-Han Ho (eds) *Sounding Off!* New York: Autonomedia, 287–304

—— (2000) 'A Secret Society Goes Public: The Relationship Between Abakuá and Cuban Popular Culture'. *African Studies Review*, **43** (1), 161–88

Milward, J. (1998) 'The Latin Invasion', in <Salon.com>, 16 August

Ministerio de Educación (1971) *Memorias del primer congreso nacional de educación y cultura*. Habana: Instituto cubano del libro

Mir, A. (1997) 'Otra tabla para el Rey Arturo. El rock en Cuba: una alternativa?'. *RyC*, **4**, 4–11

Mitchell, T. (1993) 'World Music and the Popular Music Industry: An Australian View'. *ET*, **37** (3), 309–38

Molina, J.A. (1998) 'Marginación y carnaval: la imagen del negro en la fotografía cubana'. *Estudios Interdisciplinarios de America Latina y del Caribe*, **9** (1), January–June, 133–40

Molyneux, M.D. (1996) *State, Gender and Institutional Change in Cuba's 'Special Period': The Federación de Mujeres Cubanas*. London: Institute of Latin American Studies

Monge Oviedo, R. (1992) 'Are We or aren't We?', in N.E. Whitten, Jr. and A. Torres, 'Blackness in the Americas'. *NAC*, **25** (4), February, 19

Monreal, P. (1997) 'The Economics of the Present Moment', in Centeno and Font 1997, 201–8

—— (1999) 'Sea Changes: The New Cuban Economy'. *NAC*, **32** (5), March–April, 21–9

Moore, K. (2001) 'The Bloques of La Charanga Habanera', in <Timba.com>

Moore, R. (1994) 'Representation of Afrocuban Expressive Culture in the Writings of Fernando Ortíz'. *LAMR*, **15** (1), Spring–Summer, 32–54

——— (1995) 'The Commercial Rumba: Afrocuban Arts as International Popular Culture'. *LAMR*, **16** (2), Fall–Winter, 165–98

——— (1997) *Nationalizing Blackness: Afrocubanismo and Artistic Revolution in Havana, 1920–1940*. Pittsburgh: University of Pittsburgh Press

——— (1998) 'Review of Y. Daniel 1995, *Rumba*'. *CS*, **27**, 272–4

——— (2002) 'Salsa and Socialism: Dance Music in Cuba, 1959–99', L. Waxer (ed.)

Morello, M. and Taliento, L. (1995) *Viaggiare a luci rosse*. Milano: Portoria

Moses, C. (2000) *Real Life in Castro's Cuba*. Wilmington, Del.: Scholarly Resources

Mosquera, G. (1996) '"Eleggua" at the (Post?) Modern Crossroads: The Presence of Africa in the Visual Art of Cuba', in Lindsay 1996, 225–58

——— (1999) 'The Infinite Island: Introduction to New Cuban Art', in Zeitlin 1999, 23–9

Muñoz, M.J. (2001) 'Another Forbidden Fruit'. *GI*, 23 August

———, López, F. and Lagarde, J.B. (1998) 'Timba con Globos'. *CB*, A. 31, **286**, 6

Murphy, J.M. (1988) *Santería: African Spirits in America*. Boston: Beacon Press

Negus, K. (1996) *Popular Music in Theory: An Introduction*. Cambridge: Polity Press

Nettl, B. (1972) 'Persian Popular Music in 1969'. *ET*, **16** (2), 218–39

Nicola, N. (1997) 'Porqué la Nueva Trova?'. *La Gaceta de Cuba*, 5, 34–69 [orig. pub. in *El Caimán Barbudo*, **92**, July 1975]

No Longer Invisible: Afro-Latin Americans Today (1995). London: Minority Right Publications

'Nueva salsa cubana se llama "Timba", dice su creador' (1999). *Reuters* (Havana), 12 February

O'Connell Davidson, J. (1996) 'Sex Tourism in Cuba'. *Race and Class*, **38** (1), 39–48

——— (1998) *Prostitution, Power, and Freedom*. Cambridge: Polity Press

——— and Sanchez Taylor, J. (1996) 'Child Prostitution and Sex Tourism/Cuba'. Research commissioned by ECPAT for the World Congress Against the Commercial Sexual Exploitation of Children

Oldrini, G. (2002) 'Tutti a Cuba: tramonta l'era delle ragazze facili'. *Panorama Online*, 22 January, <www.panorama.it>

Olsen, D.A. and Sheehy, D.E. (eds) (2000) *The Garland Handbook of Latin American Music*. New York and London: Garland

Ong, W. (1982) *Orality and Literacy: The Technologizing of the Word*. London and New York: Methuen

Oppenheimer, A. (1992) *Castro's Final Hour: The Secret Story Behind the Coming Downfall of Communist Cuba*. New York: Simon and Schuster

'Opus 13' (1988). *Clave*, 9, 37

Orejuela, A. (1999) 'La Orbita de Irakere: antecedentes de un hito'. Unpublished manuscript, Habana

Orovio, H. (1992) *Diccionario de la música cubana*. Habana: Letras Cubanas [English edn: *Cuban Music from A to Z*. Durham, NC: Duke University Press, 2004]

——— (1994) *Musica por el Caribe*. Santiago de Cuba: Oriente

——— (1998) 'Rumba en salsa, pop, folk, y timba'. *SC*, A. 2, 5, 14–17

——— (1999) 'La timba brava', speech at Cubadisco Music Fair (Havana), 11 May [my transcription]

Orozco, D. (1995) '"Echale salsita a la cachimba": Algunas reflexiones socio-culturales a partir de las letras de la música popular cubana actual'. *La Gaceta de Cuba*, 3, 3–8

Ortíz, F. (1947) *Contrapunteo del tabaco y del azúcar*. New York: Knopf

——— (1952–5) *Los instrumentos de la música afrocubana*. La Habana: Cardenas (5 vols)

——— (1965) *La africanía de la música folklórica de Cuba*. Habana: Editora Universitaria [first published 1950]

——— (1974) *Nuevo catauro de Cubanismos*. Habana: Ciencias Sociales

——— (1981) *Los bailes y el teatro de los negros en el folklóre de Cuba*. Habana: Letras Cubanas [first published 1951]

——— (1986) *Los negros curros*. Habana: Ciencias Sociales

——— (1990) *Glosario de afronegrismos*. Habana: Ciencias Sociales [first published 1924]

Otero, L. And Martínez Hinojosa, F. (1972) *Cultural Policy in Cuba*. Paris: UNESCO

Otero Garabís, J. (1996) '"Puerto Rico is Salsa": Propositions, Appropriations and Interpretations of a Popular Genre'. *Journal of Latin American Cultural Studies*, 5 (1), 25–31

Oxfam America (2000) 'Epilogue: Trade Partners, not Trade Enemies', in *Going Against the Grain*, <www.oxfamamerica.org>

P.H. (1997) 'Charanga renovada y comprometida'. *GR*, 27 December

Pacini Hernandez, D. (1993) 'A View from the South: Spanish Caribbean Perspectives on World Beat'. *WoM*, 35 (2), 48–69

——— (1995) *Bachata: A Social History of a Dominican Popular Music*. Philadelphia: Temple University Press

——— (1998) 'Dancing with the Enemy: Cuban Popular Music, Race, Authenticity, and the World-Music Landscape'. *Latin American Perspectives*, 100 (25: 3), 110–25

Padrón, F. (1987) 'Orquesta La 440: Título o realidad?'. *Clave*, 6, 52–3
———— (1999) 'Te pone la cabeza buena … y los piés también'. *SC* A. 2, 7–8, 27–36
Padrón Nodarse, F. (1998) '(Re)nacer arreglando un mundo: entrevista con Juan de Marcos Gonzáles'. *SC*, A. 2, 6, 33–7
Padura Fuentes, L. (1993) 'Todo lo que ud. quería saber sobre la salsa'. *RyC*, 3, 50–53
———— (1997a) *Los rostros de la salsa*. Habana: Unión
———— (1997b) 'Que tiene Van Van que sigue ahí?'. *MC*, 0, 16–24
———— (1998) 'La resurrección milagrosa de Rubén González'. *MC*, 2, 9–13
Pagano, C. (1996) 'La Timba: un nuevo ritmo'. *Revista 91.9* [Colombia], 14, December 1996/January–February 1997
Palacios García, E. (1987) *Catálogo de música popular cubana*. Habana: Pueblo y Educación
Pareja, L. (1999) 'Andy Wood, ¡Como No!'. *Variedades*, 15, June–July (London)
Pareles, J. (2000) 'Rumba, the Heartbeat of Cuban Music'. *The New York Times*, 11 June
Parker, D. (1995) *La Revolución Cubana*. Caracas: Biblioteca Nacional-Facultad de Ciencias Económicas y Sociales
———— (1999) 'The Cuban Revolution: Resilience and Uncertainty'. *NAC*, 32 (5), March–April, 17–20
Paternostro, S. (1999) 'The Revolution will be in Stereo'. *The New York Times Magazine*, 10 January
———— (2000) 'Communism versus Prostitution: Sexual Revolution'. *The New Republic Online*, 29 June, <http://www.tnr.com/>
Pattullo, P. (1996) *Last Resorts: The Cost of Tourism in the Caribbean*. London: Latin American Bureau
Paz, S. (1995) 'Entre Amigos'. *SC* [promotional issue], 13–16
Páz Pérez, C. (1988) *De lo popular y lo vulgar en el habla cubana*. Habana: Ciencias Sociales
Pedraza, T. (1998) '"This too shall pass": The Resistance and Endurance of Religion in Cuba'. *CS*, 28, 16–39
Perera Robbio, A. (1997) 'La Charanga se pasó'. *JR*, 31 July
Pérez, C.M. [1997] 'Están matando a la música cubana'. *CB*, A. 30, 278, 28–9
Pérez, L.A., Jr. (1999) *On becoming Cuban: Identity, Nationality, and Culture*. Chapel Hill: University of North Carolina Press
Pérez, R. (1999) 'Porqué La Habana no baila más'. Speech at the Cubadisco Music Fair (Havana), 12 May [my transcription]
Pérez Alvares, M.M. (1996) 'Los prejuicios raciales: sus mecanismos de reproducción'. *Temas*, 7, July–September, 44–50

Pérez Fernández, R.A. (1987) *La binarización de los ritmos ternarios africanos en America Latina*. Habana: Casa de Las Américas

Pérez Sanjurjo, E. (1986) *Historia de la música cubana*. Miami: Poesia

Pérez Sarduy, P. (1996) 'Y qué tienen los negros en Cuba?'. *Encuentro de la cultura cubana*, **2**, Fall, 39–42

——— and Stubbs, J. (eds) (1993) *Afrocuba: An Anthology of Cuban Writing on Race, Politics and Culture*. London: Latin American Bureau

Pérez-Stable, M. (1993) *The Cuban Revolution: Origins, Course, and Legacy*. New York and Oxford: Oxford University Press

Perna, V. (1996) 'Latin Lovers: Salsa Musicians and their Audience in London', in *Music in Europe*. Brussels: European Music Office, European Commission, 104–15

——— (1997) 'Se pop e folk dirottano su Cuba'. *Il Giornale della Musica*, **133**, December

——— (1999a) 'Trans/Atlantic connections. Interview with Gerry Lyseight'. *The Spirit* (UK), **6**, March

——— (1999b) 'Cubadisco 1999'. *Latin London* (UK), **2** (11), July–August

——— (1999c) 'Cuba, il 'Social Club' e Mahler'. *Il Giornale della Musica*, **153**, October

——— (2000a) 'Chi ha inventato Buena Vista?'. *Il Giornale della Musica*, **158**, March

——— (2000b) 'Sincretismi e contaminazioni', in 'Musica', *Enciclopedia Italiana* (Appendice 2000). Roma: Istituto dell'Enciclopedia Italiana, 236–40

——— (2001) 'Timba. The Sound of the Cuban Crisis: Black Dance Music in Cuba during the Período Especial'. PhD Thesis, University of London–School of Oriental and African Studies

——— (2002a) 'Dancing the Crisis, Singing the Past: Musical Dissonances in Cuba during the Período Especial'. *Journal of Latin American Cultural Studies*, **11** (2), 213–29

——— (2002b) 'Il fantasma dell'autenticità: utilità e limiti della *world music*'. *Musica/Realtà*, **69**, November, 55–77

——— (2003a) '"Ay Dios, ampárame!". Musica nera e rivoluzione cubana: definizioni e problemi metodologici'. Paper presented at the seminar *Le società latinoamericane nei secoli XIX e XX*. Dipartimento di Storia Moderna e Contemporanea, Università di Genova, Genoa, 13–14 October

——— (2003b) 'The (Second) Discovery of America: Is Cuban Music *World Music*?'. Paper presented at the Symposium *La industria discográfica en el siglo XXI. Cubadisco Music Fair* (Havana), 12–16 May (now forthcoming on Revisto *Temas*)

Pietrobruno, S. (2000) 'Salsa's Gendered Embrace: A Turn Backwards or Step Forwards for Male/Female Relations?'. Paper presented at the Iaspm Canada Conference, Laval University. Quebec City, 20–21 May

Pina Machín, E. (1998) 'Los Van Van make your Head Spin'. *GI*, 12 April (12)

Poupeye, V. (1998) *Caribbean Art*. London: Thames and Hudson

Pratt, R. (1994) *Rhythm and Resistance: The Political Uses of American Popular Music*. Washington and London: Smithsonian Institution

Prout, R. (1999) 'Jail-house Rock: Cuba, AIDS, and the Incorporation of Dissent in Bengt Norborg's *Socialism or Death*'. *Bulletin of Latin American Research*, **18** (4), 423–36

Puerta, R. (1996) 'Sociedad civil y el futuro de Cuba: Una vía no política para reducir el poder estatal', in R. Puerta and M. Donate Armada, *Ensayos Politicos*. Coral Gables: Coordinadora Democrata de Cuba

Ramírez Calzadilla, J. and Pérez Cruz, O. (1997) *La Religión en los jóvenes cubanos: ortodoxía y espontaneidad*. Habana: Academia

Ramón, N. (1991) 'El dilema de donde mover los piés'. *BH*, A. 83, **33**, 16 August, 10–13

Ravsberg, M. (2002) '"Informática 2002" en La Habana', <http://news.bbc.co.uk>, 22 February

Redhead, S. and Street, J. (1989) 'Have I the Right? Legitimacy, Authenticity and Community in Folk's Politics'. *PM*, **8** (2), May, 177–84

Reed, C. (1991) *The Cultural Revolution in Cuba*. Geneva: Latin American Round Table

Reporters Sans Frontières (2001) *Rapport Annuel 2000*, <http://www.rsf.fr/>

Resik Aguirre, M. (1996) 'Popular?'. *JR*, 8 September

Resolución 'sobre la cultura artística y literaria' del Primer Congresso del Partido Comunista de Cuba (1975), in N. Madan (ed.), *La lucha ideologica*. Habana: Editora Política, 1982

Rey, M. (2000) 'Creando confines socio-musicales: la música popular y la subculturización de la juventud cubana'. Paper presented at the Third Congress of IASPM (International Association for the Study of Popular Music) Latin America, Bogotá, 23–7 August

Rieff, D. (1994) *The Exile: Cuba in Heart of Miami*. London: Vintage

Ríos Vega, L. and García Moré, M. (1997a) 'Juan Carlos y Dan Den: locura prodigiosa trás el teclado'. *TI*, 5, 12–14

——— (1997b) 'Bamboleo: de tal palo tal astilla'. *TI*, **6**, 2–4

——— (1998) 'Marcando la distancia'. *TI*, **7**, 28–9

Rivero, J. and Pola, J.A. (1983) 'Formell: "…tengo que competir con mis propias obras"'. *BH*, 16 September, 21–2

Rivero García, J. (1979) 'Un subproducto comercial'. *CB*, **135**, March, 6–7

Robbins, J. (1989) 'Practical and Abstract Taxonomy in Cuban Music'. *ET*, **33** (3), 379–89

—— (1990a) 'The Cuban Son as a Form, Genre, and Symbol'. *LAMR*, **11** (2), Fall–Winter, 182–210

—— (1990b) 'Institutions, Incentives, and Evaluation in Cuban Music-Making', in Manuel 1990a, 215–48

Roberts, J.S. (1985) *The Latin Tinge: The Impact of Latin American Music in the United States*. Tivoli, NY: Original Music [first published 1979]

—— (1999) *Latin Jazz: The First of the Fusions. 1880s to Today*. New York: Schirmer

Robinson Calvet, N. (1996) 'No es tan tosco José Luís como lo pintan'. *TI*, **1**, 9–11

Rockwell, J. (1984) *All American Music*. New York: Vintage Books

Rodríguez Chávez, E. (1997) *Emigración cubana actual*. Habana: Ciencias Sociales

Rojas, F. [1997] 'Agenda abierta? Conversación con Alicia Perea, presidenta del Instituto de la Música'. *CB*, A. 30, **283**, 18–23

Rojas Gutiérrez, F. [1998] 'Para las niñas y pa' las señoras'. *CB* A. 31, **288**, 2–3

Rondón, C.M. (1980) *El libro de la salsa: crónica de la música del Caribe urbano*. Caracas: Arte

Rose, T. (1994) *Black Noise: Rap and Black Culture in Contemporary America*. Middletown, Conn.: Wesleyan University Press

Roy, M. (2002) *Cuban Music: From Son and Rumba to the Buena Vista Social Club and Timba Cubana*. London: Latin American Bureau

Rundle, L.B.M. (2001) 'Tourism, Social Change, and Jineterismo in Contemporary Cuba', *The Society of Caribbean Studies Annual Conference Papers*, **2** (Oxford, UK)

Ryback, T.W. (1990) *Rock around the Bloc: A History of Rock Music in Eastern Europe and the Soviet Union*. Oxford and New York: Oxford University Press

Salas, B. (1997) 'El son más largo del mundo'. *TI*, **4**, 8–14

Salas, L. (1979a) 'Juvenile Delinquency in post-Revolutionary Cuba: Characteristics and Cuban Explanations'. *CS*, **9**, January, 45–59

—— (1979b) *Social Control and Deviance in Cuba*. New York: Praeger

Salazar, A. (1998) 'Dream team de la timba cubana'. *TI*, **7**, 56

'Salsa de Ruben Blades' (1986). *RyC*, **7**, 80–81

Sánchez, J. (1997) 'Banderitas americanas en La Habana'. *EH*, 3 March

Sánchez de Fuentes, E. (1923) *El folklór en la música cubana*. Habana: Siglo XX

Sansone, L. (2003) *Blackness without Ethnicity: Constructing Race in Brazil*. New York: Palgrave-Macmillan

Santiesteban, A. (1997) *El habla popular cubana de hoy*. Habana: Ciencias Sociales

Sardiñas, M.F. (1996) 'Los tumbaos de piano en la música cubana'. *TI*, 1, 62–3

Sarmiento, L. (1998) 'Manolín, o la manzana de la discordia'. *SC*, A. 1, 4, 29–31

Sarusky, J. (1999) 'José Luís Cortés: entre el barrio y Beethoven'. *RyC*, 4, 15–19

——— and Mosquera, G. (1979) *The Cultural Policy of Cuba*. Paris: UNESCO

Schwab, P. (1999) *Cuba: Confronting the US Embargo*. New York: St. Martin's Press

Schwartz, R. (1997) *Pleasure Island: Tourism and Temptation in Cuba*. Lincoln, Ill.: University of Nebraska Press

Schwegler, A. (1999) 'El vocabulario africano de Palenque (Colombia). Segunda Parte: compendio de palabras (con etimologías)', in L. Ortíz (ed.) *El Caribe hispanico: perspectivas linguisticas actuales*. Frankfurt-Madrid: Vervuert, 171–253

——— (2000a) 'On the (Sensational) Survival of Kikongo in twentieth-century Cuba'. *Journal of Pidgin and Creole Languages*, 15 (1), 159–64

——— (2000b) 'The African Vocabulary of Palenque (Colombia). Part 1: Introduction and Corpus of Previously Undocumented Afro-Palenquerisms'. *Journal of Pidgin and Creole Languages*, 15 (2), 241–312

Segarte, A. L. et al. (1999) *La mujer en la sociedad cubana: Desafíos ante el nuevo milenio*. Habana: AUNA

Segre, R., Coyula, M. and Scarpaci, J.L. (1997) *Havana: Two Faces of the Antillean Metropolis*. Chichester: Wiley

Serpa Maceira, C. (2002) 'Despiden a director de programa radial que sacó al aire música censurada', *UPECI/ Cubanet*, 4 November, <http://www.cubanet.org/>

'Sex Tourism arrives in Cuba' (1993). *The Ottawa Citizen*, 13 March

Shnookal, D. (ed.) (1991) *Cuban Women confront the Future: Vilma Espín*. Melbourne and New York: Ocean Press

Singer, R. (1983) 'Tradition and Innovation in Contemporary Latin Popular Music in New York City'. *LAMR*, 4 (2), 183–202

Smith, L.M. (1992) 'Sexuality and Socialism in Cuba', in Halebsky and Kirk 1992, 177–91

——— and Padula A. (1996) *Sex and Revolution: Women in Socialist Cuba*. New York and Oxford: Oxford University Press

Smith, S. (1999) 'Hip hop a la cubano'. *Afrocubaweb*, <www.afrocuba web.com>

Smith, V. (1995) 'What are Little Girls made of under Socialism?: Cuba's Mujeres [Women] and Muchacha [Girl] in the Period 1980–1991'. *Studies in Latin American Popular Culture*, **14**, 1–15

Soler, A. (2003) "La 'zona roja" invade. *Cubanet*, 30 January, <http://www.cubanet.org/>

Sommers, L.K. (1991) 'Inventing Latinismo: The Creation of "Hispanic" Panethnicity in the U. States'. *Journal of American Folklore*, **104**, Winter, 32–53

Sontag, S. (1964) 'Notes on Camp', in *A Susan Sontag Reader*, intro. E. Hardwick. Harmondsworth: Penguin, 1988, 105–19

Steward, S. (1985) Interview with Arturo Sandoval. Audio tape, National Sound Archive (UK). London, 1 August

—— (1999) *Salsa: Music Heartbeat of Latin America*. London: Thames and Hudson

Stokes, M. (ed.) (1994) *Ethnicity, Identity and Music*. Oxford: Oxford University Press

Street, J. (1986) *Rebel Rock*. Oxford: Oxford University Press

Stubbs, J., Haines, L. and Haines, M.F. (1996) *Cuba: World Bibliographical Series*. Oxford and Santa Barbara: Clio Press

Sweeney, P. (2001) *The Rough Guide to Cuban Music*. London: Rough Guides/Penguin

Tabares, S. (1996) 'Textos bailables? Del corazón a los pies'. *BH* [International Edition], A 88, 9, 8–13

Tagg, P. (1982) 'Analysing Popular Music: Theory, Method and Practice'. *PM*, **2**, 37–67

—— (1989) 'Open Letter: "Black Music", "Afro-American Music" and "European Music"'. *PM*, **8** (3), 285–98

Tagliafico, D. (1999) 'In viaggio con i supernonni' [TV reportage on the Italian tour of the I. Ferrer Orchestra, Summer 1999]. RAI-TG2 Dossier, broadcast 9 July

Taylor, T.D. (1997) *Global Pop: World Music, World Markets*. New York and London: Routledge

Tesoro, S. (1993) 'Carlos Averhoff: El lenguaje de la música popular'. *BH*, A. 85, 5, 29 January, 16–17

Thigpen, D.E. (2002) 'The Buena Vista Social Club is Yesterday: The Streets of Cuba's Cities Today are moving to a Younger Rhythm', in <www.time.com>

Thomas, H. (1998) *Cuba, or the Pursuit of Freedom*. New York: Da Capo [first published 1971]

Thornton, S. (1985) *Club Cultures: Music, Media and Subcultural Capital*. Cambridge: Polity Press

Tirro, F. (1977) *Jazz: A History*. London, Melbourne and Toronto: Dent and Sons

Torres, D.I. (1995) 'Apuntes sobre el feeling', in Giro 1995a, 341–57

Torres, M. de los Angeles (1995) 'Encuentros y Encontronazos: Homeland in the Politics and Identity of the Cuban Diaspora'. *Diaspora*, **4** (2), 211–38

——— (1999) *In the Land of Mirrors: Cuban Exile Politics in the US*. Ann Arbor: University of Michigan Press

Travieso-Díaz, M.F. (1997) *The Laws and Legal System of a Free-Market Cuba: A Prospectus for Business*. Westport and London: Quorum

Trumbull, C. (2001) 'Prostitution and sex tourism in Cuba'. *Cuba in Transition*, vol. 11 – Papers and Proceedings of the 10th Annual Meeting of the Association of the Study of the Cuban Economy (ASCE), Miami, 2–4 August

'Una aventura loca' [1997] [partial transcript of a press conference by Manolín 'El Médico de la salsa']. *CB*, A. 30, **280**, 15

Urfé, O. (1984) 'Music and Dance in Cuba' in M. Moreno Fraginals (ed.) *Africa in Latin America: Essays on History, Culture, and Socialisation*. New York: Holmes and Meier, 170–88 [first published 1977]

Valdés, A. (1986) 'Formell en tres tiempos'. *Clave*, **1**

Valdés Cantero, A. (1988) *El músico en Cuba: ubicación social y situación laboral en el período 1939–46*. Habana: Pueblo y Educación

Valdés-Rodríguez, A. (1999) 'Who's buying the Cuban Phenom?'. *Los Angeles Times*, 14 August

Vélez, M.T. (2000) *Drumming for the Gods: The Life and Times of Felipe García Villamil, santero, palero, and abakuá*. Philadelphia: Temple University Press

Vicent, M. (1997) 'Los músicos de salsa en Cuba reciben sus primeros premios comerciales'. *EP*, 15 December

——— (1999) 'La Habana, ciudad vigilada'. *EP*, 3 March

——— (2000) 'Cuba descubre el negocio de su música'. *EP*, 7 May

——— (2001) 'Cuba reduce aún más la iniciativa privada'. *EP*, 4 March

——— (2002) 'El 'rap' cubano sabe a descontento', *EP*, 21 August

——— (2003) 'Subsistir en Cuba'. *EP*, 11 May

Vilariño, E. (1997) *Reforma y modernización socialistas*. Habana: Ciencias Sociales

Villaça, M.M. (2002) 'A política cultural cubana e o movimiento de Nueva Trova'. *Actas del IV Congreso Latin American IASPM*, Ciudad de Mexico, 2–6 April; http://www.hist.puc.cl/historia/iaspm/mexico/articulos/Villaca.pdf

Villar, G. (1997) 'De los Beatles a los Panchos', in Castellanos 1997, 111–17

Villaurrutía, R., Guerra, M. and Oviedo, A. (1999) *Características sociodemográficas y musicológicas de una agrupación de projección internacional: Isaac* [sic] *Delgado y su Orquesta.* Habana, CIDMUC (mimeo)

Villaverde, C. (1882) *Cecilia Valdés.* Habana: Arte y Literatura

Vinueza, M.E. (1986) *Presencia arará en la música folclórica de Matanzas.* Habana: Casa de las Américas

—— and Sáenz, C.M. (1992) 'El Aporte Africano en la Formación de la Cultura Cubana'. *Folklore Americano*, **53**, January–June, 55–80

Wade, P. (2000) *Music, Race and Nation: Música Tropical in Colombia.* Chicago and London: University of Chicago Press

Waterman, C.A. (1990a) *Jùjú. A Social History and Ethnography of an African Popular Music.* Chicago and London: University Press of Chicago

—— (1990b) '"Our tradition is a very modern tradition": Popular Music and the Construction of Pan-Yoruba Identity'. *ET*, **34** (3), Fall, 367–79

Watrous, P. (1997) 'Havana Jazz Festival: International Dissonance Aside, Harmony in Cuba'. *New York Times*, 24 December

Waxer, L. (1994) 'Of Mambo Kings and Songs of Love: Dance Music in Havana and New York from the 1930s to the 1950s'. *LAMR*, **15** (2), Fall–Winter, 139–76

—— ed. (2002) *Situating Salsa: Global Markets and Local Meaning in Latin Popular Music.* New York and London: Routledge

Weiss, J. (1985) 'Popular culture', in Halebsky and Kirk 1985, 117–33

Wenders, W. and D. (2000) *Buena Vista Social Club: The Companion Book to the Film.* London: Thames and Hudson

Williamson, N. (1999a) 'Playing to the Camera'. *Songlines*, Summer, 18–20

—— (1999b) 'Ry Comments'. *Folk Roots*, **193**, July, 21–7

Yañez, M. (ed.) (1998) *Cubana: Contemporary Fiction by Cuban Women.* Boston: Beacon Press

Yoss (J.M. Sánchez Gómez) (1999) *Los siete pecados nacionales.* Habana [Italian edn.: *I sette peccati nazionali (cubani).* Lecce: Besa, 1999]

Zamora Céspedes, B. [1997] 'Por eso me pica aquí'. *CB*, A. 30, **283**, 14–15

—— [1998] 'Ahora quieren rascarse aquí'. *CB*, A. 31, **285**, 31

Zeitlin, M.A. (1999) *Contemporary Art from Cuba: Irony and Survival on the Utopian Island.* New York: Delano Greenidge and Arizona State University Art Museum

Zimbalist, A. (1992) 'Teetering on the Brink: Cuba's Current Economic and Political Crisis'. *Journal of Latin American Studies*, **24** (2), May, 407–18

Zimmermann, K. (1998) 'Latin Music Explosion North of the Rio Grande'. *Music Business International /The Latin Report*, June, xiii

Interviews by the author

Alemañy, Jesús: trumpet player, leader of Cubanismo. London, March 1996

Alfonso, Juan Carlos: pianist, composer and leader of Dan Den. London, November 1998

Benemelis, Ciro: president of Cubadisco Music Fair. Havana, May 1999 and May 2003

Betancourt, Joaquím: composer and producer, former leader of Opus 13. Havana, May 1999

Calzado, David: composer and leader of La Charanga Habanera. Torino, March 1999

Chacón, Osvaldo: singer, former member of Bamboleo. London, November 1998

Chapottín (Nieto): trumpet player with Conjunto Chapottín y sus Estrellas. Havana, May 1999

Cortés, José Luís: composer and leader of NG La Banda. Torino, May 2000; Havana, May 2003

Cotó (Juan de la Cruz Antomarchi): *tresero*, leader of Eco del Caribe. Havana, May 1999

Crespo, Reynaldo: bass player, composer and arranger. London, June 1998

Dedeu, Amado: percussionist, leader of rumba group Clave y Guaguancó. Havana, May 1999

Delgado, Issac: singer and bandleader. Modena, October 1998

Duany Rivero, Rafael: lead singer of La Barriada. London, December 1998

Elizalde, Rosa Miriam: writer and journalist (junior ed. for *Juventud Rebelde*). Havana, June 1997

Familia's Cuba Represent: rap band, collective interview. Havana, May 2003

Faya, Alberto: musician, managing director of record company Bis Music. Havana, June 1997

Fournier, Osvaldo: professional dancer and dance teacher. London, December 1998

Frometa, Raúl: bass player, composer and arranger of Havana Mambo, formerly with the Orquesta Revé. Torino, September–October 2000

Giro, Radamés: musicologist and music writer. Havana, June 1997

González, Homero: dancer and dance teacher. London, December 1999

González, Juan Carlos: pianist, formely with La Charanga Habanera. Torino, October 2002

González, Juan de Marcos: A&R for *Buena Vista Social Club*, leader of the Afro-Cuban All Stars, former leader of Sierra Maestra. London, November 1999

González, Salvador: painter and muralist, Havana 1999

González La O, Lidia: teacher of folkloric dance at ENA, Habana. Torino, September 1999

Gutiérrez, Pedro Pablo: bass player, director of La Charanga Forever. Torino, March 2000

Kemell, Juan: composer, arranger and leader of La Barriada. London, December 1998

Linares, Maria Teresa: musicologist, Fundación Fernando Ortíz, former director of Museo de la Música, Havana. Havana, June 1997; May 2003

Lyseight, Gerry: media relations officer for Palm Pictures (UK). London, November 1998

Monzón, Seju: musician and record producer. Havana, May 2003

Orejuela, Adriana: student at CIDMUC, Havana. Havana, June 1999

Orovio, Helio: writer and music journalist. Havana, July 1997 and May 1999

Paulíto FG (Pablo Fernández Gallo): singer and bandleader. Torino, February 1999

Puente, Omar: leader of Raíces Cubanas. Reading (UK), December 1999

Piloto, Giraldo: composer and leader of Klimax, former member of NG La Banda and musical director for Issac Delgado. Havana, May 1999

Pouso, Vicente: vice-director of marketing of record company EGREM. Havana, July 1997

Rivera, Mario 'Mayito': singer with Los Van Van. Milano, July 2000

Saenz Coopat, Carmen Maria: musicologist, researcher at CIDMUC. Havana, June 1997

Segura, Alberto: president of record company Eurotropical (Spain). Havana, May 1999

Simonet, Manolíto: composer and leader of Manolíto y su Trabuco. Torino, April 1999

Suarez Galván, Alejandro: leader of Sierra Macstra. Torino, February 2000

Tamayo, Alberto: singer and leader of Tamayo y su salsa. Torino, May 2000

Valdés, Lazaríto: pianist, composer and leader of Bamboleo. Havana, May 2003

Valle, Orlando (Maraca): flute player, composer and leader of Otra Visión. Havana, May 1999

Varela, Carlos: singer-songwriter. Havana, May 1999

Vázquez, Alexis: director of Centro Nacional de Música Popular. Havana, May 1999

Viart, Marino: composer and leader of Havana Mambo. Torino, September 1999

Yotuel: rapper with Orishas. Torino, February 2000

Discography

Unless otherwise specified, the albums listed below are published as CDs.

Adalberto Alvarez y su Son
Adalberto Alvarez y su Son, Artcolor, 1993
A bailar el toca toca, Caribe, 1995
Grandes Éxitos, Egrem, 1999

Afrocuba
Arco Iris, Caribe, 1995
Eclecticism, Ronnie Scott's Jazz House, 1995

Afro-Cuban All Stars
'A toda Cuba le gusta', World Circuit, 1997
'Distinto, diferente', World Circuit, 1999

Bamboleo
¿Te gusto o te caigo bien?, Bis Music, 1996
Yo no me parezco a nadie, Ahí Namá, 1998
Ya no hace falta, Ahí-Namá, 1999

La Barriada
La Barriada, Milan Latino/BMG, 1996
(Juan Kemell y La Barriada) *Río Abajo*, Egrem, 2002

Buena Vista Social Club
Buena Vista Social Club, World Circuit, 1997

Carlos Manuel y su clan
Malo cantidad, Masucci Entertainment/ Palm Pictures, 2001

Chacón Osvaldo
Salsa afrocubana, ARC, 2001
Voy a entrar, ARC, 2003

La Charanga Forever
La Charanga soy yo, Caribe, 2000

La Charanga Habanera
La Charanga Habanera, DOM (early 1990s, no date)
Me sube la fiebre, Egrem, 1993 (re-released as *Love Fever* on Milan / BMG, 1996)

Hey you, loca!, Magic Music, 1994
Pa' que se entere la Habana, Magic Music, 1996
Tremendo delirio, Magic Music/Universal, 1997
El charanguero mayor, JML/Karlyor, 2000
Soy cubano, soy popular, Egrem, 2003

Chirino, Willy
Asere, Sony Tropical, 1995
Baila conmigo, Sony Tropical, 1997

Clave y Guaguancó, Conjunto
Songs and dances (Egrem, 1990), (re-released as a CD on Xenophile/
    Green Linnet, 1994)

Compay Segundo
Lo mejor de la vida, Nonesuch, 1998
Calle Salud, Nonesuch, 1999

Cotó y su Eco del Caribe
A mi Yemayá, Egrem, 1997

Cuarteto Patria
A una coqueta, Corasón, 1993

Cuarto Espacio (feat. O. Hernández & E. López-Nussa)
Cuarto Espacio, Ashé, 1997

Cubanismo
Cubanismo, Hannibal, 1996
Mardi Gras Mambo, Hannibal, 2000

Dan Den
Dan Den, LP, Egrem, 1990
Más rollo que película, LP, Egrem, 1992
Salsa en Ataré, Egrem, 1997

Delgado, Issac
Dando la hora, PM Records, 1992 (re-released on Qbadisc, 1995)
Con ganas, Artex, 1993
Otra idea, RMM, 1997

DLG
Swing On, Sony Tropical, 1997

D'Rivera, Paquito
Mi vida saxual, CD enclosed in the book with the same title, Plaza
    Mayor, 1999 (includes recordings by the Orquesta Cubana de Música
    Moderna and by Jesús Valdés y su Combo, the precursors of Irakere)

Familia Valera Miranda
La Familia Valera Miranda, Ocora, 1997

Ferrér, Ibrahím
Buena Vista Social Club presents Ibrahím Ferrér, World Circuit, 1999

Ferrér, Pedro Luís
100% Cubano, Ceyba Music, 2000

GES / Grupo de Experimentación del ICAIC
GES, vol. I and vol. II, Egrem, 1997

Gonzáles, Celina
Que viva Changó, Qbadisc, 1992

Gonzáles, Rubén
Introducing ... Rubén Gonzáles, World Circuit, 1997
Chanchullo, World Circuit, 2000

Hargrove, Roy
Habana, Verve, 1997 (feat. Crisol, 'Chucho' Valdés, M. 'Anga' Díaz, Changuito)

Havana Mambo
La mecaniquita, Tauri, 2002

Irakere
'Bacalao con pan' and 'Aguanile Bonkó', now in the collection *Taka Taka-Ta*, Exotica, 1998 (Holland)
'Ese atrevimiento', on the LP *Para bailar son*, Egrem, 1981. Now on the CD *Colección Irakere, Vol. V*, Egrem 1995
'Rucu rucu a Santa Clara', on the LP *Bailando Así*, Egrem, 1985. Now on the CD *Colección Irakere, Vol. IX*, Egrem, 1995

Klímax
Mira si te gusta, Eurotropical, 1996
Juego de manos, Eurotropical, 1997
Oye come va, Eurotropical, 2000

La 440, Orquesta
Horns in the Night, RMM, 1998
Spicy Traditions, RMM, 1998

Machito and his Afro-Cuban Orchestra
Tremendo Cumban, Tumbao, 1991

Manolín, El Médico de la salsa (Manuel González Hernández)
Una aventura loca, Caribe, 1994
Para mi Gente, Caribe, 1996

De buena fé, Caribe, 1997
El Puente – Live in the US (2 CDs), Ciocan Music, 2001

Manolíto y su Trabuco
Contra todos los pronósticos, Eurotropical, 1996
Marcando la distancia, Eurotropical, 1998
Para que baile Cuba, Eurotropical, 2000
Se rompieron los termometros, Eurotropical, 2001

Manuelle, Victor
Ironías, Sony Tropical, 1998

Los Muñequitos de Matanzas
Vacunao, Qbadisc, 1995

NG La Banda
Siglo I (a.n.e.), LP, Egrem, 1985
Siglo II (d.n.e.), LP, Egrem, 1986
Abriendo el ciclo, LP, Egrem, 1986
A través del ciclo, LP, Egrem, 1987
En la calle, LP, Egrem, 1990
No se puede tapar el sol, LP, Egrem, 1990
Cabaret Estelar, Caribe, 1992 (also titled *Échale limón*)
La que manda, Caribe, 1994
La bruja, Caribe, 1995
La cachimba, Caribe, 1995
En directo desde el patio de mi casa, Caribe, 1995
Veneno, Caribe/EMI Spain, 1997
Toda Cuba baila con … NG La Banda (collection of early songs) Max
    Music, 1998
The Best of NG La Banda, Caribe/EMI Spain/Hemisphere, 1999

Obsesión
Un montón de cosas, Egrem, 2001

Original de Manzanillo, Orquesta
Yo vengo de allá lejos, compilation Saludos Amigos, 1997

Orishas
A lo cubano, Cooltempo/EMI France, 2000
Emigrante, EMI, 2002

Paulíto FG y Opus 13
Reclamo por tu cuerpo, Egrem, 1991, (re-released as *Dance and
    Romance*, RMM, 1998)

Paulíto FG y su Elite
Tu no me calcúlas, Egrem, 1993

Sofocándote, Magic Music, 1995
El bueno soy yo, Magic Music, 1996
Paulíto FG, Nueva Fania, 1996
Una vez más ... por Amór, Promusic, 2000

Pedroso, Cesar (y Los que son, son)
De la Timba a Pogolotti, Timba Productions, 2001

Portuondo, Omara
Buena Vista Social Club presents Omara Portuondo, World Circuit, 2000

Elio Revé y su Charangón
Que cuento es ese, LP, Egrem, 1988
Papá Eleguá, Egrem, 1993
Elio Revé y su Charangón Vol II, Caribe, 1994

Ritmo Oriental, Orquesta
'La Chica Mamey' (1975), now on the compilation CD *Historia de la Ritmo Vol 1*, Qbadisc, 1993

Rodríguez, Arsenio
Montuneando con Arsenio Rodríguez y su conjunto, 1946–50, Tumbao, 1993

Rodríguez, Silvio
Rodríguez, Fonomusic, 1994

Rubalcaba, Gonzalo
Supernova, Blue Note, 2001

Rumbavana, Conjunto
Te traigo mi son cubano, compilation Saludos Amigos, 1997

SBS
Mami dame carne, Magic Music/Universal, 1998

Sierra Maestra
¡Dundunbanza!, World Circuit, 1994

Sintesis
Ancestros, Egrem, 1987

Son 14 (with Adalberto Alvarez)
Son, the Big Sound, compilation Tumi, 1995

Los Van Van
'Yuya Martínez', on the LP *Los Van Van*, Egrem, 1969. Now on the CD *Colección Juan Formell y Los Van Van, Vol. I*, Egrem, 1995

'Somos Los Van Van' (1982), on the LP *El baile del buey cansa'o*, Egrem, 1982. Now on the CD *Colección Juan Formell y Los Van Van, Vol. VII*, Egrem, 1995

'La titimanía' on the LP *Al son del Caribe*, Egrem, 1987. Now on the CD *Colección Juan Formell y Los Van Van, Vol. XII*, Egrem, 1995

Lo último en vivo, Caribe, 1994

¡Ay diós, amparame!, Caribe, 1995

Te pone la cabeza mala, Caribe, 1997

Llegó Van Van, Havana Caliente/Atlantic, 1999

En el malecón del La Habana (live), Unicornio, 2002

Varela, Carlos
En Vivo, Alerce, 1991

Vieja Trova Santiaguera
Hotel Asturias, Nubenegra, 1996

X Alfonso
Homenaje (a Benny Moré), Unicornio, 2002

Yoruba Andabo
Del Yoruba al Son, Series *La Isla de la música, Vol 6*, Magic Music, 1998

Various Artists
Con lo puños arriba, Egrem, 2002 (cassette compilation of Cuban rap on cassette, featuring: Familia's Cuba Represent, EPG & B f, Eddy K, Anonimo Consejo, Papo Record, Los Paisanos, Cubanos En La Red, Las Crudas)

Cuban Counterpoint. History of the son montuno, Rounder, 1992

The Cuban Hip-Hop All Stars, Vol. 1, Papaya Records, 2002

Cuban Revolución Jazz, Milan/BMG, 1999 (2 CDs)

Dancing with the enemy, Cuban Classics 2, Luaka Bop, 1991

Estrellas del Areíto (Egrem, 1979), re-released on CD as *Estrellas del Areíto/Los heroes* on World Circuit, 1998 (2 CDs)

Oru. Toques e canti della santería, SudNord/Cidmuc, 1994

Rockeros. Saliendo a flote, Egrem, 1997

Documentaries, Films and Music Videos

The list below includes films featuring music scenes, or simply quoted in the book.

P.M. (documentary), S. Cabrera Infante and O. Jiménez Leal (ICAIC, Cuba, 1960)

Memorias del subdesarrollo (fiction), Tomás Gutiérrez Alea (ICAIC, Cuba, 1968)

¡Que bueno canta usted! (documentary), Sergio Giral (ICAIC, Cuba, 1973)

De donde son los cantantes (documentary), Luís Felipe Bernaza (ICAIC, Cuba, 1976)

Música (documentary), Gustavo Paredes (USA, 1984)

Salsa (documentary), in *Beats of the Heart*, a Channel 4 TV series (UK, 1985)

Machito: A Latin Jazz Legacy (documentary), Carlos Ortíz (Nubia Film Society, USA, 1987)

Alicia en el pueblo de Maravillas (*Alice in Wondertown*, fiction), Daniel Díaz Torres (ICAIC, Cuba, 1990)

Fresa y chocolate (*Strawberry and chocolate*, fiction), Tomás Gutiérrez Alea and Juan Carlos Tabío (ICAIC, Cuba, 1993)

La que manda, music video by NG La Banda (VHS/Caribe, Cuba, 1994)

Guantanamera (fiction), Tomás Gutiérrez Alea and Juan Carlos Tabío (ICAIC, Cuba, 1995)

Socialism or Death (documentary), Bengt Norborg (Sveriges Television AB, 1995)

Yo soy del son a la salsa (documentary), Rigoberto López (RMM, USA, 1997)

Pa'que se entere La Habana, music video by La Charanga Habanera (VHS/Marakka 2000, USA, 1997)

Tropicola (docu-fiction), Steve Fagin (USA, 1997)

Global Beats in Cuba (documentary), (Rapido TV, France, 1998). Broadcast by Channel 4 TV (UK), 13 November 1998

Buena Vista Social Club (documentary), Wim Wenders (Germany, 1999)

In viaggio con i supernonni (TV reportage on the Italian tour of the I. Ferrer Orchestra), Daniela Tagliafico (TG2 Dossier: RAI-Italy) 9 July, 1999

Calle 54 (documentary), Fernando Trueba (Spain, 2001)

Los Van Van. Empezó la Fiesta (documentary), L. Mazure and A. Vega (ICAIC-ARCA, Cuba-Argentina, 2002)

Index